Advance ~~~~~
When We 1

"A poignant, vulnerable p⌷   its
giddying complexity...Ther⌷   ⌷hat
moves even as it educates. Weaving the national with the local
and the personal with the political, *Outlaws* gives us a young,
charismatic-but-flawed butch woman struggling heroically
to reconcile her own internal contradictions, trying to find
her way at the convergence of new left, feminist, and gay and
lesbian politics...and hoping to live and love with courage in an
activist world that has not yet reckoned with the radical political
implications of 'butch.'"

—**Talia Mae Bettcher**, Professor of Philosophy, CSU Los
Angeles, co-editor of *Transgender Studies and Feminism: Theory, Politics,
and Gender Realities*

"*When We Were Outlaws* is an important personal witness as well
as an historical document, written with a truly brave heart. I have
long thought of Jeanne Cordova as the James Dean of the lesbian
scene. Now there is also her keen intellectual prowess which
captures the history of incendiary times with equal measures of
passion and cool. She adds much to our understanding of those
times."

—**Mark Thompson**, former Senior Editor of *The Advocate*, author
of *Gay Spirit*, and *The Fire in Moonlight*

"1975, the SLA, *The Lesbian Tide*, and the year I came out.
Jeanne makes herstory come alive!"

—**Phranc**, "All-American Jewish Lesbian Folksinger," visual artist

"The honesty here is really admirable; discussing the
contradictions of feminism, the then real debate about violent
overthrow of the government, the huge divide and uneasy
alliance between lesbians and gay men. Many activists have

simply never told these kinds of stories—about the values and the sheer energy of the time that was so universally compelling. All this, and the no-holds barred, undisguised lesbian voice which is so rare to find nowadays."

—**Stuart Timmons**, author of *The Trouble with Harry Hay* and co-author of *Gay L.A.*

"A riveting, unique, first hand telling of a dangerous, fractious, creative lesbian time...the lesbian feminist '70s with their messy, sexy, bold social and personal visions live again on Cordova's pages; she was thick in the middle of things, as a journalist, as an activist, as a lover. It's all here: the first lesbian conferences, the first women's music festivals, first gay centers, first lesbian newspapers, first gay labor disputes, lesbians in the SLA and FBI witch hunts, Susan Saxe and Margie Adams, sex before and after endless meetings, so many firsts—debates and factions galore. Like reading a stormy and passionate family diary that also speaks of a national time. One version of these times, but what a version! Dramatic, revealing, living history story-telling."

—**Joan Nestle**, Lesbian Herstory Archives co-founder; author of *A Restricted Country*

"Jeanne Cordova's memoir is a love story set between the decay of Sixties radicalism and the rocky but energetic blast-off of the Lesbian Movement. Reacting to women of the Revolutionary Left, Jeanne was both inspired by their commitments and turned off by their rhetoric. The freedom of the independent press, Lesbian and straight, will make contemporary readers swoon with envy."

—**Sarah Schulman**, author of *After Delores and Rat Bohemia*

WHEN WE WERE OUTLAWS

OUTLAWS

a memoir of love & revolution

Jeanne Córdova

Spinsters Ink
P.O. Box 242
Midway, FL 32343

Printed in the United States of America on acid-free paper.

First Spinsters Ink Edition 2011

ISBN-13: 978-1-935226-51-2

This book is dedicated to
the queer youth of today whose activism
now gives their elders so much pride

And to my Family of Choice
who kept me alive during the rough and early years:
Ariana Manov, BeJo Gehrke, Robin Tyler,
Ivy Bottini, Sally Stewart, and Dina B.Evan
And especially to LHB who does so now

Author's Note:
A Persistent Noise
(the story behind Outlaws)

I was not born knowing how to love. It came to me late in life and continues to be difficult. Politics on the other hand came naturally, my mind attuned from birth to the ways of power and survival. Over the twelve years it took me to complete this memoir I discovered that a writer has to understand love and hate, and other primal contradictions, in order to have something to say that will interest others.

When writers sit down to write we attempt to sort the good guys from the bad and to find what cracks in the foundation of our own character may be moral or immoral. If we write authentically, we find both in ourselves as well as others. My spiritual teacher, Michael Ventura, once told me, "Writers are not nice people." Luckily, I experienced no surprise or deflation at hearing his words. I knew at an early age that I was too butch, too different, and too dangerous to be nice.

To be nice is to bore, because by definition "nice" has no shadow or shade. The father of my South African spouse was a freedom fighter - "an outlaw." The fact of her paternity drove me to investigate her further, and in the process I married her. This memoir visits many outlaws, some freedom fighters, and a few who would be called terrorists today. I am one such outlaw. I have been willing to "go too far." I needed to know and sort out these outlaws in my mind in order to discover the perimeters of my moral compass. I am not a nice person. I have too many shades. *Outlaws* takes place at the intersection of shadow and shade that differentiate between persona and principle.

I have always been fascinated by how a noisy swelling called a social movement arrives on the doorstep of an individual's life and how she responds to it. Most ignore the calling of the unfathomable energies of our times. For the rest of us—how does one recognize a social movement when it comes calling at your door? And what greatness or despair might follow should you open the door and invite it into your life? The first step must be to recognize that a stranger of importance has showed up. And I think this recognition must come from listening to the pain in your body, mind, or psyche. Where does it hurt?

The pain in my life began at the age of four with the simple act of receiving the wrong Christmas present—a toy doll. The dissonance in your life might begin more obviously: the day you were raped, the night you went to bed hungry, the day your father left home. My pain was subtle and psychic, and I could have ignored it except that I continued to receive the wrong Christmas present for eighteen years. That was step one in recognizing my social movement when it came knocking— the persistent noise in your head that tells you that the world's reality and your own don't match. The pain nags relentlessly. One might argue that never getting a Christmas present that matches your sense of self beats going to bed starving. But I did go to bed starving for two decades, haunted by the famine of misidentification.

Identity and answering the call to activism are two themes I deal with in this book. Besides the major themes and plot noted on the cover, you will also find yourself by making this journey, traveling back with me to the embattled relationship of a butch daughter/son to her Latino father; to the perils of an unrequited love affair; and to the unshakable audacity of a twenty-six year old advocacy journalist coping with a life lived at the intersections of multiple American civil rights struggles.

Speaking of difficult topics, I leave bread crumbs that mark the trail of a life story condensed here in two years that will show you the fullness of how I and other outlaw activists lived. I also talk to you about depression, pill popping, alcoholism, and unresolved parental issues so that young activists today will know they are not alone, and not think themselves rendered incapable by the false seduction of this kind of background music. Such notes are no excuse for inaction.

Each generation of social justice activists and artists comes of age convinced that the battles they face are unique to history. History is a spiral of relapse and overlaps which push the envelope of identity and liberation a new step forward, then back, then further forward. The "isms" of my youth—black nationalism, *Chicanismo*, American imperialism, feminism, gay liberationism, sexism, lesbian separatism—arose in the '60s and '70s because world consciousness was at the dawn of change over these issues. We need to realize that global "noises" like the massive contagion of democratic revolt called the Arab Spring could not possibly have taken place in the 1970s because that generation of Middle Eastern activists was overwhelmed and preoccupied with adjusting to their imposed post-colonial boundaries. The first wave of feminism, the suffrage movement of the early 1900's, could not have raised the issue of a woman's right to choose because the technology of birth control, just like the technology called Facebook, was buried in the future. Karl Marx writes that technology underpins and directs the possibilities of social change. I agree with this construct.

Today, the United States has new issues and names for new "isms." Our post constructionist vs. essentialist youngest generation, the Millennials, conduct their activism at the intersections of globalism vs. globalization, states rights vs. federalism, female circumcision vs. transnational feminism, gender disorder vs. gender performativity, assimilationism vs. cultural multiplicity, and nationalism vs. migration, to name just a few. Queer social change advocates and artists also have new "isms" and speak of transgenderism, queer theory, gender fluidity and variance, essentialism, Butchdom, and trans-malehood. The very name of the movement in which I came of age—the gay and lesbian movement—is now called the queer or LGBTQ movement. Gays and lesbians are but a majority tribe in this expanded version of people committed to the exploration and liberation of gender identity. Queer theory and transgender politics have revolutionized the way young people today relate to their bodies and society. "Queer" now includes a host of self-identities beyond gender or sexual orientation. Queer words are the forbidden words now used by those who choose to become a power that speaks to truth. And the word "gender"—used in my youth to refer to men and women—is now popularly used to define the specifics of one's performativity. Queers of color now form the vanguard of challenge to the 'heteronormative' (formerly, 'straight') world. How far we've come!

My point is that hidden in the "ism" of each generation is the seed of the next revolt. The "isms" of today have unfolded from the "isms" of yesterday as each generation begins where their foremothers left off. So activists beware—understanding what happened yesterday will show you what you can make happen tomorrow.

To tell you what happened in my yesterday, I've had to make a few authorial compromises. Real life, unlike a book, does not include the orderly playing out of disasters, victories, or morals-of-the-story. For most of us life doesn't unfold so neatly. Memoirists are forced to hunt and peck through the messy events of our lives—the loss of love, a death, betrayal by comrades—as if they occurred in a sane sequential cause and effect manner. A few events in this memoir took place one or two months before or after the dates I imply. I brought forward or moved back such dates hoping to create an articulate narrative arc for readers. Because I take historical accuracy very seriously, you will find date corrections noted in the "Endnotes" section at the back of the book. Endnotes also offer additional historical detail and relevant *chismes* (gossip) regarding some events. This section also fills in the end-of-the-story for some persons or political events that were not resolved until after the book's timeframe. Lastly, Endnotes includes comments from some of the characters in my memoir. I thought it only fair to give pivotal public players the chance to remark about their actions before mine are consigned to the ever evolving sequence called history.

I've used the real names of everyone in this book who played a public or historic role. Pseudonyms have been given to two personal characters with small roles, and notably to "Rachel" due to the extraordinarily intimate nature of our story. All representations of the people in this memoir and my relationship with them are true. Truth is necessary, it keeps us sane. Secrets bend the mind into more hurtful "realities" that never existed. Yet, in rendering this story, I have given *my* truth; others may have their own "truth of the matter."

This work is written as a novelized memoir because I wanted it to be accessible to everyone, not just academics or historians. I also wanted to present history as a living thing, not just a documentary type sequence of impersonal truths. By structuring and styling my work as a novel, I have re-created dialog that reflects the emotional truth of those long ago conversations and people, rendering dialog as correctly as memory, old tapes, papers, diaries and research allow. Paying more attention to content, I cannot claim to have rendered the style of conversation—especially among personal rather than political characters—accurate to each person's personality. It is not my wish to hurt or cause problems for persons alive or dead with whom I interacted during the years portrayed in this memoir. If I have done so please accept my sincere apologies. A memoirist has only her own truth with which to define and express her historical view, so please forgive any pain I may have caused as I have sought to find my truth.

In 1999, I sat down to write a butch's simple love story, but out popped a political drama of wider scope. I sat down to write an autobiography and out popped two sole years of my life. I sat down to write a book about what it means to grow up deleted and dangerous in American culture. A constant beacon in my life has been the reimagining of myself, or an entire generation of teens, growing up in a queer-affirming loving world. If you are one of these youth, this book is about you. And if you are one of the hundreds who lived through these times and changed history, "the kids" and I salute you.

Fondly, JC

Foreword
by Lillian Faderman

I first saw Jeanne Córdova in 1971 in Los Angeles. She was on a panel of feminists and lesbian feminists, and though I can't remember much of what was said that day—by her or by any of the panelists—she was indeed memorable. A soft-spoken panelist had just begun her comments when a couple of people in the large audience yelled "Louder!" The speaker stopped and looked puzzled. Jeanne rose from her seat: to this day I can vividly see her lift the microphone from where it sat at the long table and place it in just the right spot so that the woman might be heard. It was such a simple gesture, but it spoke volumes. It was full of grace and graciousness, and an extraordinary confidence, too. It said, "I take the responsibility for making this panel a success and the audience happy." It said, "I know I have the power to do this." It also drew all eyes to Jeanne, and it was clear that though she was only in her early twenties, she was used to having all eyes drawn to her. She was, very simply, remarkable in her style and appearance—wearing an Elvis Presley shirt with flowing sleeves, her hair combed a la James Dean, her boy-girl form lithe and graceful—a "pretty butch," as her lover Rachel accurately dubs her in this memoir; but with so much more smarts, force, charisma, and natural leadership ability than "pretty butch" would suggest. I knew that day that here was a young leader such as the lesbian movement in Los Angeles sorely needed.

Jeanne captures so well in these pages the early—and mid-1970s, when the movement that she skillfully led in Los Angeles was at its height. Lesbians of that day, particularly lesbian-feminists, were impassioned activists—angry, committed, and bold—who took a page from the Black Power and Anti-War movements. Lesbian-feminists knew with certainty that the powers-that-be were wrong and corrupt, and they were happy to tell them so, and send them to hell. As a leader, Jeanne Córdova had to figure out how to take their wonderful but unruly energy and channel it into constructive action. Her task, as she shows here, was often like that of herding cats.

Jeanne was on the scene and in front of the pack for virtually every major event or piece of business that involved the Los Angeles lesbian movement in the 1970s. She not only helped organize the 1971 gay pride parade in L.A., but she also brought gender parity to the parade—lesbians up front in equal numbers with gay men. She was a wily strategist, who used good sense as well as a wicked sense of humor for the sake of the cause—figuring out, for example, a wonderfully novel way of getting rid of homophobes who came to jeer at the parade. She organized the first—and extremely important—national lesbian conference in 1973. She was the leading lesbian columnist and reporter for what was, arguably, the most important alternative newspaper in the country, the *Los Angeles Free Press*. She was the founder and editor of one of the most vital lesbian-feminist journals of the era—*The Lesbian Tide*.

Jeanne Córdova was notably different from the usual militant lesbian-feminist of the era. For example, though she was a leader in the feminist strike against the gay male leadership at the Los Angeles Gay Center, she understood that ultimately what was at stake was the health and unity of the gay and lesbian cause, that burning the Center down, as some wanted to do, or taking it to court, as others wanted to do, would only hurt the very important cause. While many lesbian-feminists wanted to throw gay men out with the bath water, Jeanne sensibly argued that it was the duty of lesbians to "drag our gay brothers into enlightenment." She was able to make important distinctions, too subtle for many would-be leaders, between the enemy and the misguided opposition. As any good leader must, she kept her head while all about her were losing theirs.

She would do anything for the sake of the institutions and projects in which she believed. For example, when the owner of the company that printed *The Lesbian Tide* dubbed a particular cover obscene and refused to print it, she struck a deal with him. She would give him an hour's worth of tips "for getting broads into bed" in return for his printing the issue. He agreed. Of course Jeanne gave him "all the wrong information I could think of." She was a girl-butch-knight, fighting the dragons that would destroy the movement with any weapon she could muster. Like all good knights, she owned a dashing "Lionheart" that took her from dragon to dragon. Though Lionheart was not a trusty steed in this case, but a car—a red Cougar—"he" was as loved as any knight of old loved his trusty steed.

When We Were Outlaws evokes a time that will seem like ancient history to many who live in an era when the president of the United States has called himself a "fierce advocate" for LGBT rights, major American businesses advertise in queer publications, the words gay and lesbian are used often and neutrally in the mass media, and Ellen DeGeneres and Rachel Maddow have their own national television shows. To those of us who lived that time, though, it will seem like only yesterday—those years Jeanne writes about, when we were outlaws. For anyone who lived through the 1970s, this book will be a stunning reminder of how young we once were, how earnest and revolutionary and deliciously naïve.

With humor and passion, Jeanne interweaves in this book the story of her political activism with the story of her romantic adventures. She focuses particularly on a love affair that was more than an adventure—in an era when non-monogamy was requisite for any politically-correct lesbian. She shows how lesbian-feminists tried to live their politics in their personal lives—and the complications that such youthful idealism often wrought. Those who weren't around in the 1970s will be intrigued to learn of the rules of the social institutions around lesbian-feminism, how you were supposed to conduct yourself in a long-term non-monogamous relationship, the androgyny of style to which all lesbian-feminists were supposed to adhere. These rules may seem so amusing and antiquated to us now, but Jeanne presents them not just with the wisdom of hindsight but also with tenderness for the well-meaning but sometimes misguided enthusiasms of that era. She shows what happened when the idealistic theories of lesbian-feminism met the realities of life and human emotions. She shows how theory that makes sense in the abstract can create such pain and complications for those who try to live by it.

Jeanne brings great honesty to the portraits she paints in this book—even to her own portrait, which is often a painful task for a memoirist. She depicts herself as being sometimes wide-eyed, sometimes wild-eyed; sometimes a dreamer, sometimes a schemer; sometimes impetuous, and sometimes wise. Her insights into what made her tick—especially the difficult family dynamics that we are all destined to repeat in our most significant relationships—are stunning in their acuity and frankness.

When We Were Outlaws offers a huge slice of lesbian-feminist history as it played itself out in 1970s Los Angeles. It's a moving evocation of the sweet innocence and incredible enthusiasm of youth, and of a time that feels like yesterday but happened—incredibly—almost two generations ago.

Acknowledgements

This is a memoir and also a history book. I wish to thank my research editor, Lynn Harris Ballen, for her hundreds of hours devoted to bringing these political events to accurate life. And my P.C. editor, Ariana Manov, who reviewed each chapter for its political nuance. Without either of them I might have surrendered well before the twelve years it has taken to bring you this story. My thanks also to Judith Branzburg for her fine editing. No one could have wished for a more supportive editor in preparing this work for its publisher by cutting, oh, say, twenty-five thousand unnecessary words.

It does indeed take a village to birth a book. My village people are:

Don Weise, former editor at Alyson Books, who first accepted my work and lent his prodigious mind to showing me how to make it better.

Author and friend Mark Thompson, who became my coach when I was down to the twenty yard line, and helped push me through the fear of hurtling over the end zone. For his great generosity of spirit and humble wit, I thank friend and champion Stuart Timmons, who encouraged me to write "important political stories" even when he was exhausted from his own great work, GAY L.A. Deepest thanks also to "Rachel" for her uncommon courage and willingness to share our story.

My teachers and fellows at Lambda Literary Foundation's first Writers' Retreat for Emerging LGBT Voices—particularly Terry De Crescenzo, Fenton Johnson, and Katherine Forrest

—for her stalwart belief in me. Writers@Work founder Terry Wolverton, my classmates Cara Chow and "Amgen Matt"— who first validated my love scenes as "hot" from his gay boy perspective.

My lesbian writers group mates Lisa Freeman, Komal Bhojwani and Rachel Harper. Close friends, Professor Talia Mae Bettcher and Susan Forrest, who lent me their smart minds and feedback skills. Dear old friends—historian Lillian Faderman and publisher Art Kunkin.

My dyke gang LEX, the Lesbian Exploratorium Project, for hosting the launch events for this book and standing together with me through so many lesbian cultural projects.

And gracious thanks to LBGTQ archives that exist to give authors like me the primary materials from which to produce new work. Particular thanks to Loni Shibuyama, chief research dyke at the ONE Archives of Los Angeles, and to the Southern California Library.

Finally, I want to acknowledge my mother and father who first acknowledged me as "an interesting character." The sense of discipline they instilled in me—never leave something unfinished, above all, never quit—was often the only internal sensibility which kept me going. Their strength of will and purpose has been core to my life. My father died the year I finished writing this memoir. I did not tell him about this book because as a Catholic he had eternity much on his mind—lots of sins and a preoccupation with how many years in purgatory he'd have to spend before seeing my mother once more in heaven. I'd like to think he would have simply said of this book, "I never said I was perfect. You have to do what you have to do, pal. Just be excellent at it."

As a longtime journalist, activist, publisher, and author, no project has been more difficult for me than writing this book. I heartily thank my spouse, Lynn, who has endured this other lover in our lives for so long. Her acumen, multiplicity of talents, and devotion to me and Lesbian Nation continue to amaze me.

Table of Contents

Chapter 1

The Last Guerrilla Left Standing

[San Francisco]

Dateline: San Francisco Mission District-September 18, 1975

They stand separated, handcuffed yet defiant. Each boxed in, tightly surrounded by FBI agents in the underground parking lot of an ordinary apartment building.

"General Teko" by his fugitive SLA name, Bill Harris slouches— solitary, hunched like a big cat ready to pounce if the handcuffs don't hold or a captor looks away long enough for him to snatch his wife, Emily, and split.

Emily Harris, thin, mousey-haired with strung out bangs, gaunt-cheeked from fourteen months of living on the run, looks at the camera, her face caught between defiance and despair. And "Tanya," Patty Hearst by her white, bourgeois name, stands several car spaces apart from her comrades, fragile, an out-of-place urban guerrilla, teary and vulnerable, repentant revolutionary or terrified prisoner—only her hairdresser knows for sure. She is at the top of the FBI's Most Wanted list for her leadership in the Symbionese Liberation Army.

Patty Hearst

EDITORIAL:

Paper-tiger radicals?

JEANNE CORDOVA

The political soap opera of the decade closed midseason: the closing was rumored but still unexpected.

Some say the leading character was bored and feared if she stayed with the series she would be type-cast for life. The show ran just over 19 months, second in the ratings only to Watergate.

revolutionists, who have spent their lives in careful struggle, will think this bunch "cheap" — paper-tiger radicals who saw revolution as a Yellow Brick Road, skipped on the cracks and wrote "fuck you" on the Mad Hatter's dungarees to the mommy and daddy who bought their chalk. They will say a young woman's boredom made a joke of their sweat. They will

Symbionese Liberation Army members are captured by FBI. Patricia Hearst, Wendy Yoshimura, Emily Harris, and Bill Harris. *Los Angeles Free Press, September 1975*

Her chestnut locks fall smartly in waves around her face. It's a good hair day. But a bad day, perhaps the last day, for the revolution.

The camera refocuses on a bearded Bill, about to be tossed into a waiting black van lettered Federal Bureau of Investigation. His dark eyes glassy with rage, he raises steel-cuffed fists above his head, clasps them together in a power-to-the people salute. He mouths our chant: The revolution lives on!

The Feds are careful, uptight, crew-cut, muscled men in suits who do not move. The camera is watching them too. They need to play it by the book. No mistrial for these three, the last of the Symbionese Liberation Army, the last of the Underground Left, the last who matter to America anyway.

A cop knocks Bill's hands down and waves the camera away... toward Hearst, mislaid daughter of America's ruling class. Her tall, thin frame accompanies a white-on-white complexion that manages wordless surprise: Why is everyone looking for little ol' me?

That Patty Hearst is the center of the Western World's attention confirms the vacuity of the culture that that spawned her. But Patty Hearst, newspaper heiress gone rogue radical, granddaughter of press baron William Randolph Hearst of the San Francisco Examiner, doesn't interest me.

I move closer, sit on the floor to get a better look at the small screen's grainy, black and white video. My colleagues, fellow staff of the Los Angeles Free Press, huddle together in the Production Department listening to the televised news. The story that captures my reporter's instinct is that of Emily Harris, wife to Bill, college student, middle class emblem of the sixties. Emily is the last feminist left alive in the SLA. I didn't want her caught, her life cut short before she was old enough to make a thoughtful contribution to our cause. She is my last guerrilla left standing.

Her face is walled off, jaw clenched, stoic; I see she is blue-eyed. I know we are the same age, same height, same frame size, same Irish nose. Emily Montague Schwartz—"Yolanda" by her revolutionary name. Both of us recent students of political sociology, me at UCLA, *her at the U. of Indiana. Her ever-so-great immigrant grandparents came to America to give their progeny a chance at a better life. Better than what? Emily and I want to know. What if Emily Montague Schwartz is me and I am her, just another freedom fighter trying to supplant capitalism? Why is it Emily—and not me—who is today a captured revolutionary? Why does she face the end of her life while I look to a future free to be an activist in the lesbian and feminist movements?*

And why does the footage show Emily, small and frozen in her early morning jogging shorts? CBS anchorman Walter Cronkite speaks fast and furiously. The Feds spotted Bill and Emily this morning on a sidewalk as they stepped out of their heavily surveilled apartment to go jogging. I gasp! A careless California moment—jogging. Hadn't they had enough exercise running from the FBI this long and tortuous final year?

My editor-in-chief speaks loudly, declaring, "It's the end of an era!"

"Yes," I reply. "The sixties are finally over—just five years late."

"So much for the revolution," she adds. "I guess we'd better get on with the Reformation."

"Sadly true," I agree, wondering whether the Symbionese Liberation Army is to the Left what the strike at our LA Gay Community Services Center is to the lesbian and gay movement: the last gasp of a falsely united political front. The chaotic battle in my current life at the Gay Community Services Center has also just failed. The Establishment has won. Nineteen seventy-five is lopping off radicals on the right and the left. Only those in the middle are left standing.

Police helicopters, the pigs' newest addition to preying on American civil liberties, begin to leave the screen. A phalanx of wide-bodied undercover-cop cars carrying Emily, Bill and Patty spill out of the underground parking structure like tanks in a Russian parade. I bow my head, my hands covering my face.

The country has been divided for months; anti-war Leftists hoping that Hearst and her SLA anti-capitalist comrades would evade the FBI forever; the Establishment and their ilk seeing Leftist freedom fighters as simple criminals disturbing the status quo. The SLA's brain spasm of kidnapping a high-profile member of the elite class had completely buried the group's initial noble political action— demanding two million dollars from Hearst's father to feed the poor in Oakland. Randolph Hearst had coughed up the money, supply trucks with food had scurried into the mostly black township a year ago. But in the interim, the SLA had robbed several banks and left one innocent bystander dead. By now the radical group's message about the politics of poverty had been lost. Today mainstream media's sole preoccupation was—is—Patty Hearst a kidnap victim or a willing rifle-toting, bank-robbing urban guerilla? And the question my Free Press radical readership wanted answered was—what does today's news mean for the survival of the Left?

Over the last decade, we on the Left—with the Los Angeles Free Press as one of our voices—had toppled a crooked President, ended a no-win imperialist war, re-fought the Civil War and won voting and housing rights for black Americans, introduced the counterculture lifestyle in which a young person could "Turn on, tune in, drop out," and brought forth the still radical notion of "free love." These movements of the sixties were ebbing but new concepts of potential radical change had recently swept into my life, and the lives of thousands like me. From Boston to Los Angeles small cells of women had begun to gather to protest the second class citizenship of womanhood in the Western World. Homosexuals were marching in the streets to redefine gay as a way of being rather than a crime. From our successful victories in other peoples' movements, we as women and queers knew we could continue to change the world. And here I was, lucky enough to be born on the cusp of two eras. Good timing had always been a blessing in my life. There was much to be done. My people—gays—could hold a job or rent an apartment, but only if we pretended to be straight and stay deeply in the closet. For me, that was nowhere close to good enough.

A staff member turns off the TV. My editor's hand is suddenly on my shoulder. "Córdova, I need you up in Editorial. We need to cover this story. We've got ten hours before deadline."

I lift my head and shake it back to present time. "Cover what, Penny? Everything looks over to me."

"Every newspaper in the country will be all over this story." My editor's tone sounds sharp as she motions me upstairs. "That means we have to dig deeper, uncover an angle that no one else has. I want you to find Emily Harris and get her story."

Born in 1962, the *Los Angeles Free Press* was America's first underground newspaper. *The Freep* and I had been lovers—me as her Human Rights Editor and investigative reporter—for two years now. Our story was one of love at first sight.

The Freep had tracked the first anti-Vietnam street protests, the rise and fall of the Black Panthers, the drug-experimental lifestyle of Timothy Leary, the FBI and LAPD spying on activists, and every musical, theatrical, or civil rights-oriented band of brothers and sisters trying to build a counterculture based on peace, love, and brown rice. It was not unusual to step over the lounging forms of Bobby Dylan, Allen Ginsberg or Abbe Hoffman hanging out in our bead-strung hippie coffee room. And *The Freep* was not uptight about covering the newest of the radical movements, the gay and lesbian one that most papers wouldn't even credit with being an organized wave of social change. This was my movement, and at twenty-six, I'd logged five years as a pioneer gay activist. Coming out of Social Work grad school, I'd studied my Saul Alinsky thoroughly, but the father of modern urban rabble-rousing had not told me that being a front line organizer could be so emotionally exhausting. Burnout was the factor that drove me to *The Free Press.*

In the fall of '73, I felt as if I'd just been released from an emotional halfway house. Disappointments and betrayals triggered by my role as a key organizer of the National Lesbian Conference at UCLA had left me feeling battered by the very tribe of women that I'd made a lifetime vow to serve. The Conference, the largest gathering of lesbians in history, had been a moment of divination and a specific kind of hell. My own lesbian feminist newspaper, *The Lesbian Tide*, had called it, "the cloning of a nation."{1} Two thousand lesbians from forty-five American states had come to L.A. to speak their piece. Every big-name lesbian speaker, strategist and leader in the country had attended. Warring ideological groups of women from different parts of the country had fractured over the stage presence of a transsexual woman, the encroachment of the Socialist Worker's Party, the public drunkenness of superstar Kate Millet during her keynote speech, and a divisive rant by the other keynoter, Robin Morgan, author of the new bible of feminism, *Sisterhood Is Powerful*. The "shoutalong" had split our community into rabidly disparate political ideologies. The birth of Lesbian Nation at UCLA had been so psychologically labored for me, its primary midwife, that I'd run away from Los Angeles. I'd hitchhiked north to a small Sacramento music festival trying to travel anonymously while every lesbian feminist publication in the country was slicing and dicing me and the other organizers. At the music gathering I'd met a song-writer named Margie Adam, who led me to discover that I could write my way out of a nervous breakdown. I'd written hundreds of pages about depression and breaking through it. And in this healing, it dawned on me that *writing* about Lesbian Nation might take me out of the over-exposed trench of trying to organize it. Writing for a living might also feed the hunger for words and journalism that I'd left behind in adolescence. Perhaps, I hoped, I was even good enough to earn a living at it.

Returning to Los Angeles, I possessed no credentials as a reporter. But I was adamant that I had to write for my town's only radical paper, *The L.A. Free Press*. To get a job I'd have to rely on chutzpah and wit and no small amount of my mother's Irish luck.

On a busy Monday morning, I slipped past the pot-smoking receptionist and scurried through the aisles bluffing as though

I belonged, notebook in hand, searching for the Editorial Department. I knew I'd found it when the intense buzz of voices gave way to the quiet clicking of typewriters. Peering through the haze, I knew I'd be at home in a career where everyone smoked. Finally, I espied the well-known, electrically frayed and Afro-styled blond head of the famous publisher, Art Kunkin.

Before anyone discovered that I was in fact nobody, I accosted him. "Good afternoon, Mr. Kunkin." I jutted out my hand and shook his. "My name is Jeanne Córdova. I've read your paper carefully, and I am here to tell you that what *The Free Press* needs is a gay columnist—one who is also a feminist and a Chicana. Hiring me gives you three oppressed minorities for the price of one!"

Kunkin studied me intently. Minions around him stopped their chatter.

"You look the part, Córdova, but you talk pretty white to me," barked the stocky, pale-faced hippie. Turning to his built-in audience, he continued, "So, we get three for the price of one, but the question is...can it write?"

"Yes, she can!" I thrust a sheaf of articles from my paper, *The Lesbian Tide*, and my columns from the big gay paper, *The Advocate*, in front of him.

Kunkin lit up a smoke and took my portfolio. Thumbing through it, he rubbed his chin thoughtfully. Finally, he bellowed, "Douglas!" A staffer came running down the aisle.

"Douglas," he repeated. "Clear this kid a desk. Give her two weeks. If you don't like what you read, fire her." He turned back to me. "And you'd better keep your community of fags and dykes happy. We like covering this new movement." As he walked away he called back, "You don't mind being called a dyke?"

"That's what I am!" I jumped up and down thrilled that The Man—the legendary Kunkin—had hired me.

Kunkin was brilliantly ruthless with my copy and everyone else's. I admired the man because in the name of the oppressed he broke all the rules and fought the Establishment in print. But as a publisher his weak suit was finance and the times they were a changin'. A year after I joined his staff, *The Freep's* debts got the better of him and he was forced to sell his paper. He'd been one of the few people in my life under whom I was proud to serve.

Now, under new ownership in the fall of '75, *Freep* headquarters remained the same fifties-style warehouse located at 5550 Hollywood Blvd in the heart of old Hollywood. Most of the city's wealth had moved west, toward Beverly Hills, but I didn't care. After a stultifying butch adolescence in L.A.'s Stepford suburbs, any part of Hollywood was paradise to me. *The Freep's* Production Department on the first floor housed the paper in all its myriad forms. A constant stream of super-sized production boards, carried by paste-up artists whose shoes crackled with the sound of hardened wax, clogged the aisles. The carpet was so old it looked like the cement floor had been poured over it. No formal delineations marked different departments, except a flight of stairs up to Editorial. Kunkin believed that the sum of the parts was fed by the whole. Although he was no longer around, the ever-present buzz of Kunkin mania still permeated the place. Over the last two blitzkrieg years I'd risen from once-a-week dyke columnist to a three stories per week investigative reporter with a title of Human Rights Editor. Since Kunkin had left, I'd worked for two nitwit Editors in Chief who'd come and gone quickly. Finally, the new absentee publishers had given the top slot to a talented and gracious woman named Penelope Grenoble. My own cubbyhole, an eight by ten private room on the second floor, was located across from Penny's office and next to the City Editor, Tom Thompson.

A week after the world and the FBI felt safe once more now that America's sweetheart-flipped-guerrilla-action-figure had been returned to her ruling class perch, Penny sent me another urgent summons.

"You wanted to see me?" I asked dully, as I threw myself into the chair in front of her Chieftain's desk. The shock of seeing the Hearst capture had worn off, and I'd come back to reality thoroughly bummed. The news was rocking the country. Several of the slain SLA women were lesbians, news that would stun the readership of my own newspaper, *The Lesbian Tide*.{2} It was also Friday night, the night I saw the new love of my life, Rachel. But she hadn't called or answered my messages in weeks. I'd carelessly tried to juggle our personal relationship with my political life, asking her to wait. Three weeks ago she'd walked out on me. So had Morris Kight, my political godfather and founder of the Gay Community Services Center, the scene of my recent political debacle. The bowstring of my psyche was unraveling. The weekend stretched before me with no plans to see Rachel, no calls from Morris, and no political meetings. I slouched into Penny's chair, swung my boots onto her desk and emitted a depressed sigh.

Penny sat up straight behind her desk. "I just heard that Patty Hearst wrote in the 'occupation' slot in her booking report that she was an 'urban guerilla.'"

"That woman is so dumb that's probably the only job she's ever had. I hope that's not why you asked me to report in?"

"Of course not," my editor shot back. "I just had a great idea. So I made a phone call."

My usually demure editor was as wide-eyed as I'd ever seen her. Penny the Chief was a decade older than me and had a Ph.D. in English Literature. The most educated of all the staff, she was also the prettiest, not counting the guys, which I didn't. Petite—just my type—with fine features and even finer doe-brown eyes, she was a hard to resist femme package for a lesbian butch like me. Thankfully, she was straight as an arrow. This kept our working relationship uncomplicated.

"A phone call to who?" I asked dully.

"Emily Harris's probable new attorney that's who. I've been thinking. Since Hearst has gone down, wouldn't it be possible to get an interview with Emily?"

"Yeah, us and every other paper in the country."

"Well…" Penny smiled, looking every inch the editor bursting with the next big scoop. Her nicely arranged features, capped by brown rim glasses that gave her a scholarly look, were sharply tensed. "I've just learned that Harris will be flown down here, to L.A. She'll be held at Sybil Brand Institute for Women."

My mind slowly flew east, across downtown L.A. to the women's prison on the hill over looking the San Bernardino Freeway. Last year, my *Tide* staff had led a demonstration in front of the large county prison, protesting its infamous Daddy Tank, a separate wing where they housed butch-lesbian inmates.

"Emily could be held at S.B.I. for months!" Penny continued.

"So?" I grunted, wondering why the hell I couldn't get revved about the best story idea Penny had ever put on my plate. Somehow nothing seemed important since Rachel had disappeared, with no note and no good-bye. I hated bringing my personal life to work, so I hadn't told Penny.

She kept talking. "My old friend Leonard Weinglass just returned my call. He says…"

I wondered briefly how Penny had a connection with the big name Lefty lawyer who was about to step forward to handle Harris' case pro bono. But that was Penny's job—connections.

"Leonard says Emily might be looking to tell her story. But she'll only consider feminist reporters. I'm guessing, as a socialist, she won't be giving her story to the *L.A. Times*. She knows they won't print her motivations as she sees them." Penny's pale green eyes were twinkling with excitement.

"So who do you think she'll choose?"

"You!" Penny stared me down. "You're perfect. Didn't you tell me that the SLA had self-avowed lesbian members that were killed by the pigs in the Watts fire last year?"

"Yeah?" I tried to shake my gloom and bend my mind to Penny's. The accidentally televised shoot-out between the LAPD and the SLA in Watts last year had been savage. At least the Hearst arrest had gone down without bullets. "There were two lesbians in the SLA. A woman named Mizmoon and her lover Camilla Hall. They were murdered in the Watts shootout."

"So don't you see it, Córdova? As a feminist Chicana, an overt lesbian reporter, you're perfect! I want you to write Harris a personal letter saying how much *The Freep* wants an interview. Tell her about your politics. Tell her you'll write her story the way she wants it told. Wake up, Córdova. We've got a perfect shot at this. You and Emily have everything in common!"

Everything in common. Penny's words finally broke through. Much more in common than you know, Penny, my inner voice said. I'd never told Penny that my own paper, *The Lesbian Tide*, was close to underground women fugitives. I'd never told anyone that I knew these women were reading *The Tide* because we dropped issues at a safe place for them to pick up. And most of all, I'd never told Penny that armed struggle was a question I'd been dealing with personally. That I had friends who were close to these women and that I too wondered what I'd say if a fugitive sister asked me to pick up a gun for the revolution. Sometimes my heart ached to watch the pigs hunting down my sisters. These radical years I too proceeded on a need to know basis and my editor didn't need to know how close I was to the line between advocacy journalist and participant. A line which at times felt almost porous to me.

"All right, Penny. I'm in. I'll do it." I got to my feet and saluted my editor with a snap of my wrist. "It's a brilliant idea."

I turned to leave her office, embarrassed that my brain was too overloaded to have come up with the idea myself.

"Córdova," she called out to me, "I want your letter to Emily on my desk before you leave work today!"

"Whatever you say," I called back over my shoulder, as I ambled back to my cubbyhole. Closing the glass door behind me, I sat down at my desk. Penny's face pressed against my glass wall. "Today!" she mouthed.

I took paper out of my top drawer and ran a sheet through my typewriter, and waved Penny off with a silent, *See me writing!*

Dear Ms. Harris, I began. But no words followed. My mind talked to Rachel. *Where are you? When will you come back to me?*

I no longer had the capacity or desire to talk politics with anyone—not with Emily Harris, not with the Blessed Virgin Mary. Harris would be in jail for months before her trial, and possibly too blown away by her own defeat and capture to respond to any reporter. For once in my life, my heart was dictating that politics could wait until I found a way to repair my personal life. Emily the freedom-fighter had to wait long enough for me to go back, retrace my steps, find out where I'd gone wrong with Rachel, Morris, and the whole damn gay strike. I had to win them both back. I couldn't face myself, much less Emily Harris, until I'd faced my own demons. Was it only last November that my life had felt so promising and full of hope?

Chapter 2

The Hat

[Los Angeles]

Dateline: Grand View Street, Midtown, November 11, 1974

The stars pierced a crisp winter's eve the night I first met Rachel. I was covering a story at the Woman's Building, an L.A. art institute that was both a feminist venue and a lesbian hangout. Entering the courtyard's sanctuary, I strode between the pillars of the stately two-story relic on Grand View. It was packed with some four hundred lesbians mostly clad in the counterculture uniform of androgynous dress—low-slung bell-bottoms, anti-war bandanas, shirts from the Salvation Army, Birkenstock sandals, and frizzed out hair. The vibrations of "woman-power" injected the air with edgy exhilaration.

Happy to be walking on women-loving-women ground, I buried myself deep in the crowd. I could feel the electricity—the rustle of women rubbing shoulder to shoulder, the muted, sweet smother of tightly packed sisterhood. After years of activism, I was still thrilled to be part of the family of women.

We—the family—had come together that night to hear Angela Davis, the controversial former UCLA professor, read from her newly released autobiography about political prisoners, Panthers, and other purist propaganda. The woman, the philosopher, the disciple of Marx, sat on a small stool in front of us smoking a pipe. Seeing her in the flesh—the aggressive jut of her jaw, the angle of her wrist as she held her pipe, her don't-fuck-with-me attitude—begged me to recognize something familiar about her. The woman reeked of lesbian butch body language! Aha, I smiled to myself. The scuttlebutt on the gay grapevine was right—Davis had to be gay. Her forbidding black spectacles, however, seemed to ward off any invitation to a personal life, implying she was of the mind only, above the debris of human emotion.

Davis began her speech by laying a basis for what she called "an increasingly fascist pattern" in America's government. She

Courtyard of original Woman's Building on Grandview, scene of numerous feminist and lesbian artistic and political events in 1974. *Woman's Building Slide Archive at Otis College of Art and Design*

brought up examples of racism in our judicial system, like how Nixon was acquitted before coming to trial, while her black cellmate was held in prison for eighteen months before coming to trial.

The audience was half drifting, not listening too closely when, in the middle of her speech, she blithely said, "Alternative sexual orientations are a bourgeois affectation."

My pen stopped scribbling. An audible rumble, like a rolling 6.1 earthquake, vibrated through the mostly white, but mostly lesbian audience. I looked up and thought—this could be a real short night.

Angela also looked up. Her lips tightened as her eyebrows registered the crowd's response. She stopped speaking. Everyone waited.

The wave of the quake subsided. In a rare burst of collective dyke forgiveness, the audience settled back down. Whew! It was my turn to be surprised. They were not going to walk out. No white woman could have said what Davis said and still have an audience. These were volatile years, when dykes brooked no disrespect. But we also knew Davis had earned her veteran activist stripes by being jailed by the FBI for allegedly helping her political prisoner friend, George Jackson, escape. I also felt a certain sadness coming from my sisters. Somehow we accepted that this Communist intellectual was probably too cerebral to practice *any* sexual orientation.

As I pressed the stop button on my tape recorder and flipped the tape over I decided I wouldn't let Davis off so easily. I was covering her talk and book signing for *The Freep*, so it hadn't been too hard to arrange an interview with her after her talk. But I was also double hitting tonight, covering the event for my own newsmagazine, *The Lesbian Tide*. I checked my pockets and found three more cassettes. Tonight I'd strike a blow for my lesbian readership, which was rapidly growing as we picked up subscribers from college towns as far away as Duke in North Carolina. I'd make it my job to convince the Afro-haired political activist to come out of the closet.

Chewing the plastic cap of my ballpoint, I turned to study the people in Angela's entourage. I tried to spot a woman lover's body language. No one. Nada.

For now, I listened carefully to the rest of her speech, hoping the well-connected Leftist might say something about the fugitive freedom fighters she had to know. Perhaps she'd drop a comment about a change in direction of the New Left's stratagem on urban guerilla warfare. The subject interested me, as well as both of my newspapers. Many of us radical activists were groping with the question of how far to go in confronting the military-industrial complex. With the kind of people I knew, any day now I might be asked to commit more than civil disobedience. More likely, the choice would drop in front of me with no notice, and I'd have to rely on instinct. I'd be called upon to print something in *The Lesbian Tide*, or approached as a known *Tide* staffer and asked to hide a sister who was a fugitive. It was a question I had to come to terms with way down inside me where it mattered. The times were combustible, boundaries between right and wrong morphed faster than I could wake up some mornings. Last May, millions of Americans had watched those televised, but oh-so-real deaths of six members of the S.L.A. Searching desperately for Patricia Hearst, and following a three-hour gun battle, police SWAT teams moved in and fire-bombed the safe-house in South Central Los Angeles, killing six SLA comrades as thousands looked on in the streets surrounded by many dozens of cop cars. I'd felt a chill up my Leftist spine watching that day. I'd worked in Watts as a social worker, mere blocks from the torched house. After the SLA deaths, I'd spent several days holed up in my apartment, grieving because I knew that some of the dead were radical lesbians like me.

Scribbling notes as fast as I could, I lost Angela's train of thought somewhere around her saying, "It is true that women were the first group to be oppressed but...there is a different quality in the oppression that prevails under, say, feudalism, than that which prevails under capitalism." The woman could out-talk and out-think me any day of the week. At twenty-six

I was well versed in the ideological principles of most social movements of my day; but as Davis waxed on dialectically, I chided myself for not being properly prepared. I hadn't read all of her writings. I'd only skimmed her recent essays. Her resume alone made me feel, in my military father's words, like "an indolent speck on the map of life." No, I'd have to work much harder to be, like Angela, the perfect political machine—able to spout Marxist paragraphs, or better yet, quote lesbian feminist theory at the click of a microphone switch.

I reached into my pocket and checked my watch. A Masters degree out of UCLA and I still couldn't afford a new watchband. At this rate it looked like my interview would start after midnight. What would my self-made millionaire father say if he found out about my life's commitment to gay activism? In his boot-strap thinking, starting your own company and making a six-figure salary were the hallmarks of success. Luckily, he and I weren't on speaking terms. He didn't know what I was doing

Angela Davis tells lesbian audience, "alternative sexual orientations are a bourgeois affectation." *L.A. Free Press, November 1974.*

with my professional gay radical life.

I leaned against a marble pillar. Davis was taking questions now. I slipped on my sunglasses and lowered my brown suede hat. Its Australian flat brim hid my eyes so my sisters couldn't tell if I nodded off for a few minutes. Wearily, I closed my eyes.

Had I been focused less intently on Angela, and more on the audience around me, I might have noticed a woman named Rachel that night, a woman with robin-egg blue eyes studying me as closely as I was watching Angela. I might have seen that fair-skinned petite woman with blonde highlights crowning a curly mass of light chocolate brown hair talking to her friend and pointing in my direction. I might have noticed how intently she watched my lips, wondering if they were pursed in anger or in concentration. I might have learned that she'd come to the Woman's Building that night because she'd just turned twenty eight, just left her marriage, and was beginning to explore her lesbian feelings. And had I been less obsessed with work, I surely would have overheard as she asked her friend, "Who's that lovely woman over there, the one with the brown suede hat?"

I would have heard her friend reply, "Oh, that's Córdova. Leave her alone."

"She only has a last name?" the blue-eyed woman pursued the matter.

"Her first name is Jeanne," the friend answered. "But Rachel, everyone calls her Córdova. She's trouble. Forget her."

Awakening from my momentary catnap, I studied Angela's oval, plain-Jane face. Her name had been romantically linked with George Jackson, but it was a vague link, I thought, and a political one. Angela probably didn't do romance. The Communist Party line on romantic love was that it was "an irrelevant by-product of capitalism." Devout revolutionaries were supposed to meet, court, and consummate to the trumpets of the Fourth Internationale.

Fortunately for me, lesbians had a different take on sex, and also fortunately, I was born into well-arranged genes. My father's jet black hair, light brown Latino skin, and my mother's delicate placement of Irish features with well-defined dark bedroom eyes, and a ski-jump nose meant I hadn't needed to waste political time browsing lesbian bar culture to find a lover. Feminist protestations to the contrary, good looks still seemed to be a commodity among radical lesbian feminists. Being an activist leader brought dozens of women to my bed. Power seemed to attract people, and my political life put me at the center of the action which was exactly where I wanted to be.

My devotion to nation-building among lesbians was the reason I hadn't followed classmates out of graduate school into the corporate business world and life in the suburban flatlands of the now cool San Fernando Valley. Many friends had gone there eager to set up their lives in Plastic Land. I could have indulged in a professional social worker's routine, a normal life in which politics was background TV to the six o'clock cocktail hour. Normal wasn't my style. A consumer's life held little attraction. I wanted a more just world for my people. My role as a radical feminist lesbian was to spread the revolutionary word. When the revolution was over, maybe I'd move to the Valley and settle down. Besides, I reminded myself, I was indeed living with a lover, albeit in an open relationship where I'd had a steady flow of other affairs. The fact that none of them was satisfying had more to do with me, I was sure, than any of them.

Angela came to a long pause and I realized her talk had ended. Music and dancing would start now. That's what most of these newly minted lesbians had really come for—a chance to dance, to touch, to be with one another. Casting a last look back at my sisters I saw them starting to sway toward a makeshift dance floor. A small part of me envied them, but the larger part wanted to get the political scoop from Angela. I followed her toward an interview room, away from the music, away from my tribe.

Sitting in front of Davis, in the small room with two other reporters, I was surprised to see that she was only a few years older than me, no more than thirty. Her lean, taut body held itself like a trampoline that refused to be broken in. It flashed through my mind to ask her how she felt about white hippies wearing Afro hair in support of their black sisters and brothers. Quickly I decided against it; Angela looked too serious for pop-culture triviality. One of the reporters asked her if she thought prison conditions had improved in the last three years since she'd been released and started her new organization, the National Alliance Against Racist and Political Oppression.

As she answered my mind drifted in another direction. What could be so difficult for Davis about coming out gay? She had been the first political female on the FBI's Most Wanted list, had been arrested for helping Black Panther George Jackson escape, and had been widely persecuted for the lawfully protected act of preaching Communist beliefs in the land of the free. So why didn't she see that gays were part of the revolution?

She paused, and I saw my opportunity. "Ms. Davis," I said, "Black Panther leader Huey Newton said recently that the new Gay Liberation Movement was 'a friend and potential ally' in the civil rights struggle. Do you share his point of view?"

From the way she looked at me I could tell she had pegged me for a gay activist before I'd asked the question. Such was an occupational hazard for being an out and proud baby butch-looking dykelet with short black hair combed James Dean style.

"I believe that all people have a right to privacy in their personal lives," Davis said. "But there is a difference between the oppression of racism and economic exploitation…and the quality of discrimination against gay people."

My mind silently screamed, "Yeah, the difference is that economic exploitation is better than being raped for being a dyke or a faggot." But before I could rearrange my thoughts and press on, the third reporter was taking Davis back to her more comfortable subject, the Communist Party.

I wondered how to proceed. Davis would avoid calling on me now that she knew *The Free Press* had sent a gay militant. The woman didn't want to answer personal questions.

But feminism taught that the personal is political. Linking the two was a cornerstone of the feminist revolution, said Redstockings, the foremother cell of Radical Feminism. We daughters had begun to see everything in political terms. These days, smoking pot was a political statement.

I believed it was critical that Davis come out gay. It was not her personal choice; it was her obligation. How could my people walk the streets openly if our leaders remained afraid? Her coming out would make her a great role model for otherwise frightened black lesbians. In our battle to change the straight world, the cowardice of passing was the weak link in our lines. Condoning Angela's passing was no way to run a movement.

"Ms. Davis!" I shouted, jumping to my feet, "Would you be willing to say that you are gay, if you were gay?"

Davis' large eyes narrowed as if she were trying to block out an errant laser beam. With an air of detachment she studied me for a long moment that found us both sweating out an inconvenient truth.

"I'm not denying or affirming anything about my private life," she said. "Personal issues are not a relevant part of political life." {1}

She re-lit her pipe, which had long gone out.

"Next?" she said, dismissing me.

Chapter 3

Wisdom of the Cornfields 3

[Los Angeles]

Dateline: Culver City, April 1975

"Welcome home, honey!" my lover greeted me as I walked through her front door. She waved a sheaf of papers in the air like a lasso, kissed me on the cheek and announced, "I've got loads of messages for you!"

Barbara Jo "BeJo" Gehrke and I had met three years ago when she'd walked into a planning meeting of the National Lesbian Conference. At thirty-two she was six years older than me, a fact I liked. I relied on the wisdom of older women because I was almost always in over my head with some new action I'd planned and therefore looking for a soothing place to land.

"I've had a shit of a day." I hugged BeJo and dropped my cardboard briefcase on the kitchen table.

My life at BeJo's apartment was a respite from the normal stress and chaos of my political life, the place I went to retreat and gather my strength. We had the standard lesbian feminist relationship—non-monogamous—but she was my primary lover. In the jargon of the day primary lover meant the one you spent the most nights with, and the one whose schedule other secondary lovers were supposed to wrap around.

Ours was a plain, but functional, two-bedroom apartment that sat on thin legs over a carport in Culver City. It was a decidedly working-class building, but BeJo had made gingham curtains to wall out the world, and I'd spliced together an assortment of once grand wood furniture from garage sales in Beverly Hills.

"I have to work graveyard tonight, but I have an hour before I leave," BeJo said. "Come and eat. You must be tired walking in here at ten at night. I kept dinner warm."

With lush brown hair and a tall slender body, BeJo had a slight olive hue to her skin, which spoke to her German-French ancestors from Alsace Lorraine. After a stint in the Navy, BeJo had decided not to return to the farm. She wanted to be part of life in a big city where, as she said, she could "consort with intellectuals." But at five foot seven and lanky, she was every inch the farm girl she'd sought to leave behind in Iowa.

As she set the table, I looked around the living room, trying to shake off the world of politics. That was a difficult task, since feminist, gay and leftist newspapers from around the country lay on every horizontal surface. BeJo's yellow and orange plaid breakfast chairs clashed with the table's red oilcloth, but the table was extra long and sat ten bodies scrunched together. That was the important thing. *The Tide* Collective and other movement groups met here weekly.

"Karla called from New York," BeJo called out. "She said the gay rights ordinance went down again this year. Do you want the story? Your pal Robin Tyler left a message saying the press conference for Z Budapest's trial is Monday, ten a.m. sharp. Someone called from a new gay group in Texas, wants you to speak at a lesbian writers something or another. Lesbians organizing in Texas, who'd a thought it! And Penny called from *The Free Press*. She wants to see your body at the office tomorrow morning, early."

I sat at the table and watched BeJo's perfect hand-eye coordination placing silverware faster than a speeding bullet. When I'd seen how talented she was on *The Tide's* wax and paste-up boards, I'd bumped her up to Production Director.

Lesbian Tide collective members in 1974; l. to r. Features Editor Ann Doczi, News Editor Jeanne Córdova, and Production Manager BeJo Gehrke. *Photo by EK Waller, Lesbian Tide.*

"Ariana from the Westside Women's Center says we must do something about telling lesbians to watch out for the F.B.I. She says they're infiltrating the dyke community looking for Patty Hearst." BeJo stopped reading and looked me in the eye. "What's Patty Hearst got to do with lesbians, honey?"

"Uhh," I stalled, trying to think of a simple explanation for how and why the country's top fugitive had wound up in dykesville.

"You'd better give out someone else's address if you're going to drag *The Tide* into that one!" BeJo finished my thought.

I smiled to myself as I looked at her. Years in Portland, Oregon, and San Francisco had not corrupted BeJo's uncanny ability to see things pragmatically. Common sense was one of her contributions to my life.

"And, oh," she continued, "I handled this one myself. Hope you don't mind. "Karla Jay called from New York wanting to know if *The Tide* can pay her enough to make a living if she relocates out here. I laughed and laughed. Told her I'm already supporting you, the publisher, and that the paper can't support anyone."

BeJo dropped the pink message notes on my plate and went to the stove still chattering. "I love being your secretary, talking to people from all over the country fighting the military-industrial-complex. My honey..."

I cringed; it was sexist to use the term "secretary" these days. "You're not my secretary," I called after her. "You're the best production artist *The Tide* has ever had!"

By becoming a core member of the *Tide* Collective, BeJo had woven herself into the fabric of my life more tightly than the locked together roof beams overhead. And, she was one efficient woman. Whether she was balancing plates at her waitress job or making love, her body moved with the keen self-confidence of a ball player. I supervised the grueling, forty-eight hour layout of *The Lesbian Tide* every month, but I couldn't lay a straight line to save my life. When it became obvious to me that BeJo was faster and more creative than any of the professional paste-up women who volunteered each month, I'd ragged on her, telling her that her talents were going to waste being a waitress; she should think about becoming a professional in the graphics world. I told her the white-collar work world was peppered with the resumes of men who over-valued themselves and women who sold themselves short. I guess my words were finally beginning to change her obstinate mind, since she'd recently told me she'd been reading the job ads for graphics work.

She sat down next to me with a plate of meat loaf and mashed potatoes. "Oh, here's one more message. I saved the best for last," she said with a twinkle in her dark brown eyes. "That cute blonde butch co-worker of yours from the GCSC Center, Pody, called."

"I wish you wouldn't tell people that *The Tide* is insolvent, sweetie. They'll think we aren't a professional paper. Besides, I pay rent, I support myself."

"Yes, you pay *some* rent," BeJo said, handing me a full plate. "Of course, you couldn't put a steak on the table or a spare tire on the car with what's left over. Not that you ever go shopping for the house or food, so how would you know what a light bulb costs these days? "But, then..." she teased, picking up her fork, "life with you is the most exciting thing I've done for myself since joining the Navy! Stop obsessing on what people think of *The Tide*. Come into the bedroom and talk to me while I get dressed for work."

Following her, I lay down on our bed while she started in the bathroom. I breathed a sigh of relief staring at the ceiling, realizing that I wasn't on speaking terms with my parents. They would never expect a dinner invite so I'd never have to explain that I had a woman lover or that she was a waitress who'd grown up on a farm and had brothers named Butch and Spike. My family's classism was as overt as their homophobia. Since Dad had thrown me and my girlfriend out of his house when I was nineteen, I'd never had to explain my gay life, or anything else, to them. All for the best, I assured myself, as images of my ten younger siblings ran through my mind like a montage. They lived only twenty minutes away, in South Pasadena, but I hadn't been home in seven years. I wondered why it never got any easier, and if the longing for my siblings and my mother would ever disappear.

Now it was always BeJo—not Mom—to the rescue, BeJo who provided stability and a semblance of home life. Before I'd met BeJo, I'd lived in a ninety-five dollar a month one-room studio on the beach. Dinner used to mean opening one of seven cans of Campbell's soup, which I'd arranged single-file in the cupboards above labels naming the days of the week.

The bathroom door opened and BeJo sat down beside me. Watching her put each shapely leg into her stockings I remembered how I'd fallen in lust with her the night at the Bacchanal when I saw her dance. The cavern-size lesbian dance club had played Carole King's "Tapestry" all that summer of '72 and BeJo had boogied sharp and easy like she knew she was good. Being Latino, Dad had taught his kids that dancing was a primary outlet, and I'd adopted it as a primary way to woo a woman. I'd gone to BeJo's apartment that night. I was surprised to discover that she was the most accomplished femme lover I'd ever met. Old-school bar femmes were far better lovers than newly coined lesbian feminists, I was discovering. The latter, most freshly out of straight marriages, had too much political noise and correctness going on in their heads. Two months later, I'd moved in with BeJo.

"Somehow I've got to get a handle on the deeper meaning of what's going on at GCSC," I reflected aloud to her. Being news editor on *The Lesbian Tide* I'd heard rumblings about lesbians across the country walking away from working with gay men, our brothers. Were shades of this unusual political occurrence about to happen here in Los Angeles?

"Sometimes life doesn't have a deeper meaning," BeJo said. "Sometimes, shit just happens."

"Political shit never just happens, BeJo," I countered. "There's always a way to analyze the bigger political picture so that one can grasp the particulars more clearly."

BeJo stopped and studied me. "Honey, sometimes I don't understand what drives you. Most people have a life and then do activism at night or on the weekends. With you it's the other way around. It's not like they're electing women to be President of the United States these days."

"How does 'Senator Córdova' sound?" I said.

"Are you joking me, baby?" she said, slipping into a dark blue straight skirt.

"Yes and no," I answered slowly. "I've been thinking about it. But a person has to be able and willing to lie easily to be an elected politician. I dunno. Maybe it feels more authentic to stay grounded in issue-based politics. Look what Cesar Chavez did for the farm workers. And he's not an elected anything."

"You wouldn't last a day in them thar cornfields," BeJo drawled.

I chuckled. "I think they're them thar grape fields."

"Them neither," BeJo replied from the bathroom, where she was drawing on her lipstick. She consciously backslid on her feminism and put on make-up to fit in at work.

"Every Chavez needs a campaign organizer or press secretary," I continued.

BeJo sat down on the bed and took my hand. "Sweetie, some things are simple. I fell in love with you because you're good-looking. Your Elvis Presley black hair rang my bell. And now you've shown me a world of creativity and activism. I didn't even know what being political meant."

"Being political is who I am, BeJo. Besides, what does it *mean* to be good-looking?"

"Now don't go all philosophical about the meaning of good-looking. It just means cute. I figured that anyone with as much passion as you showed in those meetings had to have the same passion in bed." Her voice grew wistful as she brushed my hair with her long fingers. "Sometimes it's hard sharing you," she whispered softly.

"Oh BeJo," I groaned. "Let's not rehash this one."

She got up and went to the makeshift vanity table. "How

did feminism come up with this non-monogamy idea, or philosophy, or whatever you call it?" BeJo was a Taurus, stubborn as hell on topics she didn't agree with. "Why does this have to be the correct liberated woman's lifestyle? I've had four long-term relationships before you and they were all perfectly monogamous and perfectly happy."

"And perfectly short," I laughed, rolling over on the bed and watching her in the vanity's mirror. "Living non-monogamously prevents men from trying to own women," I explained. "Monogamy was invented by men to enslave and isolate women from one another and to protect their inheritance, their land and women as property. It's a colonizing construct, BeJo. By rejecting heterosexual marriage and monogamy, surely you can see that we're trying to build a new kind of society."

Finishing her eyes, BeJo returned to the bed. "But sweetie, we *are* women! Why can't lesbian feminists like you see that it's natural for a woman to love just one woman at a time?"

Sprawled on the bed, I realized that I'd never met a woman I thought I could be with for the rest of my life. After seven years as a lesbian and dozens of lovers, I'd given up thinking I could ever be happy with one. I seemed to need and want a complexity and depth of feeling that didn't exist in a single woman. So I'd tried to find it in several at a time. Living with BeJo was as close to being married as I ever planned to be. But I didn't want to hurt her feelings. "I suppose it's natural for *some* women, but straights argue that heterosexuality is natural for all women and that's false. Anyway, women have to move beyond our so-called 'natural' feelings. Most of them are just centuries of social conditioning, learned behavior taught by men to women to fulfill male needs."

I thought about my friends. Almost all of them were in non-monogamous relationships. And my pre-feminist "old-gay" friends who lived monogamously were harassed for imitating heterosexual marriage.

BeJo stroked my hair. "Don't you ever want to get married, honey?" She had pleading in her eyes.

"I'll get married when I'm too old to be political. Or, when dykes are free to be dykes, whichever comes first."

"What about settling down?"

I looked up at her. "Settling down into what?"

BeJo sighed. "You really have no idea do you?"

I grimaced. "What does being married mean? A white iron fence in the Valley with the RV parked in the driveway?"

"It's a white picket fence, not iron, honey. Settling down means having a good job that pays well. And a Cadillac, not an RV, in the driveway." She smiled, referring to the '62 Caddie she'd named Ramona parked below us in the carport. "It means coming home every night to someone who's happy to see you."

I sat up and kissed her. "I always come home happy to see you."

"Not every night, you don't." She turned her back to me as she slid off the bed. "Not on Monday and Friday nights."

According to our agreement, Monday and Friday were our non-monogamous nights, our "space" nights. I took advantage of them much more frequently than BeJo did, but according to our arrangement, she could have, too.

"Oh, sweetie,' I protested. "Mostly on Monday and Friday nights I'm at a meeting or a demo..."

"And screwing someone else after those meetings."

I got up and stood behind her at the vanity, kissing the soft place where her neck met the back of her ear. "Don't be angry," I whispered.

"And you're too tired to make love when you get home at midnight on our nights too," she continued. "And, what's worse, all of our friends are people we work with in the movement."

"Who else would they be?" I asked as I started to pull off my jeans and get into my pajamas.

"Friends are people you have something in common with, who like the same kind of fun that you do. And fun! Oh, there's a concept..."

"I have everything in common with my political buddies. Fun is for bored people who are seduced by capitalism's excess."

"Don't start with that socialist stuff," BeJo cut me off. "I thought you weren't a Commie anymore. It's a good thing I'm not out to my mother so I don't have to write home and say, 'Hey Mom guess what? I'm living with a Communist!'"

"I'm not even a socialist anymore. But Marx has some good ideas—"

"You're too deep, baby," she snapped, slipping into a pair of low, flat heels. "Why do you think about things that only make life more complicated?"

"How can a person be alive and not think about these things?"

"I'm perfectly alive and I don't." BeJo headed for the front door. She called back to me, laughing, "Try to be happy and don't think too much. You need more control over your mind!"

"And you're too German!" I shot back, realizing that BeJo could build a clock and take it apart in the time it took me to define the feminist meaning of time. And yet, I didn't know how to tell her that I didn't think she and I were a long term match. There were matters of the mind, as well as matters of the soul— my mind and my soul—that I couldn't share with her.

Chapter 4

_____

The Tide Rolls Out

[Los Angeles]

With BeJo gone for the night I had a few private hours to
write a story for *The Tide* about the conflict that was tearing
apart the L.A. Gay Community Services Center and, though
not for public print, sabotaging my relationship with my gay
political mentor—the Center's founder, Morris Kight.

Clad in pajamas, I hoisted myself from the bed and walked
down the hall to the second bedroom, where my child—*The
Lesbian Tide*—lived. I sniffed the smell. Fresh ribbon ink and
carbon paper mixed with cigarette smoke. I loved it. This room
was command central, the hub of my life. *The Tide* and I had
lived together since its birth in August of '71. The photos, art
boards, file cabinets, and Rolodex filled with names and contacts
of every gay organization and lesbian leader from around the
country—not to mention our expensive, new IBM Selectric
typewriter—all lived here together in a 10x10 room a straight
couple would have turned into a nursery. Not me. This was the
ink-and-thought-filled back room where Lesbian "herstory" was

discussed, chewed over, and written for our now two thousand paid subscribers.

I opened my briefcase, the thick black cardboard kind with an orange and black bumper sticker that read DYKE, in 72 point type, all caps. It sat on a wall-to-wall table made out of an eight by four-foot, black painted piece of plywood, held up by two sawhorses. BeJo had flipped out when I'd said I'd only move in with her if I could bring *The Tide* with me. To me, since growing up the definition of home had always included work; I had watched my parents pore over architectural blueprints on the kitchen table every night. Leaving work at the office might be normal to BeJo, but it was never my style. Besides, my life was about rearranging the very definition of normal. Normal said that queers were born sick or criminal. Normal said that women were born to serve men in the kitchen and in the bedroom. Normal, like my father, said that success was battling one's way to the top of the economic ladder and letting the chips—with people as collateral damage—fall where they may. Not to me. Normal was not a good reason to do anything. If my beliefs were dedicated to normal I would have committed suicide as an alienated butch teenager and certainly never founded a newsmagazine called *The Lesbian Tide*.

Like most of the good things in my life, stumbling upon *The Tide* had been an accident which occurred on the path I'd taken to avoid an unwanted destiny. After a successful year of being President of the L.A. Chapter of the national gay women's organization, Daughters of Bilitis, it had become clear to me that I was going to lose a bid for re-election—if I made one. As D.O.B. president, 1970 and '71 had seen me lead the charge to open L.A.'s first center with the word "lesbian" painted boldly on the glass door at 1910 S.Vermont Avenue. {1} But this was also the year that feminism arrived in Los Angeles, and I as D.O.B.'s leader had recently begun to spend too much time, according to the old-school membership, consorting with a new group in town called The Lesbian Feminists. Yes, I was becoming a "feminist." My sisters at D.O.B. felt threatened by this new theology that defined lesbians as "the rage of all women condensed to the point of explosion."{2} Old-school gay women, who peopled D.O.B., thought that a lesbian was a girl who slept with other girls, not a bunch of hippie "womyn" who didn't shave their legs or armpits.

Two months before our elections I'd had the audacity to invite Women Against the War to come speak at D.O.B.'s monthly meeting. I'd come to believe that the Vietnam War was politically relevant to the gay cause. The evening was a disaster—Wilma Flintstone meets Jane Fonda—a socialist plot by their own leadership, said the D.O.B.'ers. I and my small pack of "radical" members had to go.

"It's clear we aren't going to get re-elected to catch frogs," said my best butch pal, vice president Barbara McLean, who'd come west after her own stint as president of D.O.B.'s Chicago Chapter. We, the radical leadership, were meeting to decide how to greet our fate.

"No," I laughed looking around at my small pack which included Barb's lover, the D.O.B. secretary, Caren Presley. "So how do we prevent a coup and get out of here with some dignity?"

"I'm not ready to leave D.O.B.," said Caren. "We want to become feminists but I feel more at home here than I do with those strange lesbian feminists."

I thought about our dilemma. As an organized and smart pack of friends we'd come a long way. We wanted to stick together. We were also convinced that this new feminist philosophy had much to offer and that this new thing called the Women's Liberation Movement was something we wanted to be part of. It felt good and right and spoke to society's secondary discrimination against us, the fact that we were women.

That's when the future occurred to me. "Why don't Barb and I step aside as president and vice president and run for newsletter editor and assistant editor," I said. "The membership never looks at newsletter editor as anything important; it's the fifth and last officer on the executive board."

"Great idea," Barb agreed catching my drift of a new future for us. "Then we can all be the newsletter staff and create something dynamic and all stick together!"

Months later we'd put the plan into action and I became newsletter editor, demoted in the eyes of the membership. That was the beginning. Much to my surprise, I'd fallen in love with the freedom to express my thoughts and politics in print.

Six months later, my gang and I slapped a new title on the L.A. D.O.B. Newsletter, calling it *The Lesbian Tide*. The membership grew even more afraid of their now radical feminist newsletter. They voted affirmatively, and with gusto, when its staff asked permission to take *The Lesbian Tide* solo—that is, out of D.O.B. From its small beginning, I'd modeled our tiny publication's format to be that of a newsmagazine—like my favorite national weekly, *Newsweek*.

Now, four years later, Barb and Caren had been sucked into Orange County to work in a new field called computers, but Bejo and I and a new crew ran a forty-page monthly with photos and a glossy cover that was eagerly read by thousands of lesbians—both the exploding feminist kind as well as the old-school butch-femme couples of D.O.B. We were fast becoming the best lesbian paper in the country with lesbian feminist writers from San Francisco to New York wanting to be published in "*The Lesbian Tide*: *A feminist publication, written by and for the rising tide of women today.*" My newest goal was to take the paper in a truly national direction. The road to such distribution, sent wrapped in an anonymous plain manila envelope, would not be smooth.

Dateline: Downtown L.A., Mid-April 1975

The ringing phone woke me and I turned over and read the clock, eight a.m. Startled, I sat up trying to remember whose bed

I was in. The room was decorated with flower child scarves; the bedroom's doorway was composed of strings of colored beads. Of course, I thought, it was Annie's bedroom. I'd come over last night with the purpose of breaking up with my latest "short-but-meaningful-affair" as we feminists called our secondary relationships.

I jumped toward her phone hoping to catch it before the second ring woke her. We had indeed broken up last night—apparently sealed with some heavy duty closure.

"Hello," I whispered into the receiver, realizing I should have just pulled the plug out and saved myself—or Annie—an unsavory explanation of who I was to someone who could be her next lover.

"Hello is this you, honey?" the voice asked.

Oh Christ! Maybe it was Annie's other lover?

But suddenly I recognized the voice. "BeJo? What are you doing calling me here?"

"I'm calling you there because you are there," my lover replied, her tone quick and panicked. "They've stopped the presses!"

"Where are you?"

"I'm at the damn printers. You were supposed to meet me here this morning."

"Oh shit! Is it Saturday?"

"You bet it is. I can't believe you forgot. You've never missed a press check!"

I stood naked on Annie's linoleum floor, horrified at my negligence. "I'm sorry…"

"This isn't part of our non-marital, non-monogamous agreement," BeJo cut off my protest. "But we've got worse problems now. The printer is refusing to run *The Tide's* cover. You've got to get down here."

"No shit!" BeJo had my full attention. *The Lesbian Tide* had not had printer problems for months. It would take weeks to find another. There were no women-owned printers running the big web presses. "What's his problem?"

"He says the cover photo is obscene! Honey, we are really screwed. You've got to talk him out of this."

Anxiety was plain in BeJo's voice. No cover meant a late issue. Years ago I'd laid down a cardinal rule to the staff: "*The Tide* rolls out on time each month! That's why it's called 'the tide.' Nobody is allowed to get sick or break-up with a lover until after an issue hit the streets." In a movement peopled by lesbian feminists who were prone to process rather than product, *The Lesbian Tide* was famous for its stability. Our readers relied on us. And here I was breaking my own rules, ditching a lover on movement time!

"I can't talk to this guy," BeJo whined. "He's a bully. I don't do confrontation remember? That's your job."

Everything's my job, I cursed, bending to collect my boots. "Give me fifteen minutes. Meet me and brief me outside the back door of the building."

I tiptoed back into the bedroom, poking around for my shirt. The goddamn movement. What was the point of being purposefully unemployed and dirt poor if I got pulled out of bed to go to work? My boots felt raw against my bare feet. No time to find socks. I ran for the door.

"Thank the goddess you're here!" BeJo said, hugging me as we met in the printer's back alley.

"What the hell is going on?" I snapped.

"It's because of the photo of the two women kissing on the front cover."

I grabbed her hand and strode toward the pressroom. "I have a plan."

Once in the great room the pounding of the forty-foot web press, its drums thundering, drowned all conversation. I paused long enough to smell the ink, the rhythmic clatter, and the sounds of men barking staccato orders to one another. How I loved the rush and the smell of words churning through metal.

Our sales rep, Roger, waved me into his small office. The

man was wimpy, slightly built, and was nervously smoothing his thinning grey curls. He looked more tired than I was after being up all night. But anger was fueling me.

"I'm sorry about this," he offered lamely.

"So am I," I boomed. "Why is there a problem with our cover? It's a headshot. They're both fully clothed. You print this kind of photo with a man and a woman all the time."

"It's not a problem with me." Roger held his hands up. "I think the two women are...it's a fine...kiss."

I looked at BeJo and then back to Roger. "So who's got the problem?"

The man turned around and pointed to a large upstairs window. "It's his problem. That's my boss's office."

The glass cage sitting above the pressroom looked like a traffic controller's private domain. I turned to BeJo, who was wide-eyed with fright. Roger, shuffling proofs on his table, avoided my eyes. I watched his wrists move, then leaned over and spoke softly in his ear, "Roger, are you gay?"

His lower lip trembled and he stopped shuffling. He closed his eyes for a moment. His wrinkled face broke into an unexpectedly sweet smile. "Yes, I am," he said softly. "I'm not your problem."

I reached over and gave his hand a brief, soft squeeze. Then I pointed to the upper office. "So what's his name?"

"Mr. Karinsky," Roger said fearfully.

"No, Roger, what's his first name?"

"Charlie."

By that time I was half way up the stairs. The tough approach was the only kind that men respected.

"Who is it?" a thick voice boomed from behind the closed, dark glass.

I yanked open the door. My eyes focused immediately on the burly, cigar smoking, oily-faced man behind the desk. But I didn't flinch. Working class tough guys had never scared me. It was the tight-lipped, white-collar power men whose potential for violence was carefully shrouded that unnerved me.

"It's your client, the publisher of *The Lesbian Tide*," I announced myself. I stuck out my hand, "Jeanne Córdova."

"Oh," he said. Standing, he shook my hand. His palm was sweaty but his grip was hard.

I took a seat in the armchair in front of his desk, sprawling one leg casually across the other and took out a cigarette. Looking at him, I waited for him to light it. He did.

I positioned my pack of Benson & Hedges next to his cigar in the ashtray and said, "I hear you've got a problem with our cover this month."

The man rocked back in his chair. "That's not my problem. That's your problem."

I brought my fist down on his desk. Hardening my voice, I looked him in the eye. "We have a contract with you to print this issue. The whole issue."

"That contract doesn't mean shit to me." Charlie yawned, resting his elbows on his desk. "You guys are paying just above cost. I only print you to keep my staff busy."

Confrontational power play wasn't going to get me my cover, I realized. Leaning back in my chair, I asked conversationally, "You gotta a problem with sexy women, Charlie?"

"Hell no." Charlie leaned forward. "I like the woman you sent here. What's her name...?"

"BeJo…Barbara."

"Yeah, Barbara. She's got great legs."

I swung a boot leg onto the corner of Charlie's desk, looked into his deep mud—brown eyes and said, "Yeah, and that's not all she's got that's great."

Startled, Charlie studied me as though he were trying to decide whether or not we were complete strangers. Finally he smiled, showing his crooked teeth. "So, how do you bulldykes get all the pretty ones?"

"Well, my man," I teased, mentally trying to deduce how far this conversation would have to go before I got what I wanted, "that's for me to know and you to guess at."

He grunted. "How about you give me your best secrets

about women for the next hour and maybe I'll give you what you want?"

"You'll turn on our press run before we begin?"

Charlie threw back his head and broke into a laugh. "Fuck! You don't know anything more than I know, you bargaining little dyke!"

"I must know more than you know, Charlie, 'cause I'm going home with Barbara tonight and you're going home to no one."

No straight woman would let a man walk out of the house looking as unkempt as he did with his slovenly plaid shirt two sizes too small for him.

Charlie stared, speechless.

"So how about making that deal with your new best butch pal?" I continued.

"I don't want my friends in the biz knowing I printed that photo…"

He seemed to be waffling. I offered, "I'd be happy to delete your company's name from the masthead. Believe me, none of the people I know, know any of the people you know."

Charlie's ragged eyebrows knitted. He had no idea what I'd meant.

"An hour's worth of tips on getting broads into bed?"

My eyes closed for a moment of reflection on my about-to-be-sullied butch honor. "Okay. One hour. And the press runs till my job is done."

Charlie picked up his phone. "Roger?" he barked, "Tell Tom to run that dyke cover. Let's get it out of here." He dropped the receiver into its cradle. Reaching for his cigar, he leaned far back into his chair, locked his fingers behind his head and threw his own legs on his desk. "So start talking," he said.

An hour and fifteen minutes later, I stumbled out of Charlie's dark glass tower into the frying sun. BeJo was waiting for me. She pressed a cold soda into my hands. "My hero!" she joked, toasting her soda can against mine. "You saved our cover. Look, here's a copy!"

My eyes fell on the lovely sight of Gudrun and Jan kissing,

one woman's hand resting against the other's neck {3}. Noticing the light and shadow contrast, I smiled, "Wow, it came off great! Copies of this all over the country make it all worth while!"

"Makes what worth while?" BeJo knew my voice too well; she'd caught the inflection, a tiny space of regret in my voice. Her forehead knitted.

"Worth spending an hour with a sexist pig," I said, trying to keep my voice light. I grabbed BeJo's hand and

Kissing cover of *Lesbian Tide* stops the presses.
Photo by Denise Crippen.

walked her to her car. "Men are all the same. But at least I screwed him too. I told him all the wrong information I could think of!"

"Wrong information about what?"

I ignored her question. "We need a new printer, BeJo. But right now, I just want to get the fuck off his property."

"Sounds good to me." BeJo plopped into her car. She couldn't resist spreading the cover proof out on the steering wheel. Stared at our baby. Her cover's print resolution was clear and sharp. "She's beautiful," I whispered.

BeJo sighed, looking at me through the driver's open window, and said, "This is why I love you. You make things happen in the world and I'm part of that."

As her words sank into my body, so did the exhaustion of the confrontation with Charlie. The post-partum downer which always followed the excitement of getting each issue to bed was settling into me. As I leaned on her car, my legs felt weak, my will depleted.

"It's Saturday," BeJo said. "You haven't been home during daylight hours for weeks. Come home with me now and I'll make you a nice lunch and put you to bed.

As I drove home following BeJo, I felt somehow defeated. Yes, the next issue was liberated, yet a vague unrest gnawed at me. I'd told Charlie lies; things I hoped would make his dates dump him like a bag of hammers. So, I'd won. Then why did my stomach hurt? Because it was a narrowly held power, with me forced to play the only card a butch had with a man like that—other women.

My father had taught me how bullies handled the world and each other, that power was their fulcrum. When I was a child, my father's power was terrifying. There was no winning. I'd had no cards. All the power belonged to him and the man meant to be obeyed. Obedience was everything. Straight out of West Point, he treated his children like plebes, blowing reveille and making us stand inspection every morning. When he was in his early thirties he had moved his wife and five children from

Germany to the orange groves of 1950s Southern California, where he set up a marble import company and was pressured with seven more offspring.

I tried to be especially careful of his power at night when he came home for dinner. Mom always said, "The dinner table is the heart of the family." Our dinner table—an extra long "hot-dog" dispensing table that we'd borrowed from the Church and normally used to feed the masses—sat on steel folding legs in my childhood's kitchen. Sometimes at dinner, because I was only seven, or ten, or twelve, I forgot to be careful, forgot to obey. When I did get in trouble, one of Dad's authoritarian not-to-be-messed-with-or-ever-changed rules was: "You will do what I tell you to do, as long as you live under my roof." I whispered to myself that the next time he chased me with a bat, or his leather belt, I'd find a better place to hide; next time I'd be smarter, run faster, and run away. And the day I was eighteen would be the last next time. I'd run away and live under my own roof. No sir, when I got older, no matter the cost, I swore to myself, not even the Pope would tell me what to do.

Lionheart's wheels bumped, startling me. I was drifting over the lane markers. *Christ!* I hated allowing my father to leak back into my life, even for a daydream. I looked at my watch. A bummer of a day—and it wasn't yet noon.

Chapter 5

The Godfather

The tyranny and humiliation of my life under my father was the reason I became a warrior. My life as a freedom fighter in the movement for gay civil rights took a dramatic turn towards being a career path on a hot June day in 1971, the day I met Morris Kight, L.A.'s most prominent gay community organizer, and the man who would become my political godfather.

At fifty-two, Morris was an experienced anti-war, peace, and black civil rights activist. He knew how to plan large-scale demonstrations and keep them peaceful. In a fledgling movement filled with twenty and thirty-year olds, he was unquestionably our leader although he did not necessarily look the part. Of medium height with an ordinary, middle-aged potbelly, he had a shoulder length white mane so wispy that the wind blew it in all directions at once. Usually, he wore the simplest of thrift store khaki pants and shirt, one grade up from vagrant.

On that day, at Morris's invitation, I had answered the call from leaders of the infant gay and lesbian movement in New York to help plan simultaneous gay liberation marches across the nation. The marches would commemorate the last Sunday in June, the second anniversary of our 1969 Stonewall Revolt in Greenwich Village, the most famous rebellion of queer people against police harassment in modern times.

Although I'd just spent months organizing the first Gay Women's West Coast Conference—scheduled to take place on the same weekend as the march so lesbians could have their own celebration on what was becoming known as gay male liberation day —I jumped at my first chance to work one-on-one with this brilliant strategist. That he had invited me came as something of a surprise since, together with the Rev. Troy Perry of the gay Metropolitan Community Church and other gay male leaders, Morris had already set the demands for the L.A. march: to decriminalize gay sex by demanding the eradication of California's anti-sodomy laws. Maybe he and the other gay men were beginning to take their lesbian sisters seriously.

"The March route will start here," Morris said, as he spread a map of Los Angeles over the hood of a parked car. He pointed to the corner of McCadden and Hawthorn, two small streets a block east of the major avenue called Highland. "Our people can be hidden as we assemble here, yet have quick access to a main street," he explained.

Morris and the others had spent frustrating months in front of the L.A. Police Commission, begging for a permit to use the streets. But our much despised Police Chief, the calcified Ed Davis, had denied us. He'd written a letter to Councilman Art Snyder, which said, "It's one thing to be a leper; it's another thing to be spreading the disease." We hadn't made much progress in raising his consciousness. Last year he'd said, "Giving a permit to homosexuals would be like giving one to robbers and rapists." Finally we had gotten qualified permission. The march could start at 6:00 pm at night and we were to stay on the sidewalks.

One misstep, he'd warned, and the cops would be all over us.

I bent over the map. "It's a good kickoff site," I agreed. "It's quiet and tucked away, the cops won't see us gathering."

Morris nodded, his eyes still glued to the map. "We'll then emerge out onto Highland and march north to Hollywood Boulevard. Then east ... all the way to Vine."

"I see what you're doing," I said, a note of admiration in my voice. "The movie star names embedded in the sidewalks on Hollywood make the Boulevard wider; the marchers can go five or six abreast down the Boulevard."

With a wrist flourish that would rival a fag half his age, Morris drew an imaginary line east. "We shall simply tiptoe the ten blocks over to Vine Street, which is long enough to make a proper political statement," he told me. Although he was born in a no-name town in south Texas, Morris's formal speech sounded more like that of a Southern gentleman.

He pointed to the map again. "Toward the end of the route, right about here, why don't we surreptitiously lead everyone off the sidewalk and into the middle of the street?"

"Why can't we just ignore the cops and take to the streets for the whole march?"

"Because, my dear, one builds the momentum of a demonstration slowly." Morris waved his hands in a complex of spirals. "One allows it to become a ballet, a dance that builds in intensity."

I watched him, fascinated by his silver-strapped hands, each finger encased by custom-soldered turquoise Navajo rings. Much of his energy seemed to be channeled through these flamboyant jewels, and in their movement I saw the subtle orchestration of the entire march.

"I get it!" I said. "We start off gradually so that people can get into a braver mood. We build the commitment and the excitement. Then, we burst onto the street for the last few blocks."

Exactly!" Morris exclaimed, resting his arm on my shoulder. I flushed with a pride I hadn't felt since my father once

Morris Kight reigns as Grand Marshall at
gay pride march, early 1970s. *ONE National
Gay & Lesbian Archives*

watched me pitch my softball team to a no-hit shutout. That was more than a decade ago. By now, Frederick Benito Córdova had no idea that I had dedicated my life to a passion he would call a perverse and utterly ridiculous waste of time. I was beginning to feel that this man, Morris Kight, and I shared a political passion that was more familial than anything I'd felt with my father since early childhood.

"And who do you think can solve our traffic light problem?" he asked.

"I don't know. But we've got to stop those lights from cutting up the march like a segmented snake."

"Ah, dahling!" He smiled. "That's where your lesbians shall save the day."

"My lesbians?" I blinked. *Christ*, I thought. Here comes the pitch.

"Metaphorically speaking, of course," Morris added. "You *are* the premier lesbian organizer in Los Angeles, are you not?"

I had no answer for his rhetorical flattery but that's when I realized he'd asked me to join his planning committee because he'd spotted me as a "comer." Morris Kight's invitations were about results. He knew about my Gay Women's Conference and he knew that I could put boots on the streets.

I gasped, feigning horror. "You're not thinking of using my lesbians as cannon fodder at the intersections, are you?"

"Well," Morris said, dropping his voice coyly. "At the anti-war demonstrations I observed that lesbians were often the security monitors. They seemed to like that role. Ergo, I thought perhaps your people would like to stop the cars. Lesbians always protect gay men, thusly..."

"Enough, Morris!" I cut him off. "Of course we dykes will protect you."

Smiling, Morris drew a set of index cards from his shirt pocket and handed them to me. "I made you a proper card file of the intersecting streets between Highland and Vine," he said.

I took the cards with a sardonic smile; he'd come came prepared, knowing I would agree to his plan. I was about to get angry at his manipulation when I realized that two could play his game.

"One last thing, Morris," I said, and stopped my teacher as he started to fold up the map. "Since we dykes are willing to take this risk, it's only fair—for your protection, of course—that the lesbian contingent marches at the front of the march."

"Oh really?" Morris stopped folding.

"And furthermore, when the march moves into the middle of the street and unfurls the lead banner, I want some dykes holding that banner along with your gay men."

"But those men have already been chosen!" Morris's voice rose to a flabbergasted pitch. "They're all activists, they deserve the privilege."

"Morris." I lowered my voice, forcing myself to stay calm. "The TV cameras are going to be there. We need to show that we're united—gay men and lesbians together. That's what you want, isn't it?"

Morris loved the Body Politic of gay men with his whole being, he understood his people like a father, but when it came to comprehending us—his sisters from Lesbian Nation—I wondered if he meant what he said politically, or was he going to turn out to be a slippery old eel?

He inhaled deeply before speaking. "Of course, dahling," he said, his voice now back to normal. "That's what this march is about—equality. The women shall be up front. Gender parity it shall be!"

On June 27, the night of the march, despite the wide-spread rumor that the LAPD was going to shut the whole damn thing down and arrest everyone, two thousand queers showed up!

The assemblage at the corner of Hawthorn and McCadden Place was mass confusion. I passed Freda Smith, a Sacramento organizer from the Gay Women's West Coast Conference, and yelled to her, "Grab every dyke you see and tell them to look for the Lesbian Mothers banner!" I pointed toward it at the head of the march. We lesbians didn't have much in the way of signs, but at the conference Del Martin had raised the issue of lesbian mothers losing custody cases in court—an issue that scared many of us. Myself and other organizers had only convinced about half of the attendees that marching in a gay parade was also a lesbian issue. To many of these women Stonewall and the Christopher Street West annual march was a gay male birthday.

Because of my telltale organizer armband, marchers were besieging me. They were arriving by car, foot, bus, and bicycle. "Will there be trouble with the pigs?" "Who should I march with?" Most gay men looked blankly at me saying they didn't belong to any group. They'd only heard that this was gay Sunday in Hollywood. They'd hitchhiked from Phoenix, or bussed in from Colorado looking for someplace on earth to be openly gay. Even a group called the Gay Community Alliance had flown in from Hawaii.

Finally, with the sun setting to our backs, we were chanting and marching abreast down Hollywood Boulevard, every newly conscripted gay draftee shouting at the top of his and her voice. Dashing up and down as a monitor, I paused and almost came to tears. A banner carried by an elderly, straight-looking woman walking alone read, Heterosexuals for Homosexual Freedom. I wanted to salute this woman. Someday, perhaps even in my own lifetime, gays will be free, I told myself.

That day was not tonight. Uniformed cops were everywhere. Several cars had male drivers dressed in full suit and tie, plainclothes LAPD vice or Feds. The rumors of LAPD files were true—they were taking photos of every monitor and anyone who looked like they were organizers including myself.

When I was social working in South Central three years after the Watts Rebellion of '65, I'd seen many armed young men and learned that the FBI's counter-intelligence program was all over the black activist community. The Feds wanted nothing more than to hunt down every member of the so-called insurrectionist Black Panthers who they believed sought the violent overthrow of white America.

Today they were here. But today this was my people, my march.

Looking ahead I saw the march was indeed breaking up into segments, crowds were bunching up at those damn intersections. Monitors were not in place. Our people were looking vacantly at one another wondering whether or not to venture into traffic.

I rushed into the hugely jammed intersection at Cahuenga and motioned the marchers to cross. Standing alone, my arms outstretched against traffic, I tried to look like an imposing figure. An aging Ford stopped in front of me, and out of it emerged a bearded, blond guy in overalls, who screamed, "The only good fag is a dead fag! Get the fuck out of my way!"

"Ladies!" I screamed at a group of feathered drag queens waiting on the corner. "Come here, I need you!"

The frenzied fags ran devotedly into battle. "What's the matter, honey?" the group's leader asked.

I pointed toward my Aryan. "Go kiss him. Get him back into his car so our people can cross the intersection!"

The gaggle of queens descended upon the tall, now speechless blond. One stroked his arm, another pinched his butt. The muscled straight guy shrank from the queens. The only safe place was in his car. Quickly, he jumped back in, slammed the door, raised the windows, and locked himself in. Drag-phobia had saved the day!

"Right on!" I yelled to my "sisters" as I waved our marchers through the now safe intersection.

I looked forward. As planned, the head of the march was starting to leave the sidewalks and take the street. Seeing a banner reading Out of the Closets & into the Streets, I ran forward to meet Morris, arms raised in triumph.

The Los Angeles 1971 commemoration of Stonewall was the first of many grassroots events I would organize with Morris Kight over the next decades to fight for the rights of gay men and lesbians, struggling not just with the politicians but also with other gay and lesbian leaders to keep the bourgeoning movement from straying from its grass roots or, among other morasses, into the New Left of class politics. Still, it wasn't until 1974 that one of our particular efforts at making legislative change finally met with a cumulative success. One of the things I'd learned from my mentor was to think outside the box, to revel in the unexpected. But I was more than a little shook up that summer, when Morris called me and Troy Perry, the founder of the new gay Metropolitan Community Church, over to his McCadden Place haunt and asked us to volunteer to be arrested as sex criminals.

Morris had decided that the quickest way to bring down California's Penal Codes against sodomy and oral copulation— PC 288a and 286—was to get a gay, a lesbian, and a straight couple to publicly confess to these sex crimes, and trick the police into arresting us. Those couples turned out to be Troy and his lover Steven Gordon, a straight couple named Jeanie Barney and her boyfriend, and me and BeJo. I hesitated about this caper, but I'd always found it difficult to say no to Morris. Finally, I'd committed us. BeJo didn't share my readiness. She panicked when I brought the legal paperwork home for us to sign. "I haven't come out to my parents in Iowa. You're out of your mind."

It was eerily quiet in our apartment that night as BeJo and I didn't speak. I wondered if Troy's young lover, new to the movement, was making things tense at his house too. I'd noticed that Morris hadn't put himself forward. "I don't have a lover," he'd said. His role in the plan was to make a citizen's arrest and haul us down to Rampart Division Police Headquarters after the press conference.

"I don't suppose you have a back-up lesbian couple?" I asked Morris on the phone. BeJo still hadn't said yes.

"No, I can't find any other out lesbian couple willing to do this," he said. "But don't worry; our lawyers will be at the police station to bail you out as soon as possible."

The evening passed like time on a broken clock. Finally, I

heard BeJo call in to work saying she'd come down with a cold and needed tomorrow off.

By the time she and I arrived at the Los Angeles Press Club, BeJo was covered with anxiety-provoked sweat. With cameras flashing and microphones popping under the bright lights of the Press Club, somehow the risk felt surreal. I read aloud my carefully composed statement:

"I am here in the name of thousands of lesbian mothers who have stood before California Judges and heard, 'This woman is unfit, and she has no right to her child because she is homosexual.' I am here in the name of hundreds of lesbians who have been dishonorably discharged from the services, thrown out of their jobs, their homes, their churches. In the name of

Gay Felons Six speak out against California sodomy laws at L.A. Press Club. R. to L. Rev. Jeanne Córdova, Rev. Troy Perry, BeJo Gehrke, & Steve Jordan. *June 1974. Cordova Collection at ONE Archives.*

those whose lives have been ruined in the name of this Penal Code law, I demand to be arrested!"

Morris's smiling face at the end of the table gave me courage. I went on to recount the case of two women in Michigan having been arrested for making love in their camping tent in the forest. One of them had just finished serving three years in the state penitentiary.

By the end of the press conference the *L.A. Times* had shown up, but the police had not. Morris stood up and arrested us "in the name of the good state of California." He promptly loaded us into a bus bannered with the sign The Felons Six in which we took a slow but very public ride—waving and explaining our action to sidewalk passersby—through the major boulevards of Hollywood and downtown LA.

Once inside the Rampart Station a media savvy Commander Wise announced, "I will not take custody of these people. We did not see the crime in action." So it was off to the District Attorney's Office where our straight lawyer (there were no out gay lawyers in '74) insisted to the DA that he didn't need to *see* our crime in person because there was nothing in the law exempting private or consensual oral copulation.

Assistant D.A. Jacobson met with our lawyer behind closed doors for almost an hour. We felons and our entourage waited, standing with a hopeful BeJo and young Steve, while the entire D.A.'s staff gawked at us—the self-confessed homosexuals. Finally, a much distressed Jacobson went before the gathered press cameras. "Any groups or individuals who wish to change current laws in California should take their complaint to the state legislature," he said. "I didn't make the law." Then he instructed his security to escort us out of his office. Being arrested for trespassing seemed anti-climatic and not on-message. We cleared out.

Once home we printed thousands of leaflets urging gay couples to openly break these Penal Codes. Months later California Governor Jerry Brown, pushed strongly by Morris

Kight and the whole damn statewide gay and lesbian movement, signed an Executive Order overturning California's anti-sodomy laws. My mentor and I were one giant step closer to freedom for our people.

Chapter 6

Petition at Midnight

[Los Angeles]

By the middle of the 1970s the national lesbian and gay movement was at a turning point that few of us living through it could grasp. The Gay Liberation Front, a small cell of radical socialist gay men and women out of the New Left, was the first national gay organization to arise in the post-Stonewall era. But the radical politics of the GLF, which sought to lead gays into the revolutionary struggle to overthrow capitalism, had dissipated by '75. President Nixon, a powerful Leftist organizing tool, had resigned and in his place was a floppy sort of good-natured guy, Gerald Ford, who was hard to hate. College kids were no longer being drafted out of their classes to fight a war in a country most Americans couldn't find on a map. By mid-decade, anger from the masses was down, hope was up. An essential kind of pragmatism—how to get a bigger share of the American pie—seemed to seep into the gay and feminist and even the black and Latino movements. The boomer generation was growing up and they wanted apartments and cars, not marches and bombs.

Before most of us could analyze what had happened, instead of the egg-throwing radicals of the '60s, omelet-makers of the '70s were becoming our leaders. In the gay movement, the rank and file seemed to be more committed to disco in the clubs than marching in the streets. As the editor of a national lesbian paper, I began to receive stories about the new and growing wave of women's music and lesbian concerts. New York, San Francisco, and Los Angeles—the recognized go-first cities of the gay struggle—began filling up with a generation of mid-Western runaway teenagers and young men who came to the cities to find gay liberation. By now the gay movement had thrown the cops out of our bars. Politicians had called off the pigs because queer leaders were besieging city councils to pass housing and jobs anti-discrimination legislation. Slowly but surely the radical battle cry was shifting from revolution to civil rights.

Urban gay leaders were now looking for ways to get our kids off drugs, off the streets, and off the new lifestyle known as gay hustling. Tens of thousands of gays and lesbians were jumping out of the closet. It was now our leaders' problem to figure out how to meet the needs of the suddenly *visible* gay masses.

The overthrow of capitalism was not at the top of their list. No, we had a lifetime of hiding and sexual denial to make up for. We wanted to talk and be with each other in every imaginable and intimate way. Community service centers began to spring up in dyke 'hoods and gay barrios from Houston to Seattle, and San Diego to Vermont.

At first, these centers were no more than centrally located warehouses or cheap storefront rentals where activists could hold nightly meetings and queers-in-need could make their plight known to others. These centers began to replace the lesbian and gay bars as safe hubs for social life. The centers began to provide a base of operations for the movement and a population density substantial enough for organized fundraisers. Capitalism began to be harnessed, not overthrown, to take care of our own.

In the centers it was easy to see what our needs were as a community. Men young and old needed health care for sex-related diseases that was previously denied. Toss away boys needed homes with supportive parent figures, a jobs program to find work, and rap groups to establish a new sense of family. Everyone needed therapy to eradicate self-hatred fostered by growing up in the straight world. Lesbians had fewer runaways, mostly 'mannish' girls tossed out by family, but women had an even deeper sense of social isolation. We desperately needed to find one another, to talk and build family. A wide range of social groups sprang up at these community centers and gay therapists of every stripe were sought.

Into this fabric of diaspora and need, the Los Angeles Gay Community Services Center was born. It was the first of its kind in the country. L.A. quickly became the national center of gay and lesbian institution building. The city's large pro-gay Jewish population, the immense wealth of the movie industry, and the West's notion of the importance of land ownership, were factors that shaped the development of gay L.A. Borrowing from the Jewish concept of giving to charities that took care of their own, a model prevalent in the gay-adjacent Jewish community, early LA gay leaders harnessed the financial resources of wealthy but closeted men and began to buy gay properties. The entertainment industry was also heavily populated by homosexual men and women who had relationships—both distant and immediate—with gay activists.

The Hollywood Hills were arguably the largest and richest gay closet in the world. It was no accident that *The Advocate*, the newspaper that would become America's largest gay male publication, was born and raised in the Beverly Hills—adjacent barrio called Hollywood. The world's largest and wealthiest gay church was founded here in 1968 by the intensely theatrical Rev. Troy Perry. Los Angeles, with its large sprawl of ethnic ghettos, was also home base to the Black Panthers and the Brown Berets—vital race-based social change struggles upon which gay leaders role-modeled. As early lesbian and gay leaders left college, we closely monitored the nightly news. Watching the Watts riots, the Panthers looking for ways to feed their people, and Cesar

Chavez's farm workers marching in California's central valley, we quickly learned the skills of community organizing.

The Los Angeles' Gay Community Services Center was the brainchild of three Gay Liberation Front founders: Morris Kight, Don Kilhefner, and John Platania. The three were radical socialists who had piled up years of activism in the anti-war, Peace & Freedom, United Farm Workers, and black civil rights struggles. Because they were older and more experienced, Kight and Kilhefner, along with our forefathers in other cities—like Frank Kameny in New York and Jim Foster in San Francisco—had watched the early and radical black liberation struggle gradually morph into middle-class acceptance. They, the first generation of gay leaders, understood much earlier than us college kids that the radical gay movement had to eventually mainstream into a civil rights movement.

The problem was, the gay and lesbian movement was being run by radicals who only yesterday wanted to overthrow the government. In 1971 middle-class gays and lesbians had not come out of the closet or into the movement. Kight and Kilhefner soon realized that to survive and gain legitimacy, their Gay Community Services Center, now known as GCSC, would have to successfully apply for government grants just like other non-profit social agencies. But to do this GCSC would need a credentialed Board of Directors who had MSW, MFCC, and PhD degrees. Morris Kight managed to scrape together five gay men and one lesbian willing to sign their professional names on the dotted line of a homosexual organization. In 1971 GCSC opened its doors as the first gay non-profit organization in America recognized by the IRS. {1} In late 1974 it became the first organization with the word "gay" in its name to receive federal funding.

Morris asked me to join him at GCSC and sit on its first Board as a byproduct of our close political relationship, and because I was the first openly lesbian activist to obtain an MSW in Social Work, and because I was Chicana. After only two years in the struggle, I'd become a feminist and had an intuitive hit that the deep rooted sexism of the older generation of gay white men didn't bode well for women. Politely, I said no thanks to Morris: "I'm a 'lesbian primacist.'" That meant I wanted to give my primary energy to creating a strong and independent lesbian movement. This goal and building my own institution, *The Lesbian Tide*, took front and center in my life. Unfortunately, Morris's search for professionals with letters after their names did not include looking in the very new, and overly educated, feminist movement.

Morris Kight was savvy about the national political landscape and the intersections of the social change movements of our era. Intellectually he recognized that the straight world persecuted gay men because they were perceived to be men taking on a feminine role, the role of women. Yet he was too much a man of the 1950's to make the emotional leap into accepting women as political peers. He made only a few exceptions for butches. Also, Morris wasn't convinced that lesbian feminists were valid lesbians. This was a disconnect in his thinking, ergo in his political organizing, that I failed to realize in my early years with him. Not grasping the bedrock of his genderized mind would turn out to be a formidable lapse in judgment on my part and the cause of great conflict.

By 1975, Los Angeles' most prominent gay organization was housed in a pair of loosely held together 1930's Victorian houses located at the rundown end of Wilshire, the end close to downtown where street people wandered and prayed. The landlord had allowed Kight and Kilhefner to rent his buildings because they weren't fit for up-to-code housing or business. GCSC opened its doors with hippie style beds on the floor and beads in the doorways. It was a gay rap center, sleepover pad for runaways, hotbed of political discussion, and hub of L.A.'s gay community. Perhaps the separateness of Morris's and my own political paths was why Morris never informed me that he was making a dramatic right turn from radical activist to social service worker. And so, after years of hard fought campaigns with him—building the early movement and fighting the heterosexual world—I found myself, in the winter of '75, locked in a war with my political godfather. This time, our turf was personal. It was his own gay center.

Dateline: The Gay Community Services Center, January 6, 1975

"What are we gonna do if they refuse us, Córdova?"

The question came from my co-worker Pody Molina. She and I were among the two dozen staff members holding a vigil outside the Gay Community Services Center's Board of Directors meeting. The meeting had been called for 7:00 pm and it was now 9:00 pm on January 6th, the feast of the Epiphany on the Catholic calendar. Most of GCSC's lesbian employees were jammed together on the second floor landing outside the Boardroom waiting for the Directors to finish their meeting so they could have their own.

It had never been part of my life plan to work *for* Morris rather than *with* him as a peer, and I had always felt the Center was, as it was named, a gay more than lesbian center, but months after our "Felons Six" ride I found myself accepting a sorely needed part-time job working as a publicist for GCSC's Herself Health Clinic, one of the two programs for women the Center had just begun to provide. The fifteen-hour-a-week gig writing press releases paid me just enough to keep my heartfelt jobs—writing for *The Free Press* and my own *Lesbian Tide*. As a veteran activist I knew one of the cardinal rules of friendship among gay leaders was "You stay out of my creations, and I'll stay out of yours." I knew that my mentor was Chairman of the Board at GCSC. But, bluntly speaking, I needed the money. I was subsisting on $700 a month, and this was a gay job, not a straight place where I'd have to keep my political activist life a secret or be fired. Besides, BeJo was mostly supporting our apartment. I was desperate to contribute more.

What I didn't know was that GCSC was a hotbed of

political turmoil. When I arrived I found that lesbian staff was complaining that there were no dykes in decision making positions, the men had made women second class add-ons to bolster their power. The place was a magnet for dissonance between the left and the right of gay politics. On top of that, it brought the overly rich Westside gay male donors into volatile I-see-you range of the "underclass" gay clients. Besides sex, the two groups had little in common.

Quickly I decided that I should try to fly under Morris's radar, be an absentee worker, ignore the politics of the place, and stick to writing about the health needs of dykes. What could be controversial about lesbian health? Morris wouldn't even know I was there. We could continue our close working relationship on wider gay issues.

Perhaps I was naïve. Within a few months I had joined the forces of lesbian resistance.

During the fall of '74 the lesbian staff had presented the Board of Directors with several workers' petitions stating our belief that as feminist workers we had a right to self-governance. We'd repeatedly asked the Board to let us have a staff-elected management collective to replace Ken Bartley, the lone male Administrator. Bartley was one of those gay men from the 1950s who felt emasculated if a woman asked him to be a decent human being. Morris Kight's Board had rejected our notion of a management collective—the word "collective" sounded too radical and too feminist to them. But they'd agreed that a five person management team was a good idea. However, they appointed Bartley to head the team, and three other men to be co-managers with him. Tonight the Board would vote to seat the fifth and last staff representative on the management team. Tonight we'd submitted our last petition, a list of three lesbian feminist employees. We'd demanded that they pick one of the three to fill the last seat.

"The Board has to give us something," I told my co-worker.

Pody's normally fun-loving face was creased with worry lines. I shared her angst. Here we were, lesbian employees of a gay center protesting against it. Pody had recently moved to town from North Carolina and this was her first movement action. Like her Cuban-born father, Pody was blonde and fair-skinned, which made her less Latina looking than I. Both of us had been raised white, culturally speaking.

My Mexico-born father had met my Irish New Yorker mother at West Point in 1946, the year after the good war, World War II, ended. Graduating the Academy, he'd been assigned to Paris to help the reconstruction of postwar Europe and never looked back to his childhood in Texas. Raising us, he'd told us that we were Americans and he taught us Italian, the language of opera and artists, rather than Spanish.

Pody nudged my shoulder. "So how does pressure cause social change?" She motioned toward the board members sitting behind the closed doors, all of whom were in their fifties or older. "Especially with this bunch?"

I reached into my jeans and pulled out my silver Zippo lighter. "Listen," I said, as I flicked it open and spun the wheel with my thumb. "Did you hear the grate of the wheel against the flint? Metal on metal, immutable force against un-giving force equals a spark, a flame, a fire. That's the principle of dialectic materialism."

"Run that by me again?"

"It's a political theory, Pody. A process of social change spelled out by the German philosopher, Karl Marx." I took a long drag off my cigarette. "Marx says that at some point in the evolution of a thing called A, that A will be so impacted by its opposite, let's call that B, that both A and B will lose their A-ness and B-ness and evolve into an entirely different new thing called C. The Gay community Services Center is A. And we, the lesbian staff, are B—the forces of change."

"Combustible," Pody laughed. She jabbed my chest, playfully hitting the political buttons affixed to my faded blue denim political war jacket. To me each button represented a battle decoration from a campaign hard fought or a new organization founded. *Marimacha y Feliz!* proclaimed one that took the derogatory Spanish words for "lesbian and happy" and screamed it out on red letters against black. "Alpine County or Bust" said another, referring to Morris's wildly popular idea that gays should move to the small, nondescript Northern California county and take it over.

Huddled on the floor with Pody, I realized that tonight's petition might be a last ditch effort. We were desperate to get one of our own, a lesbian feminist representative, as the fifth and final member of the management team. Our patience was running thin. We didn't trust that the Board of Directors, all men except for one lone female who was barely out of the closet and called herself "a gay woman" rather than a "lesbian," would make the right decision about seating one of our choices. More than that, the petition had become symbolic. All over the country, and in other Los Angeles organizations like the Woman's Building and the Westside Women's Center, women were rising up and rejecting male, top-down, hierarchical power structures. Our petition was the latest step in lesbians trying to persuade GCSC to adopt a few basic feminist principles like collective leadership and equality between lesbians and gay men. Out of GCSC's fifteen programs, twelve were for gay men.

The irony was that although GCSC was a male-dominated agency, a new grant last fall had come from the National Institute for Alcohol Abuse & Alcoholism to rehabilitate women alcoholics. A national study had been done which showed that twenty-five to thirty percent of lesbians had problems with drinking, so the government had given the money to a gay agency for outreach to lesbians. The grant was a national blockbuster in both amount and target population; a three-year renewable funding for the staggering amount of a million dollars, a third of a million per year, a groundbreaking statement as the first federal money exclusively given to rehabilitate women alcoholics. It was also a national first because a million had never been given to a homosexual organization. A second, smaller grant had recently come to GCSC from the L.A. County Board of Supervisors for the purpose of setting up a women's health clinic, my department, the Herself Health Clinic.

Of course this kind of government funding was great news for the national gay and lesbian movement. No one could have predicted we activists would get help for our people from the very source of our oppression. But these two grants were destabilizing Morris's fledgling GCSC. Before the grants, the Center had largely subsisted on those private donations from wealthy gay men. Now this federal money forced the Center to hire almost two dozen lesbian employees. Another half dozen had to be hired for the women's clinic. So much money and so many women! Now there were twenty-nine female salaried positions at GCSC; female employees outnumbered males by three to one. The inadvertent upheaval in gender balance had come as a major shock to its Board of Directors.

"Córdova, can they do anything like fire us for protesting?" Pody asked, a hint of fear in her otherwise cheerful voice. She was the coordinator of volunteers in the clinic program.

"No way, Pody. We can't let fear sidetrack us. We have to handle ourselves calmly and firmly," I said, trying to borrow the sage tone I'd read about in the writings of community organizer Saul Alinsky. "I don't think the Board can do anything to us, directly."

A flicker of compassion passed through me. Poor newbies, I thought, studying Pody and her friend, Rachel, who had just joined us in the wait. Looking at this new woman, I saw she was petite, barely clearing five feet, and had startling blue eyes. She was definitely femme and new to the movement, I realized, because she wore earrings. This at a time when jewelry was seen as a sign of seeking male approval and "collaborating with the enemy." I vaguely remembered that she was on staff, and that I'd seen her walking around the halls at GCSC and at other events, but we'd never been introduced. I pitied newcomers. These were their first gay jobs. Surely neither of them had signed up for a pitched battle against a gay Board of Directors.

I stole another look at the petite woman, who still smelled of the suburbs. She had a lovely Irish face, and I had a weakness for ladies of my mother's ancestry. She was dressed in a gauzy green blouse open low enough to more than suggest small, well-formed breasts. Ardent feminists exposed nothing, I knew, so this also told me she was probably a lesbian-come-lately, one of thousands of heterosexual women who'd recently left a marriage and now flooded the fast growing Women's Movement.

I was a "lifer" –a lifelong lesbian, a dyke who'd never been heterosexual, married, or slept behind enemy lines. At fifteen my mother had accidentally tipped me off to my as yet unknown sex drive by pointing out to me that the birthday card I received from a girlfriend was indeed a love letter. Filing this reference away deeply in my subconscious, I managed to be pleasantly shocked and gleefully proud when my first morning after arrived four years later.

We lifers didn't need a political movement to give us permission to come out of the closet. As a lifelong lesbian, I'd trained in the culture of pre-feminist lesbian bars. I treated newbie lesbians like tourists—with a good deal of skeptical distance. Fifties bar culture held that such a woman needed, at best, a year to sort out her identity issues, and at worst, she'd dump you—as a trend or experiment—before going back to men.

I turned away from Pody and her friend and toward the ashtray next to the stairwell. I needed to sit, smoke, and think things out politically. It was now ten o'clock. The Board couldn't hide in there all night.

Damn. What were we going to do if the Board came out and announced they were rejecting our petition? Ken Bartley, I was sure, had purposely given us only a one-day notice about tonight's meeting. That meant something unexpected was up. Always have a back-up plan, I chided myself. June and I needed to strategize, and we needed to do it now!

June Suwara, the tall, quick-mouthed Director of the Peer Counseling Program, cut an imposing figure dwarfed only by her ideologically battering personality. Orange-haired with freckles, June was in her usual androgynous drag—today's version a green and black flannel thrift store shirt and a camouflage vest, replete with political buttons that bespoke her solidarity with Mao's Chinese revolution.

In my lifelong lesbian vernacular, June was butch. I thought it was odd how most lefty lesbians from the anti-war movement rarely admitted to being butch or femme. They identified with the politically neutral label "androgynous." This was only one of the many political duplicities espoused by lesbians who followed Marx or Mao, I thought. June and I were far from friends, since I knew almost nothing about her personally other than she'd been working at GCSC for two years. That meant she understood the intricacies of the politics here better than I did. And she was extremely vocal about them. All the more reason that she and I needed to be on the same page when the Board came out.

The redhead was in intense conversation with Brenda Weathers, the Director of GCSC's Alcoholism Program for Women (APW). She glanced at me, but didn't break off her conversation, deliberately keeping me waiting. I noticed that the buttons on June's khaki vest read differently from mine. The most dominant one screamed, OVERTHROW CAPITALISM, red letters on white. From what June had said to me, and from the scuttlebutt on the Center's grapevine, I knew that June was a self-described, card-carrying member of the Communist Party. Unlike me, a convert to radical lesbian feminism from a homosexual background, June was a dyed-in-the-wool Lefty with worker-based class politics. Her father was probably a union leader, while my father, a poor boy from Texas, was the president of the marble import company he'd built from the ground up. Dad used to come home at night complaining that the unions were breaking him. I made a mental note to find out more about June's background. It could be relevant to the fight ahead of us with the Center.

Studying the crowd around June, I realized that the Center's rapid hiring had brought lesbians of wildly different political backgrounds into forced proximity. Among us, there were lesbians from the hinterlands of suburbia who called themselves gay women and had grown up thinking of themselves as homosexual. This group felt that gay men were our brothers. They clashed with those among us who were feminists and felt that the cause of our second-class lives was the male-constructed world of patriarchy. These newly converted lesbian feminists were sure there was little difference between straight and gay men. Also among us were activists from the New Left who, like June, had grown up on an anti-war, down-with-the-Establishment diet. To them, being a lesbian was only the latest issue in their litany of oppressions.

Finally, June finished talking with Brenda and turned to me. "What's up, Córdova?" she asked in her usual clipped tone.

I stood up straight. "We need to talk about what to do when the Board comes out."

"That's true," June said. "Bartley let it slip this morning that the Board won't be seating me on the management team."

In composing its slate of three acceptable names to seat on the management team, we'd deliberately put June's name down as one of the three, along with myself and a quiet, non-controversial lesbian named Denise Crippen. The Board didn't know it, but Denise was one of us, a lesbian feminist. We'd strategized that the Board would reject June and me as too hard to control, so they'd have to accept Denise.

"Did Bartley say why not?"

June's freckled complexion turned dark. "He told another staffer he thinks I have hidden agendas."

"What the hell does that mean?"

"Who knows what those idiots are thinking?" June retorted. "I think he found out that I went to some of those Westside meetings to start a new lesbian center."

"That's ridiculous," I said. "I go to those meetings too. I have close friends in that Lesbian Center Collective group." It crossed my mind that Bartley was lucky June hadn't popped him one in the jaw. The man had a small, lean build, and a pushed in face that looked like it had been last been kissed during the

Ice Age.

"Why should GCSC care anyway?" June said. "A lesbian center on the Westside would take the pressure off them to create more lesbian programming."

I moved closer to June and lowered my voice. "I think the real reason the Board refused you is because you're a commie-pinko dyke," I whispered wryly.

"Yeah, probably," she agreed. "They know I'm pro-union."

"Exactly. Fomenting unionism among staff isn't a brew they want employees drinking." I blew the hair out of my eyes. I wasn't surprised to hear that the Board was going to refuse June. "What will happen if they don't choose Denise?"

June looked around the room. "That will fry everyone," she said.

I nodded. "The first thing we need to do now is spread the word. No matter what happens, keep a lid on it. No insults, no name-calling, no confrontation. The Board members are from a generation that thinks talking loud is angry."

"Anger is exactly what we should show them," June said. "Why not scare them? Fear is the only reasoning they'll listen to."

I lowered my eyes so that June couldn't read my face. Was she indirectly asking me how Morris would respond to an intimidation strategy? Most activists who knew the lay of the land politically knew that Morris Kight and Jeanne Córdova were close and had always been on the same side. June might know I was one of Morris's protégées.

"We can't take no for an answer." The belligerence in her voice amplified my fears. "Something's gotta give or some of us will be forced to quit."

"That might be exactly what they want," I cautioned.

"Last week Bartley called one of my people an anarchist hippie."

"Evolution will never reach Bartley," I agreed. "He's a mutant strain."

"He's got to go." June smacked the wall with the palm of

her hand.

"I agree. That's why it's so important that we get the fifth vote on management. We've got to curb his power."

June's eyes narrowed. "And if they say, 'We haven't had enough time to consider…'?"

"Then, you or I step forward and demand they regroup for another emergency session tomorrow night."

June nodded. "Acceptable," she said. "OK. I'll tell my group not to yell fuck you at Kight. But they'd better do it tonight, Córdova." She spun on her heel and left me with her demand.

I wiped the sweat off my brow. It was hard to believe June and I were on the same side. Goddess forbid this fight with GCSC should drag on.

By the time I returned to Pody, I was strung out. I let myself slide down the wall. I'd been awake most of last night, lobbying on the phone. Sometimes my life went by too fast like I was chasing it from behind.

"I'll go down to the liquor store and get us some beers," Pody instructed. "Do you want a downer to calm your nerves?"

I looked at her gratefully. "A cold Coke would be great."

As Pody left, I reached into my back pocket and found my back-up Darvon, which I popped with a sip of water. I'd first discovered painkillers in college. They quelled the pain of exhaustion and let my tired body keep up with my overactive brain. I closed my eyes and lit a cigarette, trying to relax. When I'd signed up for this job it was supposed to be a small, part time gig. Now it had devolved into a political mess. Why couldn't Morris and his boys toss their lesbian feminist staff a few egalitarian bones? We hadn't even been able to convince them that a man using the women's bathroom was a legitimate issue. The men's room smelled of urine. Now ours did too.

Pody returned with the beer, squatting beside me on the floor. "I've never been part of anything like this. I just came to the big city to date girls…I mean women."

"That sucks, I'm sorry. I guess we dykes found our voice with feminism and now the guys can't shut us up."

"I heard the boys brought a thirty-foot "cock-a-pillar" float to the gay march a few years ago. The lesbians must have gone nuts."

"Of course we did! The men were demeaning gay 'liberation' as sexual license," I recalled, picturing the giant, brightly colored papier mache penis with men's feet sticking out from beneath as it walked down Hollywood Boulevard. "Lesbians believe gay liberation is about coming out without being fired at work."

Pody nodded. "Yeah, or not allowing your ex-husband to take you to court and claim you're an unfit mother because you're living with another woman."

Pody looked glum. "No wonder we're still fighting with them."

She gestured toward my pocket and I took out two cigarettes. "That doesn't speak well for our odds on winning tonight, does it, Córdova?"

I puffed, trying to keep my cig lit in the stale air. "I think Morris is wiser now. He knows that men and women have to find a way to work together." I forced a smile as I reached over and tousled Pody's short, blonde hair. "Don't worry." I looked at my watch. It was now midnight. BeJo was home alone with Johnny Carson. She'd be livid that I hadn't even called.

Suddenly, the boardroom door creaked open.

"The jury's in!" June shouted.

I jumped to my feet. The bodies on the landing moved toward the door.

A shock of white hair appeared. It was Morris. Quickly he stepped aside, and, with a wave of his turquoise-laden hand, motioned a second figure behind him to come forward. All eyes fixed on the bony, bearded face of GCSC's President of the Board, Dr. Benjamin Teller, an MD psychiatrist. I kept my eyes on Morris. I knew he would be the doctor's ventriloquist.

Teller stepped toward us and stopped. The single sheet of paper in his right hand trembled. Why is this man afraid of us, I wondered, trying not to feel sorry for him. He held the power.

The good doctor coughed and cleared his throat. "Ahem,"

he began. "The Board's response to...ah...the...your petition is that...we the Board reserve the right to appoint all people to all positions, including management. Therefore, for the fifth position on the management team we have selected a person not on your list. That person is—"

A loud, collective groan drowned out the name Teller uttered. We lesbians had been disenfranchised once more. Then suddenly, everyone turned to gawk at Pody's newbie friend. Her name was Rachel. Teller had spoken her name. But I barely knew it and couldn't believe it! The Board had deliberately chosen someone who was new to the movement and the Center. Someone who couldn't possibly stand up to Ken Bartley, and worse, someone not on our list. They'd openly denied that workers had the right to self-management.

"Fuuuuck!" June hissed.

"Wow!" choked Pody.

"Shit!" someone exhaled.

The petite woman Rachel stared at us, a deer caught in the headlights. I could see the wordless question mark forming in her mind, as it had in all of ours, *Why me?*

My eyes returned to Morris just in time to see his lip curl in a sly smile. I heard him whisper to Teller, "Finish it."

"There's more," Teller said, clearing his throat. "In order that your complaints, I mean...concerns...will be represented at the highest level, and to show that we are listening to you... we have also decided to invite Jeanne Córdova to sit on the Board of Directors."

Mouths fell open once more, including my own. The landing was so still I could have dropped a full volume set of *Das Kapital* on the floor and not a single pair of eyes would have shifted away from the doctor's face. The bony-faced Teller's eyes grew frenetic, as if they were waiting for the first stone. Morris said nothing.

Slowly, confusion replaced shock on my co-workers' faces. What did this mean? The Board refuses our principle—worker self-representation on the management team—and then turns around and invites one of us to sit on their precious Board? It made no sense. I wanted to scream at Morris and beat on his conniving chest. But how could I? The man had just invited me to sit with him on his Board. I felt mind-fucked.

No one spoke. Collective shock silenced us all. If Teller's words signaled hope, how come defeat filled the air? I was afraid to turn around and face my comrades. If this was victory, why weren't we clapping?

Morris re-opened the door behind him. His motion made me realize that our audience was about to end. Remembering my pact with June, I lurched forward. In a voice that masked my fear I demanded of my mentor, "Did the Board instruct the management team to operate as a collective?"

Morris stopped, his exit halted. Above his horn-rimmed glasses, Teller's eyebrows reached toward his hairline, as if praying for divine intervention. His sheet of paper had gone limp in the humidity of our humiliation.

"No," Teller said. "That will not happen. It is believed that the workers can address their concerns by having their representative—you, Miss Córdova—on the Board."

The simplicity and genius of Morris's strategy began to unfold in my mind. He'd launched an end-run around our demands. Inviting me on the Board made me one of them. If I accepted a seat at the high table, I would be alone on the Board, silenced and cut off from rank and file employees. The same held true for Rachel's appointment to management. It was going to run as a sham, not a team.

"This is giving us nothing!" June wailed, stepping out from the pack.

The rumble of angry voices grew loud. A voice heckled Teller, yelling "Coward," as he turned away. Brenda Weathers, the Alcoholism Program's Director called out, "Give us something real!"

Damn, I thought, filled with rage. They'd told us to eat cake.

Morris hurriedly motioned Teller to return to the sanctuary of the boardroom. As he held the door open for the good doctor, his placid blue-eyes caught mine.

You screwed us! I screamed silently.

Better luck next time, he taunted with no words.

Chapter 7

The Vote

[Los Angeles]

April 24,1975

It was a gloomy mist-layered evening in April, the kind of night that wasn't supposed to happen in Southern California; I might have taken that as an omen.-

I stood at the foot of the staircase at GCSC, the boardroom beckoning me from upstairs. I'd taken the bait and joined the Board of Directors at GCSC two months ago. That had placed me in a more difficult situation, testing and stretching loyalties between my political godfather and my sisters, the workers. Now, three months later, staff versus management relations had gone from bad to worse. I was sitting in a position of supposed power, yet I felt more powerless than ever.

As I climbed the stairs to my third monthly Board meeting, I still questioned my decision. Tonight I'd purposely dressed in my best navy blazer and button down blue-striped shirt with my hair for once combed rather than tumbling. I bounded up the stairs, ready for anything.

A voice called out behind me, stopping me on the stairs. "Jeanne, I didn't expect to run into you!" It was a woman's voice, high and excited. I turned around to see Rachel standing below me, breathing heavily as if she'd been sprinting.

"I'm here for the Board meeting," I told her. "What are you doing working so late?" It was almost eight o'clock.

"I've just come out of a management team meeting." She grabbed onto the railing to brace herself. "I want to resign, I just can't take it anymore," she blurted, on the verge of tears.

My eyebrows shot up at the news. Like me, she had only been seated for a few months.

"I'm going to bring up the idea of resigning at the next workers' meeting," she continued in a hushed voice, looking around to make sure we were the only ones in the hallway.

Obeying an impulse to reach out and take her hand, I came back down the stairs.

"Why do you want to quit?" I asked.

Rachel leaned against the wall and sighed. "It's been pretty much a shell game these last two months," she explained. "The team never talks about important things. It's as though Bartley holds pre-meetings with Morris and Don and they come to policy conclusions before the so-called management team gets together. Then Bartley makes announcements to us as if he's Moses coming down from having received God's word."

"Did you bring up the move to the new location on Highland? Have they said anything about which programs are going to get which new spaces?"

"We've been asking him about the move every week," Rachel said. "The program directors have been begging us for information and hammering us with requests."

"And you've been able to tell them…what?"

"Not a damn thing," she burst out, blinking to keep back the tears. "Bartley won't tell us anything. And then tonight—" She shuffled through the stack of folders nestled in her arm. "He presents us with this!" She thrust two sheets of paper toward me. "It's a detailing of exactly where each program goes, with what staff and what equipment, practically right down to the last paperclip. This is the last straw!"

I took the papers from her shaking hand, peering at them closely. The first page had a diagram of the floor plan of the new building at 1213 North Highland Avenue. Each room was labeled with the program going into it.

"So this is a *fait accompli*?"

"Damn straight!" she said.

She was completely serious, but her use of "damn straight," a heterosexual pun, made me chuckle. My laughter brought out hers and for a few seconds we let go with each other, sharing the irony that our new titles really meant nothing. Leaning against the banister, I marveled at her tone of defiance; the newbie had grown fast, quickly figuring out that the Board had chosen her to be on the management team precisely because of her naiveté. What the Board, and most of us workers, hadn't known was that this lesbian-come-lately was well read and grounded in feminist theory. She'd evolved into being quite the worker's champion.

Suddenly, someone rushed out of a nearby room and collided with Rachel. It was April, my boss, the program director of Herself Health.

"Oh, excuse me," April blurted. Rachel and I stared at a red-faced April who was buttoning a disarrayed blouse. Her hair looked like she'd spent the night driving in a convertible.

"I'm so late," she mumbled as she ran past us and out the door.

"Well that was interesting," Rachel said, blushing.

Before I could respond, the same door that April had shot out of spewed out a second person, Brenda Weathers, who seemed to be chasing April. She did not stop to talk.

"Are all the program directors working late?" I asked Rachel.

She smiled at me knowingly. "Brenda and April are lovers!" she announced, like she'd divulged a national security secret.

"No way?" I hooted in disbelief. The director of Herself Health and the director of the Alcoholism Program for Women were sleeping together. This was indeed political news.

"They're trying to be discreet because they're both directors," Rachel said. "No one is supposed to know, but of course everyone knows."

"Including Pody?" I asked, concerned that my buddy was being played the fool since her recent break up with April.

"Yes, Pody knows. Everyone knows. Except you, I guess." Her eyes twinkled.

I smiled back, but I wasn't happy that I'd missed such significant gossip. This kind of realignment of power could have real political significance. The large, all-lesbian APW staff was a power base within GCSC. Brenda had become one of the leaders of the movement for reform, and lately she had been more vociferous about pushing us toward a more confrontational posture with the Board. She was one of the architects of the latest workers' proposal I planned to present to the Board tonight. No wonder Brenda had April's full support! If Morris found out, he'd be livid and would want them both fired.

Rachel's surprising gossip made me linger in the hallway. "Do you know why Brenda so adamantly wants APW to find another location right now?" I prodded my informant.

"Only that she still has no place to put APW's fourteen residential rehab beds."

"I heard she's worried Morris is using her APW money to fund the Center's move to Highland."

"No kidding?" Rachel raised her eyebrows. "Can they really borrow APW's grant money like that?"

"Technically, from a fiscal point of view, you're not supposed to appropriate program money for management expenses," I explained. "But social work agencies rob Peter to pay Paul all the time, hoping they can get new money back in time to meet the goals of the temporarily robbed program."

"Oh," Rachel said softly.

"Brenda is telling everyone that APW should be independent from GCSC, that a woman's program should not be subordinated to male management."

"The lesbian staff agrees with her," Rachel said. "If APW has all women clients and an all-woman staff, why can't women manage the program?"

"Because GCSC wrote the grant and the grant money flows through the Center. The Board of Directors wants badly to keep this cash flow."

"All that money!" Rachel whistled through her teeth.

"Exactly." I smiled, watching her pale eyes dance. It was fun to talk strategy with her. "I don't think Morris or Bartley care if lesbian alcoholics have their facility now or next year."

As I lingered with the newbie, the energy between us shifted from political to personal. I wondered if her smile could be any more inviting if she had fewer clothes on. Suddenly the few feet between us felt awkward.

"Christ!" I looked at my watch and began jogging up the stairs. "I gotta get into the Board meeting."

"Some other time…" she called after me.

I entered the nearly empty boardroom, taking a seat at the far end of the table, opposite its head where Morris usually placed himself. From this seat I could observe where the underlying power alliances were. I was early. The only other person in the room was Sheldon Andelson, {1}a tightly compact, square-jawed, balding real estate lawyer in his early fifties. We knew each slightly, but he was famous. I suspected he liked me and I wanted his vote so I nodded at his three hundred dollar leather briefcase lying on the table.

"Is that Spanish córdovan leather?" I asked.

Sheldon nodded back, acknowledging my overture.

He was a self–made businessman who exuded command and quiet authority. The gay grapevine had it that the multi-millionaire owned most of the real estate on Santa Monica Boulevard between La Cienega and Doheny, an exclusive mile that included several gay bars and the 8709 Club, a notorious gay bathhouse.

Sheldon looked up at the ceiling, attempting to adjust the papers in his hands to catch more light. "We must get better lighting in here," he remarked in a soft but irritated tone that suggested a secretary was standing by to take note of everything he said.

I slid my squeaky folding chair closer to him. "Why don't you have your people tell our people to buy some decent chairs while they're at it?"

He chuckled.

Good man, I thought, a sense of humor.

Like me, Sheldon was new to the Board, and, I guessed, not accustomed to being one among many. I assumed that he would soon make a judgment about whether or not this GCSC outfit was salvageable. If he chose to stay, I reckoned he'd soon be president. He was sharper than Doctor Teller and, as his rumored multiple millions attested, far more effective in the world. I liked him instinctively because he knew what he wanted and didn't lie about getting it.

The only other woman on the Board, a psychologist named Betty Berzon, walked into the room with Board member Marty Rochlin, known around the Center as a lounge act piano player. I thought of Marty as a political innocent who rarely had any idea about what the subtext of a proposal might be. Morris had recruited him, I surmised, because he doubled as a Beverly Hills psychologist in his day job and had appropriate letters, Ph.D., after his name. Marty gave me a nod and a vague half-smile, as though his mind were more engaged in deciding which Judy Garland song to sing at his club tonight. Betty Berzon looked at me and offered a stiff, "Hello, Jeanne."

In my activist life, I'd noticed that some lesbians had baffling reactions to me. Something about my attitude, looks, or reason for being, engendered strong feelings among certain women. What kind of feelings, I couldn't figure out. I'd bumped into Berzon briefly at meetings or political parties and had always gotten a strangely intense vibe from her. Whether she disliked me, was afraid of me, or was attracted to me, I didn't know.

A small pert woman in her late forties, Berzon took a seat next to Morris's chair just as the chairman himself entered the room with his arm loosely slung around the shoulders of president Teller. Morris winked at Berzon as he sat down next to her with Teller on his left. I had the uncomfortable feeling that this triumvirate arrangement was no accident. Morris, my comrade in organizing, hadn't greeted me. Usually he had a list of non GCSC-related political business to discuss with me. Tonight, he didn't even look me in the eye.

The six of us sat in the fluorescent shadows and stared at one another. I wondered where Morris had found these people. Certainly not trolling the grassroots. Three of the six Board members were shrinks in private practice, whereas I'd chosen community organization rather than the option of casework as my master's degree specialty. I'd never wanted to spend my life sitting in a room trying to help one client at a time. I wanted to organize communities to change the world. Not one of these people was politically active in the gay or lesbian movement. They were a doleful lot and felt more like my parents than my peers.

I took the yellow folder which held the latest worker's resolution out of my briefcase and laid it squarely in front of me. Maybe it was a good thing to avoid friendly chatter with Morris, since he wasn't going to like the proposal I was charged with presenting tonight. Besides, I wasn't there to make friends. I was there to represent the lesbian feminist employees and our issues. I studied the room. It was 1975 but not one of the members of the Board, except Morris, had any understanding that American women were in the middle of a revolution that was redefining our relationship with the male gender. They'd heard about gay civil rights, and thought GCSC was related to this struggle, but "feminism" was a word they'd only read in *Time Magazine*.

"Shouldn't we begin?" Morris nudged Teller.

President Teller rapped his small wooden gavel on the table. "You all now have the agenda in front of you," he said as he passed out a single sheet of paper. "I call this meeting to order."

I lowered my eyes and reviewed the agenda, which I knew Morris had prepared for Teller. Its language, in Morris's now familiar style, positing old-fashioned constructs such as "shall we" rather than the colloquial "can we" and the like. The brevity of the agenda shocked me. It had only one item: "Internal Business, Board Makeup." Surely with the worker versus management chaos at the Center there were many things to discuss.

"I'd like to add an agenda item," I spoke up. "A proposal from our employees concerning GCSC's financial bookkeeping."

Oddly, there was little reaction to my statement. No one seemed surprised. I tried to catch a supportive eye from the only other female in the room, but Berzon was looking intensely at Teller, who scribbled on the agenda in front of him. Berzon had earned her masters studying group therapy in the Big Sur-based Human Potential Movement promulgated by Carl Rogers. Despite her avant-garde psychotherapeutic career, she was still in the closet professionally. Even within the GCSC network, she didn't identify with the lesbians; she was "gay."

Marty Rocklin piped up. "I'd like to hear an update on that loyalty oath that the employees were supposed to sign. Does L.A. County Supervisor Edelman really need our employees to sign that thing? And, did they sign it?"

My mouth dropped open and the room turned suddenly very still as I saw Morris and Berzon look at me, the interloper. I was not supposed to hear what Marty wanted to know. Morris motioned to Marty, as if to dismiss his question. "We don't have to talk about that," he said.

The loyalty oath was last week's latest intimidation maneuver. The night it was passed out to the staff I'd gone home to BeJo to talk about it. Over dinner I'd told her the bad news.

"Things are crap at the Center," I'd murmured, my knife hovering listlessly over a pork chop. "Today the Board of Directors presented us employees with a loyalty oath."

"A loyalty oath!" BeJo had been shocked. "Loyalty to who?"

"To the damn Board of the Gay Community Services

Center!" I slammed my fist on the table. "Have you ever heard of anything more McCarthyite?"

I swallowed, trying to get a grip. "You know I've gone to the Board meetings, but no matter what I propose, I lose every vote."

"Well, you taught me how to handle that," BeJo said, "Expand the Board. Get new people on it to create a new majority."

"I've tried that, BeJo. I huddled with the workers and came up with half a dozen really solid names like Johnnie Phelps from the National Organization for Women, and Judy Freespirit from the Westside Women's Center. I proposed them and the Board voted them all down. They aren't about to upset their precious majority of closet case professionals."

I reached into my briefcase and pulled out a green-colored pamphlet. "A few weeks ago we got desperate and decided to print a worker's newsletter called—*It's About Time*." I handed BeJo the copy. "See there under the masthead, it says our purpose is 'to focus upon and create a feminist identity at the Gay Community Services Center (GCSC).' Even straight corporations are beginning to adopt pro-woman reforms."

BeJo ran her finger down the newsletter. "It says here that the new Board-selected management team is 'a boss-imposed structure.' So what's happened since management read and hated this newsletter? And by the way, this is a really sloppy layout. Next time ask me—"

"BeJo, the layout is not the point! More and more staff is getting involved in our campaign. Even some of the more progressive gay men are with us now. But something went wrong. Someone leaked a copy of this to David Glasscock, the senior aide to L.A. County Board of Supervisors, Ed Edelman."

"Doesn't some of GCSC's grant money come from the Board of Supervisors?"

"Yes! The Herself Health Clinic grant. That's my salary and four other women's jobs. This Glascock guy, who Morris placed in his job, appears this morning at the Center. He goes into a secret meeting with Morris and Bartley. Then Morris appears at the staff meeting this afternoon and tells us that Supervisor Edelman won't sign the renewal of our grant money unless all the editors of *It's About Time* sign a loyalty oath."

"Oh goddess, no! Who leaked the newsletter?" BeJo asked, her mouth agape.

"I think it was Morris himself. It's not like one of us accidentally mailed it to a County Supervisor's office."

"Sign the oath or else what?"

"Sign, or be fired."

"Oh shit, just like the Navy!" BeJo exclaimed, letting out a deep sigh.

Seeing a familiar hurt in her eyes, I stopped my rant, went to kneel by her chair and took her hand. Out of high school in 1960, BeJo had joined the Navy. After almost a decade of service, she and a dozen others had been hunted and harassed to admit that they were "subversive lesbians." Luck and refusal to admit guilt finally played in her favor as the U.S. made plans to invade Viet Nam and BeJo was offered a chance to get out of a trial and leave with an honorable discharge. It was one of the Navy's many great lesbian purges. The trauma had been a turning point in her life.

BeJo's soft eyes were now holding back tears. She reached for a roach, which was delicately straddling a curve in the ashtray. Tiny frags lay in almost every ashtray in the apartment. "Did they ask you to sign?"

"Yes."

"And?"

"We refused! All nine of us *IAT* editors."

BeJo smiled softly. "That's my baby. She goes down with the ship." She leaned over and kissed me.

I stood up, straight shouldered. "This ship is not going down so long as I'm on it!"

I'd declared as we finished dinner.

And now a Board member, Marty the innocent, was about to spill the real beans in front of me.

Morris spoke to Marty sharply, "The dissident staff has

refused to sign it. Let's move on."

Marty's face was askew with confusion. "You mean Supervisor Edelman didn't ask for the oath? It was only his aide's idea?"

A hush fell over the room as Morris, Teller, and Berzon looked at me, and saw me realize that the loyalty oath had been a ruse. Supervisor Edelman had never seen *It's About Time*. Morris had tried to bluff the workers! I swallowed twice, trying to stuff my shock and anger.

Suddenly Morris shifted tone and spoke to me in his coyly charming voice, "Córdoba, why don't we deal with your agenda item now."

All faces turned toward me.

Caught off guard, I managed to motion Sheldon to pass around the room my neatly stapled stack of copies of the latest worker's proposal. I took a deep breath.

"Over the last couple of weeks," I began, "the Center's corporate treasurer, Alicia Maddox, has discovered that Ken Bartley is manipulating the books." I paused. The room was so quiet that a tiny 3.5 could have rippled through the building and been clearly felt. The proposal papers were shaking in my hands.

"There are specific examples of what Bartley has done that are put forth in this proposal," I continued, scanning the page. I dared not lift my eyes. "Basically, Alicia and the staff charge Bartley with fiscal mismanagement. There are thirty-nine workers who have signed this proposal, which represents two thirds of GCSC's employees. This is something we can't ignore any longer."

A few chairs squeaked as people squirmed in their seats. I realized that I'd never get through the whole proposal by ad-libbing. I directed my fellow Board members to the last page, and summarized;

"We feel that the Board of Directors has opened itself up to a possible lawsuit from our funding agencies because Bartley the administrator has appropriated money for operations when such funds were given to us for other specific programs." In the silence of my pause I feared that everyone in the room knew exactly what Bartley had been doing with the books.

I read on. "These misappropriations may be illegal. A non-profit agency shouldn't mix federal and state grant money with other operating expenses. Many of the program directors, especially the Alcoholism Program for Women and Herself Health Clinic, are worried that the funding agencies will come here for a review, and see what Bartley is doing." I looked up. "We are worried that the funding agencies will pull their grants and close the projects down. Some program directors are also concerned that there won't be money available to pay their programs back for a long time because the priority is funding the new building on Highland Avenue."

"This is absurd!" Morris interrupted.

"Completely inappropriate," Berzon chimed in.

My voice became rushed. "Upon learning these things, Maddox didn't know what to do. She and the staff have no access to the Board since our meetings have been closed. So she took her concerns to the management team. At that meeting Bartley called her a liar, and said what he was doing was standard operating procedure. He has since closed the books to her, even though she's our corporate treasurer. After that, Maddox came to a workers' collective meeting and to me, as a Board member, showing us the manipulated records, and how there are not enough private donations coming in for Bartley to cover his tracks. GCSC is spending much more than it's bringing in—"

Morris cut me off. "Ms. Maddox is not empowered to show our fiscal records to employees!"

President Teller rapped his gavel.

"Finish reading the proposal," Sheldon commanded.

"Maddox is our corporate treasurer," I continued, my voice lower now. "She asked me to tell you that she feels she must resign. She says it's either her or Bartley because she won't be held liable for his misappropriations. Hearing this from Maddox, several project directors and a couple of management team members put together this proposal in which they call for

Bartley's resignation." I bit my lip, recalling the original draft of the proposal, which had called for the Board of Directors itself to resign for allowing such irregularities. I'd been narrowly able to persuade the workers to delete this demand and call for Bartley's resignation alone.

"Are you finished?" Berzon asked.

"In conclusion," I read, "we the workers respectfully ask that the Board take further action to correct this fiscal mismanagement within thirty days. If the Board fails to take these steps we feel we will have no other recourse but to communicate with our funding agencies and tell them what is being done with their funds. At that point, we will take whatever legal actions may be deemed appropriate."

Morris jumped to his feet. "This is outrageous!"

"You have no right to do such things," Berzon added.

I looked around. The other Board members sat with their mouths agape.

Morris glared down at me. "Unacceptable!" he shouted, raising a closed fist.

Sheldon broke in. "Ms. Córdova, thank you for bringing these serious matters to our attention. I'm sure the entire Board agrees with you that we must do our own investigation. We must have Bartley come before us immediately. I call for a vote on this proposal, now!" Sheldon motioned to Teller.

"All in favor?" Teller said in a disembodied tone.

All six of us raised our hands. It was the first unanimous vote taken since I'd been seated among them. I drew a breath of relief. Now Bartley had to come before us and explain himself. It was a start.

Morris look at his watch and nudged Teller, who tapped his gavel for order, "Next, we will take up the last agenda item, Internal Business–Board Makeup."

Feeling more relaxed; I dared to think that we were at last going to add some new people to the Board. I reached into my briefcase and found my list of heavyweight lesbian feminists who I planned to recommend. Teller also brought a stack of papers out of his briefcase and motioned to Morris to hand them around. As Sheldon handed me a copy, Teller began to speak.

"I have here a motion calling for the removal of Jeanne Córdova from the Board of Directors."

"I second this motion," Betty Berzon said.

I gasped, looking down at the papers in my hand.

Morris instructed Teller to continue. "Please read the motion into the record."

I blinked hard, forcing my eyes to scan the words, as Teller nailed my coffin. Jeanne Córdova...her interests...hostile and adverse to the interests of GCSC Board of Directors...one of the editors of *It's About Time*...a document which seeks to undermine volunteerism..."

"And I will add yet another reason," Morris concluded, his voice trembling with rage. "Tonight she brought before us a proposal saying she would consider legal suit against us!"

Too dumbfounded to speak, it dawned on me that Teller's motion was typed. They'd planned to dump me tonight even if I hadn't brought the workers' proposal. It wasn't just a reaction to Maddox and the cooked books.

Finding my voice, I jumped to my feet and shouted, "You can't do this!"

"The motion has been duly written, proposed and seconded." Berzon's face wrinkled with disdain. "I call for a vote!"

"What about discussion?" Sheldon broke in. "Shouldn't there be some discussion?"

I studied Sheldon's face as his eyes darted around the table. He was trying to figure out who backed the motion, and who didn't. He was as shocked as I was. Morris hadn't pre-enlisted his vote. Sheldon was the new kid on the block and he wasn't in the loop.

Teller brought his gavel down hard on the table. "Hearing no discussion, all in favor of the motion as read, please raise your hands!"

Four hands shot up on cue. Damn. I looked at Marty Rochlin,

but he wouldn't look at me. They had his vote in the bag.

"All opposed?" Teller asked.

I lifted my hand. So did Sheldon Andelson.

"The motion carries, four to two," Teller finished.

I was dumped off the Board and hadn't even seen it coming.

Chapter 8

_____

The Firings

[Los Angeles]

May 1, 1975

The ringing phone woke me from a deep sleep and I looked at the clock, knowing I would be late to *The Freep* again.

Pody's voice on the answering machine filled the room. "Córdova? You gotta be there. Pick up the phone. PLEASE!" Her voice sounded broken, as though she'd been crying.

I grabbed the receiver. "Po," I said, gently, "I'm here. What's the matter?"

"Have you gotten your mail today?" Her breathing was erratic.

"Not yet, it comes in the afternoon."

"Please, Córdova, go check your mail box."

"I'm in my pajamas."

"Please buddy. I just got something special delivery. I can't believe I'm the only one. Go check yours, now!"

"All right, all right. I'll call you right back."

I scurried down the stairs in my pajamas, passed the carport and out to the building's curbside wall where the metal boxes hung. Pody was right; there was a single envelope in my box. I pulled it out. Strange, no postmark. Someone must have hand-delivered it. Stranger still, the long, white envelope had the Gay Community Service Center's return address and logo. My name and address were handwritten in ink.

I peeled the sealed flap. A single sheet, three folded. It felt like a Xerox, yes, a form letter, with my name handwritten in after the "Dear... blank." It was dated, April 30. My eyes scanned the short paragraphs: "The Center's Board of Directors has... made an investigation...the nature and effectiveness of your performance in the position of Blank. Someone had written in "Publicist—Medical Services"...you have been in severe breach...your employment is terminated, effective immediately."

Terminated? GCSC was firing me? I stood paralyzed by disbelief and cold. The marine layer, L.A.'s moving blanket of heavy fog and smog, had come in off the ocean. Fear tightened the base of my throat. "In severe breach?" I choked out. This had to be a joke. My gay brothers were terminating me? It didn't make sense. Every dyke in L.A. knew about the Herself Health Clinic. I routinely stayed overtime to finish my press releases, flyers, and interviews.

Standing in the street in washed out pajamas, I suddenly felt like a homeless person: terminated, adrift, cast out. A car engine ignited and I jumped back against a wall. The car pulled out of its space, approaching me slowly. A bearded man at the wheel rolled down his window and stared at me as if to say, "You don't belong."

A sob escaped my lips. I began to run, out of the carport, up the dingy staircase, and down the hallway to BeJo's door. Slamming it behind me, I pounded the back of my head against it. So this was why Morris kicked me off his damn Board last week. They'd planned to terminate me. Christ, I should have seen it coming! I should have been a better leader. Instead, I was careless.

"Careless, careless, careless," I heard my father's voice

scolding as he towered over me on the front lawn. I was nine years old. Reaching down, he grabbed the splintered baseball bat out of my hands. "Look around you, Jeanne." He grabbed my shoulders and flipped me around to face the street. "Do you think money grows on that apricot tree there? Or maybe you think I drive to work each day and God rains down money like manna at my office. So I can spend it on the things that you kids wreck. Answer me!"

I executed a sharp about-face like he'd trained us to, and saw his angry face. "No *sir*!" I saluted. "Money does not grow on trees, *sir*! Money does not drop from heaven, *sir*!"

The man who my mother said truly did love us, glowered down at me. "And take off your hat when you are addressing your superiors, soldier."

My hand shot up to my sweaty forehead and grabbed the blue Dodger cap, "Yes, *sir*!" I emphasized the 'sir' like he said his classmates did at West Point. Every morning since kindergarten we'd had to stand inspection in our living room where we received our cadet training.

"Now tell me, cadet, why is your bat broken?"

"Mom called us into dinner last night," I mumbled, feebly. "I didn't see that a kid must have tossed it into the gutter. I forgot about it. I found the bat this morning. A car must have run over it…*sir*!" Tears streaked down my face and into my newly braced, crooked teeth.

"Are you equivocating with me, soldier?" he demanded, the veins in his neck as rigid as my splintered bat. "Are you trying to blame someone else for your mistakes? Tell me again. Why is your bat broken?"

I threw my shoulders back so the sobs wouldn't break my reply. "No, *sir*! I have no excuse, *sir*!"

"That's right!" his voice boomed. "There is never anyone else to blame. You are a Córdova. That means you and you alone are responsible for everything that happens to you. I don't want any cowards in my house."

"Yes, *sir*."

"Stand down, soldier," he barked.

I separated my heels, but my backbone refused to relax. The tone in his voice had downshifted. He hadn't pulled off his belt. He wasn't going to whip me this time.

"I'm not buying you a new baseball bat to reward your carelessness," he continued. "You're going to have to wait until you've saved enough allowance to buy another."

"Understood, *sir*!"

"For your punishment, I am giving you eight demerits. Now, soldier, you are dismissed!"

I didn't care about the demerits. They only meant walking up and down the hot, cemented backyard a few dozen times. No, my real punishment was these days of humiliation. Facing my troops tomorrow would be hard. I was the only kid on the block with a bat. Now we couldn't play ball. It would be two months before I'd saved enough weekly dimes to buy another bat. It was all my fault. Good soldiers never let their platoon down.

I sat on BeJo's toilet with the bathroom door closed, filled with the same shame I'd felt as a child. Today Morris Kight, my political godfather, had humiliated and dismissed me. Dad didn't control who I was anymore; Morris Kight did. At least, he wanted to, if I let him get away with it. I grabbed some toilet paper to dry my tears. *Pull yourself together, Córdova!* I demanded as I stood up.

I jerked open the bathroom door and marched into the bedroom. I hadn't minded being kicked off the Board. In some ways it had been a relief. But being fired, this was going too far. I lit a cig and exhaled a deep breath. What were Morris and GCSC up to? Something very strange was going down. I couldn't help but wonder, why me? I wasn't the ringleader of the "dissident" staff, or even the most vocal.

Oh shit! My cigarette fell to the floor as my mouth opened. This wasn't about just me; Pody got a letter too! Oh no—were there others?

I dashed to the kitchen and dialed Pody back. "Good, you're still home," I said as she answered on the first ring.

"It's not like I have a job to go to," Pody quietly replied.

"I got the same letter," I replied.

"Yeah, I was afraid they got you, too. I can't believe they would fire you, Jeanne Córdova, publisher of *The Tide*, dyke leader..."

"The Board must have had secret sessions, and planned this out in detail."

"Why fire me? I don't make trouble. I make people laugh," Pody protested.

"I don't know why you," I replied, truly stumped. "Why the two of us? It makes no sense."

I stared at BeJo's spick and span sink, so orderly. I needed to order my emotions to take a back seat so that I could see the parameters of Morris's plan. Where was my political brain when I needed it? Turn on the faucet, turn off the faucet. On and off, something simple was right there in front of me. I took a deep breath; suddenly, everything snapped into place. "Pody," I spoke gravely, "it's not just about you and me. If you and I got these letters, June will have gotten one for sure. There could be others..."

Pody stopped sniffling. "You mean they fired three people at the same time? How can they get away with this?"

"They won't get away with it," I said, my voice turning dark. "Get in your car, Pody. Go to the Center. I'll meet you there."

"We can't," she said. "The last paragraph on the letter plainly says, 'Call for an appointment to pick up your stuff.' They don't want us there."

"That's exactly why we have to be there, Pody! We have to confront this. Morris Kight can't fire a bunch of employees with no warnings and just expect us to roll over and take it. Get in your car, Pody. Drive to GCSC. I'll meet you there in fifteen minutes."

I slid into my jeans and donned my war jacket.

By the time I hit the cement stairs in front of the Center, I was breathing rage. My shirt was sticking half in/half out and haphazardly buttoned. I'd forgotten to comb my hair. No matter. Today would not be about fashion. GCSC couldn't dump multiple employees with no warning. IBM couldn't even do that.

The place was a mess with every office packing for the move to Highland. Quickly, I ran to the small front reception room of Herself Health Clinic. I found my boss, April, sitting at the desk. She looked at me with tears in her eyes. She held up a single sheet of white paper.

"Christ, not you too?" I said. Other than sleeping with another director, my boss was a low-key, constrained and sensible woman.

"What's going down?" she asked limply. Her voice was a hollow monotone.

A spasm of panic rippled though my chest. GCSC had fired a project director. That meant that the funding agencies would be involved. This was bigger than I had imagined. I laid a hand gently on April's shoulder. "Quick," I told her, "get on the phones. Call everyone. Tell them to come to the clinic's office."

"Here?"

"Yes, here. We have to occupy the building. The others have to come here." I barked my orders. The small reception room was filling up. But luckily we could see who else approached the room because the door was open and faced a long hallway.

"What others?" asked my boss.

"Call June and Brenda. And then every woman on the GCSC staff. And the boys who have been with us. Tell Brenda to call all her top staff of the A.P.W. Call everyone! Tell them to come here. We all need to be together."

"What a bummer," April said, looking at me like a wounded bird. "What if some of them are fired, too? I don't want to be the one to tell them." She looked at Pody, who had just arrived, with pleading in her eyes.

"Whoa...not me," Pody replied.

"April, I'll make the calls with you." I turned around. "Pody, start packing all of our protest stuff. Take all the political memos, the IAT material, the unpublished stories, our supporter's list."

I heard sniffles and turned to see Rachel standing in the doorway. "I received this in the mail!" she cried, handing me her termination letter.

She looked so helpless standing there with her shoulders heaving, tears streaking her pale face. I stepped toward her wanting to put my arms around her, but Pody stepped in between us and reached out to hug her.

I remained rooted at April's elbow, phone in hand, too stunned to speak. Why fire the woman who was the Board's own candidate for the management team? Then I remembered, Rachel had told me she'd threatened to resign last week.

Suddenly, June Suwara's wild red bob appeared in the doorway. "What the fuck is going on here!" she demanded, brushing past Pody and Rachel to come to a halt in front of me. She waved her own termination letter.

"D-Day," I replied. "The bodies are falling."

"Today is May first," she said. "It's International Workers Day. They can't do this!"

Two of the male employees who had been lesbian-friendly appeared in the doorway, crying on each other's shoulders. "I'm a program director," Enric said. "Look what I got in the mail."

Then he took notice of the rest of us. By now the office was almost full. His eyes made the circle. "Not ALL of us?" he said.

Seeing the familiar letter in Enric's hand, my shock deepened. Our guy friends, too? In recent weeks a handful of the gay male employees had begun to support us, calling themselves "effeminists," a term used by the radical left wing of the gay men's movement. Effeminists glorified in the name "gay faeries" and understood that the straight world mocked them because they as faggots identified with women. They championed feminist principles like lesbian equality in the gay movement. They were usually feminine, rather than butch gay men, and they'd become our natural allies.

A large frame filled the doorway. It was Colin McQueen, a big bear of a white guy with a great head of reddish-brown hair that was teased out into an Afro. Colin was June's assistant coordinator of the Peer Counseling Program. His socialist politics were similar to June's but other than that he was new to L.A. and no one seemed to know a thing about him. "This means war!" he hollered waving his own termination letter.

"What about me?" a small, male voice called from behind Colin. It was Jesse Crawford, the program director of the Growth Groups.

"And me? Let me through," a woman's voice called out from behind the stack of men. Colin stepped aside and Alicia Maddox, GCSC's treasurer, slipped into view.

Her presence among us was no surprise, I thought. Since Alicia had accused the Center of mismanaging funds, an accountant in a three-piece suit had arrived at Center. Bartley had told us he was an independent auditor. The day after I made my report to the Board, Bartley had told Maddox to take a mandatory "leave of absence."

The next person who walked in was a surprise. Dick Nash had been one of the original founders of the Center with Don Kilhefner and Morris Kight. Older than the rest of us, Dick was tall and lean with stringy hair he'd grown out during his years in the Haight. Since his official position was only director of the Hotline and Switchboard, I'd always assumed he'd been demoted in some previous power struggle.

"Well this makes sense, doesn't it," Dick said in his droll, quiet way. "We all got paid yesterday. So we're all fired today."

No one answered Dick. Others were still drifting in, everyone waving his or her letter. The stuffed room felt low on oxygen. I breathed shallowly. The effeminist men had taken a stand based on principle. My respect for them was growing.

"We ought to do a head count," I said quietly.

"I have," June, answered. "It's eleven."

"Eleven?" I repeated, trying to absorb the shock.

"Six lesbians and five gay men," June said.

April came forward with a hand-scrawled list. "It's almost everyone on the Herself Health Clinic staff, the Peer Counseling staff, the Growth Group leadership and three from administration."

"Who's left?" felt like the universal unspoken that bounced off the clinic's now unstaffed walls.

"What about Brenda and her APW program?" I asked.

"I'm out here," a calm voice answered from the hallway. "We're with you guys all the way!"

A loud cheer went up. I turned around to see that the entire hallway, all the way to the building's front door, was packed with nearly two dozen staff. Behind Brenda I saw her top assistants and the whole staff of the APW program.

"Let Brenda in," I yelled to those crowding the doorway.

Brenda Weathers was a tough looking dyke whose exterior belied a sophisticated, strategic mind. As she came forward, I remembered that in this past week she had managed to use the uproar over Bartley's alleged playing with the books to finally persuade GCSC to put a deposit down on a new building for her program. The new location on Alvarado Street was a broken down mess of a large Craftsman house but Brenda and her staff were already working to renovate their prospective recovery home, planning on opening it for residential clients next month.

As Brenda approached I asked her, "Where's your letter?"

"We didn't get one," she said, using the plural on behalf of the APW staff, I assumed.

"Why do you suppose that you weren't fired?" I prodded.

"Because they can't fire me," Brenda said, with a sly smile. She spoke softly, as if she didn't want our conversation to be overheard. "I've established a very close relationship with my funding agency."

My eyebrows arched. "What does that mean, Brenda?" I asked, knowing that her funding agency, NIAAA, was headquartered in Washington D.C.

Brenda leaned in close to me and whispered, "Now's not the time. I'll tell you more later." Her smile was as close to a Mona Lisa grin as a butch could pull off.

Suddenly I remembered a conversation Morris had tried to have with me at the end of last week's Board meeting.

As I'd tried to slink out of the room without showing my anger and shock over being ousted, Morris had had the unmitigated gall to come up to me. Before I could open my mouth and tell him to go to hell, he asked me, "Has Brenda Weathers or April sent letters to our funding agencies?" I'd replied with hostility, "No one's written any letters to any funding agencies. The workers agreed to wait until after tonight's meeting when I presented my proposal."

Morris had smiled that sardonic, crooked grin of his that told me he thought I was lying. Studying Brenda's face now it dawned on me. Had Brenda been in touch with APW's funding agency all along? Was that why she and her staff hadn't been fired?

Spinning away from me, Brenda addressed the crowd, "APW is with you all the way. Let's decide what we're going to do next!"

"Burn the fucking place down!" a male voice shouted from the crowd.

"Yeah!" a woman hollered. "Everyone's moved to Highland and the place is empty. Burn it now!"

"Right on!" June chorused with the others. The group was unleashing months of pent up hurt and rage.

I looked at Brenda and thought I saw the same fear on her face as I felt on mine. Burning things down was part of the revolutionary rhetoric of the day, but no such thing was going to happen here, I vowed. "Why don't we get on the phone and lobby our friends?" I countered, my mind grasping for some way to turn the clock back and make the Board reconsider firing us. "Let's spread the news. Let's divide up the community organizations and businesses and call everyone to a meeting, tell the whole community that we're not going to take this lying down!"

"We don't need no fuckin' meeting," Eddie yelled out in disgust. "We *are* the meeting. Burn the place down!"

"That makes no political sense," I told him. "What are we saying to our community with a bunch of charred embers? I say, go get more numbers, ask all of L.A.'s gay and lesbian organizations to join us. That's what we're all here for— community. Meet over the weekend."

"Meet where?" June asked. "You think they'll give us a room at the new building?"

"We can meet at APW," Brenda said. "There's a big living room."

"When?" Enric demanded.

"Sunday night," I offered quickly. "Right Brenda?"

"Yes. Sunday," Brenda agreed. "Eight o'clock at APW. Bring everyone you can!"

We weren't going down without a fight. Several people crumpled their termination letters into balls and threw them into the trashcan. One of the guys struck a match and tossed it in. Luckily, it didn't catch.

Chapter 9

My Nazi

[Los Angeles]

May 1, 1975

Morning was passing as I left my angry comrades at GCSC to head for work at *The Free Press*. Unlocking my car, I slid softly into the rich, black leather of the '67 cherry red Cougar that I'd named Lionheart, and let the sweet seclusion of my cave envelop me. Lionheart was my home on wheels, sometimes offering the only private place I had. The tightly sealed windows and purring roar of the engine blocked out the troubled day.

Parking in *The Freep* lot, I went inside and climbed the stairs to Editorial.

Penny stopped me. "You need to be here more often," she said, following me into my office. "Especially now. A guy keeps calling for you. Says he's a Nazi, and that he's the one who tear-gassed the huge rally to reopen the Rosenberg trial. He won't give me his name. Says he'll only talk with you."

"I can't handle more people blowing things up. Not today!" I waved her off.

She followed me. "I said you'd be in any minute, so if he calls back today you need to be right here waiting for him. I forbid you to leave the building until he calls!"

"I am at your command!" I joked with a playful bow and arm flourish.

Gratified, Penny turned to leave my office.

Suddenly, the City Editor, Tom Thomson, appeared in my doorway. "Pick up the phone, Córdova," he ordered. "It's your Nazi!"

I pressed the blinking button on my desk phone and stood up to take my Nazi's call. I always felt more powerful on my feet. "Córdova speaking," I said, waving Penny and Tom out of my office.

"Who'm I talkin' to?" The voice was hard and demanding.

"This is Jeanne Córdova, the Human Rights Editor of *The Free Press*. To whom am I talking?"

"You're talkin' to a member of the white race. So that means I got human rights too, don't it?"

I pegged my caller's education level at mid-high school. "Yeah, you got rights," I said. "But first tell me who you are or quit wasting my time."

"I'm Captain Joseph Tomassi," he said. His voice was deliberate and full of ego. "Captain of the National Socialist Liberation Front." {1}

"And that makes you a Nazi?" I mocked. What kind of Aryan name was Joseph Tomassi? I could just picture Mr. and Mrs. Giuseppe Tomassi Sr. getting off the boat from Sicily.

"Sieg Heil!" he said, laughing at me. "And proud of it!"

"That's nice. And how are you today?"

"Don't play with me," Tomassi barked.

"You called me, Joe. What do you want to talk about?"

"Remember the tear-gassing at the rally for those dead Jew swine traitors last month?

I blinked at the hatred in his words. A coalition of west side Leftists were calling for the reopening of the infamous Rosenberg spy case. The rally had been broken up in midstream as someone released tear gas in the building. People had run for the auditorium exits. Several had been injured in the melee. The organizers speculated that the perpetrator had been an agent provocateur, someone from LAPD Chief Ed Davis's anti-Leftist spy squad, the Public Disorder Intelligence Division (PDID) stirring up trouble. Davis denied the existence of such an unconstitutional unit, but like his Criminal Conspiracy Section (CCS), activists knew PDID was real. It was used to hunt and gather political intelligence on us Lefties. {2}

"Yes, I remember what happened in Santa Monica," I said.

"That wasn't the pigs," Tomassi said. "That was me. My army."

I swallowed and sat down.

"And the bombing at the other building in Santa Monica," Tomassi continued. "The one with the Social Workers Party headquarters in it?"

"I suppose you're going to brag that your National Socialist Liberation Front was responsible for that, too?" I said.

"That's right, chick. And I'd like a little more respect in your voice. Or else, I'm gonna call another paper."

"Okay, Joe," I backtracked. "A little more respect from me, and no more chicks from you. I'm a feminist, not a chick. Why did you call *The Free Press*?" I flipped open my tablet and grabbed a pencil.

"The *L.A. Times* wants too much proof, get me to reveal my 'whereabouts' as they say. And they ain't gonna print what I think of those Jew pigs and Commie criminals."

"What makes you think we will?"

"Because I'm gonna trade you."

I waited.

"My confession, for a story about my people and what we stand for."

"What people would that be, Joe?" His trade sounded good. *Freep* readers needed to know there were neo-Nazis alive and well in our midst.

"The people of the white race. We're an occupied people in

our own country. We don't have no rights in America anymore. That's why we've declared war on the Jew capitalist U.S. government."

"Why me, Joe? How do you know I'm not Jewish?"

"Your last name tells me you're a Spic. Besides, I saw your photo in your column. I wanted to meet a real dyke." Joe laughed. "But that's not the real reason," he said. "You're the one who writes about niggers and homosexuals and what broads want. I figure you'll understand what it means to feel like you don't have no rights. I want you to tell my side of the story."

"You want an interview?" I pulled my lips tight trying to hide my excitement. A Nazi's confession!

"That's right," he said.

"The cops don't even suspect Nazi involvement. You'd be drawing fire to yourself."

"We want the pigs and the public to credit us. I want them to wonder where and when we'll strike again." Joe's voice was low and thick.

As I waited for him to go on, I heard a click followed by several more clicks. And finally, a dial tone. Someone or something had disconnected me from my Nazi.

I spent most of the day waiting for Tomassi to call back, while knocking out a story about the trial of Z Budapest, a lesbian feminist activist who'd just been arrested for giving tarot card readings. Psychics had probably been foretelling the future in California since the gold rush, but technically fortune telling was a misdemeanor violation of L.A.'s Municipal Code, Section 43.30. The LAPD was trying to shut down the goddess worshippers' wing of the women's movement across America. Witchcraft was allegedly a threat to national security. Budapest had really been busted because she was a radical feminist who publicly proclaimed that she was a witch, and opened a prominent Goddess storefront in Venice called The Feminist Wicca. The cops said she dabbled in the occult. That made her a criminal in our Judeo-Christian country. We feminists knew that witches were prophets of the ancient goddess religion, Wicca. We'd begun the Z Budapest Political Defense Fund, and contacted the media, as was lesbian feminist tradition when political people were arrested. It had worked! The District Attorney was now talking about probation, instead of a six-month jail term.

It was mid-evening and dark by the time I shut off my IBM Selectric. I'd had enough politics for one day. The morning's debacle at GCSC was still smoldering in my chest like a hot spot in a temporarily contained fire. I wanted to get home before I, too, exploded with emotion. I needed to assimilate the day. I walked downstairs and out into the fresh night. Lionheart would take me home and BeJo would make a nice hot dinner and nothing bad could happen for what remained of this major bummer of a day.

I pulled Lionheart into the darkened Culver City carport and saw that BeJo's vintage Cadillac, Ramona, was missing. Once inside I found a note. "Sweetie," BeJo had written, "It's Friday night. Didn't think you'd be home. Fran invited me to join them at the Bacchanal. See you in bed tonight. I hopa, hopa, hope. Love, BeJo."

Damn, I'd forgotten it was Friday night. Mondays and Fridays were non-monogamous "space nights," according to our arrangement. We were in an open relationship, but feminist politics demanded honesty within non-monogamy. Sisterhood didn't include lying.

I dropped my briefcase on the kitchen table and walked to the bedroom. This was a downside of non-monogamy: all that freedom meant free to be absent when your lover really needed to talk. Who was Fran anyway? Someone from the baseball team, no doubt. Over our three years together BeJo had never gotten involved with another lover. But there had been plenty of times when she'd gone out with friends. Just to show me that she could, she'd warned.

Brooding, I went to the bedroom closet and pulled out my hidden journal. I'd filled a dozen red-covered, spiral notebooks in the short six years of my adulthood. Flipping it open to a blank page I wrote the date, "May 1, 1975," followed by, "GCSC isn't even my fight. I put dykes first by giving my energy to projects like *The Tide* and the Westside Women's Center. The Center was supposed to be a part time job, not a major war. How did I get involved with this group of macho gay male control freaks?"

I put the pen down and lay on my side, curling into a ball. Pulling the worn termination letter out of my jeans pocket, I re-read it. No mistake, Morris was the author. The tell tale sign was in the writing style: "You may have some personal properties in the Center, and *we should like you to have them.*" Morris always used the subjunctive when he meant to use the imperative. The sentence really meant, "Get your shit out of here now!"

I sat up and opened the journal again. "FIRED FROM GCSC TODAY,' I printed in heavy capital letters. "Never been fired before. Feel broken inside," I added. I closed the book, lay back down, and closed down the tears.

Hours later, I awoke, having fallen asleep in my clothes. BeJo lay next to me but she didn't stir. There was no point in waking her. In the clarity of darkness, I realized, the ache in my stomach was bitterness—bitterness and anger about Morris. How could he have betrayed me like this? We'd been allies for years. His loft home on McCadden Place, the activist hub of the gay movement, was my second home. There were few people closer to Morris, politically speaking, than me. Yet, he'd fired me. Had I been blinded by my long loyalty to him? If he was so angry and desperate, why hadn't he called me on the phone and talked to me about the situation at GCSC? Why had he avoided me? The firings had the ring of a near-panic political move, a hyperbolic stunt. Maybe a less savvy Board member had offered this ridiculous idea and Morris had grabbed onto it as a desperate bluff. Surely he knew that termination was using a hatchet where a precision blade had been called for.

How could I make things right? Pacing the hallway an idea came to me. I would show up at McCadden Place tomorrow morning. Reason with Morris face to face. Counsel him that

LA's first gay institution, which represented a movement that prioritized civil rights, could not terminate employees without warnings or notice. Remind him there were probably laws against this sort of thing. Make him understand that this could be one of the major blunders of his otherwise outstanding political life. Yes, I breathed a sigh of relief. It wasn't too late. Morris and I would find a way to wiggle out of this one.

Now, with action plan in mind, I felt calmer. Yes, being fired had all been a surreal mistake. Wearing a T-shirt and a pair of boxers, I climbed back under the covers, feeling sorry for Morris. This was way too big a mistake for me to let my friend make. Yes. I would tell him that he'd listened to the wrong advice. That the firings would drive an unsealable crack in the always fragile unity between lesbians and gay men, a chasm that the movement could not tolerate.

Turning over, I pulled the blankets snugly around my chest and wondered if Rachel might also be laying awake tonight. I knew she wasn't used to this emotional roller coaster called political life. And what about money? Penny had said yes to giving me more work. Did Rachel have another job or source of income? And why did I feel so protective about her, I wondered, as I drifted off to sleep.

Chapter 10

The Gay/Feminist 11

[Los Angeles]

May 4, 1975

I'd twice driven to McCadden Place trying to find Morris. Each time no one answered. Now it was too late. News about the firings at the Gay Community Services Center had spread like a Santa Ana wildfire across lesbian land in the L.A. basin. The dyke community—many of whom were lesbian separatists who didn't trust men to begin with—was furious. A male-dominated institution had summarily fired six women! Lesbians who had no relationship to the Center demanded to come to the workers' meeting hastily planned for tonight.

So far, the only good thing to come out of our battle with GCSC was that the women's alcoholism program was on the verge of a new life. Brenda Weathers had promptly moved her entire staff out of GCSC and into the large, ratty-looking two-story Craftsman with barred windows and a tattered paint job. Located in a seedy Latino area not far from downtown, the newly re-named Alcoholism Center for Women was no longer geographically under the thumb of the Board.

Walking into ACW's spacious living room, I was greeted by friends from everywhere, from LA's westside Venice dykes to eastside Highland Park activists. The great room was dressed with dilapidated armchairs from the fifties and broken couches with springs protruding under the seats. Posters from the civil rights, women's, and our own gay liberation movement hung on the walls in rampant disorder as if someone racing by had flung a handful of pushpins at the open spaces. The movement had no time for aesthetics.

I tucked myself into one corner of the room, standing between Pody and my best butch buddy, Robin Tyler, whom I'd dragged to the meeting to give me some objective advice. I'd met

Activist Robin Tyler addresses California rally just before November vote to defeat the Briggs Initiative. 1978. *Photo by Sue Cooke.*

Robin, a high energy, Peter-Pan type Canadian butch and a comic by profession, three years ago at a Gay-Straight Dialog. We'd been the only two self-identifying butches at the event who dared to raise our hands in a room full of rabid feminists who decried butches as male-identified. Our moment of mutual rebellion had ignited a deep friendship. She didn't work at the GCSC.

Glancing around the room, I recognized a reporter from the radical feminist paper, *Sister*, and another from LA's local gay newspaper *Newswest*. I myself would cover the story for *The Lesbian Tide*, although how I'd do that remained a mystery to me since my involvement had ruined my objectivity. I saw no one from *The Advocate*. I'd deliberately not called its publisher, Dick Michaels, or any straight press in town, since I hoped we could contain this battle quickly and keep it local.

There were close to forty lesbians in the room, yet I realized that I had only a superficial knowledge of the political background of most of them. Studying Marxist Leninism, classes I'd taken at the insistence of a Trotskyist lover two years ago, had taught me the importance of paying attention to where people were coming from politically. Knowing someone's politics helped me predict their real agenda. And this was an unusually disparate group of political bedfellows, brought together by an act of war against lesbian feminist principles.

"All right, women! Can I have your attention?" Brenda called the confab to quiet down. Despite the presence of gay men, it was common at lesbian feminist meetings to use the catchall "women."

In her mid-thirties, Brenda Weathers was short, compact and tough, with a hardened face that suggested she'd spent a lot of years behind a bottle. Word was she was from the streets and knew her drunks. Her staff, most of them also former alcoholics, was fiercely loyal to her as their mother lion. She and I had a mutually respectful, but impersonal acquaintance. Our paths had not crossed although she'd worked politically with Morris Kight five years ago in the Gay Liberation Front. In addition to being the head of the Alcoholism Program, she'd been one of the authors of the grant application. In recent months she'd played the role of one of the leaders of the rebellious staff. This made our telephone conversation this morning delicate.

"Can we meet and talk before the meeting," I'd called to ask her.

"Can't do that. I'll be coming from another meeting."

"Then let's talk now," I'd pressed. "The day we were fired you were telling me why you thought GCSC hadn't fired you along with the rest of us."

"Ah ...right," Brenda hesitated. "My funding agency knows that I know how to run this program. We've talked a lot."

Talked a lot, echoed in my mind. Past tense. Brenda had been talking with her grantor for some time. Luckily, she couldn't see my mouth hanging open in shock.

"So, you're saying GCSC wouldn't dare fire you because your funding agency told them not to?"

"I didn't say that," Brenda fenced. "I've had to protect my program. The GCSC Board has no idea who alcoholics are. And no clue how to treat this disease. I'm tired of ignorant men who've never had to deal with the struggles of alcoholism, telling clean and sober women what to do. That's what this is really about."

"So when the staff asked me to take the workers' petition to the Board and you promised not to write the funding agencies because you were going to give the Board one last chance to clean it up—you had already been talking to your funding agency, right?"

Another phone rang in the background. "Sorry, Córdova, gotta get this one, it's the emergency line."

My heart sank, as I hung up swallowing an angry retort. So Weathers had stoked the fires of rebellion because it suited her program's interest, but she hadn't been fired. I felt used.

I ordered my mind back to ACW. The room quieted down following Brenda's call to order.

"We're all here," she addressed us. "To decide what the

lesbian feminist community's response should be to the termination letters."

There was a collective moment of silence, as if we were all gathered at a graveside. The recently deceased were eleven bodies, five men and six women.

June broke the hushed mood, her green eyes blazing. "It seems to me that we were terminated illegally. Even factory workers are given warnings or reprimands. Did anyone get a warning?"

"A warning about what?" said Pody.

"A warning that your job was in jeopardy," June snapped, her thin upper lip tight.

I stepped forward. "June is referring to a set of standard rules that non-profit organizations are supposed to follow when hiring or firing people. The rules are called the personnel policies and procedures." I addressed Rachel, who sat across the room with some of her friends. "Did the topic of personnel policies ever come up at management team meetings?"

Rachel looked blank as she mouthed a simple, "No."

Everyone looked around, whispering.

No one knew anything, nor had there been any reference to PP&P's, as they were called. As a professional social worker, I knew non-profits had to have a legitimate set of PP&P's, but I wasn't thinking about the law when I got hired by the Center last fall. It had been a relatively simple process, no procedures or job descriptions. GCSC was the first gay non-profit in the country. No one in our young radical movement worried about following the rules.

"A lawyer I talked to said this is very important," June continued. "If GCSC has these procedures they certainly didn't follow them. An employee is supposed to get an official warning that their job is in jeopardy due to some specified reason."

"Does this mean we can apply for unemployment?" said Colin, the big guy with the Afro.

"Right on!" another voice yelled out. The room broke into excited chatter as it occurred to the group that there might be some immediate financial relief.

"We should all go down to EDD and apply for unemployment," I said.

June interrupted. "Even if we do qualify, I think the Center will reject our claims."

"Then they need to give us our jobs back," one of the effeminists interrupted. "It's one or the other!"

"I'll bring the lawyer next time we meet," June said.

I felt a bolt of panic shoot through me from groin to brain. A *lawyer* meant a lawsuit, a lawsuit meant court, and court meant the matter would be taken out of our hands as a community.

"That's premature, June." I spoke loudly to the entire room. "It's too early to turn this thing into a legal issue. Officially inviting a lawyer to our meeting will make the lawyer think we're asking her to represent us. That takes us a step further than we want to go."

Enric joined in, "Can't we have a lawyer come here unofficially and just give us some information?"

"Yeah, we need info," several voices chimed in.

"We should decide how to get our jobs back before we call in someone else," I argued. "Let's make a demand and give GCSC a chance to respond."

A new voice spoke up "They had their chance and they already responded." I recognized the dishwater blonde ponytail of June's best friend. Dixie Youts, dressed in the de rigueur Lefty dyke attire of work boots and flannel shirt, visited June at work often. She was a Maoist, a believer in Mao Tse Tung's Chinese revolution. "I see this issue as workers versus their bosses," she said, stepping forward. "When you're on the assembly line and they're trying to squeeze your contract and lay you off, you don't go running to them and say, 'We're giving you one more chance to give us our jobs back, pretty please.'"

"Right on! We're not gonna beg anymore," someone bellowed.

I upstaged Dixie, purposely walking into the middle of the room. "'They' are not just the 'bosses'! The 'they' that we're talking about is a homosexual services center." I projected my voice. "'They' are gay men, and the last I heard this movement is about gay solidarity." I desperately wanted everyone to treat this issue as a gay problem, not a labor issue.

"Fuck gay solidarity," Colin yelled. "They fired us!"

"I have no respect for that institution called GCSC," June added. "This is about workers' rights. They are management. They are the enemy!"

As June ranted, I cringed at her labeling gay men as the enemy. Male values and oppression were the enemy, not all gay people in management. And we weren't "alienated labor" like factory workers. But my cohorts were hurt and angry. The mood of the room was not with me. "I agree they're the opposition, but not the *enemy*. This particular Board doesn't represent the concept of a true community center. This Board of closet cases made a mistake. They are five ignorant people. But GCSC is a gay center and we're gay too—"

"We're lesbians!" a dyke's voice called from the back of the room.

"I say shut the place down!" Colin's deep voice roared.

I looked to Robin for help. She held out her hands, making the "let's talk" sign. Robin and I, and some of my peer group from the Radical Feminist Therapy Collective who were in the room, needed time to talk in private. But I couldn't ask for a recess. Something in the room felt wrong. The group's mood was quickly descending into a rage-driven place.

Looking for common ground, I tried to take the floor back. "Since we are agreed that we want to fight back," I said, "we need a name for our new organization."

As the group talked, I began to gather with my friends, but heard June propose,

"Let's call ourselves the Gay and Red Union."

Damn! I stopped in my tracks. June was proposing a name similar to the new gay group in town, a socialist gay organization called The Lavender & Red Union. I looked around the room wondering how many of her Commie pals June had brought with her. Among the crowd were some newbies, the effeminist men who'd been fired with us, many lesbian feminists from the Women's Movement, and dykes like June who'd seen action in the anti-war New Left movement. These women—from the Socialist Worker's Party, the Communist Party and other factions—were leftists first, people who had come into their lesbian identities more recently. They put what they called "the workers revolution" first. Others, like the lesbian feminists from the Westside Women's Center, had cut their activist stripes marching for abortion rights and against rape and other anti-woman violence. From my years working with them, I knew that these lesbians put women first and believed that the patriarchy was the root of all evil. Many of them wanted to live in Amazon Nation, a fantasized utopia with no men.

Still others, like Robin and I, were feminists with a homosexual past, who believed that gay men were different from straight men and that we had to drag our gay brothers into enlightenment. There were also half a dozen faces that I didn't know at all. I frowned as I lit another cigarette—not a great homogenous combination.

"What's the red for?" Pody called out.

From the other side of the room Rachel spoke with a timid voice. "The word union sounds like we're the Teamsters. Shouldn't we go with a name the whole community feels comfortable with?"

"I like the words feminist and gay," a member of the Radical Feminist Therapy Collective spoke up.

"I like union—it sounds united," Dixie retorted.

"The red sounds communist," said someone else. "I think that word confuses the issue," she continued naively, as if she hadn't a clue that blurring the issues was exactly what June, Dixie and Colin had in mind.

I wasn't entirely comfortable with the "gay feminist" term that I'd proposed, but I sure didn't support words like "red," or "union" which would re-define our feminist fight as a labor issue.

"I like 'Gay/Feminist 11'," Brenda confirmed, authoritatively. "I think that says it all."

A woman from the Westside Women's Center spoke up. "Then, to clarify," she said, and waved her arm across the room, "this group will be the Defense Coalition for the Gay/Feminist 11, right?"

Others grunted their approval, and I nodded in agreement. Our new organization's title had a substantive ring to it.

"So what are we going to do about being fired?" June broke the mood of consensus.

"I say we go in at night and take the place over," Enric called out. "And we change the locks and lock them out!"

"Yeah," his lover agreed. "Then we'll see who has a job and who doesn't."

I wondered who Enric and his lover Eddie were; where did they come from politically?

"Yeah, shut the place down!" June retorted.

"Burn, baby, burn!" Colin laughed, mouthing the chant that became popularized during the Watts Riots back in the summer of '65.

"We won't get our jobs back if we burn the place down," I warned.

"So let's demonstrate!" said June.

Knowing that the group wanted action, I tried to seize the energy, "Yeah, let's call a community wide demonstration for tomorrow."

Dixie spoke again. "I like the demonstration idea. But a one day demo ain't gonna cut it. We have to boycott the place. Everyday, all day!"

"Boycott! Boycott!" The room took up the call.

I looked to my left where my wise friends, the therapy collective, were gathered. Even they were nodding. The room wanted to do something big. The word "boycott" was harsher than "demonstration," strong enough to embarrass the Center. Maybe the word "boycott" would make them buckle more quickly, I thought.

"I'm good with boycott," I chimed in. "We demonstrate until we get our jobs back. As long as it takes!"

"Right on!" a chorus went up.

The dense air seemed to exhale like someone had popped the cork on a bottle of champagne. Boycott had resonated. Goddess forbid, I thought as I let the moment go by, that any of us linger long enough to define what we meant by boycott. I hoped we intended some loose form of ad hoc, ongoing demonstration. But were June and Dixie thinking we meant a traditional labor boycott where no one crossed a picket line? That could get far nastier than what I wanted. But no way I could get the room quieted enough to discuss the fine print. This meeting was done.

Robin nudged me. "I have to split. I'm glad this is your fight and not mine," she said and slapped me on the shoulder. "Some of these people are very far out. If I were in your place I'd get out of this fight, and soon!"

Startled by her summation, I hugged her as she left, and then sat down on a sofa, emotionally wrung out.

"You were brave," Rachel said, handing me two chocolate cookies and a napkin.

I looked up to see her smiling at me, and sighed, touched by her gentleness. "Thank you," I whispered. "Almost got my head shot off."

"I agree with what you said. GCSC is not my enemy. They hired me. But you must be tired of talking politics. I was wondering…since we're unemployed and don't have to work tomorrow, would you like to come over to my house now for a relaxing beer and talk?"

I smiled to myself. A relaxing beer at ten thirty at night? I was flattered. The woman might be shy politically, but there was nothing timid about her personal overtures. I'd arrived late in the decade of free love and had been making up for lost time by sleeping with every other woman that turned me on. Could Rachel be an every-other, I wondered. She seemed to be inviting herself to the party. Still, I was hesitant. Maybe I wanted to be the one to make the approach. Maybe I just hadn't decided it was her I wanted to approach. Or maybe I was just too worn out for any more "talk." The meeting had gone much worse than I'd expected, a narrowly missed disaster. A wave of exhaustion rolled through me.

"I'm rather talked out after this meeting," I said, studying her small, gold-hooped earrings. "And…someone is expecting me." It had just dawned on me that tonight was Sunday, not a "space" night from BeJo.

"You're a busy woman," she whispered as a friend came toward us. She turned to walk away.

"Another time?" I called after her.

"Maybe," she replied.

Gathering my things, I walked out of the building, pausing on the front porch to light up a cig. An attractive slim woman sat on the step, as if she was waiting for her ride. I couldn't tell if she was butch or femme. Sifting visual clues was much more complicated now that everyone was wearing the same damn androgynous jeans and flannel shirts. It was far simpler in the good 'ole pre-feminist days, when lesbians sorted themselves out and advertised by distinguishable dress signals. Standing in the cool night air, I suddenly felt very alive in my body, like there had to be more to life than politics. I watched Rachel walking down the block and across Alvarado Street. Suddenly overcome with regret, I ran down the porch stairs to call after her, but it was too late. Her car door slammed in the night.

Chapter 11

The Kiss

[Los Angeles]

May 5, 1975

The marine layer was burning off, leaving a rose-tinged Hollywood sky over 1213 N. Highland Avenue, GCSC's new, brick-faced office building. With its businesslike louvered windows, the edifice looked like a government-run social services agency. It was hard to believe that last week we were a radical hippie flophouse, and that over the weekend, L.A.'s best known gay organization had morphed into a "gay institution." The very words sounded so impossible together. Not a happy coincidence, I thought, for either side that today was the Center's first day open for business at its new location and it was the first day of our demonstrating.

Striding up Highland to join my comrades, I saw that our demonstration numbered about fifty strong, mostly women, but a few men, all marching in a long oval in front of GCSC's main entrance. My heart raced with excitement. I waved to some friends who'd just opened the city's first feminist bookstore,

Lesbian picketers march against L.A.'s gay center. *Summer 1975.*
Photo by Denise Crippen, Lesbian Tide.

Sisterhood. One of them carried a placard which read, Fired Workers Demand Jobs Back. Further back, the editor of LA's radical feminist newspaper, *Sister*, held a poster saying, GCSC Board of Directors Rejects Feminism.

The demonstrators' mood felt raucous, but not heavy. Good, I thought, we needed to display serious but orderly intent. Perhaps the strong words and this drastic public measure would force the Center to admit they'd made a mistake. GCSC could not afford to polarize L.A.'s lesbian and gay community. It was also terrible PR for the Center. Surely Morris could not allow this to go on. He had to give in, and soon. And yet, I was veteran enough to know that drastic measures sometimes had greater than intended drastic consequences.

Two years ago, I'd been shocked by a press release *The Tide* received from New York, announcing that all the lesbians had walked out of the Gay Activist Alliance (GAA), the city's primary gay organization. The split had happened because lesbians felt assaulted at GAA's mammoth dances where they felt forced to be with hundreds of half naked men who were all but doing it on the dance floor. The dykes had first asked the leadership men to tone down this behavior, but when nothing changed, they stopped going to their own organization's main social activity. After months of battling male domination on the dance floor and, more importantly, sexism in GAA's leadership, the dykes had staged a mass walkout. They'd gone off to form a new organization, Lesbian Feminist Liberation (LFL). The woman who had led the split was my counterpart in New York City, Jean O'Leary, a lesbian primacist who was my same age, also an Irish Catholic, and the city's top-gun lesbian organizer. She'd become president of the new LFL. And ever since, the powerful all-lesbian organization had been accomplishing great things. A similar split had rocked the San Francisco community five years earlier when Del Martin, the Bay Area's top lesbian leader, issued a riveting, now famous, letter called, "Good-bye, My Alienated Brothers." Martin's separatist manifesto said "Good-bye to the wasteful, meaningless verbiage of empty resolutions made by hollow men of self-proclaimed privilege. 'Gay is good,' but not good enough—so long as it is limited to white males only. I will not be your nigger any longer. Nor was I ever your mother." Her damning words led SF dykes out of the gay movement and into the feminist movement.

As I joined the demo and made the turn in the large oval of marchers, I chewed on the inside of my mouth. Was national gay history about to repeat itself here in L.A.? Walking out of a gay organization was not the same thing as demonstrating against one, but which was worse? Protesting in front of a gay building made the hairs on the back of my neck break into a sweat. *Christ*, lesbians demonstrating against a gay center! My nerves were working themselves. I started to doubt myself, realizing we should have taken more time at the meeting to talk about the politics and strategy of "demonstrating" versus "boycotting."

Out of the corner of my eye, I noticed Rachel walking

opposite me in the oval. She seemed to be flirting with me; her eyes lit up each time we passed each other. It was certainly easier to focus on lighter things so I looked her right in the eye and smiled back flirtatiously. As she circled she called out, her voice high and flushed, "This beats sitting in meetings, doesn't it?"

She passed before I could reply, but not before I noticed that she wore a shade of pale peach lipstick. Lipstick, I chuckled to myself, a symbol of women's "collaboration with the patriarchy." How long it had been since this woman had actually slept with the enemy—a man? Still, I had to admit, my past was littered with evidence that I liked almost straight-looking lesbian femmes.

At the age of twenty, before I'd become a feminist, I'd fallen head over heels for Gayle, an acutely feminine eighteen-year-old with butt-length chestnut hair that looked like she brushed it several times a day. There was something about rank femininity, the way these femmes flick-flicked their tresses with a snap of the neck, the way they made their earrings dance like bobby pins prancing in the air, that captured a rough element in me and made me want to lay down with them and growl with contentment. Later, as a feminist, I realized my body's tastes were not erotically correct. I'd responded by trying to go back into the butch closet, but with not without strong pangs. I'd never forgotten the day I'd taken a shoebox full of ties and carefully hid it on the top shelf of my bedroom closet. I couldn't bring myself to throw them away. Then, I'd taken off my ankle-length black leather boots and, with a bolt cutter, snapped off the gold chain that circled each heel. Wearing boots with chains, I'd been accused of being "male identified," a feminist cardinal sin. Other than this I had few dress complaints. The unisex radical feminist uniform of denim over denim, no jewelry, no makeup, felt natural to me and even rather butch—though my feminist friends called it androgynous. Femmes committing to feminism had a much tougher time. They became embroiled in an entire wardrobe change. More than a few lovers had secretly told me about their sadness over having to scuttle their makeup and every piece of feminine clothing. Androgynous, it seemed to me, was code for ill-fitting and sexless dress. Feminism too often took the romance out of lesbianism.

Did Rachel realize how badly she was breaking rank, or did she just not care? She'd certainly not gone all the way with feminist deflowering; her style was jeans but with gauzy flowered hippie blouses half-opened down to her breasts, with earrings and naturally curly blonde-brown hair. I liked her rebellion. And there was obviously something about me—not my femininity—that Rachel liked.

Suddenly, she darted out of the line, skipped over to me and whispered in my ear, "Can we talk at the break?" Her breath was cool in my ear, giving me the chills.

"Sure." I smiled. I twirled my placard, and kept walking.

A ten-minute break finally arrived and I found her sitting in the center's parking lot on a little block of cement, marked Reserved for Staff. Fellow demonstrators were milling around sipping sodas and talking with one another, but she sat demurely, legs together, looking down as if lost in a world of her own. I squatted next to her on the cement block, straddling it and facing her, stretching one leg in front of her and the other behind.

"What's happening, Jeanne?"

I greeted her with my best smile. Up close and more personal, I saw that she wore small pewter earrings with blue stones. The scent of some kind of perfume begged me to lean closer and something about the way she pronounced my first name, drawing out the end of it like the last bead in a rosary, felt incredibly sexy. Most friends called me Córdova. The sound of it on her lips made me remember that she'd no longer be around in my life everyday. We wouldn't be crossing paths accidentally at GCSC anymore. The thought troubled me. No more flirtatious notes, no more…options. I paused. The reflection of the white sky brought a translucent quality to her pale, light pink complexion.

"Well, hello there!" She seemed taken aback by my proximity. She tilted her head to the side to expose the flawless skin of her neck. I leaned closer to block the glare from my eyes.

"What?" I answered absently.

Her eyes were a dazzling powder blue, the color of a smog-free winter L.A. sky. Her lips crinkled into a come-hither smile as she laid a surprising finger on my lips as if to soothe further conversation. She studied me, a half-smile suppressing a glimmer of satisfaction.

Huddled on the cold cement, amidst the Sturm und Drang of clashing ideologies, kissing this woman suddenly seemed like a very necessary idea. I needed to kiss her to pass the adrenaline from my body into hers. My body moved forward and I pressed my shoulder against hers to let her know I was coming in.

Our lips touched briefly, brushed each other's contours. Mine parted, my tongue opening her mouth ever so slowly. Going inside, I felt as if I'd passed down this tunnel before, as if I'd known her in a past life. Time stopped. Contentious comrades became background music. The Big Bang could not have diverted my attention. I wanted to devour this woman now. Flip her over the cement block onto an asphalt bed, strip us both and take her right there in front of God and the Communists.

Out of nowhere a male voice interrupted, "How's politics, girls?"

Startled apart, I looked up to see the inquisitive round red face of Gary Franklin, a television reporter from Channel 13. I groaned. Rachel's face turned several shades paler than her previous white-on-white. The street became a street once more. It felt like all of our comrades were staring at us.

Rachel reached out to shake his extended hand. They had, I knew, worked together on a previous story. "It's good to see you again, Gary. Yes, as you can see, we are marching against GCSC."

"Can you give me some background?" Gary asked, as he took her arm and started leading her away. I heard him say, "Let's go to that coffee shop on the corner where we can talk."

And suddenly she was gone. I stood up, furious at Gary—and myself. I knew I shouldn't be kissing at a protest, not that kind of kiss anyway. My body still shook with desire. I took a few deep breaths, brushed the hair out of my eyes and numbly stumbled back toward the line. There was nothing to do but rejoin the oval and try to pretend our kiss—a kiss everyone had seen and was now whispering about—had never happened.

The next hour felt agonizingly long. I struggled to stay focused on my feet, forcing them to fall into step with the other protestors. Done with politics, I felt drained. The awe of my moment with Rachel still filled my chest. It had been so tender, not at all rough or awkward like most first kisses. The perfect fit of her mouth inside mine had drowned out the back-chatter conflict of my vast, anonymous city. I'd kissed dozens of women before, but there'd never been a kiss like that one. My fingers touched my lips. How was it possible?

Finally, another break. Rachel stood before me again, her blouse half opened, her breasts pert and beckoning. And all I could think of to say was a very lame, *Your bed, or mine?* but no, that would be too forward.

I read hesitancy in her questioning frown. "What's going on with you?" I asked, gently.

"I'm afraid to ask you again…" she said, letting her voice trail off.

"Go ahead." I smiled tenderly, watching the lips I'd kissed. "Ask me anything, the answer is yes!"

She burst out laughing. "Then I'll expect you for dinner at seven at my place tonight?"

"Sure," I shouted above the background noise. "Oh, no! What day is it?"

"Monday," she said, the pleasure on her face fading.

"Isn't our next protest meeting called for tonight?"

Rachel looked sad. "Yes, in fact it's at my house."

For a moment I hated the Gay/Feminist 11.

"Can you come early, before the meeting? I can make dinner around five."

"Sure."

"Maybe not just dinner," she added. "You could stay…after

the meeting."

"Break it up you two." Pody was suddenly beside me, slapping me on the shoulder. "This is not a kiss-in, ya know!"

The pitfalls of being a leader in the lesbian community struck me. I hated living in a fish bowl. What could I have been thinking? Would this morning's kiss get back to BeJo before I'd had a chance to tell her myself?

I grabbed Pody's arm, roughly. "I want to make it perfectly clear, Pody. That woman and I are not having a relationship. I hardly know her."

"That's never stopped you before," Pody teased.

Chapter 12

The House Where She Lived

[Los Angeles]

May 5, 1975

Rachel opened her front door and stood, hand on her hip, greeting me. Her stance was what my mother would have called saucy—not flip, not coy, but certainly a tease. Her blouse, a gauzy lavender material, clung to her breasts, opened to the third button to reveal a strand of small blue beads. The sun, streaming through the window behind her, backlit a come-get-me smile that felt full throttle opened. It had been six hours since we'd kissed.

"Greetings, Comrade!" I bowed and held up a Spanish-yellow rose. "What are you doing after the revolution?"

Rachel laughed a deep-throated easy sound. "I'm glad you came on time for this one. Welcome to my home."

Her mini-house was the first unit of a double set of duplexes located in Silverlake, a neighborhood alive with low rent housing, left-leaning peaceniks, and purposefully unemployed revolutionaries. Her place on Effie Street crowned one of the neighborhood's many small hills peppered with California bungalows. She led me through a tiny kitchen and into a large living room. The place didn't feel like an apartment, or even like she had attached neighbors, but rather like a cozy, secluded nest.

We stood awkwardly, three feet apart, in the large living room.

She broke the silence. "You look nice in red. It makes your skin tone darker."

I blushed at her compliment and hoped my brown skin would conceal it. I'd never picked a specific shirt for a date, but for this occasion I had ironed a red button-down. On the way, I'd even taken a comb to my unruly hair, since Rachel seemed the "proper" sort who would want some courtly behavior before jumping into the sack.

"You look smashing," I replied, wishing instantly that I could take the word back. "Smashing" was too archaic. I tried to take my eyes off her smile, find a topic to recover my balance. "Your living room is nice and big, all the protesters should fit in here," I said.

"Yes," she said. "Brenda said we couldn't meet at ACW anymore. My place is central to most parts of LA. Would you mind making yourself comfortable for a few moments?" She began to shuffle towards another room. "I forgot something."

"Of course," I said, wondering what she could possibly be missing. Just one more thing I'd have to take off when I undressed her.

Trying to focus on the present, I began to case the living room. With polished oak floors and off-white stucco walls and filled by a stereo, a desk, TV, and bookcases, the room felt lived in. Most of the windows were open and it smelled like a garden. A small pine table that looked like it came from some farmer's kitchen served as her desk, and a shiny black Smith Corona sat on it. Circling a large avocado-colored bean bag chair, I ran my fingers over the unusually small screen of a television that huddled in a far corner. Clearly, Rachel didn't watch much TV.

Bookcases stretched along the entire south wall and looked

like she'd made them herself, like a proper self-empowered dyke, from old planks and milk crates. The top shelf held cookbooks interspersed with file boxes. I lifted one lid—recipes. Ah, she cooked. This butch could not have too many lovers who cooked. Next to the recipes was a sprinkling of books about Oriental religions.

I made a mental note to ask Rachel what religion she was raised in. No one I knew in gay or women's movements was a practicing anything anymore, but I'd learned that a woman's childhood religion was relevant to her sexuality. I'd found that formerly Catholic lesbians had more sexual hang-ups, while Protestants sometimes did, and Jewish dykes were generally less contorted (and therefore more fun in bed.) My medieval Catholic parents had rarely mentioned sexuality. Identifying as a boy while growing up, I'd unknowingly but blessedly escaped the usual shame-filled Catholic sexual message aimed at indoctrinating girls. Rachel wasn't Jewish or Catholic; I would have picked up those clues, so she had to be some kind of wishy-washy Protestant. That was good news!

Squatting to investigate the bottom shelves, I saw that they were filled with feminist books, pamphlets and small volumes of poetry. The works of Marge Piercy, and Susan Griffin did not surprise me, but wow—Rachel seemed to have everything Sylvia Plath had ever written. *The Bell Jar*, Plath's fictional account of her descent into madness, was very popular with new feminists who were just leaving their marriages. She also had books by Robin Morgan, my favorite political poet. Aha, this woman and I might have something in common besides carnal attraction.

Portrait of a Marriage caught my attention. I pulled the memoir off the shelf. How interesting that Rachel had placed this book in her theory section rather than with the other biographies. A story of the non-monogamous marriage between the author's parents, Vita Sackville-West and Harold Nicolson, the memoir detailed the author's affairs with men and, more prominently, his mother's long and tempestuous love affair with British lesbian author and socialite Violet Trefusis. It was popular now and quite inspirational in the women's movement's ongoing redefinition of every aspect of our lives, right down to sexual politics and marriage.

I didn't believe in marriage—the complexity of who I was wouldn't fit the traditional confines of monogamy. What's more, the idea that marriage and sexual exclusivity were good, or even natural, for women had been disputed by radical feminists as early as 1967. Then too, the notion of loving, or making love, with only one woman for the rest of my life felt bizarre. I agreed with our foremothers, like Simone de Beauvoir, that lifelong sexual exclusivity was an unnatural state. That suited me just fine since I was convinced that I'd never find one woman with whom I could be all of my many selves.

Rachel appeared rather suddenly at my elbow. "Have you read that book?"

I looked at her. She'd put on some dangly green and purple earrings. "Yes," I said. "In fact, it's one of my favorites."

She touched my sleeve. "The two women were not monogamous, you know. But they loved each other over a lifetime." Her voice was low, almost reverent. "I think marriage is dated. But not commitment." She shook her head and laughed. "I sure as hell didn't like being a wife! Being the other woman sounds like a lot more fun to me!"

We both fell silent, realizing what she'd said. Rachel had to know that I lived with another woman.

"When were you a wife?" I asked.

"Two years ago in Kansas," she replied. I kept his last name, but not him."

It was my turn to laugh, and feel more relaxed. Rachel's background was familiar territory. In the last few years most of my lovers had recently come out of heterosexual marriages. With the birth of women's liberation thousands of straight women were turning to feminism as an alternative to unhappy marriages. As a butch, I had no complaints. As a feminist, I agreed with Jill Johnston's new book, *Lesbian Nation*, which shocked both the gay and het worlds by saying, "Feminism is the theory, lesbianism is the solution."

"Why did you divorce this John?"

"I didn't know a lot of things about him before I married him." Rachel's face lost its smile as her mood shifted. She started to walk away. "Come into the kitchen. We'd better eat before the meeting starts."

I followed her into the tiny room and sat down at a Chevy-yellow Formica table with two matching yellow vinyl chairs. It reminded me of my childhood kitchen in West Covina.

"Would you like a beer?" she asked, opening the fridge.

"No thanks, but I'll have a Coke if you've got one. I never drink before meetings."

"I always do," she said. "Meetings make me nervous."

"Do your parents know you're a lesbian?" I asked.

"I hardly know it myself." Rachel came toward me, leaned across the table and lit two small candles. "I just came out to myself last year. My mother may suspect, but my father wouldn't know it if I kissed you in front of him. He doesn't notice much."

"So they aren't together anymore?" Something in her story made me guess they'd split up.

Rachel turned back to the stove. "No. My father left us... when I was twelve."

In the hunch of her shoulders I saw her withdraw. A silence came between us and I hesitated, reluctant to pursue the parent subject.

"Do you like your rice plain or with garlic and butter?" she asked in a quiet voice.

"With," I said, sniffing again. It didn't smell like there was hamburger or other meat with the rice. But perhaps now was not the moment to admit that I wasn't part of the peace, love and brown rice crowd.

The rice smelled heavenly. A light sweat had broken out over her delicate and very sexy upper lip; she had to smell even better than her rice.

I reached across the table and took her hand.

"Hey Rachel, anybody home?" a voice yelled from outside

the front door. The herald was followed by the laughter of other voices.

"Our comrades have arrived early," Rachel said, withdrawing her hand. She stood to clear our plates.

"Damn politics!" I blew out the candles, choking on the smoke.

It was almost midnight when the meeting broke up. The last of our band had just walked out the front door. Empty beer bottles and soda cans were scattered everywhere.

"Some of our fellow protesters are wacko," I shouted to Rachel across her living room. I was jacked up and stomping the perimeter of the room like a disoriented boxer. We had ended up having the same argument we had had at the earlier meeting. Worse, this time June and her labor cronies had taken the unauthorized liberty of bringing a labor lawyer, Sylvia Patton, to the meeting. I wanted to keep our issues within the community. Any hint of gays suing gays in the courts was going too far in my opinion. Tonight's vote—to let this lawyer check into our unemployment, to see if we qualified—scared me. The vote had carried by twenty to ten; I'd voted with the minority. Rachel had voted with the majority. Now that everyone was gone, I had to explain to this innocent how politics really worked.

"There were too many unexpected people here tonight," I said. "I wish we hadn't allowed supporters to vote."

"Isn't that the egalitarian thing to do?" she asked.

"Yes, normally. But these others don't have the same stake in the situation as we do. Letting just anyone who comes to the meetings vote diminishes our right to decide the outcome of this thing. It was a bad decision."

"I thought it was okay. I voted for it."

"I know you did." I didn't want to get into lecturing Rachel, since mentoring wasn't the role I wanted with her.

Rachel folded herself into a miniature chair near the living room bookcase. "Some employees who were not fired were here tonight talking about forming a union," she said earnestly. "If we'd have been unionized we could not have been fired the way we were."

"Unionizing may be a fine idea," I countered. "But a lawsuit coming at a time when we are fighting for feminist reforms all over the country will just cloud the issue. A lawsuit might make people think we're protesting for higher wages or benefits from a new gay center that has no money and just moved out of a condemned building. I don't know if this lawyer cares if gays tear their community apart."

"Of course she does!"

"Don't you understand? This lawyer's from the Echo Park People's Law Collective. That's a Marxist organization, Rachel. Marxists just try to bend gay and feminist issues into mass demonstrations, or 'workers' issues.' I'm afraid they just want to have their own little workers revolution right there on Highland Avenue. She never even said she's a lesbian."

"I think the lawyer *is* a lesbian, Jeanne."

"Who she fucks is not the point." I said vehemently. "The point is who she wants to fuck over. Anyway, who wants those stupid jobs back? It's not like they paid anything. Any one of us can make a better living somewhere else."

"We can't just walk away and pretend it never happened," Rachel said. "You only worked a few hours a week at the Center, Jeanne. Some of us worked there full time and really need our jobs back."

I stopped and tossed the trash bag into a corner. What Rachel said was true. I hadn't lost my dream job. Yet, many of the others were hurting. I was being myopic.

"The Board will realize they made a bad choice," Rachel said. "They will come to their senses and realize that we're all family. They're directors of a gay center for God's sake."

I studied Rachel in her naiveté and wondered why she personally needed such hope.

"I damn well hope you're right," I yelled.

"All this anger scares me," Rachel whispered from the other

side of the room. Her voice sounded distant. "I wish you'd calm down."

The volatility of the meeting, and my own emotions, seemed to upset her. In the pint-sized chair she looked like a small child. I went to her and knelt on one knee beside her. Taking her hand, I said, "Don't be afraid of me, I'm just blowing off steam."

She stared at our hands locked together on her lap. "My father used to scream at my mother, and throw things. Sometimes he threw my sister and brother into walls."

Images of my own father chasing us with his belt floated up from somewhere inside. "I don't throw things when I'm angry," I tried to comfort her. "Well, maybe a lamp or a can of Campbell's clam chowder if I'm really angry. But it has to be clam chowder or else I won't throw it."

Rachel raised her eyes. "Why does it have to be clam chowder?"

We both burst out laughing. I relaxed and sat down on the floor beside her, still holding her hand. "Did your father ever throw you against the walls?" I asked.

"No, not me. I was the peacemaker. I would get in between him and my mother…and my siblings."

"My mother was the peacemaker in our family," I said. "Dad would lose it and come tearing after one of us with his belt or a broomstick. It was often me he caught. But my mother would try to stop him."

Rachel studied my face. She brought her hand up to my cheek and cupped it like she was holding a precious flower.

Tears began to well, but I looked away. In exile I was missing the grow-up years of my younger sibs. They still lived under my father's roof. Brother Bill, my first best friend in life, got his own apartment a few years ago. Happily, I'd come out to him and he'd often drop by to talk about girl problems and our latest romantic exploits. I desperately hoped there'd come a day that I'd get to know the little ones as grown adults with their own vision of what was right and wrong. The last thing I'd overheard before my exile was Zoey and Kathy, age eight and nine, discussing whether or not they could "catch what was wrong with Jeanne."

I swallowed a sob and turned back to look at Rachel. The last thing I'd expected on this first date was to share stories about disturbed family and violent fathers. I pictured her as a tiny girl-child standing between two over-sized parents, her arms held out to keep them from clobbering each other.

"My father wasn't always like that," Rachel said. "He was very loving, before he went to the war."

"What war?"

"The Korean war. He was a marine."

"But he came home in one piece?"

"On the outside maybe. But he was a different human being inside. Then they got divorced."

I closed my eyes, remembering my childhood prayers to the Blessed Virgin asking why Mom couldn't send my father away so that he wouldn't beat us anymore. Later, as an adult, I realized my parents were Catholics, so divorce was never an option. But he was an angry man inside.

Rachel stood up suddenly. "Let's have some music," she said, moving toward the kitchen. "Come, dance with me." She held out her hand. "I just bought this new Joan Baez album called *Diamonds & Rust.*

My mind stopped buzzing. Fathers and politics weren't the reasons I was at Rachel's house in the middle of the night. I set my Coke can aside and took her in my arms. Her perfume smelled like vanilla almonds.

"Maybe there is a better way to resolve the fighting at GCSC," she said, as she pressed the lip of her beer bottle against my breastbone. "Maybe you and I can find it together."

I brought her closer to my body. The electric feeling spread from our hands to my groin. I wondered if she felt the same. Talking became more tense. Somehow it became harder to find the right words.

The room began to sway. I'd had a beer and Rachel three or four. I relaxed into the music and caressed her back with

my hand. "You know how to dance," I said, responding to the
lilt in her step. One of the many non-romantic byproducts of
feminism, I'd learned, was that few lesbian feminists knew how
to dance well. Only old gay femmes like BeJo who'd grown
up in bar culture did. Dancing was foreplay in bar culture. If a
lesbian didn't dance, she didn't get a lover.

The evening fog sashayed through Rachel's open
windows. "Do you have somewhere else you have to be tonight?"
Rachel asked in a whisper.

"No, I don't have to be anywhere else tonight." I lowered
my lips to meet hers.

"I heard that you live with a woman named BeJo. Are you
and she lovers?"

I drew my head away from her lips. "Sort of…"

She threw her head back and laughed. "That's a pretty
simple yes or no question!"

I wrinkled my forehead and tried to step delicately. "Yes,
then. BeJo and I began as lovers but we haven't slept together
in…months," I fudged. "We are very non-monogamous."

"Just asking."

She let her forehead rest against my cheek; her face nestled
into the cavity of my shoulder. She must be four inches shorter
than me, I marveled. She was everything in miniature.

She lifted her head and smiled. "We're a perfect fit."

Her body relaxed against mine again and she ran her
fingertips over the hair on the back of my neck. Again the rush
began as my hands began to explore her back. Touching her
made the muscles around my groin tighten. I sought her lips
as my fingers brushed her nipple. She trembled and gripped
my neck more tightly. Sensitive breasts, I made a mental note.
My fingers widened to take her small breast in my hand. Her
lips opened to let me in as her knees began to disappear from
under her. I gripped her waist to hold her up. I was alive on
Effie Street, on a dance floor on top of the world, everything
else dropped away.

My legs got weak and I knew I couldn't hold her up much

longer. I steered us close to the avocado chair and whispered, "Beanbag chairs can be beds, too," and I let us fall.

Hours later, on the edge of sleep Rachel gave me a smile that lit up my insides and murmured, "Pretty butch."

"Butches aren't pretty," I growled.

"This one is," she said, tapping me on the nose.

Joan Baez's lyrics replayed all night and laid down a track in my heart.

A morning ray crept across my forehead. I lay perfectly still, feeling the tangible heat from the window's sun on my skin. Sex with Rachel had been rather supernatural, something at the core of it extraordinary and disturbing. For a few minutes, it had taken me to another world. I watched her face as the light edged across her profile and slowly traveled down the delicate bridge of her nose. Her face in sleep had the surrendered look of a small child napping.

The radiator on the far side of the room chugged for breath. I tried to sit up and look at my watch. I had to get to *The Freep*, but my arm was pinned beneath her. We were sprawled almost naked on the living room floor, half in the avocado bag chair, and half on the blond wood. The wood was warm beneath my legs. She must have gotten up during the night, after we'd fallen asleep, and covered us with a pink blanket. Shifting my weight, I tried to disengage. My boot heel scraped against the oak. Shit, we'd been in such a hurry I'd made love with my boots on. I closed my eyes against the approaching day, trying to hold onto the night. In the afterwards of her I'd felt an exquisite sense of physical and emotional peace. But today was a new day.

Damn! What would the protesters have to say about this affair? Rachel was not going to be another one-night stand. The Gay/Feminist 11 would not take kindly to me conflating the bedroom with politics. In-bed romances meant new out-of-bed power alliances. June's camp might think I was sleeping with a newbie to win more votes. The balance of power among the protesters was tense enough already. Rachel and I would have few champions in this crowd.

And what about BeJo? *Christ!* It was a space night but I should have called to say I wasn't coming home. I told myself BeJo wouldn't be jealous of a simple new affair. She didn't seem to mind as long as I stuck to our rules—Mondays and Fridays as non-monogamy nights. Rachel hadn't asked if there were any rules. This could get complicated.

Find your damn clothes, Córdova. Get the hell out of here! a disturbing voice inside me demanded.

Crawling around, I discovered my belted jeans on top of a set of Dylan album covers. Bell-bottoms had the advantage of being able to slide on and off quickly over boots. Where was my shirt? Nowhere! It must be on the floor, under the beanbag chair, under Rachel. No problem. I kept extras in the trunk of the car. Slipping into my denim jacket, I felt a pinprick scrape the top of my naked breast. An errant political button was poking through the denim. There was Rita Mae telling me in green lettered, ten-point Times New Roman, "An Army of Lovers Cannot Fail." Was my present situation what she had in mind? I snapped the jacket closed. This would have to do until I got to work and put on a new shirt in the bathroom at *The Freep.* None of my colleagues would be uncool enough to ask where I'd lost my clothes. It was still the decade of free love.

Searching for my briefcase, I crept toward the kitchen table. A cartoon postcard picturing a blonde woman dressed in a flower child headband sat on the table propped against my briefcase. I turned it over. "I want to make love with you—again and again!" Rachel's flowery script had written.

I should leave a note too. Something sweet about the night. Opening my DYKE-bannered case, I ripped a page out of a notebook. Scribbling in red ink, I wrote, "Have to go to work. See you Friday, at the meeting. It was great last night."

I looked at my note...crossed out the impersonal "it," and

replaced it with "you." Now it read, "You was great." Illiterate. Cold. I crossed out "You was" and lettered, "We were." Hmm? I murmured to myself. "We" was too…two. I crumpled the now illegible note and shoved it into my pocket.

Chapter 13

The Women's Saloon

[Los Angeles]

May 9, 1975

Late Friday afternoon found me holed up in my *Free Press* office, poring over story notes about The Lexington Six, a group of lesbian college students and feminist organizers in Kentucky who had just been arrested by the FBI. The Feds were searching for anti-war activists Susan Saxe and Kathy Power, who had been roommates and lovers at Brandeis University. In 1970, as a political action to fight the war, Saxe and Power along with three men, had robbed a bank in Brighton, Massachusetts. One of the men had shot a police officer during the robbery. The FBI now thought the Lexington dykes had information about the whereabouts of the two lesbians who were still on the Feds' Most Wanted list. {1} I'd been tipped about the story through the lesbian grapevine and had convinced Penny that the arrests had national implications and *The Freep* should cover it.

A light on my outside line began to blink. It had to be BeJo or Rachel. "What's up with you?" I said, hopefully covering both.

"I wondered the same thing. You haven't called in four days."
I broke into a smile. Rachel was a welcome break.

"Have you forgotten we have a 'relationship'?"

"Does a terrific one night stand qualify as a relationship?" I
returned my voice light and flip.

"At least a short and meaningful one," she shot back.

Remembering   the   sweet   weight   of   Rachel   falling

FBI invades lesbian land communes looking for Patricia
Hearst, the SLA, and anti-war activist Susan Saxe.
Lesbian Tide, May 1975.

against me as I'd brushed her nipples, I felt a rush of adrenaline. My body wanted her again. I had made a casual statement to BeJo over morning coffee about meeting someone new, but my primary lover hadn't asked for a name. BeJo knew that secondary lovers were supposed to fit in around one's primary schedule. Those were the rules, and I was grateful that in this new lesbian feminist
lifestyle of rapid turnover of words, concepts and practices, I had a framework of rules to cling to. Feminism had torn up my bar culture ways.

"I'm sorry I haven't called," I said, looking for a good excuse. "The *Tide* Collective has been in an uproar all week, arguing over whether or not to print Camilla Hall's poetry."

"Is the poetry that bad?"

"It's not a *quality* issue," I explained, "Camilla was a member of the SLA killed by the cops in Watts last year. I went to her memorial service." I blinked trying to hold my composure as images of the two young lesbians suffocating in the house filled with teargas flashed through my mind. {2}

"I remember watching that on TV. Was she a lesbian?"

"Yes, a radical lesbian feminist. So was her lover, Mizmoon who died with her."

Rachel gasped. "I had no idea there were lesbians in the SLA. Does the FBI know?"

"As usual, they were the last to know. But since Watts, yes." I fiddled with my pencil, trapping it inside the phone cord. "It took the pigs almost a year to put the SLA's sleeping arrangements together. Everybody was sleeping with everybody. Just like us."

"I guess they were practicing non-monogamy too," Rachel joked.

"Once they figured out the lesbian angle, the FBI has been raiding dyke communities all over the country. They think we dykes are hiding Patty Hearst."

"Do they think that every lesbian in the country knows every other lesbian?"

"Yeah." I grinned to myself, pleased at how quickly Rachel's mind pulled things together politically. "All the activists anyway. They're acting like there's a national lesbian network that's hiding fugitives of radical groups."

"Is there?" Rachel asked.

My lips froze. *Shit!* It dawned on me: I shouldn't be having this kind of conversation over a *Free Press* line! From tidbits I heard, but purposely never written about, I knew that lesbians across the country had both knowingly and unknowingly helped hide radical feminist fugitives. But, this was certainly not something to talk about with a new lover on a line that could be tapped. *The Freep* had printed stories alleging that FBI Director J. Edgar Hoover had a secret Counter Intelligence Program (nicknamed COINTELPRO) whose purpose was to spy on American activists and anti-war groups. So I knew the Feds had wiretaps on thousands of phone lines belonging to the alternative press. I might not be the only one on this line with Rachel!

Instinctively, I swept the Lexington Six notes off my desk and into a drawer. Some of my info had been smuggled to *The Tide* by friends of the Kentucky dykes.

Rachel broke into my silence. "The Feds must think all lesbian feminists oppose the establishment."

"Millions of anti-war Americans do." I laughed dismissively. "That's no big news."

"What a ridiculous stretch of logic," Rachel said. "Where did you get Camilla's poetry? Do they use the U.S. Post Office?"

My hint to break off this line of talk had been too subtle for Rachel.

"We shouldn't talk about these things," I mumbled.

In the silence I could tell her feelings were hurt. Yet, I wasn't about to tell her—on or off the phone—that *The Tide's* information from underground sisters was left hidden under the rubbish in a broken milk carton by the weedy overgrown side of the Westside Women's Center. Not even *Tide* staffers knew this, although I personally distributed copies of *The Tide* each month to a dumpster behind a Venice grocery story for our underground comrades.

I told Rachel, "Would you believe that Camilla's poetry was delivered by little underground boll weevils who burrow up in various parts of the city and bring me news?"

She laughed. "Why don't you ask those same little boll weevils to burrow you over to my house?"

"Ah…" I laughed, caught off guard. "I need one more hour to finish the story I'm working on."

"So, I'll wait here for you to pick me up. We can go to the Women's Saloon."

The new, self-avowed women's restaurant was the talk of the town; it even had "good food politics." I didn't know that food had politics, but I had heard that Rachel had gotten the job as chief cook and that Pody was working there too as a waitperson.

"That certainly sounds like a date." I stalled, a bit rattled by her proposal. I usually appeared with BeJo in public, and appeared only in the bedroom with other lovers.

"Are you afraid BeJo might be there?" Rachel's voice was edgy.

"Of course not," I hedged truthfully. I knew BeJo had a softball game in Venice on the other side of town.

"But you don't want to walk into a public place together?" she pushed.

My throat tightened. "What's the big deal if we drive over in two cars? Anyway, I might have to go do an emergency interview later tonight. In case that happens you'll have your car."

"I'll see you in an hour," Rachel gave in. "In case you've forgotten I'll be the one with the purple carnation."

Damn. I hung up. An argument over a first non-date. Not a great start. No time to think on that.

I reached for the Lexington papers, spreading them out again on my desk. I actually had to write two stories, one for *The Freep*, and one for *The Tide*. *The Freep* would, of course, run an unabashedly pro story calling the Lexington Six "freedom fighters." These women had stood their ground and taken the 5th Amendment, refusing to talk to the FBI. They would not rat out their friends, friends who might, or might not know where Saxe or Power was hiding. The prosecutor had cited them for contempt and tossed them in jail, where they would stay until the Grand Jury adjourned—which could be months or years.

Thank the goddess Penny had taught me reporting skills because *The Tide's* story had to be different. It still often bent my mind having to write re-angled versions of the same story in two different ways within hours. But *The Tide* had large subscription bases in university towns and it was urgent to spread the word that the FBI had gone from Lexington to poking into the Colorado, Connecticut, and Oakland lesbian compounds. The Feds could be in L.A. next week *The Tide's* story would focus more on the lesbian background of the women and point out that the FBI's investigations amounted to an urgent call for lesbians to unite nationally against the coming grand juries, which would use sisters to snitch on other sisters. I intended to push The *Tide* Collective to print an editorial, my words saying: "We support the Lexington Six in their refusal to testify before the Kentucky grand jury. We urge women and gays to politically and financially support those sisters who defend our freedom at the price of their own."

I knew my point of view would be controversial. Not all of the *Tide* staffers, much less our readers, were radical. Many of them were middle-of-the-roaders. Persuading them to vote agreement about printing Camilla Hall's poetry had come at a large cost. To convince the group, I'd read them a note from Mizmoon, whose real name was Patricia Soltysik and who had grown up in Los Angeles. Mizmoon, Hall's lover, wrote that she'd attended the National Lesbian Conference that I'd helped organize at UCLA in '73. "I'm grateful for the *Lesbian Tide*," her note said. "I read it whenever I can get it. Thanks for continuing such great work." She'd signed off, "In sisterhood, Mizmoon."

I'd showed my sister staffers a photo of Camilla, a blue-eyed blonde with that whole-grain-wheat-from-the-Midwest face. Both lovers were younger than me. The majority of the staff had agreed to print Camilla's words as her good-bye, arguing that everyone deserved a eulogy. Yet, two important staff members, our best copy editor and BeJo's assistant layout woman, had left *The Tide* over the issue. They walked out saying that by supporting the SLA women we were getting "too radical." They disagreed that Camilla and Mizmoon were "the good guys." They were also afraid that the cops would be at our door. I was disappointed because I knew that tough times called for tough courage.

Camilla Hall must have sensed her future. She'd sent her poems to *The Tide* asking us to print them upon her death. We ran her poems, one of which ended with the lines:

It's my turn soon, I feel it coming
Rumbling and stumbling but on its way at last!
Others have gone (especially you)
And I won't be left again.

I will cradle you in my woman hips,
Kiss you with my woman lips,
Fold you to my heart and sing:
Sister woman, you are joy to me.

I sat back in my chair staring at the poster of Che Guevara on my office wall. Che's inspiring words had successfully resulted in the Cuban revolution and had made him a hero to my generation. His radical ideas had helped spawn the Marxist urban guerilla movement in the United States. Yet, to my knowledge, only a few handfuls of lesbians had made a commitment to take up arms. Typing the last page of my story, I wondered what complex combination of factors—personal and political—made a woman pick up a gun and become willing to lay down her life for her beliefs. I'd learned from my father that violence was part of life. I saw politically motivated violence— cop killings, Nazi bombings, student protests—all around me these days. There was little talk about armed struggle in the gay male movement, but there certainly was some in the intimacy of radical feminist circles. It was the kind of topic one discussed only with close and committed friends. Where I would draw the line if asked to commit? Were Camilla and Mizmoon the saints or the fools among us?

I heard a snap, looked down, and saw that I'd broken a pencil clutched in my fist. I should make up my mind, I thought, before some kind of political violence crossed my path. If push came to shove, what would I do?

The Women's Saloon & Parlor, located on the rumbled block of 4900 Fountain Avenue in East Hollywood, was fast becoming the new hangout of L.A. lesbian feminists. A relatively unknown redhead named Colleen McKay had opened the place on behalf of the Feminist Research & Reading Society who wrote on the sidewalk advertisement board that the new restaurant was "a way to invade society and create a place that reinforces what feminists believe." No one knew any of these researching society-mates of Colleen's, except her eccentric artist lover Sidra, but after Colleen announced that she had sold her Jag to buy a proper stove for the restaurant, everyone simply referred to her as the owner.

The eatery was a cavernous room decorated to look like the offspring of a fifties diner mated with a hippie coffeehouse. Twenty mismatched wood tables were flanked by assorted chairs that looked like they'd been pulled, two at a time, from various garage sales between Beverly Hills and Orange County. The walls were thinly whitewashed with patches of brick and concrete poking through. A periwinkle hand-painted quote from one of Judy Grahn's poems {3}was lettered on a wall. The words, "the common woman is as common as the best of bread, and will rise," greeted each woman as she walked in. Men, common or exalted, were not allowed.

I strode toward the bar cocky and sure. No men was fine with me; walking into women only places—like the Woman's Building and the Westside Women's Center—made me feel proud. We'd carved these safe houses out of parts of the city discarded by men and capitalism. It was one thing to work with gay men politically, but socially they had their turf and we had ours.

Leaning against the bar's long solid wood counter, I canvassed the tables, glad that I'd arrived before Rachel. I positioned myself so that I could see her come through the front door. I'd pick her up at the entrance. That made it somewhat like a date.

A tape of mixed music, now playing Janis Joplin's "Me and Bobby McGee," was on full blast. Perhaps Rachel and I would dance—a good excuse to touch her.

"I'll take a Coke, with lots of ice," I said to the flannel-shirted bartender who looked eighteen.

"Comin' at ya," she replied.

I turned back to the crowd and watched Pody serving three tables full of GCSC fired employees and our supporters. They were ordering off a calligraphied menu which bore condiments such as "handmade mayonnaise with fresh herbs from The Yellow Brick Road" and tofu in many different incarnations. Under the menu's logo, it said the Saloon featured "gentle spirits, art, crafts, plants, and etcetera."

Pody and I saw less of each other now that we were no longer working together. I wanted to go over and say hello but hesitated. Sometimes I thought Pody flirted with me and it made me uncomfortable. It's not like butches never crossed the line and slept with one another; feminism insinuated that butch/femme pairing was heterosexist. To be truly egalitarian butches should sleep with butches, and femmes with femmes. A ridiculous conclusion, I thought, twirling the ice cubes in my glass. No wonder everyone was having "short meaningful relationships."

I also resisted the urge to approach Pody because she was serving June's table and I didn't want another argument tonight with my orange-headed nemesis. The Gay/Feminist 11 and the protest against GCSC had become a hugely popular, community-wide issue. The Saloon's staff wanted to make it policy not to serve anyone who voiced support of GCSC.

Ever the Latina charmer, Pody, now happily single, seemed to be flirting with everyone. Now she stopped at another table, leaned over, and flirted with a woman with a sweet smile who looked something like BeJo. Watching her intently, a new possibility dawned on me—maybe it wasn't Rachel or me that Pody was interested in—maybe it was BeJo. Perhaps that's why I'd heard a particular undertone in her voice when she pronounced BeJo's nickname. And, BeJo had referred to Pody as "that cute blonde butch friend" of mine. Suddenly, it clicked! Yes, BeJo and Pody. I no longer needed a thermometer to define the warm air rising between them. And yes, I'd feel less guilty about Rachel if BeJo found someone to date. Maybe she'd be happier with me if she were happy, part time of course, with someone else.

I turned back to the bar and ordered another Coke. Penny had warned me that I might have to work later tonight, so no beer for me. A certain high level *Freep* source might call her for a last-minute interview with a particular friend who was coming into town. I didn't want anything to encroach on with my time with Rachel, but I also didn't want to jeopardize the interview. Politics never took a backseat to date night.

Energy shifted in the room, and I turned to see Rachel. She strolled through the door confidently, clothed in a powder blue V-neck and tight black jeans. I watched the silver of her hooped earrings catch a reflection from the ceiling's galvanized pipe, and saw to my delight that she wore the Rita Mae Brown "Army of Lovers" pin from my jacket that I'd left in lieu of a note the other night at Effie Street.

Rachel's eyes swept the room and I waited, flushed with pride that it was me she sought. Finally, I called out to her. As she approached me her face was radiant. "Hi, babe," she whispered and came in close to kiss my cheek.

I reached out, and she slid into my arms. "'Babe'? How sexist!" I teased. Her skin felt like the finely brushed Egyptian cotton I'd once felt on an expensive set of sheets.

Rachel tucked her head into my neck and planted a string of kisses along my collarbone. "Perfect fit," she repeated, allowing her head to rest on my shoulder.

"We can't just stand here making out," I said, embarrassed.

"Do you want to go back to my place now?"

"I thought you wanted a proper date?"

"That was before I touched you." She laughed.

"There you are!" Pody pounced on us, grabbing Rachel out of my arms. "There's trouble in the kitchen," she said. "We need you, Rachel!"

The Saloon was a do-it-yourself café. Customers were supposed to go get their own silverware, napkins, coffee and ice water from a common side table. It didn't hurt to bring a sandwich if one was hypoglycemic or otherwise impatient. Pody had told me that tempers had flared the first couple of nights over the almost nonexistent service.

I ambled back to the bar counter, wondering what level of crisis would keep Rachel and for how long. I wanted to find us seats at the tables, but June was still over there, with her new loud supporter, Dixie Youts. After the last Gay/Feminist 11 meeting, I'd realized that June and I came from two different worlds. I had five years working in the gay and lesbian movement alongside gay men. My newer identity as a lesbian feminist wasn't going to erase that. What world did June and the others came from that made it okay to close down a Center serving homosexuals? If she meant what she said, her politics would never fly with me.

Rachel's return interrupted my thoughts. "Come back to me," she said.

"Did you solve your crisis?"

She picked up a menu from the counter and pointed to an item that read, Rachel's Lentil Curry.

"Far out! You've already made headlines."

"They couldn't find the curry powder," she explained. "And then I got called into a debate with the waiters who were arguing about whether it was sexist, or not, to serve Sweet'N Low because it implies that women should be thin."

The music started up again with a slow one from Carole King's "Tapestry," an album that seemed to be playing everywhere these days.

"Dance with me," I said, pulling Rachel toward the makeshift dance floor between the tables.

She snuggled close. "When I came back, what were you thinking about?"

"June, and GCSC, the protest and Morris Kight." I said.

Rachel's eyebrows arched in surprise.

"He used to call me all the time, but doesn't anymore," I said. "My real father doesn't talk to me since he found out I'm gay. Not that we were close before that, but I can't go home anymore to see my younger sibs. Morris has been like a father to me." Intimate words seem to fall from my mouth when I was around Rachel. Why did I trust her so easily?

"This fight with GCSC must hurt you more deeply than you've let on."

"Maybe so." I looked away from her. "Morris is a swishy fag and I'm a butch dyke. We both stand for freedom to exist outside our gender roles. Hell, I'm one of his protégées." I turned back to look behind Rachel's eyes, wondering why she cared.

"Since you weren't close to your Dad, were you and your mother close?"

"On a surface level, no." I shrugged. "Yet on a psychic level she can read me. Every time I'm really down, somehow she knows it and calls. But she can't seem to figure out whether to relate to me like a daughter or a son. So that's been awkward. I didn't see much of her growing up. There were twelve of us so I kind of got lost in the crowd."

"Good Lord!" Rachel gasped. "You have eleven brothers and sisters?"

"Hey, the music stopped playing," I stepped away from Rachel.

She brought me back close and whispered, "I want to know who you are, Jeanne. Whatever you tell me is between us."

Her body pressed against mine and I let myself relax into her.

"So what do you want to know about me that hasn't been garbled by my reputation?"

"I did hear on the grapevine that you used to be a nun?"

I winced, and pulled back. I knew the rumor was out there but I rarely spoke of my spiritual life, God or the convent to activist friends. I wanted to slap myself upside the head for all but inviting her into this topic. "Yes, that's true." I managed a tight grin. "Never took final vows to become a full-fledged woman of the cloth, but I did enter the convent right out of high school. In fact the novitiate radicalized me."

"Why on earth did you want to be a nun?" she prodded.

"I was a simple parochial kid from a medieval Catholic family. Loving God or perhaps Mary a little too much was my real and only motivation." I laughed at my own Virgin joke, hoping to distract Rachel.

"Then what happened, why did you leave...what do they call it...religious life?"

I smiled at Rachel's use of the correct term, and wondered how or why she'd studied Catholicism.

"I managed to make one crucial, though accidental, decision that directed the course of my future life as well as the exit from the one I was living. Have you ever heard of the order of the Immaculate Heart of Mary nuns?"

"Yes, I have read about them! They were a very pro-feminist and radical order, correct?"

"That's my order, yes, and proud of it!" I nodded, pleased that she knew. "I almost went into the cloistered Carmelites, but back in 'sixty-six the IHM's were thought to be liberal, even radically so about supporting the modernization of the Church by the Vatican II Council. When I was at the novitiate, a group of priests were suddenly coming to Montecito and teaching us one-shot classes about the Viet Nam war and our duties to go into 'work in the vineyards of the Lord' –which meant in the ghettos among the poor. So they sent me to the vineyard of Watts the following year. But later I realized there was something surreptitious about these theologians who would suddenly drop into our sacred off-limits grounds—teach—and be gone a few days later. Years after I left, I put those teachers' names together with my new political knowledge and I realized they were radical anti-war activists, priests like the Berrigan brothers or laymen being hunted by the FBI over war or race issues."

"Your timing is rather amazing. I'm so jealous," Rachel bubbled in my arms.

"It wasn't all exciting new thoughts. Falling out of love with God, falling in love with Mother Superior's lay friend, Connie, learning about the international hypocrisy of the Holy Roman Church and how it wouldn't let the IHM sisters become feminists or modernize, or go out and correct the grossness of poverty, racism, and dead boy soldiers shown on TV every night..."

"You're still angry after all these years?"

I stopped talking. Rachel was right. I hadn't really come to terms with those radicalizing years, not spiritually.

A silence followed us around the dance floor.

"Do you ever miss the convent?" my new lover asked.

Shocked, I lost my step and landed a foot on hers. "I never thought about it," I lied, then paused. "I guess once you've heard the call you never get over it."

"By 'it' do you mean God?"

"Yes, he was the It of it. Although it feels strange now to use the masculine pronoun. But, yes. It was an intimate love. My mother taught me how to have a personal relationship with God. I'm finding that's a rare knowledge."

Rachel stroked my neck intently, her roughened fingers familiar. "I experienced a personal relationship with God... when I was studying Buddhism. I wanted for years to become a Buddhist nun."

"Really?" It was happening again. When Rachel and I were together secrets seemed to come out as if they had been laying in wait. "Why didn't you enter an ashram?"

My new lover sighed. "Eventually I shrugged it off as a teenage phase. My mother the atheist would have had a stroke if I'd mentioned it out loud."

"We never would have met with both of us behind the walls," I said, kissing her eyebrow gently.

"I love your hands on me," she said. Her eyes were half-closed with happiness.

Out of nowhere, Pody reappeared. "Phone call for you, Córdova," she said, slapping me on the back. "You can take it in the kitchen."

"Back in a minute, sweetheart," I said to Rachel, knowing that the phone call had to be from Penny. I'd had to give my editor the Saloon's number. Fuck; I didn't want to leave Rachel.

As I walked to the kitchen, it occurred to me that I'd called her sweetheart. The word had simply fallen out of my mouth. Tonight's date was being unexpectedly intimate. That scared me, but I wasn't ready for the night to end.

"Penny?" I barked into the receiver.

"Yes, it's me," Penny replied. "Thank God, I found you. Our source, Donald Freed, finally called. His source is in town and wants you to meet him tonight."

Freed, a playwright and an investigative journalist who'd just co-authored *Agony in New Haven: the Trial of Bobby Seale and the Black Panther Party*, was a known associate of radical Leftists, including some who were fugitives. Two weeks earlier *The Freep's* City Editor, Tom Thompson, who'd been doing a series of articles about CRIC, the Citizens Research & Investigation Committee, and its discovery of LAPD secret spying squads, had told Penny that Donald Freed had a fugitive comrade who wanted a meeting with the paper. Freed's source had asked for me, by name, to do the story. I'd promised Penny I'd be available, whenever and wherever. There'd be no second chance.

"When?" I asked Penny, hoping I'd misheard.

"Tonight. Now."

"Fuck, Penny," I whined. "I'm in the middle of a very important date."

"Fugitives can't wait, Córdova. I've got the directions. I don't want to give them to you over the phone. Are you sober enough to drive to the office, pick them up, and then go do the interview?"

"Of course I'm sober, Penny. I never drink on the job. But when I see this Freed I'll give him a piece of my mind for his outrageous interruption."

Penny paused, wondering if I was being facetious.

"Then, I'll see you in a few minutes?"

"You're at the office this late?"

"I've been waiting for his call. This is important, Córdova."

I hung up. Damn the revolution! It was making mincemeat of my personal life.

Rachel was at the counter talking with the bartender when I returned to her.

"Who was that?" she asked. I could already see the hurt in her eyes.

"My editor," I said gently, as I pulled her away from the bar.

"Oh, just your editor," she said, relaxing into my arms. "So... can we go home now?"

"Not really." I paused. "Remember when I said I might have to do an emergency interview later tonight? Well, later is now. I have to go cover a story."

"Cover a story at eleven o'clock on a Friday night?"

"Someone very important just came into town."

"Meaning I'm not?" Rachel took her arm off my shoulder and walked back to the bar. "Another beer. To go," I heard her order.

Her switch from intimate to chilly took me off guard, but I followed her and hugged her, pressing my chest against her back, and whispered gently, "It's with someone running from the cops. That's why I had no warning."

She turned to face me. "So it's really not someone else you're seeing?"

"God no! I was digging being with you tonight."

"Really?" She turned and started to walk away toward the kitchen. "Even straight men limit themselves to one lover per night," she shot back over her shoulder.

I was shocked. My new lover really hated surprises. One moment she was supportive, the next moment, furious.

"The woman is pissed with you," Pody said to me as I turned to leave. "You'll do serious time behind this one."

Chapter 14

A Somewhat Larger War

[Los Angeles]

May 9, 1975

The alley behind the apartment building was dark and chilly. I stuffed my tape recorder and tablet under my arm and lit up a smoke. These buildings were once studio apartments but had been converted to offices in the post World War II boom. With their stone exteriors and carved moldings, one could recall the glamour of old Hollywood. Up close, the structures were horribly run down. They were strewn all over the now poorly kept parts of east Hollywood, six—and seven-story reminders of cinema's golden age when the lower echelons of Dietrich's or Gable's entourage were assigned to bunk in these studio apartments with built-in Murphy beds and electric coffee pots. I got my love of architecture from my engineer father, and I wished I had the money to restore the once lovely brick structure in front of me that had cracked green serpentine marble walls. I could see it through the broken glass of the lobby's rear door.

I waited for my source as instructed. Donald Freed had a lot of street cred but these days one could never be sure someone hadn't been turned by the pigs or the FBI. Were he and *The Freep* on the same side? Could the cops be using him, and indirectly me too, to trail his leftist fugitive friends? Still, I was the Press and could probably babble my way out of this if the cops sprang from nowhere. I'd dumb down, use my baby face to say I had no idea what was going on, or who I was meeting. Until now, turning down Penny's assignment hadn't crossed my mind. A good reporter had to take chances. The better the story, the more risk had to be taken.

Leftist circles said that Donald Freed ran with Bobby Seale, the leader of the Black Panthers. Being a white boy, Freed had founded and led Friends of the Black Panther Party, a group of white intellectual activists who sympathized with them. The street said that Freed also had contacts within the urban guerrilla group, the Weather Underground (WUO) and relayed messages for them.

The WUO, founded in the late sixties as the Weathermen, took its name from a line in Bob Dylan's song, *Subterranean Homesick Blues* which proclaimed, "You don't need a weatherman to know which way the wind blows." Earlier, they'd split off from the radical student movement's leading organization—SDS, Students for a Democratic Society. The Weathermen had supplanted SDS's prominence as the vanguard of the New Left, and were committed to the overthrow of "imperialist America" by any means necessary. The group, which included respected radical women like Bernadine Dohrn and Kathy Boudin in its leadership, saw themselves as the spark that would lead to a "prairie fire" of revolution led by working class youth. Knowing their lives would be harder, the WUO had made the strategic decision five years ago to go underground in order to avoid infiltration into their ranks by Hoover's FBI. They also sought to avoid arrest as indictments were being leveled against several members, and going underground would give them the secrecy they needed to bomb sites representing the Military

Industrial Complex—like the Pentagon! The alternative press was printing stories alleging that the FBI's illegal spying unit, COINTELPRO, was calling the anti-war movement a threat to national security. This was their excuse to disrupt legal protests, even while Nixon's White House flatly denied using agent provocateurs and other moles. Despite the war

having officially ended, two or three leaders of the WUO were still high on the FBI's Most Wanted List. {1} It was difficult, even for the alternative press, to cover these fugitives. So when a source like Donald Freed, who was constantly being hounded by the LAPD's Criminal Conspiracy Section for "harboring" fugitives or alleged possession of illegal weapons, called *The Free Press*, we went to any lengths to accommodate them.

I buttoned my denim jacket tighter around my throat, wishing I'd brought something heavier. I could be standing here all night if something went wrong.

A man's voice called out of the darkness, "Nice car, how long have you had it?"

I dropped my cigarette and looked around. Nothing, no one. I took a deep breath and said quietly, "Glad you like my car. I'm from *The Free Press*."

A beam from a flashlight hit my left arm. I'd been instructed to wear my Press badge on my outer left sleeve. A figure appeared from behind a parked car. "Come with me," he ordered. He took my arm and led me quickly toward a door, where he removed a board from the blocked side entrance. A street lamp revealed the shape of another figure ahead of us. My guide bent down to a crossbeam away from the door frame. The second figure held open another inner door.

"You've got to wear this." The second voice was that of a woman, who held a dark-colored bandana in front of me. Turn around," she spoke commandingly. "Everyone has to come in this way." She tied the blindfold over my eyes.

"Everyone?" I asked, adrenaline running as my journalist mind kicked into gear. Perhaps I wasn't the only invited guest.

"Sorry we have to put you through this. Bummer, huh?"

Her voice sounded tired.

"No way to have a life," I tried to joke empathetically. This could have been my life too if I'd made certain choices, stepped over the thin red line between activist reporter and revolutionary participant. Was I crossing that line now?

We seemed to walk up several flights of stairs, then back down and up again. If they were trying to confuse my sense of direction, they did a good job. Finally, a new pair of hands gripped my shoulders, stopping me.

The authoritative woman spoke again. "Unbutton your jacket, we have to frisk you."

I loosened my jacket and yielded to the invasion. A woman's hands slid across my trunk, and up and down both legs. I held my arms out away from my chest. The woman rubbed her palm carefully across my back looking for wires.

Again we walked the corridors and through doorways for what seemed like minutes. The carpet under my feet smelled of stale urine and some kind of burnt chemical. Cooked heroin, I wondered? Was this building also a junkie safe pad? A door close to me clicked open. Hands pushed me through the doorway and sat me in what felt like a metal folding chair. My blindfold was removed.

It didn't take long to adjust my eyes to the darkness. The room seemed purposely wrapped in shadow and was small like a prison cell. The windows were covered with newsprint. The source of dim light was a large flashlight hanging from the wall on a nail. The floor and walls were mud brown. Quickly I made out six figures who sat on metal chairs arranged in a tight circle in the middle of the room. I realized the flashlight had been placed high up the wall. Its dim light couched everyone's face in shadow. The group continued speaking in low tones even as I sat in a chair against the wall. A male figure sitting within the circle and to my left seemed to absorb the energy in the room. The others were in a listening posture and deferred to him when he spoke. I wondered if Freed, my source, was even in the room. He was the set-up conduit and since underground Leftist matters were conducted on a need-to-know basis, and Freed already knew the nature and purpose of the meeting, maybe he was advised not to attend. As people talked, they called the central figure "John." I heard snatches of other words and caught the name "Cinque." Many underground activists who had FBI jackets used aliases, even among themselves. Blacks, like the SLA leader Donald Defreeze, used African names like Cinque, the leader of the rebellion on the slave ship Amistad in 1839. Anglos used names out of American social struggles, like John Brown, the abolitionist.

I overheard someone say, "We have to find better methods to protect the others." Would he be referring to Bill and Emily Harris, I wondered, the two SLA members last reported to have custody of Patty Hearst? Probably not because the Weather people didn't like the SLA. Still, the FBI had accused the Harrises of planting pipe bombs under police cars parked at the House of Pancakes in the Northern California town of Highland last month. Bill and Emily—and Patty—were still at large. I was flattered that they spoke even in hushed tones in front of me, but I heard no other words that I could unravel.

Suddenly, the man called John turned to me. "Come forward," he said, pointing to the single empty chair in their circle.

I changed chairs, confident that John was the person who had sent Donald Freed to find me. John had probably sent for the others too, since only Donald seemed to know him. I wondered if the others were representatives from different New Left groups or other alternative press, like me. It was clear there would be no introductions.

"So, you're Córdova," he continued. "It's a good thing you look like your photo." His words fell clipped and quick with a New England accent, as he referred to the headshot that ran with my weekly column in *The Freep*. It dawned on me that I'd been chosen because my politics were in alignment—I was listed in the masthead as Human Rights Editor—and because they could be certain it was me who showed up.

"We like what you've been writing about," John continued. "About Irv at the JDL, the socialist struggle in Portugal and the farce against Joan Little. Those who have gone to ground appreciate your efforts on our behalf." He stuck out his hand and shook mine.

"I'm sorry they caught Shoshanna," I said, referring to WUO comrade Patricia Swinton whom the FBI had just captured. By now I'd read and written so much that they all felt like family. Swinton was charged with allegedly being part of a plot to bomb a National Guard Amory in 1969.

"That's OK, Alpert won't be testifying against her," said John. "They've all gone through too much together for too many years."

"That's good to hear," I replied. "But I'll have to cover the trial either way. Freedom of the press. The sword cuts both directions."

"I understand," said John. "That's why you're in your life and I'm in mine." I thought he smiled ruefully in the dark. His spectacles rose and fell on his nose as he remarked, "The luxury of objectivity is a false one."

He turned from me and nodded to the woman who stood by the door. Then he addressed me. "In a few minutes, I have to move out of here. So here's what we want you to tell your readers, our comrades and friends."

I interrupted, "What is life like living underground?"

"Life?" I glimpsed John's teeth as he smiled ironically. He seemed amused by my question. "It's not romantic and I don't have time to tell you; even if I had the time, I wouldn't tell you anyway. I summoned you here to give you a message."

"Can I ask questions afterwards?"

"Sorry, no time."

I reached to flip on my recorder.

He reached across me. "No tape," he said, snapping it off. "They can trace voices too well now. You don't want the FBI coming to *The Free Press* demanding your tapes, do you?" He leaned toward me, wearily resting his chin in his hand. "Just remember what we tell you," John said, taking back the lead.

"Is Bernadine safe?" I couldn't resist asking about their feminist leader.

"She's far underground and clean," he said. "And she's going to stay that way. They ought to leave her alone."

"But they won't," I interrupted.

"Just listen please," John snapped at me. "We have little time. Let's focus on our message."

I decided to shut my mouth.

"We want you to tell the comrades that we in the vanguard who know the consequences of our actions are questioning revolutionary armed struggle as a tactic. We think the time for that might be over in this country. Historical conditions no longer warrant them."

John leaned back in his chair. His shoulders seemed to sag. His voice slowed. "The war is over, the campuses are quiet, and Nixon has gone. The SLA has given the radical left a spurious name. We want supporters to know we remain responsible and committed to revolution. But we want people to think carefully before they take up weapons. We are re-examining the effectiveness of urban guerilla warfare. That's what we want you to say for us."

The commanding woman leaned over my shoulder and whispered, "Have you got that?"

Pen scribbling, I was shocked. "What you're saying is a departure from the WUO's past affirmation of guerilla warfare."

"That's right," John confirmed. "We're not telling comrades what to do. We are just saying objective conditions have changed, and to think carefully. We don't want people dying for no reason."

I flashed back to The *Tide* Collective's argument earlier this week about supporting the radical left. Good thing my sister staff members would never know about tonight.

"John," I said, "why did you call me in, why aren't you just issuing a manifesto?"

"We are not yet ready to issue a comprehensive statement

on this subject. We are still in-process, doing historical research. But this is a life and death tactic so we want comrades to know we are changing, adapting, as always to objective conditions. We'll publish a document when we've concluded with our definitive position."

John pulled away from me and addressed the whole group. "Then, that's it. Córdova will stay with her." He pointed to the woman guard who'd led me to them. "The rest of us are leaving now."

No one else spoke. The woman behind me put her hands on my shoulders. The others stood. The meeting was over. A few shook John's hand and muttered, "Thank you for coming."

"Wait." I reached out and tugged on John's sleeve. "Who shall I say told me this, who can I quote?"

John was already up, but looked down at me. "Tell them we as a collective are saying this."

"We, who?"

"The Weather Underground," he answered. "Their brothers and sisters in revolution."

The group moved one by one toward the door, leaving me alone with only the woman soldier.

John was the first out the door. He turned around and told my guard, "Wait ten minutes, take her back down. Then go home."

"Understood," my guard said.

The door closed softly and the woman with the authoritative voice sat down beside me. Her eyes looked tired beyond her years.

We sat in silence for a few minutes. I was too shocked to probe her for more information. I'd finally met the underground Left! The picture wasn't romantic. At its core "revolution" wasn't pretty or easy. People died, lives were ruined. The gay and lesbian movement was no stranger to tragedy either. Too often our victims, sissy boys and masculine women, were young "soldiers" killed or driven to suicide as teenagers. For them, I had to stay strong.

Finally, the woman put her hand on my shoulder and said, "Thanks for doing this, Córdova. Sometimes all we have is the press." {2}

Chapter 15

The Strike

[Los Angeles]

Mid-May, 1975

The phone on my desk at the *Freep* rang.

"Córdova?" It was Pody.

"Yeah, buddy, what's happenin'?"

"I just got a call from June. She said our lawyer, that Patton woman, called her and told her to get the Steering Committee and our supporters together for an emergency meeting tonight. Patton has bad news. And I heard a rumor yesterday that the Center has just hired a new administrator of Women's Programs, the main grant writer of the alcoholism abuse program, a dyke named Lillene Fifield."

Stifling my anger at the idea of "our lawyer"—we never voted to retain a lawyer—I realized we had a problem.

"That's bad news already."

"What is?"

"Hiring someone new in a position called 'Women's Programs' signals the Board has no intention of giving us our jobs back. They're moving ahead, hiring new staff, to replace us."

"You can't know that for sure," Pody said. "That doesn't seem to go with the other news I've heard—that our demonstrations are beginning to slow down donations to the Center. That's good news for our side, isn't it?"

"Yes. Slow money would mean Kight has to come to the bargaining table soon." As an organizer I knew that donors needed a clear line of sight. When there is controversy, they don't stop to sort out whose fault it is. They just stop giving.

"Okay. See you tonight then at Rachel's...same place as last time." Pody hung up.

Christ! Not at Rachel's, I thought. It wasn't a Monday or a Friday, not a space night between BeJo and me. That meant I'd have to see Rachel but not spend the night. Difficult. Awkward. I looked at the calendar on my desk. Damn. I should have called Rachel by now. I hadn't given her much thought since I'd walked out of the Saloon a week ago. My life often felt like a movie reel of individual shorts with no narrative thread.

For instance, lately I had been working on a piece for the *Freep* about the rape victim, Joan Little, and other battered women. I'd already written one news article about the murder charges leveled against the twenty-year old Black woman who was in a North Carolina jail on a breaking-and-entering charge. But now she was charged with murder for stabbing her jailer the second time he came to rape her with the same ice pick he had used to rape her the first time. I'd explained to Penny earlier today that I wanted to do a second piece—an advocacy article urging that the Little murder charge be dropped to self-defense. {1}

"It's not good enough the way the law reads now, that women don't have the right to strike back unless they feel their lives are at stake," I'd told Penny. "Repeated rape is sufficient cause to strike back. If a perpetrator gets killed or severely wounded in the process, that's justifiable self-defense. This kind of law should be part of a woman's right to control her own body, part of the privacy right that the Supreme Court gave women when they ruled we have the right to abortion three years ago!"

Penny had studied me, thinking—I supposed—that one day she might have to get my ass out of jail. She'd teased, "You never bring gentle people to the office to play with." She was referring to the phone calls, letters and occasional surprise visits that my dyke column generated from angry straight white men.

She'd given me the go ahead. "Write it the way you feel it, Jeanne. Write it for all the abused women who need to hear that they have rights."

My ardent feminist chief had turned to leave my office, but she paused at the door, saying, "What I came in to tell you is the new *Freep* owners have demanded that I cut another ten percent of our editorial inches and give it to advertising. So I need tighter copy from you."

"Got it," I'd answered, noting the worry creasing her forehead.

After my first year with the paper, Penny had promoted me from dyke columnist to Human Rights Editor and investigative reporter. She'd also gotten our previous owners to publish my first book, *Sexism: It's a Nasty Affair*, a compilation of my columns. She'd edited it herself and I had used my clout as a key reporter to champion her promotion from City Editor to the first female Editor-in-Chief. We were each other's champions—often against *The Freep's* sexist male staff and now, the new porno outfit that had just purchased us.

And battered women were just one of a dozen on-going projects and stories. I lived in an eternal present. How to connect the dots?

The long driveway fronting Rachel's bungalow apartment was peppered with protesters and our supporters. It looked like she was throwing a block party. Heading for her door, I felt my thigh and groin muscles tense up. Funny how the body has a memory of its own. I was turned on just thinking about the last time I'd been on Effie Street.

"Want a taco?" Pody approached me at Rachel's door

Hacking a path through a sexist jungle

'I predict homosexuality will be the life-style of the future'

JEANNE CORDOVA

Photo by Mark Sullivan

SEXISM—It's a Nasty Affair by Jeanne Córdova, New Way Books, 79 pages, $2.

In an earlier era, Jeanne Córdova might have been sent to the stake and burned as a witch, a heretic, or something equally anti-Establishment. The authorities from both the church and the state would somehow have nailed her. She certainly would have been a threat to a male-dominated environment. She still is.

Jeanne Córdova is the sort of woman (and don't call her "girl," "chick," "broad," or "baby") that a male chauvinist, gay or straight fears. Not only is she petite, pretty, and soft spoken, all of which in our American concept of feminine beauty is acceptable, but she's also angry, talented and a crusader. And that won't do at all.

Pepper this with the knowledge about their virility and sperm count are prone to view loan of Arc as "an uppity bitch." Susan B. Anthony as a "frustrated old bag," and Jane Fonda as a "commie cunt," they'll have to dig deep to unearth a fresh put-down for Córdova.

Rising Tide

As the original editor of the feminist, lesbian publication, *The Tide*, and a fiery columnist for the *Los Angeles Free Press*, a paper noted in large part for its discreetly draped massage parlor ads, Córdova is best known for her uninhibited, right-on essays that explore and explode everything from newspaper sexism to the Victorian mentality of our rulers.

Sexism—It's a Nasty Affair is a gathering together of some of the best Córdova writing. Columns, poems, manifestos. They range ing degrees, provocative. They are uncompromising in their refusal to accept women as one-dimensional creatures and adamant in their desire to kick over a millennium of sexist hang-ups and taboos. All insist on the merit of knowing women on a real basis.

Córdova has a sharp eye for official hypocrisy, private bigotry, and a wicked pen for pricking balloon heads. Her assaults are frequently murderous. Meet Sebl Bill Baltance, Bobby Riggs, and a kennel of male supremacists are skewered with wit and accuracy. Sometimes, reporting on the high and mighty, she gets them unaware. For example, L.A. Police Chief Ed Davis, describing how he was first attracted to his wife, "I was 17, and she was 15. It

The book is dotted with poetry and includes a moving eulogy to the 32 persons burned to death in New Orleans' Up Stairs Lounge holocaust. Much of the writing is clever in striking the heavy with the light, and *Sexism* can be read in easy spurts.

In person, Jeanne Córdova reflects the personality that illuminates her prose. She's something of a creative thinker and dismisses the notion that gay men and women are "the same."

"They [society] look into the bedroom and say, 'Aha, two people of the same sex sleeping together. They're the same.' We are not the same. That's one reason so many gay women split from the male-do-

get together. The fight for the decriminalization of our loving."

Born in Germany, daughter of a CARE official, Córdova is alert to her roots. "I enjoyed all the middle class privileges." It comes as a bit of a revelation to realize that this woman some call 'a very political lady" was once destined but she remained by a cloistered nunnery.

"Actually, if it weren't for the spirit of commercial change that was on at that time, I'm sure that where I'd be today." Behind convent walls, sealed in a vow of silence is where many people would like to see her.

Round, Not Flat

The columnist is fierce in her belief that the status quo, in any form accomplishes little—except the perpetuation of the status quo. "It took 75 years for the Catholic Church to agree with science and infallibly admit that the earth was round and not flat."

Her view of the changing sex scene is clearly set out in Criswell fashion. "I predict homosexuality—most specifically, sexuality without reference to gender—will be the dominant sexual life-style of the future."

To the question, why can't gay men and gay women work closer together, the writer exclaims, "We can, but I feel I have more in common with the feminist movement. But I repeat, on those issues that involve our legal rights, we should fight and stand together. I define myself as a lesbian separatist."

Sexism—It's a Nasty Affair is a gutsy little epic, relieved by reflective moments that say in much so economically. On the importance of never forgetting the New Orleans tragedy:

Remind us in anger
Remind us in strength
And remind us in love

The Advocate reviews Sexism—It's a Nasty Affair—first book written by early *L.A. Freep Press* dyke columnist, Jeanne Córdova. *July 1974. Reviewed by J. Moriarty.*

---

carrying a large bag. "I'm Robin Hood tonight."

My eyebrows rose. "Is that whole bag filled with food?"

"Yep!" Pody smiled broadly. "I liberated it from All American Burger, my night gig. Sometimes I bring food to the demonstration too. I figured there would be hungry people tonight."

"Is money getting that tight for people?"

"Yeah, for those who haven't found jobs yet, which is about half of us. Between my hours at the Saloon and the burger joint, I'm just making it. Some folks are giving blood downtown. The Red Cross pays ten bucks a pint. Hope our unemployment checks start kicking in soon. You're welcome to come to Dixie's on Wednesday nights and to June's on Saturdays. They're offering free spaghetti dinners!"

I suddenly felt very lucky even though I was just meeting my nut of seven hundred a month. To replace my GCSC pay I'd snapped up a fourth story a week at the *Freep* and I'd started doing collections at the new women's abortion center, the Westside Women's Clinic in Santa Monica. I also realized that I was somewhat out of touch. I didn't have close social friends among the strikers. The little free time I had was spent with friends who were involved with other political projects.

"There's June," Pody pointed out, as I stood in Rachel's kitchen. "She's got that lawyer, Sylvia Patton, with her." The dishwater blonde attorney was clothed in jeans, Birkenstocks, and a worn leather jacket. She had the Silverlake hippie look. In her mid-forties, she was older than most of us, and probably, yes, a lesbian.

June and others pushed in to station themselves along both sides of Rachel's large living room. Some stood while others sat on the floor or furniture, including the green vinyl beanbag chair where I'd first undressed Rachel. Finally, I spied Rachel emerging from the bathroom. She hadn't come to greet me and now she walked past me muttering, "Glad you found time in your busy schedule to come to our meeting." She planted herself against a wall on the opposite side of the room from me. I tried to catch her eye, but she refused to look my way.

"Let's get to it," June announced loudly, and I saw her eyes narrow with intensity. She walked into the middle of the room. The lawyer followed. "You all remember Sylvia Patton from the Echo Park People's Law Collective," June said. "We asked her to look into us getting unemployment benefits. Now, she has that news for us."

Why was June bringing the lawyer back without the group's permission? We hadn't voted that we wanted legal representation. This was an internal fight between lesbians and gay men. We needed to settle it ourselves. I was about to object but I held myself back. I figured I might as well hear what she had to say.

"The news is bad from the Department of Unemployment,"

Patton began in a strong low voice. "The Gay Community Services Center has denied all your claims."

The room hushed. No one had expected the Center to deny us.

Patton continued, "The Board of Directors, according to my informant, sent a silver-haired, older man down to EDD and contested them."

I sucked in my breath. Morris had to be personally very angry to have gone down there himself. Bad move, Morris, I thought. Fear and ego had clouded his judgment.

"Does this mean we won't be getting any money?" Pody asked, fear in her voice.

"I'm afraid that's exactly what it means," Patton said. "But don't worry; I've filed a counter to the denial. They are in the wrong. The way they fired you all without letters of reprimand in your personnel files, or any warnings. The fact that they operated without PP&Ps. We have a strong case. We will win this one. But it will take four, maybe five or six weeks."

Everyone was speechless. I looked at Rachel. She stood perfectly still, dumbstruck. The Saloon, she'd told me, paid minimum wage.

"Fuck GCSC!" Enric cried out.

"We want our money now!" Colin bellowed behind me.

"Yeah, make 'em pay!" June yelled. She seemed to tolerate authority even less well than I did.

"Hold on," Patton interrupted, "There's more." She bent down to her briefcase, snapped the latches and brought up a powder blue covered staple-bound booklet, some thirty or forty pages long. "GCSC has just published this piece of propaganda. It's called, 'A Report from the Board of Directors of GCSC.' It's been sent to community groups all over town." Patton flipped through the pages. "The Board claims that all the firings were justified because you have been 'fomenting dissidence.' They say they were investigating you trouble-makers for weeks before they fired you and they had to get rid of you to save the Center."

The word "dissidence" shocked me. Morris was the only

Board member who knew how to use the word in proper political context. And it was becoming clear to me that the bonehead decision to fire us had not been a spur of the moment impulse. No wonder the Board had dumped me—I'd have blown the whistle on their planning. I felt my face get hot as hope drained through my torso, down my legs, and congealed into a block of concrete holding my feet to the floor. I'd foolishly hoped Morris would realize the mass firings were a mistake. That he'd be ready to negotiate by now. But, no—they were launching new missiles. *Damn, Morris!* This meant I'd have to continue to do battle with my political godfather. I couldn't walk away from this fight.

Someone grabbed the blue book from Patton. It circulated through the room. The rumble grew. Out of Colin's huge, bulky frame, came the yell, "Burn, baby, burn!" echoing the Watt's Riots slogan.

The room took up the chant, "Burn, baby, burn!"

June called for attention. "What are we going to do about this?"

For a fraction of a second my ears had picked up a rehearsed tone to June's question. Had she and the lawyer already talked out a plan?

"What can we do?" asked April.

"We can call a strike!" June shot back. "Then they'll know we're serious."

The word "strike" sounded ominous to me. "What does a strike look like?" I asked Patton, my voice calling for attention.

The room fell into stone quiet.

Patton remained in the middle of the floor. "The demonstration line will look the same as it does now. But calling a strike means something more serious. It means we sue the Center for wrongful termination. It means we initiate a formal lawsuit. The protest line becomes a picket line. And it won't stop until they come to the bargaining table to negotiate with us."

"And everyone who crosses the picket line will be scabs!"

Dixie Youts proclaimed. "We treat GCSC like a supermarket that exploits its workers. The picket line stops anyone from going in to do business. GCSC is no different from Boeing or IBM. The Board of Directors are capitalist pigs that exploit their workers. It's about the bosses versus the workers."

June followed. "If we keep the picket line strong into the fall, the Center's funding agencies might drop their grants for next year. I say, close the bosses down!" Her cropped head jerked rapidly as she spoke.

Hysteria mounted. I grasped where June, Dixie, and the lawyer, were headed. They'd already made up their minds. Tonight was a setup to get their agenda passed. They'd admitted defeat—we were not getting our jobs back. All that was left, in their minds, was to turn the demo line into a picket line and spread labor consciousness throughout the gay community. They wanted to change the language of our fight with the Center. I had to suppose that Patton, like me, knew that language defines and controls a movement, so they were trying to use language to redefine the nature of our battle, using words like "strike" and "scab" and trying to have us see our selves as "workers" rather than feminists. My suspicious hackles were up because I feared that, like other Leftists I'd worked with, they sought to use various gay or feminist issues as a punctuation mark on the road to a socialist revolution. This made me furious. Nobody uses my movement! I vowed. Gays are more oppressed in Communist Russia and Cuba than we are in America. Capitalism wasn't the enemy of gay civil rights. Their enemy was not our enemy, and neither was GCSC.

Controlling my anger so I could speak calmly, I walked to the middle of the room. "Our fight is about lesbian feminism versus male-dominated hierarchy. Our struggle with GCSC is not about salary or better working conditions. It's about women's struggle to be treated equally," I pleaded with my comrades. "Besides, our jobs are not the only important thing. GCSC is the only out-front gay address in the city of Los Angeles. It's a symbol of safety that calls to homosexuals all over the country.

Its existence makes life safer for each one of us in this room. GCSC isn't a supermarket. It's the place my gay baby brother might go to ask for a bed when my Catholic parents throw him out. It's a place for kids who are beaten in high school by their peers for being faggots."

"I've got something to say here," Rachel's tentative voice broke in.

"Go ahead," said Patton.

"When I left my husband two years ago," Rachel began, "I heard about GCSC. It was the first place I went to when I thought I might be a lesbian. And I was no teenager. I was twenty-seven years old."

"I went there too!" Pody called out. "If GCSC closes because we call a strike, won't that be a big defeat in the eyes of the straight world?"

June ignored Pody and turned directly to me, her freckles aflame. "If you still believe in GCSC, Córdova, why don't you just cross the picket line and declare yourself a scab?"

I fought to keep my cool. I had to stay clearheaded. "This isn't about me or any individual, June. Sure the Board was wrong to fire us. Was that illegal? Of course it was. So let's change the place and replace the Board. Let's just argue to get unemployment but not sue demanding punitive damages and back pay. Ruining the Center fiscally means there won't be any jobs. Not for us or anyone else." Surely everyone in the room knew that GCSC didn't have money. Was it only me who knew that the wealthy gay attorney, Thomas Hunter Russell, had loaned GCSC the down payment to move into the new Highland location? "Let's keep our focus on changing, not destroying! Our goal is to get feminists into management and on the Board."

"GCSC will never offer our jobs back," June retorted. "We have no choice but to strike!" She slung her arm around Patton's shoulder, raised a clenched fist, and yelled to the restless crowd, "I say we vote now. To strike or not to strike!"

I racked my mind—what alternative would appease the escalating anger? I held my space in the center of the room. "I say we demand they come to the negotiating table. Now! We use the threat of a strike as leverage to get them to bargain with us."

"Oh right, Córdova," Dixie retorted. "They won't even grant us unemployment checks."

"But I'm sure if you grovel," June said, her hands on her hips mocking me, "Because Morris Kight likes you, he'll resign. And we'll all fly to heaven in a capitalist Lear jet!"

"What planet were you born on?" I screamed at my nemesis.

June took a long step toward me and shouted in my face. "We don't need scabs on the Steering Committee, why don't you—"

Patton wedged herself in between us. "Break it up you two!"

Dixie grabbed June's arm. Pody pulled me away.

Enric called out, "It's time to vote!"

"Yes, vote!" June flung her words at me.

"Wait a minute! You can't vote on something without us!" a woman's voice yelled.

Everyone turned toward the kitchen to see the tanned face of Elizabeth Elder, the co-coordinator of volunteers at the Center, enter Rachel's apartment. Elizabeth's normally restrained composure had been replaced by a tear-filled, sad expression. She was followed by three more of the Center's employees, Charlie Jones, Eddie Culp, and Terry Pearsy

"Why are you all so late?" someone asked. The four of them were among a group of current GCSC employees who regularly attended our meetings, even though it could be dangerous for them to do so.

"They fired us today!" Elizabeth screamed. "All four of us. Ken Bartley picked us off one by one," she said, sobbing full-flow now. "Late this afternoon he brought us in separately…but told us all the same thing. That GCSC wouldn't be needing our services anymore. Pack your things and get out! He was almost that blunt. So we came here."

Once more the room fell into a shocked silence.

"Fuck!" I yelled, wanting to slam my fist into a wall. The

Center was unrelenting in its crackdown. The Gay/Feminist 11 were now the Gay/Feminist 16.

June asked, "Why were you fired?"

"Bartley said we were inciting the staff. Trying to persuade the other employees to join the Service Workers Union."

"But Patton says employees have the right to form a union," Rachel said, confused.

We all turned to face Patton. "Yes, you have that right," she said.

"These firings sound illegal, too," I said. "Did they give any of you a written warning to cease and desist?"

"Nothing," Elizabeth said, folding herself into a heap on the wood floor. She looked like she'd just had a close friend die. "It came out of the blue. Just like the day they fired all of you."

The room exploded with rage. "Vote! Vote!"

"Is everyone ready?" Patton called out. Between the denial of the benefits and now these additional firings, the Board's timing had played right into June's hands.

I watched the room shift, bodies moving from one place in the room to another as the ideological factions among us "dissidents" began to coalesce, each behind their spokesperson. Pody, Rachel and some of the others came to stand with me, forming the feminist camp. Across the room, June had most of the guys, and all of the socialists. Their camp also had the hotheads, more numerous than thoughtful. Over by the Plath-congested bookcase stood a third group, a smaller and silent minority. I didn't think they'd grasped the difference between what I was proposing and the strike June wanted. They just wanted their jobs or unemployment checks and were content to let others determine how to wage that war.

"This has to be done by secret ballot," I demanded, seeing the writing on the wall, but hoping privacy might top peer pressure. Some shrugged, others nodded. Rachel went to her desk and took out paper. She and Pody began to tear it into little strips. The strips made their way around the room. Pens and pencils appeared. People sat on the floor, or bent over to scribble on a friend's back. No one talked or consulted a neighbor. Rudy took off his faded fedora and passed it around the room. The votes were collected. Patton called out. "Does anyone object to Enric and Alicia counting the votes?"

No one replied. Alicia would be fair, I knew. The two of them made their way into Rachel's bedroom and closed the door. I listened intently for the rustle of unfolding paper or conversation, but heard nothing.

"Do you have a cigarette?" a hushed voice asked.

I turned to face Rachel. In the intensity of political maneuvering, I'd forgotten she was in the room. Now she was standing close enough to touch.

"I'm nervous," she laughed. Apparently, she'd forgotten her anger at me.

"Me too." I smiled for the first time that night.

"Can you stay a little afterwards? I'm somewhat shocked."

"Sure," I said, surprised, but delighted. "I can stay as long as you want me to."

Colin and Alicia reentered the room.

"We're finished," said Alicia, her voice registering no emotion. "The ballots are 18 to 10 in favor—of calling a strike."

Chapter 16

A Double Bed On the Ocean

[Los Angeles]

Mid-May, 1975

"Don't you have some place to go?" I asked Pody, who was thumbing through a book in Rachel's living room.

My new lover was at the kitchen door saying good-bye to the last of the protesters. Now we have to call ourselves "strikers," I thought glumly, wishing Pody would disappear so I could fall into bed with Rachel and forget the vote I'd lost.

Pody looked up from her book and around at the empty room. "Oh! You want me to leave. You're staying here with Rachel!"

I stared back at her. "The meeting is over. Why don't you go call BeJo or someone else who wants you to clog up their space?"

Pody snapped her book shut and slipped into her coat, trying to hide her shock. "You mean you don't mind if I called your...ah...BeJo?"

I also couldn't believe the words had fallen out of my mouth.

I blamed my anger on the bad vote. But it didn't matter—it was too late. "If that's what it takes to get you out of here…" I forced a smile. "You were going to call her anyway, weren't you?"

"Well, I've been wanting to. I was going to talk to you first to see how you felt."

"Well now you've talked to me." I slung my arm around her shoulder and walked her toward the kitchen front door. "See you around buddy."

Returning to the living room, I fell into the green beanbag, waiting for Rachel, and hoping I wouldn't regret giving Pody the green light. She was always hovering around me and Rachel, or me and BeJo. She already felt like a brother…ah…sister-in-law. Better Pody than if BeJo started dating someone I didn't like.

Rachel leaned against the doorjamb, looking at me from across the room. "Hi," she said tentatively, greeting me personally for the first time tonight. "That was some meeting." She sounded spent.

"How do you feel about the vote?"

"I don't know. Shocked, I suppose. Frightened. What does calling a strike actually mean?"

I tried to sit up in the green bag-chair. "It means we've crossed a line. That the struggle with the Center has reached the point of no return. And it means we voted to define this as a labor issue. The battle line has been drawn." I slammed a closed fist against the vinyl been-bag chair. It gave off a loud smack.

Rachel sat down in the small chair next to the stereo, still across the room from me. "I've never been in a strike before," she whispered.

"Neither have I." I slouched deeper into the beans. "At least not on the workers' side. My dad used to come home at dinnertime cursing something he called 'the unions' for not loading marble on ships for his next job. That's the first time I heard the word union. They were the bad guys."

"Me too. My father sometimes came home saying he couldn't get paid until the unions had okayed his jobsite."

Rachel's voice wavered. Her face was pale, her lips a flat line. I wanted to comfort her, but she was holding herself, both arms wrapped around her body as if she didn't want me to approach.

"And another thing, this means I can no longer go over to McCadden Place and talk to Morris. When he gets this strike news, negotiating a settlement will be his last priority. I know him, he's going to fight. "

"Meaning he's going to fight with you?" Rachel asked.

Her question took me aback. I almost knocked over my Coke. "Of course not. This isn't personal. I'm talking about the movement. Either way this goes, the movement is the big loser. This will tear our community apart."

Rachel started to cry. She looked so frail. Was it best to keep things between us strictly political?

"What's going to happen to us?" she said, wiping tears from her eyes.

I shook my head. "I don't know. In the five-year, mostly turbulent history of our infant gay movement no one has ever called a strike against a gay organization. People will be shocked."

Rachel began to rock herself in the chair. "I don't want anymore breakups in my life. I left John two years ago and I was so happy to find the movement, and the GCSC. I never thought there could be an us versus them. This is my new gay family. Aren't we supposed to be united-we-stand, divided-we-fall?" Her voice had grown plaintive, the question like a suppressed wail.

I began to wonder what I really knew about Rachel. Was I getting in deeper than I wanted to be?

"This doesn't mean the end of the world, sweetheart," I said. *Damn!* There was that word again. It came out so naturally when I was with her. "In New York City the lesbians don't work with the gay men anymore. The entire dyke contingent walked out of the Gay Activists Alliance and formed their own organization. None of the dykes in San Francisco work with the men."

"But that's never happened in L.A., right?" Rachel's eyebrows begged.

"No. Not on a community-wide scale."

Rachel covered herself with a blanket slung over the back of her chair, the same pink one we'd slept beneath. "It frightened me when June started calling you names, like scab. The two of you almost came to blows."

I climbed out of the beanbag, crossed the room, and knelt in front of her chair. "We didn't almost come to blows." I rested my hand on her legs. "We were just yelling out our differences. I'm not gonna punch June. Especially since she's so much bigger; she would've decked me!" I laughed, trying to pry a chuckle out of Rachel.

She folded herself even more and lowered her head. "John used to hit me," she whispered.

"John?"

"My husband."

I fell into a sitting position on the floor. So it was the volatility of the meeting that had spooked Rachel. "Is that why you divorced him?"

"Yes. Fighting takes me back to my father's house." She spoke quietly. "Growing up in my family, volatility meant violence."

I wasn't sure what to say. "In my family it only meant someone was stealing the meat off your plate or 'borrowing' your favorite toy. Unless, of course, it was my father's anger." I emitted a hollow laugh.

Rachel stared through me vacantly. "It was always my father," she said. "Screaming at my mother, or sister, or brother. Sometimes he'd hit my mother. One time he stood there holding my baby brother, dangling him with one hand, screaming at her, 'I'll throw this kid into a wall if you don't…do…whatever!' I was so terrified I ran to the nearest wall so I could catch David."

No wonder Rachel was so frightened; she thought there had almost been a fight in her home tonight. It was becoming clear that this woman was not cut out for political hardball. I didn't know whether to wrap her in my arms or move further away.

"And then he left us," Rachel went on. "That's when they

divorced and our family broke apart."

"That's not going to happen here," I soothed. "We are strong enough to weather this."

She tried to smile, but her eyes were distant. "Tell me more about why the New York dykes walked out on their gay men?"

I leaned against a windowsill. "It's an ideology now, a philosophy called lesbian, or dyke, separatism. On one hand, lesbians separating from gay men could be a healthy, even necessary, phase. Like the straight women who birthed feminism and felt they had to leave the world of men in order to clearly grapple with the new world order of women. Maybe we lesbians have to divorce our gay brothers and go organize on our own for a few years. Maybe that's the only way women can be free enough to explore who we are and what our politics and issues might be. Some lesbians feel we need to remake a world that's not male-dependent. They say as long as we work together, we'll never know what our own issues might be. For instance, is sexual liberation really a lesbian issue? Most lesbians see our freedom to make family and keep our children in court decisions as more critical than sexual freedom. Maybe by our withdrawing, the gay men will learn to value women. I have mixed feelings about lesbian separatism. As a political movement, we need to move forward with our gay brothers. Personally, I have no close gay male friends, and my world feels complete without them. But regardless of how lesbians choose to live, *my* politics are about building gay or lesbian organizations, not destroying them."

I leaned down to re-tie my shoelace, hiding my face from Rachel. I didn't want her to see the defeat in my eyes. Yes, tonight's vote pitted me against my political godfather, and that hurt. Worse yet, now I had to stay the course and pretend to fight for that miserable GCSC job I never wanted in the first place.

"Calling a strike was not the right tactical move," I continued. "It shuts the door behind us and locks Morris and the Board—and us—into a pre-defined tunnel of response." My tone hardened as bitterness crept in. "I *hate* what happened tonight!"

Rachel stood up suddenly. "PLEASE, don't get angry again!" she snapped. A different voice had emerged, this one filled with a tough, clipped ring. Abruptly, she walked toward the kitchen.

I followed a few steps behind. "So why did you ask me if this was about Morris and me?"

"I'm finished with talking about fathers tonight," Rachel said in the same disconnected voice. "Let's skip it."

"Does skipping it mean you want me to leave?" I asked brusquely.

Rachel stood at the sink with her back towards me. "I'm still mad at you," she said, now washing the dishes.

"Mad about what?" I asked.

She turned around. "You walked out on me at the Saloon. Has that slipped your mind in less than a week?"

"I'm here with you now, aren't I?" I countered, softening my voice.

"You could have called after your midnight interview to ask me if I got home safely. Did I even cross your mind?"

Rachel was right; she hadn't crossed my mind that night. "I got out of there at three in the morning," I offered. "I assumed you were—"

"We've only been dating a few weeks and already you take me for granted. So I'm just saying—not tonight."

"Fine," I snapped back, walking to the kitchen table. I started slamming my notebooks and papers into my briefcase. Just as well—tonight wasn't a space night from BeJo anyway. Grabbing my jacket, I walked out, leaving the kitchen door wide open.

A week later, I was back at Effie Street, watching the moonlight fall onto Rachel's back porch. The front door to her duplex sat level with the street but the hill dropped away sharply at her backdoor creating a long, steep staircase up to the rear. The back stairs were steep so everyone avoided them, preferring the kitchen access in front, but I liked the back door, imagining it was my own private entrance. I climbed the staircase and sat on the cement porch landing overlooking the city. They say lesbians bring a U-Haul on their second date, but I was already U-Hauled with BeJo, so I'd just brought an apology.

Rachel had called me today, leaving two messages at *The Freep*. But I'd been too busy, maybe still too angry at being all but thrown out, to return her calls. Nonetheless, as I'd left a late night meeting in Silverlake, Lionheart had driven me to Effie. Seeing the place dark, I figured Rachel was either asleep inside or out on a date. It was Friday night and I was actually free from politics and work, yet alone.

Sitting on the stoop of the staircase, leaning against her bedroom's wall I felt close to Rachel. Pulling out a smoke, I watched the almost-full moon make its journey across the sky. The muted light from the street lamps cast shadows on the Spanish stucco houses below, many with their original roof tiles from the '20's. Dad had taught me how to tell the difference between new tile and old. The old ones were handmade and wider at one end. Mexican craftsmen shaped them by putting the wet clay on their bent thighs and rounding them. The wide end of the clay narrowed as the thigh approached the knee. The new tiles were of identical widths on both ends, no doubt shaped by a machine.

Old things were better than new things, Dad always said. And the best are the old things that last, he'd tell me with a smile and a twinkle in his eye; that way you'd never need anything that was new. He was talking about cars and buildings, but he'd also been married to the same woman for a quarter century. So far, not much of the old had lasted with me. My stint in the convent had been short. So had relationships. The only part of my life that had weathered was my political life. Perhaps it wasn't the smoothest of moves to have arrived on Rachel's back step in the middle of the night. I should have returned her call, at least left a message that I might come. Yet, I hadn't wanted to commit. Using a sidewalk phone booth in Silverlake was not a safe late night bet.

Now that I'd arrived, I was content to sit on Rachel's steps, deciding how to make my presence known in case she was inside. I leaned against the wall wishing I could thought-control the beanbag chair to leap through the open window above me and bring me comfort on the damp cement steps. Buttoning my jacket against the encroaching marine layer rolling in off the Pacific, I thought about my first night with Rachel when we wore the grooves off *Diamonds And Rust*. Was Rachel the diamond and I the rust, I wondered? Was I rusted shut emotionally? Perhaps she was right. I wasn't taking her for granted, but dumping her at The Women's Saloon and not calling to check in with her was inconsiderate.

I lit another cig and stared into the night. So far, a personal love had not worked out in my life. The first love of my life had been God. I was seven years old the day I knelt in front of the jewel bedecked statute of the Infant of Prague and took the first vow of my life. At the side altar with Mary's little infant son Jesus, I'd made the sign of the cross over straight-cut bangs that fell over my eyebrows. At age seven I had reached the "age of reason" and according to the Holy Roman and Apostolic Church I was old enough to make a statement of faith, old enough to receive Holy Communion, and old enough to be a martyr. Since dying for my faith and taking that short cut to heaven didn't seem to be an option in America, I could still take the long route and promise Mary that I'd enter a convent and devote my life to knowing and loving her son.

"I give you my life," I whispered to my tiny Infant King with the crown on his head. "From this moment forward, I belong to you."

I knew it would be another ten years, the day after I graduated from high school, before I could literally enter a convent, but my promise felt natural and solid, clear and compelling. I knew that a vow was a promise that you keep forever. "Once a priest, always a priest…according to the law of Melchizedek," the Bible said. I had no doubt that my vow would fill me up for a lifetime.

Ten years later, I'd read the life and times of every Catholic saint ever thrown to the lions. I'd spent most of high school on the softball diamond, or in the small on-campus chapel at Bishop Amat. On September 6, 1966, I entered the IHM novitiate. The Montecito estate south of Santa Barbara was everything that Sister Veronica Mary IHM, my high school mentor, had promised it would be in her poem. It was indeed "a place apart where the saint might forgive and the sinner might praise. Where I was myself, not conscious of paltry pettiness."

But it was also the mid 1960s. By the time I got to my "place apart," the novitiate had become part of the chaos of American political life. Daniel and Phillip Berrigan, and other anti-war radicals, were using the novitiate as a safe house to run from the FBI. The endless stream of strange visitors made for great classes but little solitude. My order was at war with L.A.'s hyper-conservative Cardinal McIntyre because they were agitating for feminist reform within religious life. My ecstatically wonderful life among women who were committed to celibacy and covert lesbianism was a contradiction I could have enjoyed. But witnessing up close how regressive the Church was and that it was never going to even try to change poverty, war, or the second class status of women, threw me—a naïve teenager—for a grown-up loop. My faith in the Holy, Roman, and Apostolic Catholic Church had simply imploded.

The silence of the night outside Rachel's duplex was like a "grand silence" at the novitiate, reminding me of the hundreds of lonely nights at Montecito begging the Almighty Universe to show me a new path. A year after I'd finally left the convent, I became distracted by the twenty-year-old joy and angst of being a college student, testing my new found gay identity, and a new decision to become a professional social worker. But it was not until October 3, 1970, the night I walked into the Daughters of Bilitis, that I was to fall in love again. This time with the cause that would indeed reveal my life's promise.

I looked down at the steep bank of ivy that fell away from Rachel's duplex. The sweep of the city lay in front of me. Perhaps, I reflected, I was too much in love with the sweep of the movement, my new cause, to have room in my heart for a single individual human being. It felt so much larger, so much more filling, to love a cause. People—women—would leave you, but a cause was with you forever.

Being married, even to a woman, didn't suit who I thought I was. Marriage was a counter-revolutionary lifestyle. Was Rachel a white picket fence kind of lesbian? I wondered as I studied the abrupt landscape of her backyard ivy that seemed to fall down the hill out of control.

Love was too complicated and time-consuming in my life, but sex was necessary. Sex with Rachel felt particularly necessary. Embedded in her jade bushes, I questioned whether the blissed-out feeling I'd had with her could develop into something deeper. Pulling the leaves off the jade branch next to me, I counted, she loves me, she loves me not, as I denuded a branch. At the Saloon and again the other night, I'd called her "sweetheart." Sweetheart was what my father called my mother. Sweetheart could mean staying for breakfast.

I shivered inside my jacket. The pre-dawn cold would come soon. I'd be frozen by breakfast time if I couldn't think of a way to get Rachel to open the door and take us to bed. How would my father have awakened my mother if she were angry at him?

I jumped up and leaned over the porch rail facing her bedroom window. I took a deep breath.

"Jesse, come home, there's a hole in the bed
Where we slept; now it's growing cold.
Jesse your face, in the place where we lay
By the hearth, all apart, it hangs on my heart.
And I'm leaving the light on the stairs
No I'm not scared; I wait for you"

A light flicked on in the bedroom. The porch door opened a crack, and Rachel's face peered out.

"Jeanne?" she called, drawing out my name like a prayer.

"Yes, it's me."

The door opened wider, revealing her body. "I can't believe

you're doing this." Barefoot in the dim porch light, Rachel was dressed in a sheer blue nightgown gathered in pleats under her breasts. Her hair was curled every which way from sleep. In the dim light, she looked dazed and vulnerable.

"Grab a blanket and come out and watch the stars with me."

Her figure disappeared for a moment, and then re-emerged from the darkness with the Nepalese quilt draped around her shoulders. Squinting, she reached for my hand. I sat her down on a stair, and sat myself on the stair behind her, wrapping the quilt around my shoulders and folding her inside it with me.

She leaned back into my arms. "I won't ask what you are doing here," she said, shaking her head.

"I came for you." I nuzzled my lips against the back of her neck.

"That didn't keep you at the Saloon."

"Don't start. Please. That was work. Leaving had nothing to do with what I wanted."

Her body tightened and pulled away. "Listen to what you say, Jeanne. Don't you even know yourself? Leaving to do the interview had everything to do with what you want. Politics is the life you want, that's where your priorities go."

I stopped myself from launching into further defense. "I thought you'd understand. I'm sorry," I whispered. In our silence, I traced the letters l-o-v-e-r on her back. "I didn't realize my leaving would upset you so much. I'm an activist. The revolution is not going to wait until after we've had dinner and watched Ozzie and Harriet."

"The movement is your lover," she said.

The warmth from Rachel's back, pressing into my chest, quieted my mind. I watched the shadows flicker in her curls. I hadn't come tonight to talk about the revolution.

"That's what my father always told my mother when she asked him to spend more time with us," Rachel said. "He'd say, 'I've got important work to do. Can't you see I'm earning a living?' He had other priorities too. Eventually he left us altogether."

I gathered Rachel closer. "I'm not leaving your life, I'm entering it."

"I want a relationship with you, Jeanne," Rachel said. "Not a fling." She reached behind her and pulled my hair.

I almost asked what she thought was the difference between a relationship and a fling. Two nights a week instead of one?

Instead I sank back into my earlier thoughts, saying, "The stillness reminds me of praying. Look down there." I pointed to the avenue below. "The street lights are the candles. The tiles of the roof tops are the villagers in meditation, the nuns at Chapel."

We were both silent. Our chapel radiated below.

I leaned forward, my mouth an inch from her ear. "When I was fifteen," I began, "I was backpacking in Yosemite with other camp counselors. We were up very high in the Sierras and one afternoon we walked into a beautiful mountain valley called Tuolumne Meadows. We made camp and then I wandered off by myself and walked far into the middle of the meadow. I took off my clothes, all my clothes, and lay down. The tall meadow reeds combed me like they knew we were going to do something sacred together."

I trailed off feeling my face blush. I'd never shared what happened that afternoon with another human being.

"Go on."

"I lay there flat on my back, naked in the grass and prayed, '*I dissolve into the earth; my cells let go of one another. I am home in the earth. I am one with God.*' And I kept repeating this...my dissolution prayer, over and over for hours. Time passed and I began to feel my body dissolve and become the dirt and the stones and the reeds. I lay there dissolving into the earth all afternoon. I thought about the last stanza in a poem that a nun I loved wrote, 'I became God's—And this began to be my only boast, and I guess shall always be.' And, finally I understood what she meant. I felt a total surrender of identity. I was no longer separate. I lost consciousness and felt like I was sleeping inside the earth, having a meltdown of being."

Rachel shivered in my arms.

"When I came back to camp, the sun was rubbing against the pines on the west ridge of the valley. So yes," I said, rubbing the chill off her arms, "I miss the transcendent state that comes more often in religious life than anywhere. The longing never dissipates, no matter how much one doth protest."

"No, it never does," Rachel said, reaching back and caressing my cheek. "I'm glad you didn't stay behind a wall."

Her textured hands stimulated my skin like fine grain sandpaper; they felt like a razor's edge bringing each tiny pore to life. Lowering my face to her neck, I breathed in her scent of patchouli oil and cupped her breasts in my hands. Rachel reached with both arms and clasped my neck, her chest opened up. "I love you, Jeanne," she said, dragging out my name like it was a foreign word on her tongue.

I took her nipples, pinching each softly between my fingers. Rachel's breathing quickened and her fingers tightened in my hair. Pulling to one side, I studied her profile in the moonlight, watching her open mouth looking for mine. Gently, I released her breasts and eased my body out from behind her. I wanted the full length of my body on hers. I wanted to touch every part of her.

I flipped the quilt over us and lay down over her, pressing my palms against the chilled cement to hold my weight above her. Rachel leaned back and I was on top of her, drawing her tongue into mine as I searched for absolution of my longing.

Suddenly she gasped, "We can't do this out here. Come to bed, Jeanne."

I propped myself onto my elbows but refused to break contact. "Go, go," I murmured, my lips on hers.

Staggering upright, kissing and dragging the quilt behind us, we made our way through the porch doorjamb, across the living room and into Rachel's bedroom.

Nearing her bed, she pulled open the snaps of my shirt. Moonlight through the bedroom window fell on her face and breasts as her robe slipped to the oak floor and I saw her through the sheer blue gown. Reaching into the shadows I scooped the small of her back with one arm, while my other outlined her mouth and the thin upper lip that I'd come to claim. I lingered at the barely defined cleft in her chin.

"Everything in miniature," I marveled aloud. Her freckles had dissolved in the darkness, but I could still see the light in her robin-egg blue eyes. I reached down, picked her up, and folded us onto her bedspread.

"It's a good thing my bed was only a few feet away," she laughed quietly into the night. "This is so much easier than the stairs."

"I live to make things easy on you." I pressed my body against hers.

"I hope I'm alive to see that day."

"Don't go back to that subject."

"Then come back here where you were." She reached inside my unbuttoned shirt and clutched my naked shoulders. "We don't need this anymore," she said, flinging my shirt across the room.

Untying the blue cotton ribbon in the front of her gown, I whispered, "This beats dying and going to heaven."

"Then I'll give you some seeds to take to heaven." Rachel kissed me delicately in each corner of my eyes as though her lips were planting. "There. Now, wherever you go, my seeds will be with you."

In the dark, my hands defined her body; she shuddered in my arms and would not let my fingers leave her. Later in the dark, she took my nipples in her mouth and sent me on my own spiral. I called to her, not realizing that her name would always be a part of this act. "I'm here, Jeanne," she answered. "I've got you." I could tell by her breathing that my rush had again prompted hers. I kissed her roughly and she didn't hold back. Baez's rhythms felt ragged compared to the fine joy of us coming together. I reveled in the moment, knowing again the holiness of Tuolumne, of dissolving and letting go. Worlds dropped away, leaving me to wander my own infinities.

I try to call out again but no sounds come. I lie rocking on a double mattress bed in the ocean. I've gone down into the void, sunk through to the other side of the world and resurfaced, baptized, on another ocean. The double bed is covered with blinding white cotton sheets. The sun, hot and delicious on my naked skin. Yet, there is no glare. I see perfectly. The sheets yield against my back and sway with me. Pink and gray swallows play in the sky above my bed. They caw to each other, "Who is this woman who floats in our world?" Perched on the corners of the mattress, they wait with me. They are the companions of my original self. I await their absolution. Now I belong to them, the ocean, and what poetry my soul allows. The lull rocks me to sleep.

"I've got you, Jeanne. I've got you," a voice echoed from afar.

Small, sharp pains encased in my shoulders. I opened my eyes to see walls. Shadows. A poster of Angela Davis flickering in the moonlight. The pecks were Rachel's fingernails, clutching my shoulders.

"Whoa! Your nails," I called out, reaching up to loosen her grip.

"Are you back with me, babe?" Rachel's voice asked.

"I think so. Haven't I been?"

"I don't know," Rachel says. "I've been holding you. You cried for a long time."

Cried? I shook my head, trying to clear it and glanced around the room once more. Should I ask Rachel if she'd been to the double bed on the ocean?

"Where did you go? Is something wrong?"

"Wrong? No, no." I smiled at her. "It's been a long time since everything was so right."

"That's wonderful." Rachel smiled, her lids half closed. "Do you want me to plant more seeds?" I shook my head. "Then I'm going to lay right here beside you, skip work, and get some sleep."

She turned over. "So, hold me…" Her voice drifted off even

as she spoke.

I cupped her with my body, my ankles clutching hers, and wrapped my arm between her breasts. So many years after the mountain meadow, I felt like I'd dissolved again. "Rachel?" I whispered, breathing softly on the back of her neck, "I love you."

Chapter 17

The Gospel According to Joe

[Los Angeles]

Early June, 1975

I woke early to watch the first sunlight fall on Rachel. As always in her bedroom, the room felt utterly peaceful as though someone had pressed the mute button on the world. I savored her body, watching her chest rise and fall in sleep, noticing her eyelids twitch as she dreamed. Running my fingers over her breasts, I pressed my lips to her naked shoulder, inhaling her patchouli oil and the seclusion it offered.

The phone rang. *Damn!* Jumping out of bed, I dashed to her living room to stop the noise. Instinctively, I picked up the receiver.

"Córdova?" the voice asked.

"Penny, is this you?"

"I'm sorry I had to call!" My editor sounded upset. She had a list of my lovers' phone numbers in case of work emergencies. "Didn't you get my message? The FBI was here yesterday. And your Nazi is calling this morning."

"It's Saturday, Pen. I didn't get your message. What did the FBI want? What about Joe Tomassi?"

"How quickly can you be here?"

I looked through the bedroom door at Rachel's profile. My lips tightened. Leaving her felt wrenching. For a second *The Freep* didn't feel nearly as important as reveling in bed with Rachel. The revolution promised no ration book of joy.

I heard Penny gasp. I'd never hesitated before.

"You're coming in aren't you?"

"Of course," I said sharply. "Be there in ten."

Walking back into my mute world, I looked for my shirt. Rachel stirred. "Who was that?" she asked groggily.

"There's a problem at *The Freep*," I said, kneeling beside her sleep-soaked body. "I've got to go handle it."

"Hurry back to me," Rachel mumbled and turned over.

Making for the kitchen door, I stopped to grab my Dyke-bannered briefcase. Some dyke, I thought to myself. I'd missed a call from my editor. Tucking my shirt into my pants, I looked around for a comb. A yellow legal pad was propped up on the kitchen table. A note read: "Good morning Jeanne. Couldn't sleep. Wrote you this letter in the middle of the night. Please read it if you wake up before I do."

This time I wanted to leave a note as well. "My heart stays with you," I printed in large letters, no exclamation mark. I propped the pad against her bedroom doorjamb. Grabbing her letter, I let myself out the door, jumped into Lionheart, and sped down Vermont to the 101.

With the Freeway's wind in my hair I started to feel sane. Now it felt good to leave Effie Street for more neutral ground. Gaining distance my heart stopped racing. Driving was the pause between the action, the commercial break, in my life. Had Rachel heard me whisper those over-the-line words "I love you" the night before, or had she been asleep? The words had pushed out without conscious permission. Sex with her threatened to dissolve the instinctual divide I'd kept when bedding previous lovers. In bed with other women, I'd always had a sense, even after climax, that I wanted to be on to the next thing. This was new territory for me. Lionheart changed gears, merging into the 101 North as I pondered a non-monogamous factor I called slippage. Slippage was the slick spot in the rapid gear-change of emotion often necessary in non-monogamous life. The goal was to change gears without hitting a slick that led to a wild swerve.

Emotional gear-change wasn't new to me. I was reared by a calmly consistent but emotionally distant mother, and a moody, rage-prone father. I'd had to learn to gear-shift often, rapidly, and with no hesitation—to develop a survivor-oriented split psyche in relation to those that fed me. But slippage in my adult romantic relationships was proving just as troublesome. Here, slippage was the gap between the spoken and the unspoken feelings toward one lover not fully revealed to the other. Here, slippage was slick enough to send my relationship car spinning out of control. This morning I'd allowed slippage by not telling Rachel, when she'd said, "Hurry back to me," that it was Saturday, BeJo's day, so I wouldn't be returning to Effie Street. And before this damn day was out, I'd probably hit another slick. BeJo still thought I was seeing several women, not just one.

Checking my speed, I braked slightly. Non-monogamy was hell on coupledom—even for butches like me who were naturally suited to the practice. It was hard on most of my lesbian feminist friends. Feminism taught that sexual exclusivity was a male invention. Women should take ownership of their own sexuality and dispense it as they chose, without restriction by government, men, or even other women. Coupling exclusively was imitating heterosexuality, colonizing a sister, and otherwise just plain wrong. Yet most of us had grown up in the 1950s. Feminism aside, non-monogamy still *felt* like cheating. Our political beliefs were contrary to our emotionality. What was a dyke to do?

Ahead I saw the Hollywood Boulevard exit. Swerving Lionheart toward the far right lane, a minute later I pulled into *The Freep's* parking lot. It was time to shift into work gear, to box emotion away. Rachel and I had simply been overwhelmed by chemistry. I-love-yous needed to be left to the night, where they belonged. I reached into the glove compartment, found a comb, and ran it through my rumpled hair. Taking a visual in the rearview mirror, I saw myself calm and collected, ready for battle. I'd almost blown my duty, but I wouldn't let that happen again.

Penny met me on the stairs up to Editorial. "Come with me, now!" she said, turning around and pushing me toward her office.

Cornering me in the chair opposite her desk, she lit into me. "It's a good thing I couldn't find you because that means the FBI couldn't either." She stood over me, wagging a finger. "But they might be back with a search warrant."

"Searching for what?" I blurted out.

"You, *The Freep*, and Donald Freed, our source on your story."

"Christ!" I whistled through my teeth. The paper had run my article last week breaking the news that some in the Weather Underground Organization apparently wanted to float their doubts about the future necessity of armed struggle. {1} The story was controversial. Heavyweights from the New Left had called City Editor Tom Thompson and Penny herself either singing my praises or questioning the paper and me as unacceptably printing false news about a core precept of the underground.

"Two guys in suits came in late yesterday, demanding that we produce you," Penny continued.

"What did you tell them? Are they coming back?"

"Not yet. They are talking to our lawyers today looking for grounds to pull a search warrant. We told them you weren't here, which thank God you never are. And that we won't reveal our source, go read the First Amendment."

I smiled at my editor, grateful that she always had my back. In the newspaper world that didn't happen all the time.

She studied me thoughtfully. "Córdova, have you seriously considered what you'll say and do when the cops or Feds do come with a warrant? With the kind of stories you're doing for us now, that time may come. We'll protect you of course, but have you thought about…."

"Jail? No, Pen. I actually haven't given it a moment's thought. You know me. It ain't happening unless it's happened!"

"Jail can be lonely, Jeanne."

"You'll bring me magazines and chocolate, won't you?" I laughed.

Penny didn't smile.

"I hear prison is a good place to write a book. Maybe you'll publish a second book of mine?"

"I'm begging you. You need to take this seriously," she said quietly, now calm behind her desk.

"Maybe I'd make a special request to be thrown into the Daddy Tank at Sybil Brand,'" I joked. "I'd be right at home with the other butches. That would make a good book."

Penny didn't appreciate my literary ambition. "Does *anything* scare you, Jeanne?"

I twitched in my chair, anxious to be out of Penny's office and this conversation.

My jauntiness withered. "Actually, I am afraid jail will be cold. I lose my nerve when I'm cold." The fear of being physically cold had haunted me since my birth at the Bremerhaven port of embarkation in far northern Germany.

Penny stared, about to ask more.

Thompson's huge frame appeared at the doorway. "Phone call, Córdova. I think it's him! He referred to himself as 'Córdova's Nazi.'"

Praise be, I mumbled. I hadn't heard from Captain Joe Tomassi of the National Socialist Liberation Front in weeks. I thought I'd lost the story.

Dashing into my office, I picked up the blinking line. "Where have you been, Joe?" I said casually. "I thought you'd changed your mind about our interview."

"Ain't no way," the surly voice replied. "The LAPD got a little closer than I thought they would. So I had to lay low for a while. Get some things organized." He muffled a cough. "You still up for meeting me?"

"Sure," I said. "But I'll need proof, Joe. I just can't write that you were behind the tear-gassing of the Santa Monica Civic Auditorium and bombing of the SWP offices on your say so."

"What kind of proof?"

"The exact chemical mix of the teargas. An accurate description of how you went about it."

"No problem."

"As for the Socialist Workers Party bombing, I'll need the bomb components. Right down to the type of detonator. Where exactly it was placed. And why your group chose the SWP in the first place."

"We met the Socialist Workers' Party on the streets in Boston and Pasadena when they were pushing the busing of them niggers into our neighborhoods," he explained. "That integration crap is being shoved down our throats. Besides, we needed bombing experience so we can work up to hitting the Jew-infected Fairfax area." He spat out the last words like he wanted to kill.

"Sounds like you've got a lot to say, Joe," I said, wanting desperately to get the guy on tape. "When can we do the interview?"

"Thursday at three p.m.," he shot back.

"Where?"

"You drive that red Cougar of yours east on the 10, all the way to El Monte."

My heart stopped. Joe knew Lionheart; he was watching me. My throat closed up as I swallowed a fuck you that threatened to erupt.

"On the corner of Valley and Garfield there's a Sears and Roebuck store," he continued. "You know where that is?"

"I know the location." It wasn't far from the Plush Pony, a Chicana lesbian bar in Alhambra, a town Latinos were steadily moving into.

"At exactly three p.m. you drive around the parking lot to the back of the building. At the far east end of the lot there are never any cars. There's a tree. You park underneath it. You turn off the car and wait."

I was amazed at the public nature of his choice, hiding in plain sight. "How will I recognize you?"

"You won't," he said. "I won't be there." He laughed. "You think I'm a fool? How do I know you won't tip off the LAPD? They're already out to kill me."

"I'm a reporter. I don't blow my sources."

"My people will see your car and meet you. If they see anyone in the car with you, they won't approach. I mean anyone. There won't be any interview. You got that?"

I didn't like Joe's tone of voice. "I'm bringing my tape recorder," I replied. "You got that?"

"Good. I'll give you pictures. But no camera."

"Don't push me," I snapped. "I'm the one who's doing you a favor, remember?" My bully-in-chief father had taught me, punks had to be confronted early on or they'd mop the floor with you later. It had come in useful in my early twenties, when I'd been a social worker and probation officer and worked the ghettos. I stayed silent.

"Three o'clock, Thursday," Joe said.

The line went dead. I held onto the receiver, my mind reeling from the fact that I'd been talking to someone who might have already killed people. What if I pissed him off during the interview? With the name Córdova maybe he was expecting me to be Italian. What would he do when he saw that my skin was brown? Light brown, true enough, but not white.

Penny opened my office door. "Jeanne? Did you get an interview?"

"Yeah sure." My voice rang hollow. "He's one hell of a flipped out white boy."

Me editor sat down in front of my desk. "When is the interview?"

"Next Thursday."

She pursed a pencil on her lower lip. "While you were on the phone, Jeanne, I gave this interview a lot of thought. I won't have my reporters going to secret interviews with right wing murderers. Jack Margolis has to go with you. Tomassi will recognize Jack's name and photo from his column next to yours."

"You sent me to Donald Freed's source alone."

"That was different. Freed and his friends are on *our* side."

I studied the tightness of Penny's jaw line. I respected Penny's opinion, but my gut said this time I had to disobey her. Sometimes she was simply too white and too straight. She didn't understand that most gay people risked their lives on a daily basis coming out of the closet. She'd never been in the front row of a demonstration with LAPD mounted troops trampling us. She hadn't been with me in my beat up yellow Vega the night a drunken bigot had attacked my car when I was on my way to a lesbian bar, shattering the windshield with a crowbar and threatening to do the same to me. Penny didn't know about street courage.

"I've written fifty-four stories for you, Penny. Many of them turned out to be more hazardous than they first appeared. I'd think you know by now that I can handle myself. You have to trust that, Penny. The man was adamant. I need to go alone."

Behind her wide specs, Penny's eyes grew small. Her thin lips formed a very straight line. "And I say, adamantly—this Nazi can't dictate the perimeters of safety for my writers. This guy is a fanatic at best, and a mental case at worst. If you show up with Margolis, he'd have to let Jack be present."

No, he wouldn't have to, I thought. "Joe isn't going to meet me himself. His people will find me and take me to him. He knows my car. His people won't approach if they see someone with me."

Penny jumped up. "He knows your car? Come on, Córdova, I can't say yes to this!"

Suddenly a thought crossed my mind and my face relaxed.

"OK. So you're officially on the record as telling me not to go. What I do with my time is my business. Now you're off the hook if something happens."

Penny threw up her hands as she walked to the door. "It's not my neck I'm worried about."

"Don't worry Penny," I called after her. "The guy likes me."

As I headed east on the 10 toward El Monte, my mind was focused on the story I'd be writing about my Nazi. I hadn't gone to *The Freep* this morning so I wouldn't have to lie to Penny's face or block Jack from getting into my car. No one, not even BeJo knew where I was going. As a back-up precaution I'd left a note with the details stuffed in Robin's mailbox. In the note I'd left Penny's phone number and told Robin to use it if I didn't call in by nine tonight. I passed the Cal State LA campus and kept reminding myself that Joe Tomassi and I had developed a good rapport. Breathe slowly, I told myself, as Lionheart raced with my heartbeat. Get a grip. Butch out.

That Joe's National Socialist Liberation Front had bombed the Socialist Workers Party when both groups had the word "Socialist" in their names was one of those ironic leftovers from Hitler's brilliant propaganda ploy, when he'd changed the name of his German Workers Party to the National Socialist German Workers Party. Playing on the popularity of the word and concept of socialism in Germany in the 1920s, Hitler had created a confusion of his group's identity with the identity of the largest political party in his country, the German Social Democrat Party. By putting the word "National" in front of the word "Socialist," he could claim he championed equality for everyone who had German blood.

Sure enough, Joe's henchman had found me parked in a tree-covered empty corner of the Sears and Roebuck lot in El Monte. The teen-aged blond had blindfolded me, stuffed me into the back seat of his car, and handcuffed me!

I'd asked the burly youngster, "Are the cuffs really necessary?"

He'd answered with a thick, dumb sneer, under which I detected an eastern European accent. "How does it feel to be someone's prisoner, Miss Press?"

"That's Ms. Press to you!" I'd retorted.

The steel handcuffs cut into my wrists, and I worried that soon I wouldn't feel my fingertips. The cheap vinyl car seat was sticking to my jeans. No way to begin a new friendship, I thought, as I tried to keep from falling over as we rounded corners. Nauseous with car-sickness, I wondered where the bravado was I'd shown Penny last week.

The air was scented with diesel fuel and deep-fried tortillas, the smell of El Monte, a semi-industrial, Chicano barrio ten miles east of downtown L.A. I tried to distract myself with thoughts about my personal life: the half-life I led with Rachel, and the lack of definition I maintained with BeJo. I was still in shock over having whispered "love" to Rachel and still in dread about reading her letter. I'd buried it in the last drawer of my desk and quickly gone into a state of denial. I hadn't been able to pick up the phone or answer her calls for days. Yet we'd run into each other at the last protesters' meeting and the minute the last striker had walked out of Effie Street we were underneath her bed quilt of many colors. Neither of us wanted to even mention the strike against GCSC, the tension of which had increased as our side had doubled the length and strength of the picket line outside. As I'd feared, renaming our boycott and calling it an official "strike" had given June's camp more leverage to be tougher. They'd begun actually turning people away, not letting even clients in need cross the picket line. But so far, no one had crossed the line into violence. That was *the* line I was watching.

My Marxist training had taught me that violence was one of the characteristics that defined the border between how one treated "the misguided opposition" and how one treated "the enemy." The former were people in the struggle on your own side who were simply misguided. The enemy was people who were truly on the opposite side—whose politics was in principle unacceptable. Captain Joe Tomassi and I would never be on the same side. People like Tomassi were the enemy, fundamentally opposed to our beliefs. The misguided opposition was GCSC, or any of the constantly squabbling gay, lesbian, and feminist groups who sliced and diced ideological purity with each other. All of us were still members of the same tribe. Someday, I knew, gay men would realize that feminists were their sisters, that gay men suffered "homophobia" because it was also rooted, like hatred of women, in a sexist society. And on that day the Center would include the word "lesbian" and finally become the Gay and Lesbian Community Services Center. That day would come, I felt sure, as long as none of us crossed the line into violence.

The vehicle came to a stop and the front passenger door opened. The car rocked as though someone had gotten in. But nothing was said between the two people in the front seat. As we started up, I sniffed the air again, smelling cologne. I suspected the new passenger was Tomassi himself, but I stayed cool and said nothing. We had already begun to play cat and mouse. It was a game I could play well.

I clamped my teeth together, hoping I wouldn't throw up before the game started face-to-face. Besides, I reflected, bouncing helplessly, Joe could kill me. If he could throw a pipe bomb into an occupied building, disposing of me would not ruin his day. But right now, I comforted myself, I was worth more to him alive than dead, since I was writing about his ego-driven deeds. Nevertheless, I couldn't wimp out; the ante in this game was nerve. I'd already decided to save my bottom line question—"So Joe, what have you got against Jews?" for last.

The car halted and the driver killed the engine. "Don't get out," he snarled.

The passenger door opened and the cologne left the car. I could smell that we were still in the San Gabriel Valley, since the atmosphere had a similar ratio of smog to oxygen as when I'd gotten in the car. I waited patiently, assuming that my driver had a plan for how he was going to get me out of the car without calling attention to the fact that I was a blindfolded, handcuffed woman. *Be alert*, I told myself. My chance to memorize his license plate was coming soon.

The front door opened, then the back door. The driver slid in next to me, shutting the door quickly. He skillfully unlocked my cuffs and removed them, then my blindfold.

"We're going to get out now," he said, trying to sound commanding. I could hear the teenage tenor in his voice. "I'm going to take your arm and we're going walk calmly into a nearby diner like we was boyfriend and girlfriend."

"Whatever you want, honey," I said.

As we got out he turned to retrieve my tape recorder and notebook. I calmly memorized his license plate: TP573, California.

We sauntered across a nearly deserted parking lot and through the back door of an anonymous looking, rundown structure. I couldn't read any signage on the front of the building. Once inside I surmised we were in a dingy diner whose popular day had come and gone with the Third Reich. The place was empty except for a couple of old men at a table near the front.

The driver stuffed me into a tacky green Naugahyde booth immediately inside the back door. He stood awkwardly beside the booth, guarding me as if I weren't here of my own free will.

A waitress with tired blond streaks came to the booth. "Whadya have?" She stared at my driver asking, "Are ya comin' or goin'?"

"We'll have two Cokes," a deep voice answered from behind me. The waitress left and a solid figure with a linebacker-size chest swung into my booth. "I'm Joseph Tomassi," he boomed and stuck out his hand, "Capitan of the National Socialist Liberation Front."

"I'm Córdova," I replied hurriedly, forgetting to lower my voice to mimic the authority in his.

"I could see that," Tomassi said, as he pulled a piece of newsprint out of his fatigue jacket pocket. He laid my *Freep* column with its photo on the table between us. "You're cuter than your picture," he decided. "But too young."

"I'm older than I look," I retorted, flustered. Meeting Joe had made me lose the offense. "Older than you are!"

Despite a heavy black mustache, Tomassi had a baby-smooth face set in a warm brown complexion. He looked Latino with a fairly recent Native American ancestor to whom he could credit high, wide cheekbones. With his shoulder-length hair, black with almost feminine curly locks, and rough unkempt side-burns that came almost to his chin, he looked more like a Samurai than a Nazi. A most improbable Aryan.

"I'm twenty-five," Joe almost shouted.

"You don't look anything like I thought you might," I said, keeping the tone of my voice high and friendly like a chatty-Cathy feature reporter.

"Yeah?" Joe grunted, warily. "Whadya 'xpect?"

"Older," I said. "More..." I paused, cautiously noting his set of coarse, dark eyebrows knitted tightly together over cold, glassy eyes. Bomber eyes, I thought. Keep this boy smiling.

"You mean I don't look like him?" Joe pouted like a boy.

"Oh no. I mean, yes. You do! With the mustache and black hair and all. But...you must be some kind of prodigy to be so young and a captain and all."

My compliment soothed Joe. "You're right. I joined the American Nazi Party when I was fourteen."

I waited, hoping he would continue on his own. I prodded. "Tell me about your family, Joe. Where did you grow up?"

"We're here to talk about my politics," Joe exploded, banging his fist on the table. "I'm not gonna talk to you about my mom or dad so that can write up some kind of psychoanalyze that I'm a Nazi because my father and I hate each other."

"Do you?" I persisted.

Tomassi hunched forward. "Don't mess with me, Córdova." His cold eyes narrowed.

I wondered if Joe glared to hide his vulnerability, like I did sometimes.

He snarled, "My dad was in the Army and I was proud of him and that's all I'm going to tell you. So get off it!"

Hmmm, I pondered. Going parental wasn't a good idea. Most criminals didn't care for Mom or Dad.

"We have to talk about some kind of background, Joe. People will want to know where you came from, what you wanted to be when you grew up, that sort of thing."

Joe had withdrawn. His stiff shoulders saluted the back of the booth bench, as though he was deciding if our interview was over before it began. Finally he exhaled, "I wanted to be a cop."

"Are some of your members cops?"

"Most are from the Klan or the Minutemen. But yeah, some are LAPD."

"Did you enter the police academy?"

"No," Joe said. "By the time I matured into high school, I knew I wanted to bring down the government. And I saw that the cops are the political soldiers of the government. So I knew I couldn't become a cop. Instead I joined The National Socialist Party."

"The American Nazi Party?"

"I was the head of the El Monte Chapter by the time I was twenty."

"So you've had this ideology since you were a teenager?"

"Had what?"

"A Nazi point of view…about the world?"

"Damn right," Joe answered. He snapped his fingers for the waitress who appeared quickly and refilled his soda glass.

"Just so I'm sure to get the record perfectly clear, Joe, exactly who do you see as your enemy?"

"The Jew capitalist U.S. government!" Joe banged the table again. "Assimilation of the darkies into the white race will lead to nothing less than global cultural regression, the Dark Ages revisited." His jaw muscles rippled.

"So why aren't you still with the Nazi Party? Why did you break away from them and form your own splinter group, this National Socialist Liberation Front?"

"The party ousted me. They were paranoid that I had too much control," Tomassi recounted. "I found out the Party was playing ball with the U.S. government. They were collaborators. Taking money from Nixon's people to disrupt the Independent Party's presidential campaign. That just ain't right. They think their job is to hand out literature and educate white people to take their power back. They don't realize that the masses of whites won't rally around a wimp-assed educational program. White people can no longer even recognize our enemy. They've been blinded into apathy. They no longer have the guts. So groups like mine have to wake our brothers up by force, and train them how to use violence against our enemies. People are going to be hearing about my army."

Good. I'd obviously gotten Joe on his favorite topic—violence. "Is that why you tear-gassed the support rally to reopen the Rosenberg trial?"

"Where's my Fifth Amendment?" Tomassi toyed with me.

"You blew it off when you asked me to interview you," I snapped.

"Okay, I won't deny it." Joe laughed, his massive chest heaving.

"And did you also pipe bomb the Santa Monica headquarters of the Socialist Workers Party?" I pressed.

"They were both successful missions," Joe confirmed. "We been goin' out to the desert to practice on trees and things, but dealing with crowds is different. I can't expect my men to be perfect without live practice. We need hands-on experience."

I studied Joe. "People could have been killed in the SWP building or in a stampede during the tear gassing..."

"Just Jews or Trots," Joe snorted. "They ain't people."

My breath caught. I slumped in my seat. I was running into violence, or the threat of it, on almost a daily basis being a radical activist and reporter for the Left, struggling with "the question of armed struggle," as we called it. One day someone on my side would ask me to prove my loyalty with a gun. I had to know—before that moment occurred—what would I do? My personal problem with violence was that it didn't stay political. Political principles got lost when you killed somebody's family or friend, or even a bystander who happened to be in the wrong place at the wrong time. Perhaps I was capable of bombing a political target, but could I ever point a gun and shoot someone, even if they were clearly "the enemy"? Shit, I couldn't even feel good about violence against Morris on a picket line.

"I got a garage full of guns," Joe offered. "In case you were gonna ask." He leaned toward me, looking to the left and right, and whispered low to me, "Nazis see the human race divided into different breeds. Man is part of the animal world, not above it. He has to perform within nature's laws. The Chihuahua is different from the German Shepherd. They are not equal; each breed has its own role." Joe's features seemed to come together and formed a volcanic crater. Gone was his lost-boy affect. In this moment I saw that hatred formed the core of Joe Tomassi. Here was the mean in him. He hated everyone who wasn't on his side—Jews, blacks, gays and Catholics were just at the head of his list.

In a moment of recognition, I realized that hatred for one person or hatred for all of humanity must be made of the same essence. Then came the disturbing thought—maybe my motivations and Tomassi's were similar. I hated my father. Hated him for twenty-six years of humiliating me for who I was. And on top of my anger toward him, I'd also accumulated a rage at the heterosexual world for its humiliations of my people. Was my hate somehow the same as Tomassi's? Was that why I was able to recognize it? I shivered in the booth's summer heat. Joe was studying me, his eyes fixed on mine. Perhaps rage was always a cornerstone of activism.

What I really wanted to ask Joe was what made him go to war against the world. I knew he would balk at this personal question, but it was also one I asked myself. I was sure that the political wars of my life were good ones. I was on the side of human rights, the right side. But I knew I had little understanding of my internal war between BeJo and Rachel, safety versus sexual attraction, or the subcutaneous war between my father and me. In these wars, I wasn't sure who I was fighting or why.

Trying to move out of my own confusion, I asked, "How many men have you got in your Nazi Liberation Front?"

"Enough," Joe hedged. "And they're all young guys, ready for action."

"Can we expect more bombings?"

Joe threw his arms up and laughed. "Do you want an invitation to the next one?"

I twirled the flat Coke at the bottom of my glass and decided to call Joe's bluff. "Why not? Since I'm now your favorite reporter. Yes, I would like to be on the scene."

My dare excited Joe. He leaned forward, bringing his face close to mine. "We're looking into that Commie center, The Midnight Special Bookstore," he whispered.

I pulled away from Joe, shocked to hear the name of the well-known activist bookstore in Santa Monica. Like Sisterhood Bookstore was for feminists, it was a haven for Leftists.

Then he stopped and leaned back away from me. "Let's slow down and see what you write about me first." Joe waved again for the hapless waitress.

"Do you want to order German chocolate cake with me? I love German chocolate," he added.

I broke bread with Joe, wondering if he knew there was nothing German about the cake in front of us. Between bites, my Nazi detailed his goals. He told me he thought whites were an "occupied people." He and his kind would build an international coalition which would act as the leadership for all of Aryan Nation in America. At the coalition's core would be a leadership organization composed of his NSLF, which would meet and plan political strategy. "We have workshops on weaponry and how to use explosives," he explained. "The anti-war movement has taught the Establishment what can happen when the masses get their shit together. Now the government is aware that the possibility of revolution exists. Only what we have in mind is white-power instead of this power to the people crap."

I noted on my pad the parallel of how both the far right and the far left had come to the same conclusion, that violence was the only effective means of forcing political change. The goals of the two were opposite, but the strategies similar.

The strategy, according to Joe's gospel, would be "to incite blacks to riot in the streets." This would get white people riled up enough to put down the blacks. "The whites will say, far out!" he explained. In the confusion, National Socialists will move in and take control of the government. Law enforcement people from federal to local would turn his way once they saw that his Nazi army wanted to preserve the domination of the white race.

In his diatribe I recognized our own FBI's strategy of using white people's fear of anything black or brown, even Martin Luther King's peaceful NAACP, as unspoken permission for the government to kill minority activists like the Black Panthers. But Joe's thinking that all whites would approve a fascist take over of their government struck me as farfetched as the SLA's philosophy that all workers in America would side with them in an inevitable socialist revolution.

"Leaders of revolutions get killed," I said to Joe, pausing to let my words soak in.

His mouth fell open and he stared at me as if I'd just taken away a toy. A wrinkle of little boy vulnerability moved almost imperceptibly across his forehead. Then the glassy-eyed look brought the curtain down over whatever humanity Joe had left. Abruptly he slid out of our booth and stood up. "I don't think I'll see my thirtieth birthday," he said, staring down at me.

I reached out, alarmed that he was leaving. I had more questions. "What about a second interview? We just scratched the surface today."

Joe reached into his pocket and tossed a bunch of dollars on the table. That's when I saw the pistol in his belt, a square-handled gun that looked like a German Luger. I could swear I almost heard his heels click together.

"I'll call you when I can," he said. "Just remember, the future belongs to us who are prepared to suffer the consequences of disrupting the silence of darkness."

Later that night, I awakened from sleep bathed in sweat, frightened by the remnants of a dream. Trucks on a freeway were chasing me down a long narrow exit ramp. Nazis were taking over the Hollywood gay community.

Throwing back the covers over BeJo's sleeping form, I saw the clock: five a.m. I searched the darkness for something to take my mind off the truck terror, and then I remembered Rachel's letter. There had to be some sweetness there.

Tiptoeing out of the bedroom, I entered *The Tide's* office, closed the door behind me tightly and turned on the light.

Earlier BeJo had made me a big dinner and we'd talked all evening. I'd had no privacy in which to read the letter. Over the meal BeJo had had told me that Pody had called her.

"I think she likes me." BeJo had smiled, her chestnut eyes blinking coyly.

I'd winced, deciding not to tell her that I'd given Pody permission.

BeJo had also asked me, "Are you getting serious with this woman, Rachel?"

"No," I'd answered. "I may be seeing someone else too." The sentence had fallen out of my mouth, appropriate to nothing and no one.

"Good, I don't like it when you focus on just one woman. Besides me, that is. I worry things might change."

I tried to correct my lie. "I've decided that this woman, as you call her, *is* going to be my next. Nothing to worry about," I'd concluded, "Just another affair."

There it was—slippage over a fine meal of meatloaf and potatoes.

"Then stop sneaking into the house at midnight like you did last week," she continued.

I picked up the salt and shook it vehemently. "You think

Pody's cute, don't you?" I tried to sound casual. "Did she ask you out?"

"She's not bad." BeJo also tried to sound casual. "A little silly, but cute."

"She's been hinting around, trying to ask me if you were non-monogamous too."

"Why wouldn't I be, if you are?" BeJo pounded the table with the pronged end of her fork.

"So, I told her you slept with any butch that asked."

"You what?" BeJo swatted me hard with a kitchen towel "Tell me you didn't say that!" she menaced.

I ducked further blows. "Of course I didn't say that."

We'd both fallen asleep a few hours later, but now, in the early hours of a new day, I was awake and alone. Opening the drawer I had stuffed the letter in, I brought the folded yellow sheets under my desk lamp and read,

Jeanne, after each time we see each other i can only think of you with delight and joy. i walk around my house, around the streets, in the hills, thinking of you. i find it is absurd for me to try to do anything else. my mind is one track...

but in today's dawn, i am filled with many mixed feelings, remembering the joy and pleasure i felt with you and inside myself when we made love...my thoughts and feelings are as scrambled as the eggs I would like to be making for you right now...the caution and withdrawal that is inside me...the wanting to protect myself and knowing that in some ways it is too late. i already have let the feelings i have for you "out." my agenda had been to not care about anyone beyond a certain point. lying with you in bed last night, i realized that i have crossed over that point. i guess all that i am saying is that it is scary to me now, jeanne. i see that fear on your face too.

i want you to know: i like you, love the feel of you, think you have a beautiful smile, love looking into your eyes, care about you and your feelings a great deal, and...i love you.

i want to hurry and wake you...but i will wait.

Rachel

Whoa! I dropped the pages on the black lacquered desktop. So much in a short paragraph that stepped over so many lines. My chest felt suddenly expanded. She liked me as well as loved me! And yet…I pushed back away from the desk. Wasn't this too much, too soon? And Rachel also sounded more afraid of love than I was. I had assumed I was the wingnut in our relationship and she was my rock. But this letter wasn't written by a rock person.

Rachel seemed afraid of being involved and involved with me in particular. I was sure the lesbian grapevine had informed her of my past, so perhaps she was afraid of being just another in a long line of Córdova's ex-girlfriends. This I could understand, and could prove to her otherwise. Yet the other fear she was talking about seemed to be a deeper caution that was her own. "My agenda had been to not care about anyone beyond a certain point." That sounded like a decision rendered before we'd ever met. When? Why? And over who? Rachel had never talked to me about such a "certain point."

I slumped in my chair, conflicted between confusion and joy. The woman said she loved me. But, Christ, did I want that? Lust was one thing, love was another.

I heard sounds from the bedroom. Quickly I tossed the letter into my briefcase.

BeJo's head poked through the door, "Good morning, honey, want to go out to breakfast?" she said.

I turned my back to her afraid she'd see the ambivalence written all over my face. "Sure," I called to her, "that sounds like a good idea."

Chapter 18

The Picket Line

[Los Angeles]

June 10, 1975

It took me a week to get Tomassi's story out of my insides and into an article. Penny had bumped it up to a cover story, my first! I'd paid the price internally, but was now excited about seeing Joe's evil deeds, and my byline, splashed all over the front page of next week's paper. Working late that night at *The Freep*, I ended up passing out on the cot I kept stashed along the wall in my office.

My ringing private line woke me. Falling out of the cot, I stumbled to my desk, and managed a disoriented, "Hello?"

"Is that you, Jeanne?" The intimate tenor of Rachel's voice soothed me. "I thought you would be long gone from the office by now."

"No, I'm still here."

"I guess I need to schedule myself in as a story," she said. "Did you forget it was Friday night? We have a date...I mean... we were supposed to see each other."

"Of course I didn't forget." I tried to remember what day it was. "It's still early...isn't it?" I rubbed my eyes, looking around for my watch.

"It's ten pm," Rachel said.

"Really?"

"Do you still want to see me?" I heard the doubt in her voice.

"Of course." The thought of crawling into Rachel's bed and holding her felt reassuring. I paused, not sure I wanted to describe, or re-feel, my time with Tomassi.

"Is something wrong?" Rachel asked.

"I've had a tough week," I said, my voice dropping low. "I saw good and evil staring me in the face. Only the good guys lost and the bad guys won."

"What are you talking about?"

"I just finished writing about a Nazi who wants to kill everyone who's not white, and he's still walking around free. But this afternoon, I listened to a judge sentence Z Budapest to jail and forbid her from ever reading the Tarot again. The LAPD is trying to criminalize goddess-worship, yet it can't put a Nazi behind bars. Where's the justice in this country?" My words fell out in a small, tired voice. I was hunched over, my chin resting on my desk. "I'm so tired of fighting the pigs, Rachel, and seeing our side lose. I just want to sleep for days," I whispered hoarsely.

"I heard about the Z trial. I'm sorry we lost that one, babe."

"The good guys are supposed to win in the end."

"You need to get out of that office." Rachel's voice was firm. "Come over here right now."

I wiped my eyes with my shirttails. "Okay, I'm coming."

I opened Rachel's kitchen door without knocking. Her apartment felt like the only safe space in my universe. She hugged and kissed me before I collapsed onto her yellow padded chrome chair.

"We don't need to talk politics," she said, scrambling eggs

at the stove.

"Good," I mumbled.

"Besides, I've been wanting to ask you something about our relationship." Rachel brought plates and took the chair beside me. She reached over and brushed the hair out of my face.

"Our relationship?" I mumbled, concentrating on getting my fork to bring the eggs to my mouth. I was so tired, I couldn't see straight.

"There's something I don't understand."

I watched Rachel's mouth move. I loved watching her lips when she spoke. They were fine, thinly shaped, ribbons of seduction.

"Jeanne" She jostled my arm. "Are you listening?"

"Sure." I leaned back against the kitchen wall. I could stay awake if I just rested there a bit. "Go on, sweetheart."

"What I don't understand about our relationship, Jeanne, is that when you're with me, you are usually totally with me." Rachel's voice slowed as if she were aiming for precision. "And I love that. But when we're not together I feel like there is no connection between us. Like, I don't exist for you. You haven't responded to my letter. You are on my mind all the time. But I don't know that I am on your mind at all. That you even think of me."

Think of me, think of me. The words bounced in a row through my mind like sheep jumping a fence. How peaceful life would be if I only saw Rachel's lovely face in front of me. Such a sweet thought I remember thinking as my eyes closed.

A loud knock woke me up. I sat up in Rachel's bed, the morning sun daring my eyes to open. Rachel must have put us to bed last night. Now she threw on a robe and scurried out of the bedroom.

I heard another voice. Then, Rachel gasped, "Oh no!"

I put on a bathrobe and boxers I'd taken to leaving at Rachel's and made my way to the kitchen. Delene, a friend of

Rachel's and still an employee at GCSC—one of our several moles there—sat on my yellow chair, huddled in tears with her head on Rachel's shoulder. The soft-spoken butch lived in the fourth bungalow a few doors down.

She looked up, startled to see me; her gaze drifted behind me toward the bedroom, and then returned to me.

"Oh. Hi, Córdova," she said, her tone flat as a piece of lumber.

"What's going on?" I asked the two of them.

"Delene just came to tell me...us...that GCSC is going to file an injunction and a restraining order. They want to stop the picket line in front of the Center."

"Fuck," I said, leaning against the kitchen's doorjamb. Delene didn't seem to want me interrupting her moment with Rachel.

"Can they do that?" Rachel asked me.

"They aim to try," said Delene. "This morning I overheard Ken Bartley and Don Kilhefner talking about going downtown to the courthouse."

"That surprises me," I said to Delene. "Kilhefner is supposedly sick and on leave."

"I'm sure it was him," Delene answered without looking at me. Seeing me in a bathrobe seemed to bother her.

Rachel looked up at me. "Can we do anything, Jeanne?"

I moved to Rachel's side. "Have you told anyone else on the Strike Steering Committee?" I asked Delene, using the protestors' now more formal name.

"No, I came here first."

"Then I need to make some phone calls now," I said.

Rachel clasped my hand tightly, even as she held Delene with her other hand. "Don't leave," she whispered in my ear. "We need more time together."

"I won't. I'll make the calls using your phone." I smiled at her before going to the living room.

As I left I overheard Delene crying, "I'm so scared they're going to fire me next for being friends with you."

Thirty minutes later I hung up on my last call. I'd spoken to our lawyer, Sylvia Patton, and the other strike leaders, June included. We had all agreed—GCSC was not going to get away with stopping the picket line. We had agreed to call everyone in the community and meet in front of the Center in two hours. We'd show them a picket line longer and louder than it had ever been!

I was about to reenter the kitchen when I heard Delene's voice whispering to Rachel. "Just be careful. You seem to be getting in pretty deep with Córdova. She's never with one woman for very long."

My feet stopped.

I heard Rachel answer, "It's too late, Delene. I'm already in love with her."

I grinned from ear to ear. So just trot yourself home, Delene.

She continued to Rachel. "Others think you might be too influenced by her politically, but I don't care about the politics. I just don't want you to be left with your heart on your sleeve."

"Don't worry about me," Rachel answered. "I know what I'm doing, and I'm proud to be with her, especially politically. The others can keep their opinions to themselves."

I heard chairs move, but decided not to go in and say good-bye to Delene. The door opened and closed. Seconds later, Rachel rushed into the living room and jumped into my arms.

"I'm so glad you're staying," she said.

I kissed her long and deep. "Have I told you that you make me very happy?" I bit her softly on the ear.

"Come back to bed with me."

"We can't yet," I said, sad about the loss of an afternoon in bed with Rachel. "I just called half the town and they're calling the other half. We've marshaled a double-down session this afternoon on the line to show our defiance. You and I have to be there."

As Lionheart pulled to the Highland Avenue curb, Rachel and I saw the picket line already in full swing. The circle was packed much tighter than usual. Women, and more men than I'd ever seen on the line, were bumping into each other. I counted almost fifty bodies. Smelling the sweat of acrid anger, I heard the chanting, "What do we want? Close it down! When do we want it? Now!" An Afro-headed lesbian in denim and work boots hoisted a fresh red painted placard. "Say NO to the Gay Community Scabbing Center," it read. A long-haired hippie fag dressed in a flowing gauzy skirt was on top of the news and mood of the day. His sign shouted, "No Injunction Will Stop Us!" Among the men, I saw a number in black T-shirts and figured they must be from Michael Weinstein's group. Weinstein, a fiery, quick-talking, ex-New Yorker in his twenties was the head of a new gay socialist organization. He and a few of his radical sidekicks from the Lavender and Red Union had recently come to support us. The strike was becoming a national cause célèbre among gay socialists in the country. It was the gay movement's first labor confrontation. And, goddess help us, the last, I swore under my breath.

I was relieved to also see radical dykes from the Westside Women's Center, bringing plenty of additional women's bodies. Their bell-bottom jeans, beaded earrings and necklaces, and Birkenstock sandals, were easy to spot. I greeted the leadership of the Westside Center. Their presence felt heartening to me. I let go of Rachel's hand and lock-stepped into the circle, and raised my fist in time with the chants.

Suddenly, an elderly gay man opened the front door of GCSC and poked his head out. He stared at us for a long while, his expression confused and befuddled, as if to say, "What does this mean?"

A *Tide* staffer, a socialist feminist who worked with BeJo in circulation, responded by walking up to him and sticking her banner "Sexist Board Has Got To Go" in his face. I broke out in an anxious sweat. If the courts shut the picket line down, where would all this rage go? And if GCSC closed down, where would people like this elderly gay man go?

Two hours passed under the flat summer sun. The sizzle from the sidewalk made its way up through our boots and sandals as if trying to further fuel the line's rage. Suddenly the mood picked up. I heard chatter, felt ripples of anxiety. Morris Kight was approaching the building from the south end parking lot. *Shit!* The picket line had finally caught the Chairman of the Board, between us and his own front door.

As he came toward us wearing his usual baggy slacks and thrift store shirt, silver hair pasted to his forehead, I had a moment of dissonance. I felt as though I didn't know this man. Yet it had always been Morris and me concocting civil disobedience, staging demonstrations on the steps of the Park Center headquarters. It was Morris and me attending each other's birthday parties, which always turned into movement fundraisers. *Christ!* I knew the names of each tree in his McCadden Place memorial garden, each named after an historical figure like Oscar or Eleanor.{1} Somewhere and somehow Morris's politics had changed and somehow I had missed it. The founder of L.A.'s Gay Liberation Front—named in solidarity with the Vietnamese National Liberation Front—had left his radical roots. He'd sold out, left the ranks of the oppressed and evolved into a bureaucrat, an Establishment social worker, ever-hungry and willing to compromise for the next government grant.

"Hey chief scab," a picketer called out. "How was your lunch? I hope you choked on it."

But wait…the jeering seemed to be directed not at Kight, but at a woman with him. Tall and lean, she froze in her walk at the jeer "chief scab." The woman, I knew, was named Lillene Fifield and she'd just last week been appointed Director of Women's Programs. The new title and position at GCSC made her the top woman employee, hence to us strikers, "chief scab." Fifield was the only lesbian to accept a job at GCSC since the firings. Therefore, she'd become the focal point of lesbian disgust. Still, I was shocked at the vitriol aimed at her. A sour feeling crept into my throat. As the tall, long-faced woman tried to sort through the line, picketers deliberately blocked her path. In the blink of an eye the circle opened to swallow her. She kept a stone face, never saying a word. Engulfed, she was jostled and pushed. Finally, she got close enough to reach out and grab the handle on the front door. Ms. Chief Scab was absorbed into the building.

I wiped my forehead, relieved that I had been on the north end of the circle and not close to the rage surrounding her. I had no personal gripe with Fifield, but the woman had knowingly put herself in the line of fire. Still, sister against sister violence was hard to swallow even from a distance.

My attention turned to Morris. What would he say or do to get through the line? And what could I do to help—or stop— him? Did I want to help, or stop him?

My godfather was trying to negotiate through a clump of male picketers. *Do something*, a child voice called inside me. That's when Morris caught my eye. He tilted his head quizzically, studying me as if I were as out of place as a polar bear on a beach. It was the first time he and I had come face to face on the picket line. He opened his mouth as if speak to me. But his eyes shifted suddenly and fixated on something behind me. He gasped, as if witnessing a horror. His normally pinched-pink face went white. A turquoise-studded hand shot up to cover his mouth.

I turned around.

A male picketer behind me had a sign pointing dead center on Morris. He came closer, his voice raging, trumpeting the words on his placard, "Down with the KKK: Kight, Kilhefner, Ken!"

Fuck! I gulped. Turning back, I faced my mentor. The man had marched in the South with Martin Luther King against the Ku Klux Klan. Rosa Parks had been his friend, his "saint liberator." An expression of horror had settled on his face. He shuddered and stumbled against the center's wall. I fought down an adrenalin-fueled impulse to rush to him. My heart wanted to save him, but politics glued my feet to the ground. *You're the man*, I wanted to scream at him. *You're the only one who can stop this travesty. Do something!*

But the sun's hot glare glazed out the distance preventing Morris and me from connecting again. GCSC's door suddenly opened from the inside. Someone reached out and grabbed him. My erstwhile friend disappeared into the forbidden zone. I kicked a picket stick out of my path. *Damnation!* It wasn't my job to save Morris Kight. He'd kicked me out of his house, just like my father had seven years ago.

Memory tugged me back to another hotly glaring summer afternoon when I was nineteen and had taken my lover Judy home to a party at my parents' house. The family seat was now in San Marino, the Beverly Hills of the San Gabriel Valley, a well-lawned enclave that was haughty about everyone who wasn't rich and white, except my Mexican father, now a multi-millionaire, and a few dozen wealthy Chinese families. Judy, a petite working class dyke from my gay softball team, wore Frank Sinatra black wing-tipped shoes and combed her brown-gold hair straight back in a ducktail. With her '50s hairstyle, blue eyes and classic features, she looked like a butch version of James Dean in *Rebel Without a Cause*. Back in '68 I was a newbie to lesbian bar culture and had not yet learned that the whole world was divided into butch and femme. I was neither, and simply attracted to Judy's kind welcome of me as "the new college kid" on the team. We both played infield and had simply dropped into bed. Judy had introduced me to the men's department at Sears just a few weeks before and now we bought all our clothes there. It's not like I was asking Dad to accept a pot smoker into his house or a bad-mouthing anti-war Democrat. No, I was just coming home for dinner. And yes, it had somehow escaped me that Judy's very butch attire would leave no room for parental denial.

As we walked through the large, carved wood front door of the family mansion no one stopped us. Dad was upstairs, I was told, hiding as he tried to avoid the crowd and to ponder how he, a private intense guy who hated noise, had fathered twelve children.

I could feel my mother's blue eyes following Judy as we partied with my siblings on the backyard veranda. Watching her troubled eyes was my first clue that the day would not end well. *You've never brought someone who **looks** like a homosexual to our home, Jeanne,* she seemed to be telling me. I didn't think Mom would know what a butch looked like since she was still calling me a tomboy. Fortunately, Mom was too gracious to be impolite to any guest. I'd hear about it later, her eyes told me. Older brother Bill gave Judy more than one sideways glance, but my younger sibs crowded around me oblivious of my unusual friend.

Somehow fate placed me in the house next to the telephone in the downstairs foyer the very single moment that Dad chose to descend the spiral staircase above the phone box. Judy needed to make a phone call. I had walked her to the phone. I could feel him coming before I saw him. The hairs on my back of my neck were jumping to attention before I heard his polished black dress shoes hit the top stair. Paralyzed with fear, my first instinct was to run. Dad couldn't meet Judy and me alone like this— separated from the protection of my mother and siblings! But fleeing was too humiliating. I was a grownup now, paying my own way through college. I ground my teeth like a trapped bear cub. Now he was close enough to see Judy perched on the embroidered chair next to his serpentine marble telephone stand.

"Hi, Pop!" I feigned as he hit the bottom stair.

He came toward me, staring at Judy like she had the word *atheist* tattooed on her forehead. The wrinkles on his forehead seemed to bulge out instead of in. Something was wrong. He was standing too close.

"What's this?" His voice was tight and dry as he pointed to Judy.

A thumping began in my chest. He couldn't talk that way to a friend of mine. "This-is-my-friend-Judy-Whiting," I said all in one syllable. "Judy, this is my father."

Judy stood to greet him.

Dad studied Judy: saw the shoes, the cowboy silver buckle on her belt, her Sears men's pants and button-down seersucker plaid shirt. He turned to me. "What the hell is she doing in my house?" he screamed.

"We just…ah…Mom said come home for the party…we won't be staying very long—"

His hands were on Judy before I could finish the sentence. He'd grabbed her by the back of her belt with one hand and dragged her through the foyer like a garbage bag, flung open the front door and tossed Judy's size two frame onto the front grass. Though the open door I saw Judy's knees crack the ground; she rolled over trying to break the Dad's velocity. Then he turned to me.

"Don't you *ever* even think of bringing someone like that home to my house again!" he screamed at me.

I raced through his damn front door toward Judy, turning mid-step to scream at him, "And that means I won't be coming home ever again either!"

Dad slammed the door in my face, disappearing into his own forbidden zone, a zone I hadn't returned to since.

"Fuck them both," I said out loud, still marching in the picket line.

"Fuck who?" Rachel had dropped out of the circle and come to my side.

"Morris Kight and my father," I shouted over the din. "Let's get out of this place."

The next day I asked Rachel to come to my work to have lunch. I felt closer to her now and I wanted to show my new lover off to my *Freep* mates. Walking her back out to her car after sandwiches at my desk, we strutted hand-in-hand down the middle aisle of the production department. Despite the *Freep*'s progressive politics, it wasn't every day that the office witnessed an open display of the Left's newest radical issue—homosexuality. Rachel didn't care that people stared. I loved that about her. Walking alone, she was feminine and could easily pass as straight. Yet she gripped my hand and lifted her chin defiantly, telling a room full of beaded, bearded lefties, "Here come the dykes!" I was proud she used me as her badge.

Approaching Bryan's reception desk, I felt a sudden shift of energy. A peculiar hush had dampened the twitter directed at strolling dykes. Something felt different, oddly wrong. I stopped, bidding Rachel to halt too, as I studied Bryan through the glass wall and open door. The boy was sitting straight-backed in his chair, his body language rigidly contained. Bryan was never contained. Two men in dark suits with abnormally block-shaped heads and closely shaved flattops stood in front of his desk. Definitely not our readership. Penny's words "men in suits…" rang in my ears.

I crouched down in back of the art boards pulling Rachel with me. For a split second, I wondered if *The Freep* was just having a bomb scare with the LAPD come to warn us. But no, Brian would then be flapping his wrists. "Those men don't belong here," I whispered to Rachel. "Go sit on that stool over there," I pointed to a layout desk. "Pretend you work here. You don't know me."

I spun on my boot heels and raced back upstairs. In my office, I rushed to find my keys and bent over to unlock the last drawer of my desk. I had to dump my rack of cassette tapes.

"Miss Cordova, I assume?" a deep voice threatened.

I straightened up kicking the bottom drawer closed. Pitching my voice toward casual, I asked, "Who wants to know?"

Bryan's dark-suited strangers glared at me. For big guys they'd vaulted the stairs quickly. One of them was a short and broad-shouldered line backer; the other was an enormous giant.

"We're with the FBI," the extra testosterone came from the lineman. "You interviewed Joseph Tomassi?" he said. But he wasn't asking. The giant held up the front cover of the paper's cover story with Joe's picture—and my byline.

"Oh, right." I smiled, trying to feign some emotion besides fear. *Where was Penny!* "Would you gentlemen like to sit down?"

"We won't be here long enough to sit down," the shorter football player with a choking red tie answered. "And neither will you if you don't give us the tapes of your interview with that Nazi."

I parried for time. "What tapes? There are no tapes."

"Nobody memorizes all that Marxist crap without tapes," Mr. Red Tie barked. "We can arrest you if you don't give them over. He's a fugitive, young lady."

Young lady—made me snap. Nobody called me that gender-fucked appellation except my father. And suddenly I was standing again with Judy at the front door of my father's house, my cheek stinging from his slap. The old, dark pain snapped me out of my fear. The fear, not the punishment, was the thing to conquer, I told myself.

My fear melted. I threw my shoulders back into soldier stance. Time again, to stand or fold.

"We will arrest you!" the giant bullied. "Choose carefully, jail is not pretty especially for you pretty types."

I sat down calmly. I was an investigative reporter. I would not give up a source. Not to Dad and certainly not to the Feds. "Where is your search warrant?" I said, hoping that Penny or Tom were on their way.

"If that's the way you want to play it, we'll get one," the shorter guy reached forward and picked up the phone on my desk and dialed. He spoke into the receiver, "Then get a judge out of his martini. We need a warrant up here at *The Free Press* now!"

I sat, cornered and cooked.

And suddenly, Penny's high-pitched decibels came screaming into my office. "What is the meaning of this invasion? I'm the Editor in Chief. You can't come in here."

Burly Tom stomped in behind her. "This is a newspaper!" he shouted. "Have you ever heard of the First Amendment?"

The suits turned toward Penny "A search warrant is on its

way," red tie thundered.

Penny didn't pause to catch a breath. "Leave my reporter alone!" She flapped her arms like a mother hen in heat. "Get out," she scolded Hoover's finest. "Get out of here until you have a warrant."

Tom circled in back of the agents, as Penny steered them away from me.

"Come into my office," Penny demanded. "How dare you try to intimidate my reporter!"

Whispering hoarsely, Tom leaned his black-bearded face close to mine, "You need to get the fuck out of here."

Through the glass between our offices, I saw Penny thrust a phone into an agent's hand. "Call my publisher, right now!" I heard my demure Chief scream. "Make a formal request."

Frantically, I unlocked my bottom drawer, grabbed the tape rack, threw my denim jacket over it, and crept down the hall behind Tom's huge blocking frame.

Instinct made me turn toward the never-used back stairwell. It led to nothing but the distribution department's endless stacks of back issues...and a small cargo door that opened to the alley. Tom had to know it too. Distribution staff met me with frightened eyes. Bryan stepped into the alley. Bless Penny who must have briefed him in advance about the only possible escape route.

Bryan handed me keys. "Tom says to take his car. They're watching yours in the front lot. Penny says don't come back until she calls you."

"Thanks Bryan. " I released the cargo door as it snap-locked behind me. Jumping behind the wheel of Thompson's sorry brown Dodge, I stoked the ignition and put it in drive, fleeing east down Hollywood Boulevard into Silverlake.

Protecting a Nazi was not on my flight path as a reason to flee the FBI. Joe would go down soon, my gut told me. In the meantime, I had to defend the freedom of the press. Under our Nixonian government the press was often the only "power to the people" avenue left to us.

Chapter 19

The Falling

[Los Angeles]

Early July, 1975

Our mood was playful as we plopped back into Rachel's bed. We'd awakened early to take a joint shift on the picket line, but she'd lured me into cancelling the day's meetings and coming back to Effie Street on her day off by promising a matinee movie and dinner—like normal lesbians on a weekend. It had taken a few months, but Rachel and I had finally found a consistent groove with intimate time together, although I suspected that she still wanted more.

"I can't believe I'm seeing you in the daytime." Rachel bounced on the bed. "And I have you all to myself!"

I smiled, loving the way her face radiated with happiness. A fleeting thought burned in the back of my mind. It was a Saturday. Rachel didn't know I was supposed to go home to BeJo tonight. I'd resolved to push our afternoon until early evening.

"You're in a lovely mood," I said, leaning back against the

mountains of pillows. "Any particular reason?"

"Can you keep a secret?" Her voice had dropped to a conspiratorial whisper. When I nodded, her eyes twinkled and her mouth puckered, like a cat that had swallowed a canary. "The night before last Pody and I did a guerilla action against GCSC!"

I lit a cigarette. "What kind of action?"

"I was having dinner with Pody at the Saloon," she began. "All she could talk about was BeJo, BeJo, BeJo. Is it true that you gave her permission to date BeJo?"

I saw a twinkle in Rachel's eyes. She was happy BeJo was dating. "Yes, it's true. Except now Pody wants to join The *Tide* Collective. That's pushing things too far since I don't hear any commitment to lesbian journalism from her. But let's not change the subject, what was your surreptitious action?"

"It was Pody's idea." Rachel squirmed on the bed. "She's furious about losing her job and GCSC contesting our unemployment checks. As am I."

"Go on."

"And we started talking about Lillene Fifield. About how the Center is now saying to the community, 'See, we do have women's programming, we even have a new Director of Women's Programs.'"

"And...?"

"It was early. We decided to drive to GCSC. She said she knew what kind of car chief scab drove, and where the higher-ups at the Center parked."

"What in the name of the goddess did you do at GCSC?" I demanded, my voice strained.

"We were angry!" Rachel said. "Maybe we had one too many beers. Lillene deserved it. She's the only lesbian who's crossed the picket line and taken a job. One of our jobs!"

"What did you do, Rachel?"

"We let the air out of some of their tires in GCSC's rear parking lot, the one in back of the building. Pody knew which cars belonged to which people."

"Damn! It's a damn good thing nobody saw you, and —"

"That's not all we did," Rachel interrupted.

I sat up straighter. "There's more?"

"We slashed the tires on Lillene Fifield's car. I stood guard; Pody brought a strong knife…from the Saloon. She stabbed the tires. All four of them."

"Score one for our side!" My right fist shot up, clenched, saluting the incendiary political posters on Rachel's bedroom wall. For a moment I wished I had been with them.

"Then you think it's okay?" Rachel asked. "I wasn't going to tell you. Pody said to keep it secret."

"You damn well better keep it to yourselves," I replied, hearing my tone change. I stabbed out my cigarette and got out of bed. The thrill of excitement had evaporated. I wished Rachel hadn't told me her news.

"We told a few of the other strikers. They want to do more…"

"Christ, Rachel, don't tell me about *others*! You and Pody were damn lucky a cop car didn't spot you. It would look very fucked up in print: *GCSC Strikers Resort to Vandalism*."

"I'm sure no one saw us." Rachel's voice was small.

I started to pace. In my gut, something didn't feel right.

"They can't prove anything if no one saw us." Rachel crinkled herself into a small package on the bed.

I studied her face, afraid for her, and for myself. She certainly was a newbie. Word would soon leak out—there were no secrets in political fights—and people might think that June or I put Rachel and Pody up to this.

I came back to bed and took her hands in mine. "Rachel, promise me that this will be the last time you give in to personal outrage. Personalizing our issues with property violation will take the focus off our valid goals. I thought you understood that."

"Of course." Rachel was huffy.

"Tell Pody I said to cease and desist!"

"I just didn't think about it that. No more guerilla actions."

"None," I said gently, as I left her and started to pace again. "Something about this strike feels out of whack to me. Like the injunction coming so quickly. The Board of Directors always seems to know who is doing what and what we're thinking. It's as if someone tells them what moves we're about to make."

"What are you saying, Jeanne?"

"I'm wondering if there isn't an agent provocateur among the strikers or the unnamed 'supporters' who show up at our meetings. What do we know about them?"

Rachel sat up. "I thought we all knew each other."

"Only by first name. What if there was a government agent sent to GCSC to get himself employed, just like Nixon sent agents into civil rights organizations like the Students for a Democratic Society and Viet Nam Vets against the War? And he, or even she, is provoking the strike? If you look at the strike's potential to destroy the Center, and if I was the FBI wanting to get rid of this radical hotbed of dykes and fags, I might send someone in there to try to implode it from the inside out."

Rachel stared at me in shock.

"What do we really know about each other's backgrounds? There are a lot of people in this fight who I don't recognize from past movement campaigns."

"Like who?" she asked.

"What do you or I know about Pody or June or Dixie? And that Colin McQueen. Have you seen he always carries the same sign on the picket line? Even takes it home with him. The one that says, Shut it down or we'll burn it down.

"Now you're scaring me."

Rachel's timid voice snapped me out of my thought process. I had been mostly talking aloud to myself. Looking at her, I frowned, realizing, perhaps too late, that I was more familiar with the atmosphere of paranoid hostility unleashed by the Viet Nam War and the Civil Rights movements. Every night on the news political fugitives and feminists were being arrested. The FBI had just captured two lesbians on their wanted list, Susan Saxe and Katherine Powers; they were still hunting for the kidnapped newspaper heiress, Patricia Hearst.

I put out my cigarette and lay down beside her. "I don't mean to scare you." I stroked her forehead.

Rachel started laying kisses on my face. "You can provoke my body with very little effort," she murmured. "Does that make you my own personal agent provocateur?"

I lay on top of her and smiled as I fingered her lips. "If I am your special agent, I'm not undercover, and it's no secret. When Delene saw me in my bathrobe that morning she nearly choked. I'm sure she's told everyone by now."

Rachel unbuttoned my shirt and brought her lips to my chest. "My boss at the Saloon also knows about you and me."

"Is that a problem?"

"She doesn't like that her employees talk about the politics of GCSC all day. Or that her staff voted not to serve any of the scabs. She says politics is bad for business."

"So, she doesn't like that I'm politically influencing you…"

"No," she said and she played with my hair. "But the staff not wanting any scabs in the restaurant, that had nothing to do with you."

Having no allies for our relationship felt threatening, but I didn't want to worry Rachel with more problems. Especially not now.

I slid off her long enough to pry open her blouse buttons. "It doesn't matter. We're not having a three-way with Colleen," I joked as I held Rachel's breasts and massaged her nipples. An urgent rush tingled up from my feet to my groin. My mind shut down.

She murmured, "I love you, Jeanne, more than the storybooks speak of love."

I forgot about Nixon, agents, employers, and the movie we were supposed to see. Making love to Rachel felt like reading a book with no last page.

I awoke to the smell of our sweat mixed together, a scent

that made me want her all over again. Turning over in bed to find her, I instead found empty space next to me. The room felt hot and closed. It felt like early evening.

"Rachel?" I called out, suddenly afraid. "Where are you, Rachel?" I called more loudly. A dimly remembered panic seized me. The anxiousness felt old, the vacant space beside me haunting. *The place beside you has always been empty*, a frightened child-voice said inside me.

That's not true, I answered the voice. *Rachel is here. She's probably sitting out on the back porch. Go, look for her.*

She's left you, the scared voice repeated.

"Get a grip, Córdova!" I demanded aloud, my voice filled the room and bounced back to me.

I willed my body to break out of its paralytic state. Sitting up, I found my jeans, put my legs into them and hurried to the back porch stairway. No one. I circled back through the living room and out the kitchen door. The driveway was empty; Rachel's old blue Buick was gone. Coming back into the kitchen, I closed the door behind me. My breath came in fast, shallow gasps.

She's gone! the child voice repeated.

I opened the kitchen door again, inhaling the smell of the grass, the dirt and the trees. I told myself, *Get a Coke from the fridge and go sit outside on Rachel's back porch.* Yes, that's exactly the right thing to do. Watch the last rays of sunset. Lying around in bed had simply disoriented me.

I looked for a glass in Rachel's cabinet. There on the sink. A yellow legal pad with a note from Rachel. I grabbed it.

Hello Jeanne. I went to the store for groceries. Thought I would make dinner for us tonight. See you soon! Love you now! Rachel.

My breathing slowed down. *Told you so*, I chided the panicked voice inside. Rachel was here all along. Standing barefoot in the kitchen, I realized I couldn't leave Rachel, not tonight, no matter what day of the week it was.

I made myself a Coke with ice, and quickly I called BeJo. Thank the goddess for that new invention, the answering machine, and the fact that BeJo was working late this afternoon.

I left a message, telling her I was at Rachel's and not feeling well. I didn't want to make the long drive home to Culver City tonight. I would see her tomorrow.

As I explored Rachel's house, waiting for her to return from shopping, I realized that staying tonight would be the first full day I'd spent with Rachel. First waking up together. Then the picket line. Then coming back home to Effie Street. *Home to Effie Street.* The thought made me happy, although I realized my concept of where home was had shifted from BeJo's to Rachel's in the space of a day. More slippage.

I grabbed a soda and took myself out to the back porch to watch the sunset. As I turned on the hose to water her potted plants, it came to me how much I'd needed a haven in my life and had found it here at Effie Street with her. Yes, I purposefully didn't call or stay connected when I wasn't with her because I didn't want to bring the rest of my life here. My activist life was about fighting for the freedom and dignity of my people, my tribe. Yet, my world with Rachel was about peace and safety, about personally getting filled up. Deep down I feared that if my two worlds came together I might have to choose between them. Looking up, I saw gold and orange-laced cloud strata settling behind the clay roofs. There was no way to integrate my intimacy with Rachel and still keep my life's commitment. And I couldn't abandon either one. It was best to keep my two worlds compartmentalized. Today I'd allowed myself a rare exception. Even I had a right to be an indolent speck on the map of life for one twenty-four hour day.

Another hour passed and Rachel still hadn't returned. The backfire of freeway trucks sounded in the distance. A chill had sprung up. I listened to my breathing. Once more it had become anxious and shallow. Rachel will return any minute, I told myself, buttoning my shirt at its collar. Sometimes I got "the panic" at night when I woke up alone. Somehow I didn't believe I was real unless someone lay beside me verifying my existence.

How long did it take to buy tomatoes and potatoes? I should go and look for her. Yet, I had no idea where the nearest market was. Under my parents' roof, chores had included an endless amount of dish-washing, ironing, and scrubbing the floors, but my mother had never taught us to shop or cook. There was barely enough time in the day for my mother to clothe, feed, and bed so many of us. Certainly there was no time to indulge in the luxury of culinary skill-sharing or bedtime stories or any kind of touchy-feely love.

She distributed her maternal love in between the short supply and high demand for her attention. I rarely saw her in the mornings during the mad scramble for school. To brush my teeth I had to shove my way into the bathroom, stumble over bodies, and throw a sibling or two into the bathtub. We were assured that Mom loved us by looking in our lunch boxes and finding an extra Hostess cupcake.

By high school I'd given up interpreting desserts as Mom's love. But I never gave up waiting every night for her to walk into my bedroom and tuck me in. Lying in bed, I would pull the sheets over my head, curl into a ball, and pray a rosary of the same words. *Just wait a little bit longer. She'll come. Tonight, I'm sure she'll come. Close your eyes and wish for it strong enough.* Once every few months, when the babies in the nursery had fallen asleep early, and no one else had a fever or a broken arm, my mother did come into the bedroom that I shared with my older sister. On those rare nights, she'd sit on the side of our double bed and ask Dominica and me what we'd learned in school. Dominica would spout about undiscovered planets in the solar system and I would tell Mom that I'd hit a homer or pitched a no-hitter. Mom didn't know much about the stars or softball, but on those rare all-alone nights she'd sit with us attentively as though we were the only two children in her universe. My mother was a lady, a woman who wore gloves and hat to church and never made a public display of emotion. But on those rare nights she'd break rank and lean over our bed to kiss us goodnight. Her long black curls would fall on my face as she'd peck our foreheads, admonishing, "Don't cause each other any more trouble tonight. Let's not sleep with your bat, Jeanne. Dominica, give me that book. Now close your eyes nicely my little ones. Let the angels sing in your heads and take you to heaven for the night."

Then, she'd be gone—until next semester or so—and I'd save my stories for the next time she'd return. As we grew older, Dominica and I had learned to tuck each other in at night as we debated why girls could not be Presidents, and whether or not the universe really had large black holes that sucked the life out of everything.

I tilted my Coke back and sucked the last drops dry. Ah Dominica, I whispered to myself, I hope you're doing better at this love thing than I am.

Shadows filtered through the palm fronds on Effie's downward slope. I felt wetness on my face and reached up to brush the tears off my cheeks. The pink and gray streaked marble slab that formed the homework desk in my childhood bedroom, the waiting room, was all too vivid. In the years since the angels had sung to us, Dominica had grown up to become a professional space explorer. Neither of us had married. I wondered if we'd both spent too much of our lives building invincible shields against wanting something that we couldn't have.

The marine layer's chill was progressing so I went inside just as the kitchen door opened. Rachel smiled from ear to ear. "I forgot how crowded markets are on weekends. How does pasta sound to you?" she said, putting the groceries on the table.

Rachel and I ate pasta and made love all night, our first domestic evening together. I woke at dawn with a feeling of complete piece of mind. Studying her profile beside me in bed, I wondered, why Rachel? She was entirely dissimilar from my usual call to arms: she was not a stunner like Charlotte, nor blessed with Sharon's dramatic personality, Gayle's charm, or BeJo's grounded common sense. Rachel had a fragility I found unnerving. Yet I was inexplicably drawn to protect her. Somehow it was becoming hard to deny she was *everything* I wanted. Was this called falling in love?

The thought jolted me and I sat up suddenly and pulled away from my sleeping lover. My stomach raced into a weightless descent. I felt like a satellite knocked out of orbit, falling through space, dizzy with joy. But the operative verb was *falling*.

Fighting for balance, I braced my arms against the wall. The dawn light bathed Rachel's lucent white skin, her face relaxed in sleep, like a small girl-child afraid of nothing and no one. And now I felt another part to this feeling, a song of loving her. The music in my head became louder than my sense of falling. It sang notes as delicate as the poppies in Tuolumne, and as fresh as the earth. Like my favorite Yosemite meadow, the song had no sides, no ceiling or floor. My mouth opened in awe. I wanted to burst out singing.

These feelings felt too huge for Rachel's bedroom. I vaulted out of bed, ran into the living room, and threw open the west-facing curtains. I wanted to let the whole world in on my joy! What to say? What to do? Should I wake up Rachel and tell her? No! If I did I wouldn't have any more defenses. For months Rachel had been an adventure. Now she was an imperative. What if I told her and she was more frightened than I? She'd said in her letter that love scared her. She'd told Delene that she was in love with me, but would she, could she, show up if I came to her open-hearted at high noon on a normal weekday? Maybe she only wanted me because I was rarely here. Besides, falling in love meant that one was ready to move forward, had a plan of action. I had no plan. I wasn't ready to tell BeJo and lose my safe home with her; I wasn't prepared to take my life apart.

This time my stomach dropped with a thud—the thud at the bottom of the well after the fall. I closed the curtains.

Chapter 20

The Plaintiff

[Los Angeles]

Mid-July, 1975

A week later, still blissed out from the shock of admitting to myself that I'd fallen in love with Rachel, I was back on the picket line. A car screeched to a stop in front of the circle of protesters. I turned to see Pody jump out of it, balancing a large stack of documents in her arms.

"Come and get 'em!" she called out to us. "I've got the lawsuit!"

The line broke up as we rushed her, grabbing the documents.

"Hi, Córdova!" She greeted me with a warm smile as she pushed one into my chest.

"Thanks," I said, flipping through the pages somewhat fearfully. I had very mixed feelings about gays suing gays in court.

"I've tried reading it," Pody continued. "But I can't make heads or tails of it. Can we grab lunch later so you can explain it to me?"

Studying Pody's face, I felt my throat tighten inexplicably. "No!" popped out of my mouth. As her face fell, I added curtly, "I have a meeting later," and turned my back. Picking up my placard, I fell back into the picket line, stunned at what had just happened. Seeing Pody's grinning smile, the reality that she would soon be fucking BeJo had hit me. BeJo had told me this morning that Pody had invited her to a concert. Then she'd asked if I minded if she started going out with my buddy. I'd reacted with nonchalance and BeJo had dropped the conversation quickly, although I could see she was secretly pleased that my terse response meant I was jealous. Was I jealous?

Anger filled my body as I marched resolutely. It was time to stop putting friendship energy into Pody. Continuing to be pals with someone who would soon be my lover's other lover felt unsafe. I kicked an abandoned placard out of the way. It hadn't occurred to me that saying it was okay for Pody to date BeJo would end our friendship. It was one thing to accept non-monogamy intellectually. In practice, sharing the same woman didn't feel like a path to trust-filled friendship

I slapped the lawsuit document against my thigh. Why hadn't someone published a book on the rules of non-monogamy? I certainly couldn't blame BeJo. She'd given me more than I'd given her, and had always acted well within our rules. Apparently, that didn't mean I was happy with her decision. As for Pody, she'd stepped into her own damn problem. If she'd truly valued my friendship and confidence, she could have chosen someone else. I continued to stomp, annoyed with my own rigidities.

Tuning out the noisy picket line, I opened the legal document. Here was a real problem, a bunch of queers asking "the Man's" court to arbitrate a fight amongst us. This was more fucked up than struggling over non-monogamy. Fanning the stiff pages of Patton's brief, my eyes fell on a paragraph. Our lawyer had written, "The Board of Directors voted to nullify their own Personnel Policies and Procedures in a secret, seven-hour session held the week before they terminated eleven workers on May 1st." *Christ!* There it was in black and white. The Board had nullified their own PP & P's in order to fire us. I slammed the document shut. The PP&P's weren't a random bylaw that a Board of Directors could void or suspend. They were boiler plate permanent for a non-profit. GCSC had acted outside the law! With our lawyers bringing this up in the lawsuit, a judge would have to rule that the Center had fired us illegally. We would win in court. We'd get our jobs back! Breaking out in a wide smile, I let out a whoop and jumped in the air.

But wait. My brain skipped to Step 2, and my exuberance faded; it would take *years* for our lawsuit to be heard in court. The way things were going, GCSC might not exist in two or three years. I had heard that wealthy gay male donors on the Westside, confused by the strike, had begun to stop giving. Other donors were calling upon both sides to "get your shit together" before they'd resume giving. Word about the lawsuit had also made the rounds among public funding sources. The Feds and the State would not give more public grants until the "gays vs. gays" strike was resolved. Yeah, so we'd ultimately win in court, but what would we win—a financial settlement from a gay organization that couldn't pay its rent? And if the Center were by some miracle still alive in two years, we strikers would have moved on with our lives. None of this spelled victory.

Lost in my downer mood, I reopened the document at page one. If I read the lawsuit from cover to cover perhaps I could find some crack in the door, some tiny piece of information that hinted at something I could do to effect an out of court settlement. The bold-faced words at the top of the page made me freeze in step. It read:

Plaintiff; Córdova Et. Al vs. Defendant; Gay Community Services Center

My chest deflated. There it was, my name, "Córdova," suing a gay organization. I stumbled out of the picket line choking with humiliation. Why had Patton used my name to lead?

Bending over, I felt sick to my stomach. I clenched my jaw

against the rage. I couldn't stay out here in public. Breaking into a sprint, I ran down the street, away from the strikers, away from the line. Running toward the privacy of Lionheart, I threw myself into the driver's seat, rolled up the windows, and snapped the locks. My fists pounded the wheel. "Why my name?" I screamed out loud. The words whiplashed against the window and blew back in my face.

Christ! I'd worked so long to build trust and a solid political reputation with my people. They trusted my name based on my track record. A half decade spent creating a united gay and lesbian front to challenge heterosexual normalcy. Thousands of hours building new organizations, brokering inter-group conferences, writing and publishing, to build and shape an L.A. community that could move our civil rights forward. And now it was all ruined, decimated by a single line of type in public print for all posterity: "Córdova" had sued her town's gay community center.

I jabbed the rigid leather in the middle of the steering wheel. When and how had people come to perceive me as the strike's leader? I never would have led in this direction. My chest heaved as my breath broke into sobs and I stared at the blank instruments on the dash. Where had I gone wrong?

A knock on the passenger window startled me. I unlocked the door, and Rachel slipped into the car.

"Jeanne," she said, as she reached for me, her hand turning my chin toward her and cradling it. "Why so sad, what's happening?"

"I'm glad you came." I hugged her. "Have you seen this terrible thing?" I grabbed the lawsuit off the console between us.

"Yes," she said. "I was pleased. Finally, GCSC will know we're serious."

I flipped it open to page one and pointed. "Why do you think my name is on the top, like I'm the fucking leader of this strike?"

"Don't tell me that's what's upset you," she said, reading

the page. "Look down, here, further on the page," her finger pointed, "the rest of us are all listed."

"But why is my name first and up there?"

"Probably because you're the highest ranking. You were a member of the Board of Directors."

"Oh!" I muttered, realizing Rachel's answer was probably a good one. "But our damn lawyer should have made an alphabetical call. She could have put April Allison's name first."

Rachel shrugged and reached for my hand. "Yes, she most likely was using you because your name is the most widely known."

"I've called Patton's office six times in the last two weeks. If I'm such a ringleader, why can't I even get our own lawyer to call me back?" I retorted. "The woman doesn't like me. I don't support her labor versus the bosses way of framing this. She's sure found a way to lock me into her box," I screamed. "Morris has beaten me again."

Rachel looked at me. "What is this really about?" she asked calmly.

What is this really about? A lifetime of warring with Dad was reverberating in Lionheart along with my fists on the dash pummeling again. I saw him in my mind in the bleachers at the last championship game in high school. He'd sat directly behind the catcher so I'd see him with every ball I pitched. It was the bottom of the tenth, overtime, game tied, no hits, no runs, no walks. My perfect shutout game. But then…I heard the loud crack…the batter connecting to my curve. It was supposed to drop sooner than it did. I turned at the mound watching the ball fly out of the park dropping so far I could barely see it. Still, I kept watching. I couldn't bear to turn back knowing I'd see Dad get up and leave.

"Jeanne," Rachel shook me. "This isn't about Morris. This is about something the Center did wrong. You're not to blame."

I fell back against Lionheart's worn leather, my body spent. "Let's not talk about the lawsuit anymore," I said, as I gathered her into my arms and kissed her roughly. Rachel found my tongue, responding with her body reaching across the console. A tightness in my groin spread throughout my body.

"Come home with me," she said her eyes glazed, matching mine. She knew that lovemaking would make the pain go away.

I looked back toward the picket line, desperately wanting to go to Effie Street to jettison the rage. But my mind was obsessed. I couldn't let go of the lawsuit. I couldn't make love or sleep—until I found some hope, some answer, about what I could do to solve the goddamn strike.

That's when I remembered. I had a meeting scheduled this afternoon. There was hope. Rachel saw my shift in mood.

"Please don't tell me you have a meeting," she'd groaned, her body pressed against mine.

"I do," I said. "And I'm late and it's way out in Venice."

"Take me with you? I don't want to leave you now."

"I don't want you to either. But I can't take you. It's a closed session at the Women's Center, called by others."

Rachel re-gathered herself, opened the passenger door and walked back to the line. I knew she wasn't happy.

I steered west absentmindedly—heading for the Westside Women's Center. Hope drove me. My best peer friends had called the meeting. They'd know how to advise me.

The WWC, as we called it, was located in a 1920's Craftsman style house in Venice with a sloped roofed and wide front porch. It was the third incarnation of L.A.'s principle Women's Center. The first had opened early in 1970, at the dawn of feminism, at 1027 South Crenshaw Boulevard in mid-town L.A. Then a new site called the Venice Women's Center opened as an off-shoot of the Crenshaw Center and the two coexisted for six months until Crenshaw closed. In 1974 the Venice Women's Center relocated to Hill Street which was on the northern border of Venice, a ragtag community of radicals, hippies, and the homeless, which stretched along the Pacific. Its pack of rebels now included us radical feminist dykes. WWC was headquarters to dozens of lesbian and feminist groups that met seven nights a week and all weekend. It brought together women working in anti-racist and anti-war efforts; academics and grassroots community organizers. Rumor had it that more than a few fugitives—from the FBI and the civil wars in Latin America—used the WWC as a center for drop-offs and pickups of people and information not condoned by the US government. It was also a halfway house along the Underground Railroad that tracked between suburban heterosexuality and lesbian liberation. These years it felt as though dozens of young housewives were hearing the clarion call of feminism and were rushing to take their place in a wildly growing Lesbian Nation.

Entering Santa Monica on the Westbound 10 Freeway, I knew that my only chance to find a solution to the strike and my angst lay in talking with my circle of political peers at this unique meeting. The group was composed of four other lesbian political leaders who'd come of age with me in the culture of lesbian feminism, veteran dykes who'd survived their own similar battles. My close friend, Ariana Manov, had called the meeting. Judy Freespirit and Jane Herman, members of the powerful L.A. Radical Feminist Therapy Collective, and Kate McDonough, Director of the new Westside Women's Clinic, would all be there. Goddess bless!

I felt Lionheart speeding, tapped the brakes, and settled down for the drive out to the ocean. The women I was meeting with were all femmes, I reflected, except Kate. In the gay male movement and back in my old bar dyke days, butches had the power. But femmes were the leadership running the lesbian feminist movement. This made sense to me. It was always the most oppressed that held the rawest anger in a social change struggle. Therefore they made the best leaders. Drag queens and a stone butch, arguably the most oppressed of gay men and dykes, had thrown the first punches at the Stonewall Uprising. Housewives had started the feminist movement because they had the most to gain from it. In my lesbian feminist movement it made sense that lesbian femmes had the power. As women and

Some of the founders of Westside Women's Center on Hill St.
Top row: Jane Herman (Radical Feminist Therapy Collective),
Simone Wallace (Sisterhood Bookstore), Maureen Hicks. Middle
row: Gahan Kelley (Sisterhood Bookstore), Judy Freespirit
(Radical Feminist Therapy Collective) Linda Torn, Sherna
Gluck (Feminist History Research Project), Ariana Manov (Free
Venice). Bottom row: Cheryl Diehm (editor, *Sisters*). *1974.
Photographer unknown. Córdova Collection at ONE Archives.*

lesbians they had experienced the most personal discrimination
from their ex-husbands and male lovers. As one of only a handful
of national lesbian butch leaders, I was an exception. It was a
privilege to belong to this group of powerful women who had
both intellect and political savvy. Some of them had become my
"family of choice" since I'd been exiled by my biological family
as a teenager. After my father threw Judy and me out, I knew I

had to find a new family. A group of friends with whom I could have Christmas dinner, celebrate a birthday, and call in the middle of the night when a lover left. Every gay person I knew had a similar story about being emotionally, or literally, exiled. To gays, family of choice was not a substitute. It was a necessity.

Ariana had called today's meeting to take action around the FBI's arrest of the "Lexington Six" and other dykes who they thought were withholding information about lesbian Leftist fugitives Susan Saxe and Katherine Powers. Defending our community against the FBI and its notorious Grand Jury was the topic of the meeting. And, I hoped that after today's political agenda, my buddies might be willing to stay and listen to my personal problems about the GCSC strike.

The strike had become much more than my personal problem. Contention over it was spreading throughout the community and becoming problematic for everyone, including the Westside Women's Center. Ninety percent of the lesbian feminist community had terminated relations with the sexist gay Center. Scabs—who included any woman or gay male who publicly sympathized with GCSC—were no longer welcomed at the WWC, the Women's Saloon, the Woman's Building, the Women's Switchboard, or other lesbian group or gathering place.

Last month there had been a bitter showdown here at the Westside Women's Center initiated by a small group of women who called themselves the Lesbian Activists. The group's leadership came out of Chatsworth, a tiny, no name dot on the map in the San Fernando Valley. Lesbian Activists had applied to use the Westside Women's Center as their regular meeting place. That was no problem, since most lesbian and many feminist groups in the city met at the Center. But the group's newsletter, *The Lesbian News*, had declared itself neutral in the GCSC strike. This was a very big problem. Last month, they were denied the right to hold their meetings at the WWC.

They'd been deemed "not feminist enough."

Feeling ostracized, the Lesbian Activists had retaliated by calling for an end to the GCSC boycott in their next edition of *Lesbian News*. Oddly, and despite their newsletter's name, the group identified themselves as "gay women" rather than lesbian, and said that both sides in the strike were equally guilty.

There was also a small but vocal minority of strike-phobic dissenters within my own collective at *The Lesbian Tide*. A member of this minority, a good writer named Jan Sappell, had

Publishers on a Boat. Córdova (driving), *Lesbian Tide* publisher rides with Jinx Beers (back, right), soon to be *Lesbian News* publisher. *Big Bear Lake, California, 1974. Photographer unknown. Córdova Collection at ONE Archives.*

quit last week over *The Tide's* openly pro-strike coverage of the almost three month old, divisive strike. Two more of *The Tide's* staff members were wobbling. Even BeJo had demanded we publish a graphic in our last issue that called upon both sides to "Shut Up and Compromise!" {1}

I hadn't told anyone, including BeJo, that I too had been thinking about modifying *The Tide's* boycott of printing only one side of the GCSC story. We'd received, but hadn't yet printed articles written by GCSC people, scabs, or sympathizers. A week ago, Chief Scab Lillene Fifield had submitted a written essay—an emotional appeal calling for "an end to this insanity that forces sisters into silence and withdrawal." I was sitting on her submission. How much longer could I, as a journalist, justify dismissing the other half of the story? *The Tide* had solidly called for feminist reform at GCSC, but had also denounced random violence, and not called for more radical demands like "closing the boss-controlled gay center." We were a monthly publication, and events had moved too fast between the boycott and the strike and we'd had no time to print my careful distinctions between the two strategies. The paper was editorially run by BeJo, Annie Doczi and me—with a large number of newbie skilled volunteers who came and went every six months. Yet we prided ourselves on being a reliable publication. *The Tide's* pride was my pride. To me that implied a pact, an oath to my readership to render the news, *all* the news, about lesbian feminism. It was also getting harder for me to stand up under the pressure of the gay male community. Many gay men in town, including leaders I'd worked with closely on mixed gay and lesbian issues, were accusing me, because they knew my name, of trying to destroy the Center.

I wiggled over to the Fourth Street exit, turned south, then west to 237 Hill Street, and pulled Lionheart into the parking lot next to the Westside Women's Center. Bounding up the stairs of the porch, I stopped for a moment to pay homage to the sign nailed to the front of the building, L.A.'s original sign from the city's first women's center. The large red letters painted against a white background bore the simple words The Women's Center. Tucked into the "o" of "Women" was the insignia of the feminist movement—a raised, clenched fist encircled by the ancient symbol for female. The late 'sixties radical feminists from Boston had borrowed the clenched fist from the power-to-the-people salute of the Vietnam anti-war movement, who had, in turn, adopted it from the Black Panthers during the civil rights struggle. The Panthers had copied the clenched fist from the anti-fascist movement in the Spanish civil war. A proud symbol of past defiance, incorporated and modified to be our woman-power symbol, had been popularized in America by appearing on the cover of Robin Morgan's anthology, *Sisterhood is Powerful*, five years ago. I puffed out my chest, knowing it bespoke women's identification with minority people all over the world.

I opened the door, walking into the front living room which was lined with folding chairs. Posters of women of every size, color, and shape were pinned to the walls. The room exuded safe familiarity, like a true family living room of multi-ethnic worldwide women. Staring at four closed doors that used to be bedrooms, I wondered which of the rooms held my meeting. I didn't want to barge in on someone else's private group meeting. Would Ariana's meeting be in the rear bedroom where I occasionally met with members of the Radical Feminist Therapy Collective over political issues? In their opposition to the psychiatric Establishment, radical feminist therapy groups had sprung up all over the country teaching that the silenced realities of living under the patriarchy—rape, sexual abuse of children, beating of women in the home, violence against gays and lesbians, and institutionalized racism—were societal crimes and not the job of one victimized woman to "adjust to" in therapy.

Opening the door, I heard "Hiya, Córdova Kid!" as Ariana broke into a warm smile, calling me by her pet nickname. Sitting on the carpeted floor in a circle, everyone smiled and jostled around, opening a space for me.

She summarized for me. "We've decided to hold a community-wide educational forum on September 25, to defend our community against the Grand Jury's abuses of political dissidents, and using its power and secrecy to intimidate witnesses and fish for evidence." Ariana Manov's day job was counseling poor, domestically abused, and raped women while she helped create a battered women's shelter, the first feminist one in Southern California. By night, Ariana did what she termed solidarity work with Central American causes. I shared almost everything, personal and political, with Ariana, but her solidarity work was something she shared with no one.

"The purpose of the forum," continued Judy, "will be to raise political consciousness. To explain to women how the Grand Jury system is part of the government's national program of repression, and how we should respond to it." Judy Freespirit was tacitly recognized as Queen Bee of the Westside radical lesbian feminists. She was short, fat and round, with tight curly locks that sat atop an ever-smiling face. "We need to tell our sisters how these Grand Juries have been used to fragment movements, to create mistrust and make us suspicious of one another. We'll give them the background on how FBI probes and Grand Juries were used against Martin Luther King and the NAACP."

Judy epitomized the radical feminist practice of women changing their last names to reflect who they wanted to be, rather than their father's identity. At thirty-eight, she was the eldest among us. She and I had been neighbors last year, sharing adjacent studio apartments overlooking the beach, so she knew me well.

Jane Herman chimed in, "We'll tell them about the FBI's probe into the Lexington and Connecticut lesbian communities. How that's resulted in sisters being hauled before Grand Juries, and now, jailed for refusing to talk."

I interjected, "At the forum shouldn't we pass out a list of attorneys in L.A. who would be ready to take a dyke's case pro bono if she receives a subpoena?"

"Let's make a list, but don't hand it out. That would make those lawyers advance targets," Ariana said.

"Women will want to know that a Grand Jury has been opened in Los Angeles," I said.

"Indeed!" said Jane, her long, proud chocolate tresses bobbing in her indignation. "The FBI has opened a Grand Jury in every city where Saxe or Power or the SLA was known to have hidden."

"They're really looking for Patty Hearst," Ariana said. "Not finding her has been a huge national embarrassment to the FBI. They are not letting anyone's constitutional rights get in the way of capturing the SLA fugitives who are hiding her."

"We need to tell everyone that the government thinks that women break more easily than men," said Kate McDonough. Kate's new Westside Women's Clinic had been harassed with death threats and repeatedly vandalized.

Jane jumped in. "The Feds think women can't handle the pressure of being in jail. They say that appealing to our so-called natural nurturing and humanity makes us crack more quickly."

"Lesbians need to be psychologically prepared not to fall for this crap," I said.

Two hours later, we reached consensus on our plans. We'd designed a creative flyer, using the format of a real grand jury subpoena. Assignments were parceled out, and we'd decided who would say what at the public forum. Last but not least, we'd formalized our group, naming it: The Feminist Offensive Against Repression, FOAR for short.

"All right," recapped Freespirit. "Let's do some centering and then do some personal work with Córdova."

I folded my hands on my lap. The process known as centering, a feminist therapy term, created a space into which we could pool our energies, our love for each other, and our trust. During centering each woman told the others where her head was at—this week, this day, this hour. If a woman was so un-centered that she couldn't come into shared group energy, personal time was called for her to talk about what was so painful. That's what

I felt now—too blasted away by seeing my name on the lawsuit that I couldn't let that energy go.

Jane turned to me. "What do you need, Córdova, to get centered today? It feels like your energy is all over the map."

I released a pent-up sigh. I could let these women see the real me. I wasn't smarter, more politically astute, or more courageous than any of them. I tossed my copy of the lawsuit into the center of the circle. "This is what is fucking up my life. That's the lawsuit that the strikers filed against GCSC. Look at page one."

Judy picked up the document with one finger, disgust written clearly on her round, freckled cheeks. "Aside from its very existence, what disturbs you so much?"

"My shock and hurt are blocking me from finding a solution to this political battle." I stumbled over each difficult word. It was never easy for me to show personal pain. "I knew the lawsuit was coming. I think we're doing the right thing given GCSC's lack of cooperation, but seeing my name on this printed court document makes me feel so...so...devastated." The last word came out barely audible as I bought up my knees and my head fell into them.

"Devastated by what...exactly?" Ariana asked.

"I don't know!" I wailed putting my hands over my ears. "Being singled out, being the first name. Something about being a 'plaintiff.'"

"What does that word mean to you?" Jane asked.

"Plaintiff means the voice of one crying alone in the wilderness. Plaintiff means complainer," I muttered through tears. "I've been complaining for months. No one is listening to us!"

"You mean no one is listening to you?" Ariana interjected.

"That's right," I choked on my words. "I feel like a complaining, whimpering victim. Like I have no choices. I don't know what to do."

Judy reached out to caress my arm. "You mean you want to do something to make it all go away, but you feel powerless."

"Exactly!" I bellowed. And then, it hit me. "Yes!" I screamed. "It's the goddamn powerlessness!"

Ariana stroked me on the back of the neck and I leaned my head into her shoulder and let my tears flow. Sobbing deeply, a huge sense of release blew through me like someone had sucked out a boulder lodged in my lungs. I realized I wasn't "confused" about the strike. The feeling of confused depression was born out of my perception that I had no power. I'd forgotten that leading means freeing oneself to take action. That's what makes a leader—the courage to take risks. I'd known this since leaving the convent. I'd almost always been the first horse out of the box. Somehow, in the negative conundrum called The Strike, I'd rendered myself choice-less and therefore powerless.

The room gave in with me and was silent.

Jane whispered, "Poor you," voicing her words in the tone a mother might use to comfort her child. Silly words for grown-ups, I thought, hearing them addressed to me. But soothing and womblike. I felt cradled.

Kate echoed Jane's condolence. Ariana stroked my forearm. After some minutes, Jane handed me a Kleenex. I wiped the mucus from my nose and lifted my head to look at the faces around me. Everyone was listening to me.

"Are you ready to take your power?" Judy's tough invitation brought me back into focus.

Gazing into her warm eyes, I nodded. "Yeah, I'm ready… for…whatever."

The group fell into thought.

"In that case, the nerve of that Board!" Jane blurted out.

Jane Herman didn't believe in suffering silently. One of her affair-mates had it that she gave all her lovers an instruction sheet, map included, before she allowed them into her bed. "What would happen if you told the lawyer, Patton, to take your name off the lawsuit?"

I reached for the document lying forlornly in our circle. "If I asked her to take my name off this, she'd bring it up at the next meeting and call me out publicly. She'd ask me if I want to renounce my role as a striker. Word of my defection would leak and be great gossip. When the Center finds out there's a rift among the strikers, or that I don't believe in our position, it will weaken the picket line, and our position. Everything!"

"What if..." Judy spoke softly with quick, terse words, "the Radical Feminist Therapy Collective called Alan Gross, GCSC's attorney, and offered to mediate the strike? We've mediated between other groups in town."

Part of the role of the RFTC was to keep peace within sometimes fractious groups at the Women's Center and elsewhere in the city. They'd successfully mediated a disagreement on *The Tide's* staff a year ago.

I studied earth mother Judy. She didn't know the players in this situation. In my mind's eye I saw Morris laughing derisively when Alan Gross brought RFTC's offer to mediate to him. Morris and Gross would dismiss the offer assuming a bias because RFTC was a lesbian group. After all, it came from women—the weaker sex.

"That wouldn't work," I explained. "I'm sure Morris would pull the corporate papers of the WWC and see that I'm the Secretary of it, at least my title, though not reality. That makes me an officer of this non-profit, which overlaps strongly with the Radical Feminist Therapy Collective. Way too much conflict of interest. He doesn't respect lesbians anyway."

Everyone laughed, remembering how a year ago we'd sat down to draw up some necessary legal documents to renew the Westside Center's non-profit status. Since officers were required by the State, some of us activists, myself included, had blithely inserted our names. But no one knew who the officers of WWC were. In practice the center was mostly run by the Radical Feminist Therapy Collective. The words "Board" or "Director" were never used. Such structures were patriarchal, and therefore anathema.

Kate swung into the discussion. "GCSC was dead wrong to fire all of you. Even General Motors doesn't fire people without notice! I agree with Córdova that this struggle is not primarily a labor issue. But each side seems to fear and distrust the actions and motives of the other side."

I beamed, happy to be in a room full of lesbians, away from June and her ilk, who defined the strike as a worker's issue.

"In other words," Jane said, "is it a feminist Center or a homosexual Center?"

"Being a gay Center is not a bad thing," I said. I thought of my little brother, Jerome, who I was sure would grow up to be a gay man, one who might need GCSC someday.

"Why are we attempting to reform GCSC," Judy continued, "and make it acceptable? Why work with men at all? We have what amounts to a lesbian center here on the Westside."

I paused. "Some lesbians want to work with men. Gay men have the money—from other rich gay men and their visibility to get grants—therefore their programs get funded." My shoulders drooped, I was suddenly discouraged. "Hell, that's how we lesbians got into this mess in the first place. Social change doesn't always proceed in a straight line. Sometimes it just jags to the left and then jags to the right and loops back on itself and the good guys get hung with their own rope."

Again the room went quiet, each of us lost in our own thoughts.

"I don't care for the analogy about hanging, Córdova Kid, but I'm with you," Ariana broke the silence. "Maybe you can find some common ground and make some peace overture without selling out the strikers."

All heads turned toward Ariana, trying to follow her thinking. Plump and pink-faced from a Slavic-Irish heritage, Ariana was good at nuanced strategy.

"What are you talking about, R?" I said calling her by my nickname for her.

My friend studied my face. "You want to know what you, Jeanne Córdova, can do about the strike, right?"

I racked my brain. "Yes?"

"You've told me that you and Morris Kight used to be very tight personally, right?" she prodded.

"Used to be," I said. "Past tense."

"Well," said Ariana, "why don't you reach out to him based on your past political and personal relationship? Admit to him there's been a lot of hurt and misunderstanding on both sides. Get him to come to the table."

I laughed aloud. "Ariana, you must be nuts!"

"What's so crazy?" she shot back. "You know him well. You've been with him on the same side for years. You're his protégée. If he won't listen to a mediation offer coming from a bunch of radical dykes like us, he may listen to an offer coming from someone he at least used to respect and trust."

"Ariana," I wailed, still astonished. "That would mean crossing the picket line!"

"I don't mean talk to him when he's at the Center. I mean go to his house."

"You know it doesn't matter where he is," I retorted. "He could be asleep at the North Pole and I'd be technically crossing the picket line no matter where I talked to him."

"I know that." Ariana looked around the room. "And I wouldn't be suggesting crossing any picket line under any circumstances except possibly this one. You've already been branded a traitor by the gay men. Could you can stand up to possibly being branded as such by sisters?"

For a moment my mind left the room, remembering the afternoon four years ago when I'd had the audacity to stick the word "lesbian" on the masthead of my new publication—*The Lesbian Tide*. No other women's publication in the world had risked using the word lesbian on its cover. I had proven then that I was willing to stick my neck out; was I willing to risk it again to save the unity of the greater L.A. gay and lesbian community?

I studied Ariana's face. "Are you honestly suggesting that I dive into the deep end head first?"

"Yes," Ariana answered without hesitation.

I looked around. All the heads in the room were slowly nodding agreement.

I whistled through my teeth. "I know Morris. He won't cave if we keep picketing until Christmas. I'm gonna have to run with this idea. I'll try to find a way to do it without publicly jeopardizing the line or the issues. But if anyone finds out, or Morris blows my cover, I'll have to publicly say I've gone rogue and don't represent the strikers."

Judy nodded. "That's the only ethical way."

"What if he won't take my call or slams the door in my face?"

"You'll have to cross that line to find out." Ariana's lips curved into a rueful smile.

Chapter 21

_____

The Arrangement

[Los Angeles]

Late July, 1975

The sun baked the broken asphalt as I strode through *The Free Press's* Hollywood Boulevard parking lot. The glass front door was marked 5850.

"Thank the Goddess you're finally here!" Bryan gasped as I tried to pass his reception desk. He and his great brush of flowing yellow hair sat at a desk awash in messages, manuscripts, and mismanaged chaos. Bryan was as feminist as any man could be, but also a drama queen.

"What's wrong?"

Bryan was close to tears. "There's nobody in Editorial. Penny is gone, and so is Tom! She said you'd be here when I opened. You're supposed to take over!" His mouth quivered, blond curls bobbing with emotion.

"Calm down, nobody's dead." I spoke firmly. "Just give me the editorial messages." Penny hadn't given me notice that I was representing the paper today. I would've combed my hair.

"Where are Penny and Tom?" I asked, afraid the question would set him to tears again.

"They were summoned to a meeting with the publishers in Beverly Hills!"

I stopped dead and looked at him. "No kidding? Did they say anything more?"

"No, that was it. She sounded worried."

I wound my way through Production and ascended the stairs to Editorial feeling vaguely threatened by Penny's meeting with *The Freep's* new owners. The paper had been an integral supporter of the New Left since its birth in 1960 when it was founded by Art Kunkin as an anti-Establishment, anti-war, progressive alternative to the *L.A. Times*. But since our government had pulled out of Viet Nam two years ago, it had been hard to find politically oriented advertising money to keep the paper going. Burdened by loans and fighting to save *The Freep* from bankruptcy, last year Kunkin had been forced to sell us to two sex industry types, known to staff as "Don and Troy," of New Way Enterprises LTD. I figured any firm calling itself an innocuous name like "new way," which said nothing about who they really were, meant "sex" in L.A. porn code-speak. Since the war's end our advertising had become increasingly dependent on sex toys and sex-driven classified ads. As a result, there was a growing schism between our two kinds of readership, those who cared about civil rights and those who bought the paper for its sexual opportunities. Penny and I had talked about how long *The L.A. Free Press* could continue this way. And what folding would mean for the movement and our lives as civil rights journalists.

As I walked into my cubbyhole office, my spirits lifted at the sight of an American flag embroidered with the slogan, "Stars & Dykes Forever." I hung my war jacket on a nail next to my Venceremos Brigade poster.

Flipping through Bryan's messages I saw calls from all over the country. One from the attorneys of captured lesbian fugitive Susan Saxe. Last month *The Tide* had printed her quote upon being captured, "The love I share with my sisters is a far more formidable weapon than the police state" on our cover. *The Freep* had me covering Saxe's trial. Other messages were from political trials and battles being covered by fellow *Freep* writers.

The last two messages were from Rachel, repeating, "Where are you?" I reached for my calendar. Had I missed any Mondays or Fridays with her? No, it was Friday and I was supposed to see her tonight. I smiled transporting myself to her bed at Effie, lying with her under the Nepalese embroidered bedspread.

Before I knew it, I was tilting back in my cast-iron swivel chair and dialing her number. It was getting harder to see her only twice a week. I missed her. What we did in bed together and how we did it gave me a kind of dual spiritual and physical satiation I'd never known. Dynamically we were each other's perfect yin and yang. Would my political life ever slow down long enough to find out if we could be similarly connected out of bed?

Her answer machine clicked on. Damn. But then I heard the soft intimacy of her recorded voice, reeling me closer to leave a message.

"Once upon a time," I whispered into the machine, seized suddenly by the need to tell Rachel that I loved her. "There were these two tiny dykes. I mean they were very, very, tiny dykes—maybe only six centimeters high. Plus, they were teeny, tiny orphan dykes all alone in a big storm on the ocean in a teeny, weenie little orphan boat that used to have a big mother boat, but had gotten lost—"

BEEP. The machine cut me off.

Dialing back, I pondered my plotline, continuing. "And the baby orphan boat spoke to the teeny, dyke with curly yellow hair saying, 'Look. You two are alone in the sea. You need to hang on to each other. If you don't get out of this storm, your lives could be very short.' But the yellow-haired dyke answered the orphan boat, 'Go tell that to the dumb black-haired dyke at the stern. She thinks she's sailing this boat.'

"And the teeny, weenie orphan boat said back to her, 'I can't speak for you. Go tell her—"

BEEP.

Damn!

I looked up to see Bryan passing my door, looking at me quizzically. I re-dialed.

"But the yellow-haired dyke said she was too afraid of losing her balance by walking across the rocking and rolling boat in the storm all the way to the stern. So the orphan boat said, 'I'll help you!' And suddenly, a great calm came upon the sea."

I could feel the BEEP coming.

"And so they all lived happily ever after, my love. In case you missed it, the moral of the story is that you should always listen to a boat when it talks to you. I just want you to know that I... ah..." My tongue refused the words "love you."

BEEP.

I fell back into my chair grabbing a stack of paperclips. I twisted them furiously. Fuck tiny orphan boats, I thought, bending a clip into a tight square. Emotions are insignificant in the course of great political events, I paraphrased Angela Davis. If Rachel needed a bleeding heart poet for a lover she should have picked someone like Pody who had nothing better to do with her life than write poetry to BeJo. If I spent my life composing verse, *The Lesbian Tide* would be a one-page leaflet.

I flipped on the Selectric and began a story.

"Do I need an appointment to see the Human Rights Editor?"

The sound of her voice stopped my fingers. I swiveled around.

Rachel leaned provocatively against the doorjamb, tilting her head against the wood. Her powder blue eyes winked invitingly. I sat still and stared. She was a shaft of joy in my life.

"Why do I love you so much?" she asked.

I jumped out of my chair. "Because I miss you desperately!" Circling my desk, I grabbed her and pressed her into the wall.

"Go sit down." She pushed me away. "I want to talk."

"Talk?"

I returned to my chair. She leaned toward me over the desk.

Her blouse fell away from her neckline.

"I came to confirm that you are coming to my house tonight. I don't like calling you at home. BeJo answers the phone frequently." She sat down in the chair across from me. Suddenly, the twinkle left her eyes and they looked quite serious. "There's something important we need to talk about, Jeanne."

I grimaced and shut my eyes. "Good news or bad?"

"I think its good news. I hope you do too, darling."

Startled at her new term of endearment, I rolled it around in my head. Darling one-upped sweetheart. Darling was what my father and mother called each other. Darling probably meant staying past breakfast! I liked it—but her tone left me unsure. "Did you get off work early today?" I changed the subject.

"Yes. I thought you might be able to leave early and we could go to a movie this afternoon or do something normal like other people do."

"I'd love to," I said, "but I'm watching the shop. Penny is at a meeting. I'm in charge until they get back."

"I'm always waiting for you."

I was taken aback by her sharpness. This felt like long-held anger.

"I'm here now, sweetheart," I offered.

"Until when?" she retorted. "The next ten minutes? Until midnight tonight?"

I reached across the desk and took her hand.

She leaned forward. "Seeing the joy on your face and in your eyes when you just now looked at me, I know you love me. That's why I don't understand why I see so little of you. It's always the police, or the Feds, or the gay revolution. I'm growing weary of this, babe. I need more from you, more time together...a fuller relationship. I want us to go away together for a whole weekend, to the desert or the beach. Or even stay home with no phone calls, no meetings, and no politics."

I started to sweat, but couldn't think what to say. I'd felt full and satisfied with our nights together making love.

"Why don't we sit together at night and read, or go to the

beach together on the weekends?"

A spasm of panic churned my stomach. What would Rachel and I say to one another if we sat on a beach for a whole weekend? I couldn't imagine what we would talk about for two days, especially if we couldn't talk politics. But I had to come up with something. "I've got a great idea for how we can spend more time together!"

Rachel's face brightened.

"How about you join The *Tide* Collective? Then we'd work together every Thursday night and probably some weekend days too." My voice grew excited. Sharing my child with Rachel was a brilliant idea. Why hadn't I thought of it before?

"That's an outrageously bad idea, Jeanne!" Rachel pulled her hand out of mine. "Why would I want to join a group of your present and ex-lovers? That's not what I meant by us having a personal life!"

The stomach spasm tweaked again. I tried to mask my hurt. Rachel didn't want to join *The Tide*...my family. Sure there'd be some problems to work out with BeJo, but I'd fix that. Other lovers of mine had joined the staff.

"I want more time with *you*!"

Damn, I whistled under my breath. Time was the one thing I didn't have to give. I could barely juggle my work as it was. More time with Rachel meant less time for politics or giving up my arrangement with BeJo.

"I've been meaning to ask you," Rachel said as if she'd read my mind. "When we first met you told me that you and BeJo were very non-monogamous. What exactly does being very non-monogamous mean?"

I gulped, somehow feeling a trap was being laid. Was it time to be honest with Rachel? Now that I was in love with her I wanted her to trust me. "About four or five women a year," I answered honestly

"Is BeJo the reason you won't spend the weekends at my house or go away with me?"

"Of course not," I dodged her question. "It's about time. I

don't have extra time. What does BeJo have to do with you and me?"

I fiddled with a cig, tapping both ends on the desk. My feet dug into the carpet. This was dangerous ground. Sure, BeJo and I had arranged days and nights, but BeJo dividing up time seemed to be the only way to live a non-monogamous life.

Rachel saw my forehead wrinkle, saw me holding my breath.

"Why do we only see each other on Monday and Friday nights, Jeanne?" she asked. This time she didn't drag out my name.

"You and I spent most of a weekend together—"

"Once," she stopped me. "Do you spend particular nights of the week with BeJo?"

My brain scrambled. D-day had arrived. *You love her, no slippage.* "Yes. Okay. We have…an arrangement," I blurted.

"An arrangement?" Rachel dragged out the word as though it described a disease.

I stood up, came around the desk, and fell on one knee in front of her chair. "It started long before I met you," I explained, cradling her hand. "Years ago, BeJo and I decided, so that we'd know where each other were…"

I felt Rachel's body start to stiffen.

"Stop. Jeanne. What is the arrangement?"

"Geez, Rachel."

"Tell me." She wouldn't let it go.

I forced the words to come out. "That we see our other lovers on Mondays and Fridays."

"*Other* lovers. And you spend every weekend with her?"

"I can't remember the last time I was home…I mean, with BeJo for a whole weekend. I've always got meetings and marches on Saturdays and Sundays, even the nights…"

"But in theory, your weekend arrangement is with her."

"That's an empty theory," I defended. "I'm with you Friday nights and Saturday…"

Color had left Rachel's face. Without a word, she brushed me aside, got up and walked, slowly and deliberately, to the door.

I sank back on my haunches. The "arrangement" wasn't even about BeJo and me. I'd been living with the same arrangement since I'd ended my monogamous lifestyle in 1970. Since feminism I'd always lived non-monogamously, having two, occasionally three, lovers simultaneously. That's how feminists were supposed to live outside of patriarchal colonization. We weren't supposed to be living behind white picket fences. We were radicals. We were engaged in political revolution.

Rachel stopped at the door, and turned around to face me. "Do you have a beer in this place?"

"I'll go check," I said, walking past her and into the hallway, anything to get away from her staring at me so forlornly. I started down the hall knowing full well that no one drank at the office. Damn! I kicked the wall outside Penny's office hard enough to make my ankle ache. I should've told Rachel weeks ago. Now it sounded like I'd been lying, and at least by omission, I had. But now that she knew, what now? How did other lesbians schedule their non-monogamous lives? Surely, they didn't spontaneously decide each night whether they'd lay their head down in one lover's bed or the other's. That would be emotional and structural chaos. Surely other non-monogamous dykes had pre-planned arrangements.

Stalling for time, I walked into Tom Thomson's empty office. The problem was that Rachel wasn't seeing anyone else. At least, I didn't think she was. Other than that first night over her bookshelf, we'd never discussed monogamy, never broached the subject. I'd intentionally never wanted to know what she did on nights I wasn't with her.

Pausing at Tom's desk, I felt my stomach muscles churn. Thinking about Rachel with another woman had never crossed my mind. But now the thought made me sick to my stomach.

Thinking about previous lovers with their other girlfriends had never bothered me. Picturing BeJo in bed with Pody felt... acceptable.

I heard Rachel's footsteps behind me. Momentarily, I froze, unable to turn and face her. Apparently, she'd figured out the

Editorial Department was empty and there was no beer.

"Jeanne?" she called softly, dragging my name out like a joint of the finest Colombian as she put her arms around my waist and laid her head between my shoulder blades.

I turned around slowly. She raised her eyes. They were red and tear-stained.

"Your arrangement with BeJo has to end," she said simply.

I cupped her face in my hands and kissed her lips.

"Yes," I sighed and promised. "I know."

Chapter 22

Crossing the Line

[Los Angeles]

Mid-August, 1975

"Rachel?" I spoke excitedly into the receiver. "I just spoke to Morris Kight on the phone."

"Morris called you?"

"No, I called him. About the strike."

"Why on earth?"

Quickly, I told Rachel about the meeting at the WWC and Ariana's suggestion. "Someone has to cross the line and talk to Morris. Let him know that our side wants a negotiated peace."

"Whoa, babe, I'm worried about you. Why you? And I'm not sure the strikers want a negotiated peace!"

"I know, I agree. That's why I have to make them believe that Morris called me. That he wants to sue for peace."

"My God, that's quite a stretch in thinking."

"Who else is going to make this leap?" I asked.

Silence. Then, "No one."

"Damn sure, no one. Including our attorney."

"So what did Morris say? Will he do it?"

"He seemed shocked. I heard him stop breathing for a second. And then, he pretended my call was the most normal thing in the world, just like old times. He's open to sitting down and looking for a resolution. He said to come today."

"How can you just cross the line? You'd be a scab, wouldn't you?"

"Not if my only purpose is to talk terms about the strike. Someone has to cross the line in order to negotiate. Technically, yes, I should get the Strikers Steering Committee to elect me to negotiate for us. But that's never gonna happen. Plus, they're fixated. They're demanding that any offer to settle must be initiated by GCSC. So that's exactly what you and I are going to do—initiate."

"Wait, what do you mean you and me?"

"I want you to come with me. How soon can you meet me in *The Freep's* parking lot?"

"Did he say to bring me?"

I sighed, realizing that she was scared. "I'm sure he knows you and I are lovers. He'll just think I brought you because we spent the night together, and I made a sloppy personal decision in bringing you."

"Are you making a sloppy personal decision?"

"No, darling. It's better to have a witness. This way he can't wiggle out of this later and say he never promised what he did, or that the conversation never happened." Secretly, my asking Rachel also had to do with moral support.

"Having a witness cuts both ways. It puts me in a potential hot seat."

"I know." I paused and took a deep breath.

Rachel was silent. Then she said, "The strike hasn't gone well has it?"

"No. It's quite stalled. But," I added, "if it ever comes out publicly that you were there, I'll say it was my idea. I talked you into it. But you can't trust Morris. He might use it against you."

"I have nothing further to lose at the hands of Morris Kight,"

Rachel said, letting out a little whistle through her teeth. "If there is a breakthrough I want to bear witness."

"Thank you, sweetheart."

We agreed to meet in the parking lot in one hour. I spun around in my swivel chair, giddy with hope. I sorely wanted to convince Morris that working collectively with women within GCSC would not be the end of his world. At long last, the Great Strike might begin to end today!

The red light on my private line began to blink. Damn, it was probably Rachel calling back to say she'd changed her mind.

I picked up. "Rachel?"

"Is this Córdova?" a deep, male voice asked.

My brain jumped around. Few men had my private number. "Joe?" I asked out loud.

"Yeah," he answered. "This is Tomassi."

"What a surprise. How are you?"

"Skip the chat, I'm in a hurry. I want to do another interview."

I drawled the two syllables out slowly. "Oh-kaay. Are you up to something new?"

"We're getting ready to bomb that Bookstore in Santa Monica I told you about. I want you to cover it for me."

"The Midnight Special?"

"Don't say that name!" Joe yelled. "They're tapping your phone."

"Sorry, I forgot."

"I can't talk now. That LAPD Criminal Conspiracy squad is dogging me. Meet me later this week."

"When, where?"

But Joe had already hung up. Christ!

I strode over to Penny's office.

She looked up. "Córdova, you look like you've just talked with a ghost."

"Worse," I said. "Tomassi just called. He wants to blow up the Midnight Special Bookstore."

Penny stared at me. We both knew the Midnight Special was one of the major Leftist think tanks and meeting spaces.

"When?" she whispered.

"Apparently not until after he and I meet again," I said, with a sense of relief. "I think he wants pre-publicity this time."

"Thank God! I'll call the bookstore right now and warn them." Penny sat back. "They can decide if they want police protection."

"He wants me to meet him, do a second interview. He'll call back to set up when and where."

Penny's face grew pale; she leaned back in her chair. "That's a very bad idea, Córdova. I'm not going to let you go to him again. But you should stall him; let him think you'll do another interview. We have to draw the line here. I must call the bookstore and warn them. And I don't like it, but with this new information I need to call the police too."

I stared at Penny, nodding dumbly. My Nazi was evolving into a serial bomber.

Seeing Rachel standing next to Lionheart lifted my heart. She looked particularly fetching in a loose flowing skirt and a tight fitting paisley blouse.

"Allow me." I ran to hold open my car door for her. "And good morning to my partner in subterfuge." A part of me wanted to flip her over into the back seat and make love right now.

In the car she leaned over and kissed me, asking, "Have you talked with BeJo yet about adjusting your arrangement with her?"

Her question hit me like a left hook. I'd had Morris, our strategy session and a serial bomber on my mind. I sure wasn't focused on a pow-wow with BeJo.

"No," I said, turning over the engine. "Preparing for Morris today, a bunch of other meetings —time has gotten away from me." In truth I hadn't seen much of BeJo over the last week. The one evening we'd had together, I'd tried to find the right words but the prospect of a prolonged deep and meaningful night of process had felt overwhelming. I hadn't brought up our arrangement.

"We don't have time for personal things right now," I snapped. "We have to talk about how to approach Morris."

"All right," she gave in, her voice small. "We'll talk about 'us' when you come over tonight."

I nodded absently. It was Monday—Rachel's night.

"Are you sure you want to do this, babe?" she asked as I pulled onto Hollywood Boulevard.

I nodded. "I'm sure. This might get everyone's job back. If the strike carries on into the fall, the picket line will wane. If it never resolves there will never be lesbians again at GCSC."

"But it's your reputation on the line. You have a lot to lose if this gets out."

"My political reputation is strong enough to take the hit."

"You'll be called a turncoat, a traitor. They'll kick you off the Strike Committee."

"I should be so lucky! I read through the whole lawsuit document last week. I found no other cracks in the door. This is the only way."

I parked Lionheart a half block north of Morris's well-known loft address, 1428 N. McCadden Place. Multiple other cars provided good camouflage. Surveying the street, I was suddenly anxious; my skin broke out in a cold sweat. What if Morris was setting me up—just so he could publicly say, "Jeanne Córdova crossed the picket line"? What if he had Don Kilhefner or Lillene Fifield in there with him?

I turned to Rachel. "Please, go and knock on his door and see if he's alone. I'll wait in the car. If he's alone, wave at me to come. If you see or hear someone in the background, make up an excuse and come back to the car. Don't go in. Tell Morris I've lost my flat brimmed leather hat and think I might have left it here last spring. You came to check if he's found it."

"That's lame."

"It is. But it gives us deniability; if you see others inside don't cross his threshold. Tell him you'll wait while he looks for my hat. Then walk back to me."

Rachel chuckled and took my hand. "It's a good thing I love you."

We sat studying each other. If we were caught the strikers would call us scabs. In the wider L.A. community of dykes we'd be outcasts, open to public ridicule. Seeing her flushed face, I began to have second thoughts. Was she doing this more out of love for me than political commitment? She kissed me on the cheek and opened the car door, and walked toward the line of fire.

Nestling back into Lionheart's protective leather, I watched Rachel approach Morris's building, command-central to L.A.'s most powerful gay leader. The post World War II construction boom that revitalized Hollywood had skipped over his two-story Craftsman bungalow. The outside of the structure looked like the wood had wrinkled from heat and rain exposure, and hadn't been painted since the Depression. Friends of Morris's, myself included, thought he was nuts to move into the dilapidated structure. When he'd first seen it, he was delighted with its "fabulous possibility!" The first floor had no walls, it was one huge room that could, and often did, seat seventy or eighty people at a meeting. The first floor's ceiling was partial, only jutting out over the back one third of the house. It created a second floor room that looked like a loft bedroom. Movement people never went up to the second floor. That was Morris's personal space.

Although I couldn't see them from the car, I knew that in back of his house Morris had two smaller but equally rickety structures that housed his vast collection of movement memorabilia. My mentor had visions of rehabilitating all three buildings and turning them into a museum of gay art. Today, they were shacks.

I sighed, realizing that I missed the days when Morris and I were close. Both of us were political centrists dedicated to grassroots organizing and almost always on the same side. With him I'd been constantly challenged, always learning new ways to think, strategize, and win. But this time, we were on opposite sides and I knew Morris was dangerous. My mentor had an almost frightening power to both create and destroy. And he'd taught me, "Never make yourself an enemy of someone whose bottom line is lower than your own. You'll always lose." Yet, here I was, about to face off someone whose bottom line was so low I sometimes couldn't see it. Life had been simpler when the straight world was our common enemy.

I saw Rachel knock on his door. A few seconds later, it opened. They were talking. Suddenly she turned and waved me toward her. I bounced out of Lionheart. Striding up the rickety wood-planked porch, it suddenly came to me that my mentor had chosen the new Highland Avenue location for his beloved Gay Community Services Center because it was only a ninety-nine yard pass from his McCadden Place house. Morris could finally be in two places at once.

The front door was ajar. Inside I heard Morris talking to Rachel, being his usual loquacious self. I inhaled and pushed the door all the way open.

Morris rushed me. "Ah, dahhhling, Jeanne Córdoba!" he greeted, and bowed as though I was Columbus returned from the New World. He was the only person I knew who pronounced my last name in its original Spanish form.

"Good afternoon, Morris," I said and bowed slightly, wondering why my body language became formal when I was in his company.

"Come in, come in, dear woman!" Morris waved his turquoise-studded hands with a flourish. "This house is always honored by your presence!"

For a few seconds his florid greeting stupefied me. I was always initially ill at ease around Morris, as I had been around my father. Perhaps it took a few moments to sort out my contradictory feelings and put them away. Most of us thought of Morris Kight as ageless, sprung from the head of Zeus full-grown as the effeminate alter ego of Alexander the Great. He was something of a genius and had practically invented gay liberation in L.A. But he was just a fallible man. I needed to remember that.

My replacement father ushered me in with a tilt of his head and a grand, gathering sweep of his arm, much the same gesture as my father had employed when welcoming important people into his home. Both men had been poor boys, born the same year in similar no-name Texas towns that neither liked to talk about. I inhaled the familiar smell of musty old papers—history mixed with contemporary sweat and food.

"This is Rachel." I stumbled for a late introduction, seeking to regain my center.

"Yes, wonderful woman!" Morris boomed at Rachel. "Your new lover," he continued expansively, but I did not miss that his voice lowered, or that he studied my face intently as he announced Rachel's position in my life.

Morris was also the J. Edgar Hoover of the gay movement. He knew everything about everyone. He knew each person's espoused political views, and he knew what he or she actually did. He knew where every major gay activist slept at night and whose bed they got out of in the morning. Bedroom knowledge translated well into political power. Unlike Hoover, Morris didn't have to keep files. He kept everything in his head.

"I'm not here to talk about my personal life," I interrupted, seeking to abort personal connection. "I'm here to talk about the strike."

"Yes, yes, of course you are." He shooed Rachel and me toward the sitting area with its sagging flowered couches. No one knew what Morris Kight lived on. He'd never held a paying job, he didn't have family money. When he did have money he'd order more political leaflets, not paint. We all assumed Morris drew disability checks having somehow convinced the government that he couldn't work, "compensation for discrimination," as some of us full time activists who were receiving government aid called it. Other than that, Morris appeared to live off the kindness of strangers.

I stood next to his dilapidated sofas. "Before we sit down, Morris, we have to come to an understanding. Rachel and I were never here. We never met with you. Do you agree?"

"Yes, yes," he bowed again, "of course. That's the way it must be. Come. Sit. We'll talk. Forgive these papers everywhere. The Stonewall Democratic Club has been meeting here with members of L.A.'s City Council."

"I hear you're angling to elect a pro-gay City Council President," I replied, wanting to let Morris know I was plugged in about his most recent political endeavors.

"Yes, yes, quite exciting. You really must join this new Democratic Club. We're working nationally as well as locally. We need lesbians…especially of your caliber."

Why was Morris pressuring me to join his new political club, I wondered, feeling my face pinch with annoyance. He knew I couldn't ignore the picket line and join any new organization he founded, much as I understood its importance and might well want to be a part of it. We both knew that Jerry Falwell's evangelical movement was growing so fast in the United States that our movement had to come out of its city-state mentality and learn to fight on a national level. That meant this strike had to be solved so that lesbians could rejoin gay men for these battles.

Rachel and I took our seats. I said, "Morris, I don't think you should look forward to me or other lesbians joining your Democratic club right now. The timing sucks, don't you agree?"

Kight lowered his head and rubbed his forehead between his thumb and forefinger. "Yes, yes, I suppose so. Another time then."

Morris noticed that the beautiful, large Navajo tapestry hanging on the wall opposite had caught my eye. "It's from Truchas, New Mexico," he said. "Fabulous, isn't it?" A smile spread across his face. "And how are your parents?" he continued. "Such a wonderful family,"

My mental discipline flew out the front door for a moment. I felt flattered. Morris was a student of ethnicity and had asked me countless questions about my background. He seemed particularly fascinated with my father's Spanish-Mexican roots. But then I remembered who I was talking to. Watching my godfather parry and thrust, I realized that greatness often bred dissemblance. Most of human intercourse is mundane, so geniuses had to affect performance to pretend that they fit in socially. But Morris would get no buy-in from me today.

"Let's talk about the Center's family, or lack thereof, Morris. The strike has gone on for months. The Center is bleeding to death."

"It's a flesh wound." Morris waved as if he were swatting a fly. "Your lesbian community will bleed to death faster than the Center."

My backbone stiffened and my voice dropped into a dark place. So he wanted to play hardball. "If you men are so concerned with the health of the lesbian community, why did the Center reject the Westside Women's Center's offer to mediate?"

"It was felt that the staff of the Women's Center was not neutral."

"'It was felt?' That is pretty damn passive, Morris. You mean you decided to reject that offer."

"If there is going to be negotiating," Morris spoke cautiously, "it needs be between the dissidents...I mean, the former employees...and the Center's Board."

I hated Morris's dismissive word, "dissidents"; it was his way of not recognizing the strike. I leaned forward. "If the Strike Steering Committee formally called the Center through our lawyer with an invitation to come to the negotiating table, would your side say yes?"

Morris pressed his hands together. "Yes, I would say yes. What the Board would say, I don't know."

"But, you could persuade them."

"The Board would say yes, if in fact I would bring them terms and agreements we could live with."

I lit a cigarette. Now came the devil and the details. "Terms such as what?"

Morris looked me in the eye, "We would want the picket

line dispensed with—"

"That's our strongest weapon," I interrupted. "That's not gonna happen until the ink is dry on an agreement."

"Then you'd have to stop the harassment, the tire slashing and the shoving of our staff through the picket line to the front door."

"That could happen as soon as there is an agreement to talk," I said. "The Center would have to agree to stop trying to get a legal injunction against the line."

"Agreed, only as long as talks are going on," Morris said. "But all of you have to stop sending letters to our funding agencies."

"We'd agree to that if talks were going forward in good faith." It was time to move the demands to stage two. "The Center would have to stop contesting our right to unemployment checks."

Morris drew a sharp breath. "If we did that, we'd be admitting guilt in the wrongful termination."

"Then, as soon as we reach a settlement. You'd have to let our people get those checks."

"Agreed." Morris's eyes flashed. "Then, you dissidents would have to agree in writing that there would be no further treasonous attempts to take more programs out of the Center."

I stood suddenly and began to pace. For a moment, I'd seen the contorted face of my father in Morris's expression—a demand that I give in to his authority. As I turned back to face him, I saw him run his jeweled fingers through his hair. The femininity of the gesture erased my father's countenance. Unlike Dad, Morris had never tried to humiliate me personally.

The mutiny of the APW was one of the few victories of the strike. I chose my words carefully. "What's done is done Morris. We won't go any further down this path. And that was not treason."

Morris's eyes narrowed. "That was our largest grant. The Center needed that funding."

Dwelling on this bitter pill was not putting Morris in the frame of mind to make other concessions. "Speaking of money,

Morris, how much are you willing to offer in order for us to accept an out of court settlement?"

Morris gasped and pointed a ringed hand toward the rotted timbers of his roof. "We have no money! Not since this vile and violent picket line."

I sat down. Money could be a deal breaker. Despite my objections, the struggle to reform had become defined as a "strike"—not a gay versus feminist issue. Compensation was a central topic at the strike meetings. "The Center would have to pay back wages, as is the norm in strike settlements, and would have to pay some kind of severance to those who chose not to return."

"Impossible!"

"Perhaps the Board will have to go sell themselves on Selma," I quipped, referring to Hollywood's male hustler street. "A public commitment of money has to be the backbone of the settlement. Morris, you did fire us! Did you think you could get away with firing eleven people just because you want to? This is not some agitprop like making Alpine County a gay state! GCSC is not your own little back pocket group of buddies. You have to take legal responsibility for that. There's no other way to make it up to people."

"We have done nothing to you people that requires compensation!"

"There has to be some token amount offered."

"GCSC is barely scraping by. I'm sure you know that."

Morris harangued me about the Center's finances, or lack thereof, for the next twenty minutes. His information only confirmed my on-the-street calculations. I'd made it my business to know what donations were coming into GCSC. The picket line had destroyed what little reserves they had. Morris wasn't lying. They had no money. As he talked, I pondered. Personally, I thought it was wrong to demand retribution money from a gay institution—no matter what the reason. It was a charity, for God's sake. But I couldn't concede without at least token payment. June and the others wanted their pound of flesh.

Stalling for time, I lit another cig. Morris, I knew, had begun to cultivate a few rich closet-case gay men in town. These patrons would donate to see this strike disappear. "Let's say, Morris, hypothetically, that both sides agree to a settlement sum of X dollars. The Center could start off by low-balling us; show us some records that reflect the nothing you have. The strikers would lower their demand. Then, GCSC agrees to the lower sum of Y but stipulates that because the Center receives donations over time, you need to pay down the sum over time. A long time. Like, five years. That way the Center can absorb the cost, without crippling financial damage in the here and now. And to the strikers, a symbolic justice will appear to have been served."

Morris's face had darkened. "Justice! Payments!" He bobbed indignantly in his chair. "We will not agree to such words!"

Finally, Morris stopped bobbing. "You'd have to drop the lawsuit, of course," he continued, as I watched his eyebrows try to work their way from shock to appeasement.

"Yes, that would be our last move," I agreed. "In return the Center's Board enacts standard employee Personnel Policies and Procedures."

"*The Lesbian Tide* would have to call off the community boycott," Morris continued. "You'd have to convince lesbians to return to the Center."

I sighed. "Yes, Morris, *The Tide* would call off the boycott, but GCSC would have to back up reconciliation with real and public change. The Center would have to seat one or two known feminists on your Board. You have to offer everyone their jobs back and put some of the Gay/Feminist 15 into management."

"Ahhh," Morris let out a long slow breath. "That will not be possible."

Morris's narrow-eyed glint considered me as mine countered his.

"What exactly is not possible?" I asked, realizing that a deal breaker was on the table.

The man leaned back in his armchair, his voice trying too

hard to sound nonchalant. "Perhaps I misunderstand. I had assumed that few of the dissidents would want to return to work at GCSC."

"That's quite an assumption." I hid my surprise. "How few... had you assumed?"

"Very few."

I sat back, flummoxed. The possibility that GCSC would settle but NOT offer strikers the option to return had been so remote that it hadn't even been raised in meetings.

Morris saw my confusion. "How many of the strikers might want their jobs back?"

"I'm not sure," I hedged, looking to guess at a number.

"Do you want to come back on staff or to the Board?" Morris asked.

"No Morris, I wouldn't go back if the Center was the last gay bar open on the planet. I'll never work for the Center again."

"That's excellent," he sighed. "There is a lot of strong feeling against you as being the leader of the dissidents."

I started laughing. "Morris, I am anything but the leader in this circus!"

"The Board thinks you are."

"Do you think I am?"

"No, we've worked together too long. I know your politics. But my Board perceives you as such. And politics is perception."

"If my not coming back were a condition from your side, I could insist to the strikers that I can't return due to *The Tide* needing me." I drew a quiet breath of relief. My returning, if only to seal an agreement, would amount to conscription to purgatory.

"We couldn't take back any of the other ringleaders either," Morris continued flatly. "Not June Suwara, Dick Nash, Eric Morello, Colin McQueen, or April Allison. Certainly none of the women associated with the alcoholism program can return."

"You've just named half the strikers! That's hardly acceptable."

Morris continued his voice dropping into a conspiratorial

tone. "There are, among the dissidents, people who want to bring down the Center."

"Most of the women are separatists," I defended, "who don't want to work with men unless it's in a feminist context."

"Those aren't the people I am speaking of," Morris replied. "There are people in your group who want to overthrow the Board of Directors and shut down GCSC. They have hidden agendas."

Suddenly, Morris stood up. "Tea anyone? How do you take yours?" As he took teacups down from his makeshift kitchen selves, I knew I'd stumbled upon my godfather's real bottom line: he didn't want any of the major players back at the Center. Power meant everything to Morris. He had to maintain his power as GCSC's dictator. He would make other compromises, but not that one.

Personally, I didn't care if Morris ran his own Center until the millennium blew past us. Apart from illegally firing feminists, I thought GCSC was a good thing, even an amazing thing. At the birth of our movement I hadn't conceived that gays in L.A. would ever have their own government-funded social services center.

What disturbed me most about both Morris and my father was that each had the power and skill to shape his passions into a finely-honed laser beam that de-materialized any obstacle that stood in his path. In my father, this formidable power was focused on becoming a business success. Morris's saving grace, in my eyes, was that his laser intensity was most often focused on the human condition and what he could do to improve it. That said, I also knew that the secondary focus of Morris's laser energy was his own ego. It was an almost separate entity inside him that fed on raw power.

I sat back in the cushions and listened to the sound of boiling water on Morris's stove. Was I the pot calling the kettle black, I wondered? For years I'd fought tooth and nail to keep *The Lesbian Tide* on its ideological lesbian feminist course —my course. Was the house of my own ego a neighbor to Morris?

Early on I'd realized that politics was heavily influenced by ego, and denial of it was the hallmark of real egomania. Owning one's ego was the only way to keep it in check. There was no fortune to be made in giving up a career to work on behalf of one's people. So ego was the lubricatory currency, when altruism ran dry. My ethics dictated that it was all right to be partially motivated by ego, as long as it did not become the sufficient or determinative cause of my political actions.

Rachel grabbed my hand and whispered hoarsely, "He doesn't want any of us back!"

"Shhhh," I whispered, as I squeezed her hand to let her know I heard her but couldn't take my focus off Morris to acknowledge her feelings.

My mentor returned with teacups and pot, and bent over the coffee table to serve us.

Rachel said caustically, "I don't care for any, Morris."

"I don't drink tea," I said, putting my hand over my cup.

"Ah," said Morris as he filled his cup and sat down comfortably.

"Look Morris," I resumed. "We can't spend the day here. Someone is likely to come by. What about the jobs? GCSC must put the right to return to work on the table."

"We will make that pretense only if we can be assured that none of the ringleaders will accept the offer."

I picked up a pen and tablet. "Give me those names again."

Morris repeated his hit list. Scribbling the names, I realized it was a safe bet that most of the named hated GCSC too much to authentically want their jobs back anyway. But how to tell the likes of June and the others that the Center would only make the offer if it was guaranteed they won't take them? Pride and ego would make them want to say, "No way!"

Aloud I said to Morris, "I'll make this work. You have a deal."

"You can persuade your side?" Morris parried.

"Persuading them will take whatever credibility I have left. There's deep anger…"

"On both sides…"

"But yes, I'd be willing to give it all I've got if I knew it wasn't in vain, that the Center would accept."

Morris sipped his tea. "How will I know if you've succeeded?"

"When you get the final phone call from me asking you to call your lawyer to call ours to negotiate."

"I'll want to hear from you at that this point that our terms are agreed upon."

I stood up. The room's stuffy heat was laying heavy on my head. "I understand," I said to Morris as I held out my hand. "Maybe this is where the good faith comes in."

"Quite so," Morris shook my hand, "Let us begin."

Chapter 23

Front Seat Rapture

[Los Angeles]

Mid-August, 1975

Rachel popped the caps off her beer and my Dr. Brown's cream soda with a bottle opener she carried on her keys, her only butch accessory. Driving away from Morris's we'd stopped at a liquor store for some celebratory drinks.

"How on earth do you plan to convince the Strikers Committee to come to the table?" she asked. "Your promises to Morris took a lot of clit!"

I laughed. "The difference is, Morris really *has* the power, and I'm faking it. Here's the plan. I'm going to tell Patton that Morris called me—because we know each other. That he feels he can't lose face by formally calling her and risking a loud, fat, public 'No.' I'll tell her that he's desperate to settle and that I think he's ready to give us what we want if the strikers take the first step and issue a public invitation."

"But he's not."

"That's the hard part," I thought aloud, bringing Lionheart

to a stop in *The Freep's* parking lot. "You and I have to get the strikers ready to settle for much less than what they...we... want."

I killed the engine. Rachel leaned back against the passenger door and brought her legs up on the leather seat between us. We felt victorious. We had confronted the enemy and forced him to promise the strikers a public apology and to come to the negotiating table. My adrenaline was high and Rachel's folded legs offered a new challenge. She looked particularly beautiful in that moment, her face flushed from the day's excitement. The blue of her eyes was highlighted by a sky-colored blouse. She was right; we didn't see enough of each other in daylight hours.

"I wouldn't go back to work for the Center if it were the last gay place in L.A.," she said. Her shoulders shook like she was trying to ward off a chill.

"What's wrong?" I asked, watching her fingers start to pick at her nails like birds desperate for crumbs.

She sighed. "I feel rattled. You and Morris sounded so angry at times, and I hate that we had to do this so secretly, behind everyone's back."

"Not all activism is as fucked up as this," I tendered. "This strike ranks as one of the most contorted I've ever been involved in." I reached for her feet and began to massage them. "But you, darling, will have to grow a thicker skin if you're going to stay in politics."

"Maybe I'm not cut out for this kind of high tension." She reached down to the floor, producing another beer. "I haven't slept well since the day we were fired. Politics is a thrill, but there's so much pressure..."

I uncrossed Rachel's legs, leaned over and snuggled my face against hers. "How about the pressure of my body on yours?" I asked, flipping the radio on to a soft music station.

"I'm serious," she said, stroking my hair. "I'm trying to sort things out. When this strike is over, I need to decide whether or not I want to be an activist."

I began to undo the top button of her blouse.

She slapped my fingers. "Stop that, babe. Do you seriously think you're going to make love to me in a parking lot? My father would take a horsewhip to you!"

Now lying on top of her, I proceeded with her buttons. The session with Morris had revved me up. My body needed to unwind. I traced her collarbones to the place where they formed a shallow hollow at the base of her throat. She smelled like the wildflowers in the mountain meadow of Tuolumne.

"Oh shit!" I said. "I almost forgot something really important. Reach over me and open the glove compartment. It's a little brown box."

I heard the glove snap open. "Is this it?" she asked.

"Open it. It's a present for you."

"What's the occasion?"

"It's a just because present. Just because we've been lovers for almost three months, and just because it says how much I love you."

Rachel lifted the lid and took out a small, carved jade-stone heart on a gold chain. She looked at it for a long time. Finally she threw her arms around my neck.

"I love it." She kissed me on the lips. "It's the perfect size for me."

"The right size," I replied, gathering her close, "tiny, but lovely." Watching the radiance on her face gave me a deep sense of peace. The feeling was not a condition that permeated much of my life, yet I was beginning to associate this fulfilled state with being with her—even when we weren't making love.

"It's precious. Where did you get this?"

"From the Hopi reservation in New Mexico," I answered. "I've been saving it for a long time…until I knew who in my life it belonged to."

She bent her neck toward me. "Can you put it on?"

I fastened the chain before settling back onto her chest. My jade heart dropped into the hollow between her collar bones, filling the space. "Delicately carved to size," I whispered. My head on her breasts once more, I could hear Rachel's breathing quicken as my hand stroked her thigh.

"I guess this means you really do love me?" she whispered.

I lifted my head. "That is why I asked you to join *The Tide's* staff. I do want to see more of you."

Rachel took my face in her hands. "Seriously, Jeanne, I can't sit in a room every Thursday night with BeJo and other women you've slept with. I'm not like you. I'm not cut out for this non-monogamy. At least not with someone I'm in love with."

My heart started pounding as I listened to Rachel's words. Neither of us had told the other, I'm in love with you. *In love* went a step further than simple loving. It meant your body parts tingled when you heard that person's voice, your skin gave off the wild scent of no return when you touched.

"Does this mean you've changed your mind about non-monogamy?" I asked, my voice troubled.

"It seemed like the right thing, what feminism says about not being possessive. But my heart feels otherwise. I should have stopped seeing you when I realized you lived with someone else."

I groaned. This was definitely not the topic my body wanted.

"You promised me we'd see more of each other after you talked with BeJo and broke off your arrangement. When is that going to happen?"

I flinched. "I'll talk to her."

"You told me that last week."

"Forget it." I sat up. My body couldn't take anymore false starts.

Rachel pulled me back down on top of her. "We're not finished," she soothed, wrapping her arms around my neck. "I love my heart. And I'm touched that you want to share *The Tide* with me. I know it's the centerpiece of your life."

"So," I stroked her cheek, "you're just saying no to joining because you're viciously jealous?"

She fell back against the passenger door laughing. "You'd better finish what you started, or you'll see vicious!"

I spread Rachel's legs apart and adjusted myself on top of

her, my left foot braced against the steering wheel. She brought up her skirt and wrapped her legs around my waist. Fleetingly, I was grateful that I'd parked close to the building and in the staff section. Free love at *The Free Press* meant never having to apologize for when, where or how much.

I pried loose the rest of her buttons and pressed my lips into her breasts searching for the root of what made me want Rachel so much, and so often. I'd never felt so physically gripped, so captured and compelled by a lover. My enslavement mystified me. The answer had to lie somewhere beneath the chocolate-toned freckles that lay over her pale skin. Tension gathered in my calf muscles and groin. My longing sought relief. I kissed her hungrily, and pulled her more tightly against me. My hand yanked her skirt up to her waist. I felt the fabric of my shirt rip, but her mouth on my nipples made it okay. I struggled with her knotted belt until it finally gave. My palm slid over her belly, my open jeans zipper scraped my knuckle as my fingers entered her and pressed a path. Her hips moved under me. My breath came tighter and shorter and I found her clit with my thumb.

"Jeanne," she gasped, expelling my name with her breath. "Come to me." She pulled my head up bringing my lips to hers as she cried out again, "Don't let go!" With my other hand I gently cupped her mouth stifling the echoes of her orgasm. I sucked in her scream, filling my lungs with the sound of her pleasure. As her passion subsided, mine rose. She cupped my ass in her hands and pressed me against her thigh. The locus of power shifted between us, and the rush washed through me, forcing my mouth off hers.

Then tears came, as they almost always did with Rachel—out of joy or pain, I wasn't sure. It was a grief that slept underneath who I was. First, the pounding drive. Then, the simple release. The intensity between us brought out both the feminine and the masculine in me, making them conscious of each other as they struggled for separation. In those moments I was safe—spirit without constraint. It felt like fate yet came as shockingly as a rogue wave rises out of the sea. Catching my breath, I realized that making love with Rachel fed my need to feel. This was the mystery of our connection. She was the time and place for me to feel.

My sobbing eased and I rolled to Rachel's side, still clinging to her. Did she know that I found peace through her? I was too afraid to ask her.

"Jeanne," she tugged my hair, "where are you?"

"I'm here," I murmured, as I gathered her into my arms and began to rock us. "I love you."

She started singing softly in my ear, the words from Keith Carradine's surprise new hit about uneasy lovers. Humming along, I followed what I knew to be Rachel's thoughts behind the lyrics as she sang about giving love away when one's lover wasn't free.

As she finished the last chorus line saying I'm easy, yeah I'm easy, I teased her. "Yes indeed, easy is the perfect work for you! You could come if I blew on you."

Rachel smacked me playfully on the mouth. "Those aren't the words I was hoping you'd say."

"I'm calling you easy from now on..."

"Only between us," she whispered. "I'm not this way with others. And you shouldn't talk; you're only seconds behind me!"

A ray of the slanting sun fell on Rachel's forehead, bringing out gold strands in her hair shining against the dark upholstery.

"We should get dressed and go home," she said. "I can't believe we did this in a car."

"Not yet," I protested, still feeling weak. "I can't stand right now, my legs are too wobbly."

"Just a few moments then." Rachel relaxed and I sank back into her and drifted.

A chill rippled down my half-naked back. Lionheart was shrouded in twilight. Still lying on Rachel, bonded together by sweat and orgasm, I realized my legs were bent at the knees; my feet were poking out of the driver's window. I brushed her lips and woke her.

Kissing my fingers, she whispered, "It's late, we should go."

I lifted the jade heart from the hollow in her neck. "This is my way of saying that when I'm not with you, I'm practicing delayed gratification."

"Excuse me?" Rachel laughed her deep throaty laugh. "I didn't hear anything delayed about your gratification."

"I meant emotionally," I said. "When I'm not with you, I'm still with you."

Rachel studied me; her words came cautiously, "Is this your way of committing? Are you saying you want to be monogamous with me?"

I boomed out playfully, "I'm saying, I shall have no other women before ye!"

Rachel tensed. "What about BeJo? You haven't even talked to her yet."

"I meant...no other women besides BeJo. We never make love anymore, so yes monogamously."

Rachel began to squirm as though she wanted me to get off her. "That's not good enough anymore, Jeanne," she said, enunciating each word slowly.

I lifted myself off her. "All right," I blurted. "I'll talk to BeJo tonight."

Rachel was sitting up now too, arranging her skirt and blouse. She stopped abruptly. "What do you mean, tonight?"

I sat up too, surprised by her question. "It's BeJo's birthday. I'm taking her to a movie and a surprise party tonight."

Rachel stopped dressing. "It's Monday night. *Our* night together."

"Shit!" I let out a whistle between my teeth. In the excitement of seeing Morris this morning, I hadn't made the connection that tonight was indeed BeJo's birthday and it was falling on a Monday night! That meant I should have exchanged Monday for Tuesday this week with Rachel. But I hadn't. Denial and slippage had me cornered now.

I looked at Rachel. She'd stopped moving altogether. "Are

you telling me you seduced me in your car knowing you had to leave?"

I tucked my sweat-wrinkled shirt into my jeans, realizing I didn't have time to go home and change. "Of course not," I defended, "I forgot what day it was until I saw it was dark." I was moving quickly now, panicked by having glanced at my Timex. I was always late to meet BeJo, but never on her birthday.

I couldn't look at Rachel. "I'm sorry," I mumbled. "I can switch tonight for tomorrow night and be with you tomorrow." I opened my driver's door, got out and scurried around to Rachel's door. "Come on," I opened the passenger door. "I'll walk you to your car."

But Rachel sat still, looking straight ahead. "You'll walk me to my car?" she repeated, speaking to my windshield, her voice oddly icy.

I leaned forward offering to help her out. Then I saw her face, a moment ago radiant with joy, now vacant. Its usual pink color drained, her jaw set tight as if she was in physical pain— this was a look I'd never seen.

She turned to stare at me, waving an arm across the front seat. "So what's this called?" she asked her voice strident, "Fuck 'em and dump em? You forgot you were going to leave me until after you practically raped me in the front seat of your car."

Stunned by her words, I looked around the parking lot hoping we were alone. I knelt down beside her and whispered, "How can you use the word rape? WE were making love! You took my clothes off too. I wouldn't leave if this were not a big occasion—"

"And what kind of occasion was this?" she screamed, jumping out of the car and knocking me on my ass. "A meaningless fuck? You're not interested in spending weekends with me. You're never going to break your arrangement with BeJo!"

I scrambled to my feet and reached for her. "Of course I am! I'm sorry my timing sucks—"

"Get out of my way!" Rachel stepped away from me. She ripped the jade heart off her neck and threw it at me. "And you can keep your damn heart. You have no idea what a normal relationship looks like. You make me feel like a whore!"

Rachel began running barefoot across the asphalt toward her own car. I stood, momentarily paralyzed, knowing I should go after her, yet knowing she wouldn't listen if I did. I could hear myself making up an excuse on the phone to BeJo about why I was blowing off her birthday. I couldn't do that to BeJo, not after the years she'd been through with me. And yet, I ran after Rachel.

"Rachel!" I screamed, "Wait, don't go like this," I swerved, breaking my run to avoid colliding with a homeless man pushing a shopping cart, staring at me through his matted dreadlocks.

By the time I reached Rachel's green sedan, she'd locked the doors, gunned the ignition, and thrown the car into reverse. I heard the transmission pop and I quickly jumped out of her way.

Chapter 24

The Cuckoo's Nest

[Los Angeles]

Mid-August, 1975

It was cool in the darkened movie theater, and it took me a while to distinguish BeJo's silhouette from the crowd. I crept wordlessly into the empty seat next to her.

She bent toward me and whispered, "I was afraid you were going to blow off my birthday."

"No way! I was—"

"Tell me later," BeJo cut me off and turned back to the film.

I couldn't tell if she was angry with me. Not even her mother's funeral could interrupt BeJo from a movie. To the farm girl from Iowa, Hollywood's world of film was comprehensively compelling.

I slumped deeper into my chair. BeJo and I had recently settled into a new, slightly modified non-monogamous routine. She was now seeing Pody on Monday and Friday nights when I was with Rachel, but we still rigidly observed one of the cardinal rules of non-monogamy: Don't ask for details. I closed my eyes and stretched my legs. My nerves were shot and I was exhausted. Leaning toward BeJo, I pressed my shoulder into hers seeking to recapture the sense of equilibrium I often felt when I was with her. In BeJo's company, I was unconditionally okay. So different than with Rachel, where I often felt like I was struggling to stand on quaking ground.

I dug deep into my jeans pocket and fingered Rachel's jade heart, which I'd picked up from the asphalt in *The Freep* parking lot. Touching it made me feel closer to her as I slouched back into the slanted theater chair and closed my eyes. I'd never loved a woman so completely before; from her ankles to her forehead, I loved every sinew that held Rachel's body together. And in the process, I'd given Rachel a part of my soul.

I opened my eyes to find Jack Nicholson staring at me, trying to convince the audience that he wasn't a mental case. It had been BeJo's birthday call to see *One Flew Over the Cuckoo's Nest*. She liked tormented leading men. I stole a look at BeJo and screwed my face into a frown, hoping it looked like I was captivated by the movie. In a way, I was. I, like the protagonist in the film, also felt desperate, crazy, and afraid. My craving for Rachel had become something of an addiction. The vulnerability this realization exposed in me frightened me. But there was also a delicious thrill to spinning out of control with Rachel. I'd always liked living on the edge. But this edge could lead to chaos, and I knew chaos and politics didn't mix. Something in my life had to give between Rachel and BeJo, or I'd be the next one checking into a cuckoo's nest.

Finally, the credits began to roll. The lights came on. It was time to face BeJo. My breathing quickened. Non-monogamy was such a bitch.

"That was some weird flick!" BeJo said disapprovingly as we strode through the theater's lobby. "I'm so glad you showed up—now you can explain it to me." BeJo was dressed in her uptown clothes, a designer pair of charcoal slacks, which her long legs justified nicely, and a silk blouse. She didn't approve of denim on birthdays and was more than willing to put politics aside to dress for special occasions.

"I'm sorry, I had a long day with Morris Kight," I mumbled. "We had a negotiation. It was intense—"

"Don't try to sidetrack me with politics."

"All right! After Morris, I was with Rachel and—"

"I don't need you to spell it out!" BeJo retorted, as we both squinted under the lobby lights. "Jesus Christ, you still smell like her."

I winced, unsure how to interpret her remark. "I didn't think—"

"You're right, you didn't think." BeJo's voice came out unusually shrill. "It's my birthday, Jeanne. I know you're sleeping with her, but why did it have to be tonight? Your timing sucks big apples."

I hooked my thumbs in my belt loops. I felt like a clod, hurting BeJo's feelings on her birthday. "I'm sorry, BeJo."

I opened the lobby door for her and we walked onto the street together. "The trouble with your mind is that it's too complicated." BeJo read my ambivalence. "If I had a mind like yours, I wouldn't understand myself either. But hey…that's why I love you."

"So, it's not my body?" I quipped, anxious to make the most of light talk.

Reluctantly, BeJo put her arm around me. "Your body is okay, but your face is adorable. Let's get real, honey—I've been in the Navy. I've had the very best."

"Speaking of sex, how's Pody treating you?" I was still hoping to keep the topic light.

"Lower your voice!" BeJo commanded. "Pody is just fine in that department."

"So, you don't miss me so much anymore?"

"Don't be putting words in my mouth," she snapped. "You're still my primary lover. I've got my priorities straight, unlike some ditherheads I know."

"Ditherhead is my word, you can't use it on me," I teased.

BeJo laughed as we ambled across the street and came to her

car. "That's another reason I fell for you. I've got a whole new vocabulary since I met you."

"By the way," I said, holding the door open for her. "Thanks for not inviting Pody to your birthday party."

"It's our party," BeJo replied. "Let's leave the others out of it."

BeJo's party was at David's, a restaurant on Melrose, a fifties queen's bar with red flocked brocaded wallpaper and an interior dark enough to hide my guilt. My friend Robin had picked the location because she knew the piano-player. She had persuaded him to let us use his piano to sing songs to BeJo.

Two hours passed, with BeJo and I having gratefully little privacy among her friends and mine. As the evening drew to a close, Robin came up behind me while BeJo was opening her presents.

"You look pale as a white dyke," she whispered in my ear.

My buddy liked to tease me about being half-Mexican. In return, I called my Canadian-born friend a foreign alien. But tonight I had no snappy comeback.

Robin picked up on my flat affect. "What's going on with you?"

I turned to her, suddenly realizing that Robin was my reprieve. Maybe she could help me figure out what do about Rachel, and what to say to BeJo. Robin had had dozens of lovers.

"We have to talk!" I whispered under my breath, afraid of drawing BeJo's attention. My eyes had filled with tears.

Robin put her arm around my shoulder. "Poor baby dyke is bummed out?"

"When can we get together?"

"Lunch on Wednesday?" Robin offered.

"I'll come to your place," I agreed.

Getting dressed for bed BeJo thanked me for her party and

gave me a goodnight peck on the cheek. She was more than tipsy, but sober enough to keep her distance. She clicked off the lights and turned over. I let out my breath, grateful that she hadn't wanted to make love. I wasn't sure I could have brought myself to that party.

Lying next to her, I waited for the rhythm of her breathing to lull me but I couldn't keep Rachel and the parking lot out of my mind. Would she take her jade heart back the next time I saw her? I turned away from BeJo. Her breathing had become regular. The woman was a staunch pragmatist. Tonight, she could do nothing about the state of "us" so she'd simply fallen asleep. I knew she was trying to wait out my relationship with Rachel, just like she had out-waited others before her, but I also knew she was angry about Rachel in my life.

I'd been straddling the divide between lovers since I'd come of age in the world of love and sex. Since high school, there had been many who I had loved and lost: Donna, the gym coach who'd left to teach at another school; Kathy in my junior year; leaving the convent with the loss of a value system and a way of life; and then gay life and dozens of overlapping women, all carefully balanced against one another. By age twenty-six, I was sure that people didn't stick around, and that love didn't last. It was best to have backups. Until now. Until Rachel. Rachel, who had crept into my life through the back door I'd left ajar in case I needed to skip out. Rachel, who'd absorbed so much of me that I hadn't thought of dating another woman since the day we'd kissed in the GCSC parking lot.

And now I knew I was in trouble. My balancing act couldn't last. Actually, my mother had first warned me about the instability of non-monogamy. When I was a child, she'd told me about the Colossus of Rhodes, a huge bronze statue of a warrior straddling two sides of the harbor of the Greek island city, with the ocean lapping dangerously between his two legs. Ultimately, the warrior had split, his balance rocked by earthquakes, and he had crumbled and fallen into the sea. The moral of that story: decide which shore you want to live on before you end up swimming with the sharks.

I parked in front of Robin's building and took the elevator to her second floor condo. Beachwood Canyon was where the rich people lived in substantially better digs than my *Tide* and *Free Press* salaries could afford. Someday I'd live here, I promised myself, when gay people were free and I could devote some time to climbing above the poverty line.

Robin was standing in the doorway, already talking. "So, the kid has come home," her voice boomed down the corridor. She was dressed in her usual work-at-home attire: T-shirt and men's boxers. "Come in. You're wasting my air conditioning."

Six years my senior, Robin was one of the few people in my life that I allowed to treat me as her junior. After years of her insisting that I was like her younger brother Bobby, I accepted that we were never going to have any other kind of relationship. Besides, I no longer had an older sibling. Dominica had left early for Stanford and was studying to become one of the first female rocket scientists. In my father's eye, her rare achievements only compounded my queer-sheep status. Off in her high-security orbit, Dominica seldom invited sharing. Like a good, over-protective brother, Robin was always in my business.

She grabbed me by the shoulder and tossed me into a soft, black silk couch that rested on plush, silver wall-to-wall carpet. "Sit!" she ordered, "Put your feet up. What do you want to drink?"

"Coke, please," I murmured, sounding small. I fell back into the cushy sofa and threw my legs on a matching black ottoman. Robin's place was my home away from home because it bore no resemblance to my reality. With its silver-and-chrome-on black theme, picture frames, and chandeliers, I called her condo The Chrome Palace. It looked like the home Peter Pan might make for himself if he'd ever grown up and moved to Hollywood. Robin had invited few of our mutual activist friends here, and it was a comfort knowing I always had a place to hide from the movement.

She returned from the kitchen and dropped a bucket of ice

and six-pack of Coke on the glass table in front of me. "That should last you for a little while."

"You're always so gracious," I replied. "Makes me feel wanted."

Robin came to rest on the black and gray striped armchair facing me. "I graciously had to send a crying Patty out of here with Tito so you could come over and soak my shoulder," she retorted. Patty Harrison was Robin's live-in femme wife of seven years, although they were now non-monogamous and Robin slept with other butches. In fact, three years ago I was her first butch lover. Tito was Robin's gay male roommate, a fellow comic. He specialized in domestic salvage operations for Robin.

"Patty could have stayed—" I started to protest.

"No way," Robin cut me off. "She still gets hurt when I pay attention to you."

"Patty is genetically dramatic," I rebutted.

"Let's not re-wash our old linens." Robin waved away our past, which began with a show biz-intensive, six month drama lesson during which I'd lived with the two of them in a three-way love affair propelled by Robin being in love with me, me being infatuated with Patty, and Patty still in love with Robin.

"So. Why are we depressed today?" Robin leaned forward, confronting me. "Me, I have lots of things to be depressed about. ABC has cancelled my pilot, Tito wants to move out, and Patty says she's going to leave me if I don't give up my butch lovers!"

"What do you see in butches that I don't see?" I queried, my eyebrows raised. Robin was the first butch I'd met who was attracted to other butches.

"You didn't come here to talk about my lovers," Robin shot back. "Why are we depressed? We have Rachel. We have BeJo." Robin paused, squinting at me. "Are we also seeing someone else?"

"Isn't that enough?"

Robin's eyes danced. "There's no such thing as enough. You know me."

"We're talking about me!"

"Yes, yes. You'll have to keep reminding me."

I laughed. Even when I was on a bummer Robin never bored me. "That's okay; I don't really want to talk about it."

Robin vaulted out of her chair. "Do you want lunch? I've already started chicken soup. It's as good for the heart as for the body."

"I'll eat whatever you make," I said standing up.

"Good little dyke." Robin nudged me along into the kitchen.

She placed what looked like a pan with holes in its sides on the stove and turned on the flame. Watching her maneuver her tools confidently, a sexist thought occurred to me. My pal would make some butch dyke a good wife. Robin was surely a gay man born into the body of a lesbian, the very definition of what I called a "faggot-butch." She stopped clanging her instruments. "How are you and Rachel doing? She was so nice to give me her recipe for Cornish game hens last night. We're getting together next week to make penne putanesca. For a femme, she's a sensible woman," Robin babbled on, snapping the green things off the carrots. "Not gorgeous though, like Anderson or some of your other lovers. Or brilliant, like me. What do you see in her? She must be a good cook…"

"Don't insult my predilections just because you're not attracted to femmes," I scolded. You're the homo homosexual here."

Suddenly, I realized what Robin had said. "Wait—when did you see Rachel last night?"

"After BeJo's party. I went to the Saloon."

"Why didn't you tell me that when I walked through the door? You withholding little motherfucker! What did she say? Did she give you a message for me?"

"No message! Nothing, I promise!" Robin responded quickly to my desperate, angry tone.

I sat brooding on a barstool at the counter. No message meant Rachel was still angry with me. I sucked in my breath. Damn! I wanted so badly to reach out and touch her, tell her I'd talked to BeJo and everything was going to be all right.

Robin came to my side and slung her arm around my shoulder. "That's why I didn't tell you right away. I knew you'd be depressed if there was no message. Then we wouldn't have any fun."

"Robinnnn…" I wailed, "What if she's not speaking to me?" My voice echoed in the Chrome Palace.

"Why wouldn't she be speaking to you?"

I turned away and slumped on the barstool. "Yesterday, right before BeJo's party, we made love in the front seat of my car…in *The Freep's* parking lot."

"In the parking lot?"

"No one saw us."

"Then what did you do?"

"I…I sort of left."

"Does sort of mean that one part of you got out of the car and another part of you stayed with her?"

My fingers were engaged in pulling one hair from my head at a time and laying them in a line on the tiled counter. "No that's not what it meant. I mean…after we both climaxed, I saw what time it was, and I freaked…and just left."

"You mean you abused a woman in a car on the street and then left her to drive herself home?"

"How can you say *abuse*? We both came!"

Robin raised one eyebrow. I winced and dropped my head.

"Yes," I said quietly. "I had to leave."

Robin's eyes bulged. "You left her?" She backed away. "Have I taught you nothing these last years?" she yelled, waving a brass spoon in my face. "I thought I had taught you how to dress. How to act. How to treat a woman. I never should have graduated you! You're supposed to be a gentleman-butch. No wonder she's not speaking to you. I wouldn't either!"

I looked up at Robin. She had bragged publicly that I was the first graduate of "The Robin Tyler Good-Grooming School for Young Butches." Now she was yanking my degree. That demotion I could take, but her words *You left her?* resounded in my mind. I shut my eyes and pictured Rachel's expression when she realized I was asking her to get out of my car. Again I saw her lower lip quiver; her eyes grow wide with shock. *Christ!* Maybe my body had just wanted a quickie; maybe in my lust I'd just compartmentalized away my emotions, denying them to both of us.

Robin was still jabbering, "…and no! I'm not going to call her to apologize for you."

"I didn't mean to hurt her," I lamented. "I never thought she would take it so personally."

"You are such a heartbreaker, you little shit," Robin grumped, throwing a clump of carrots at me. "Get over here and cut these up," she ordered, returning to the stove. "But all is not lost. I'm sure she'll forgive you. She's obviously obsessed with you, too." Robin shook spices into the pot. "Romance isn't good for the movement. We shouldn't let ourselves get distracted. We're in the middle of a revolution."

"That's right!" I agreed, straightening my shoulders. "But life isn't just about the movement. Don't we need to find balance between the personal and the political?"

She stared at me. "Have you skipped meetings to be with her?"

"I've been late here and there," I equivocated.

"That's a bad sign; bad, bad, bad." Robin looked at my uncut carrots.

I waved the knife over them. "Do I cut them vertically or horizontally?"

"Give me that!" Robin took her carrots and knife back. "Just sit on the stool. Don't touch anything!"

I lit a cigarette. Robin cut the carrots horizontally.

"Hell hath no fury," Robin continued. "That's another reason why I don't date femmes—since Patty. Punishment, major punishment! A butch just slams the door behind her and leaves."

"What can I do, Robin? I'm in love with her. I want to be with her. What am I supposed to do about BeJo? "

Robin looked up, an idea dancing in her green eyes. "Do

what I did. Move them all in together! That way you could be with both of them."

"That's ridiculous, Robin!" I belched. The thought of Rachel and BeJo under the same roof made my guts twist. "These are radical times, sure, but that didn't work with you and Patty and me. Need I remind you?"

"Maybe that was because of you!" Robin persisted. "It did work with Judy and Patty and me."

"Yeah, for three months!"

"That's because we didn't like Judy that much…"

I brought the conversation back to me. "Robin! I feel so confused, what am I going to do?"

"You're not confused, you're scared! You're afraid to let go of BeJo because she provides a rock for you to run aground on. She's your sanity, your stability."

My lips parted to deny her, but instead I said, "That's a crude way to put it." BeJo and I were domestically compatible and we shared *The Tide* and loved newspaper work.

"She chose you. You are not in love with her," Robin charged.

"So what? She lets me live my life the way I want to live it. Does it really matter why we choose to be with someone? It's all so irrational."

"Maybe you needed a nurse when you met BeJo," Robin continued. "And now, you don't need a nurse anymore."

I said nothing. At times, I hated my big brother.

"How close to the edge is Rachel with you?"

"I never quite know where I'm at with her. Except that she's in love with me, too. At least she was before last night."

"What would you do if you were in Rachel's shoes?" Robin challenged. "In love with someone who lives with another woman and is more interested in the world of politics than the world of domestic bliss? What would you do if you were her?"

"I guess if I were Rachel…I'd cut off my left hand to save my sanity." I stared at the lit burner on the stove. "I would write her…I mean me, a long, definitive Dear Jeanne letter. An I love you, but…letter saying, 'You're a case of diminishing returns, a bad bet.'"

Robin sliced the heads off a bunch of long green stalks. "So why isn't she writing you that letter?"

"Maybe she is." I closed my mouth, dumbstruck by my own words. I stared at the noodles boiling on the stove. My flippant self withered. Good God...what if Rachel was doing just that? I rotated off the bar stool and began pacing the room.

Perhaps all my dallying with Rachel was a subconscious playing for time to find out if we were emotionally compatible as well as having this kind of almost religious physical connection. I'd wanted time to know what she was like in her domestic habits. Time to see what we had in common now that the strike might soon be over. Time to let my guard down. How come Rachel wouldn't give me a year? It had only been three months. What if I tried to apologize tomorrow and she slammed the door in my face?

I fell back onto the bar stool and looked at Robin, my face pale, my voice low. "I feel nauseous," I said holding my stomach.

"Córdova! Don't you dare throw up all over my lunch!" Robin yelled and slammed a lid on her noodles.

"What if she's writing me a good-bye letter?!" I screamed at Robin.

"Calm yourself," Robin demanded. "Rachel's a femme, isn't she? Femmes never go all the way when they leave you. They do it slowly, one finger at a time. But it's clear you're coming down to her finish line. So what are you going to do about it?"

"Cry?"

"Not good enough."

"Shoot myself?"

"Not helpful."

"I can't leave BeJo totally. Not yet, anyway. "

"Does Rachel really need you to break up with BeJo totally?"

"She didn't say that. She wants weekends with me. She wants me to break off my non-monogamous time arrangement with BeJo."

"So she did give you an ultimatum."

"Do you think so? It sounded more like a request."

"Femmes always tuck their ultimatums in like tight sheets on a bed you can't get out of."

"Yeah," I said, remembering, "that was her tone of voice."

"So go pack your Brylcreem and move in with Rachel over the weekends. See what happens."

"What about BeJo?"

"It sounds like you're not *with* BeJo anyway. Maybe she won't notice you're gone."

I stopped pacing. "That's comforting."

"So let me ask you this," she said, slamming some silverware in front of me. "Are you prepared to lose Rachel?"

My cigarette fell out of my mouth. Panic began in my lower gut and traveled to my mouth: "Good God, no!"

"There you have it," Robin concluded. She shoved a bowl of soup toward me. "So do the deed and get back to your politics!"

She sat down beside me and started eating, "Enough about women! Tell me what's new with the strike? Now that's something to be depressed about. I don't know whether you should trust Morris…"

Out of one fire and into another.

With trepidation, I opened the door and let myself into BeJo's and my apartment. Hearing the shower running, I tossed my briefcase on a chair and sat down in the breakfast room to wait for my live-in lover. Robin and I had spent the rest of the afternoon talking about the coming showdown negotiation with the Center. Instead of going to *The Freep*, I'd come home early, determined to catch BeJo before she went to work. And I was also determined to find Rachel tonight, and bring her the good news—that I'd broken the arrangement with BeJo and I was free to spend weekends with her.

The coffee pot was brewing next to the sink and cookies were baking in the oven. This was a good sign. Cookies in the oven meant BeJo wasn't baking the nails for my crucifixion.

That she'd forgiven me for almost blowing her birthday. I'd created quite a mess. How to begin the discussion with BeJo?

"Where were you all afternoon?" BeJo sailed into the kitchen, a towel wrapped around her. "I called *The Freep* and they said you hadn't come in all day." She sat in the chair next to me and folded her arms across her breasts. "It's not like you to skip work to be with Rachel," she quipped pointedly, her jaw tightly set.

I squirmed in my chair. The cookies were a dodge. BeJo was still pissed. How like her to warm me up, get me off guard, and then drop the Sword of Damocles on my head.

"I wasn't at Rachel's. I went to see Robin. We had some things to discuss."

"It seems I never know where you are!" BeJo retorted. "You could be in jail for some political thing for all I know. Are you and your gang really going to throw bricks into the Pussycat Theater that's showing the snuff movies? {1}Have you already started that? Or, you could be with some new lover in San Francisco. You're like a prairie fire that turns with the wind."

"I wasn't in jail and I'm not seeing someone new," I replied, seeing my opening. "I'm only seeing Rachel. I don't intend to see any other women."

"What you intend to do and what you actually do are often two different things. Sometimes they're three or four different things."

I cocked my head to one side, knowing this combative tone between us wasn't a good way to start. I spoke to her gently, "Would you rather I was seeing others besides Rachel?"

BeJo was silent for a few minutes as she stirred her coffee. "Of course," she said, her eyebrows seeming to fold in on themselves. "That way you wouldn't fall in love with her. I know you, remember, honey?"

"Then you know that I said right from our beginning that I couldn't be monogamous." I spoke softly, and stopped myself from adding, *because I was never in love with you.* Truth be told, I probably couldn't be monogamous with

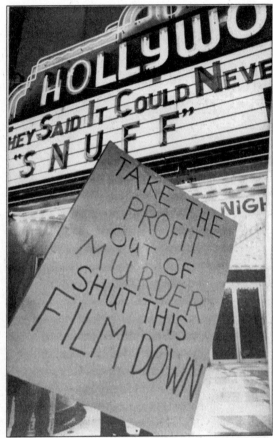

Protest at Hollywood Boulevard theater
showing "Snuff" movie that depicts sexual
murder of women. 1975. *Photo by E.K. Waller,
Lesbian Tide.*

anyone even if I was in love. Except maybe Rachel.

"And you know," BeJo continued, "that I think this non-monogamous lifestyle is a bunch of horse manure. It's just plain old *unnatural*. Besides, when we first met you were in no condition to date even me, let alone others."

I studied BeJo's soft, deer-like eyes, warm and full of love, as they had always been.

I fell down on one knee in front of her chair and took her hand, holding it in her lap. "You knew I'd get better eventually," I said.

BeJo studied my face as we exchanged memories of the dark times when we'd met, a few months before the National Lesbian Conference in '73 at a meeting of the organizing committee of

Raising the banner at historic National Lesbian Conference, UCLA. Event drew two thousand women from forty-five states. *1973, photo by Dorthy Nielson, Lesbian Tide.*

the conference. Quickly, BeJo had joined the group. "Just to hang around you," she'd later confessed. After nine months of exhaustive preparation, a devastating betrayal by my program co-chair and Trotskyist lover, and the highly charged arguments of national warring dyke tribes, I simply crashed into a full-blown nervous breakdown. Bringing together the largest dyke conference in history was politically explosive. Hundreds of lesbians favored a total separatist withdrawal from the world of men while other hundreds simply wanted to be open about being gay at their jobs without being fired. Amidst the politics, my personal pain was having a woman I loved deeply hang me out to dry publically as a Trotskyist in front of my own lesbian nation. Traumatized, I'd driven out of L.A., ending up in an isolated town up the Pacific coast. It would be seven months before I could face the world again. {2}

I'd spent the first three months of those emotionally pain-racked days lying on a couch at my friend Margie's house in Lompoc, listening to her write songs, convinced that I would be a dysfunctional vegetable for the rest of my life. Finally, I'd returned home to BeJo's apartment where all I could do was mark the rising and setting of the sun as I crouched in random corners of her living room rocking myself to sleep. For the next few months, it was BeJo who crept around the edges of my secluded hell and tended to me. BeJo who hovered over me like a lover-mother hen, helping me glue together the pieces of my fragmented psyche. BeJo who held my hand every morning and every night as I stared vacantly at the television. BeJo who made me eat and eventually took me out for long drives in Ramona to get me used to the world once more. If she hadn't been there for me I surely would have committed suicide or checked into a mental farm.

I owed BeJo my life—that I knew. But how much of my life? The whole thing? Forever? As I knelt on the carpet in front of her we slowly wiped away each others' tears.

She took my head, bent it to her and kissed me on the forehead. "Jeanne I know you've been healthy for a long while now. I know you need more in your life than I have to give. I've stayed with you hoping to make it last as long as it could. I've grown to a new level with you learning how creativity and intelligence work in your life and now in mine," she said, using her free hand to smooth my hair back. "That's why I've never made demands I would have with another lover. I know I am not enough for you."

"Don't say that." I turned away from her. "I hate it when you talk that way."

"Then tell me you're not in love with her."

"Why does that matter to you and me? I just want to spend more time with her on some weekends. You're dating Pody. You'll probably want to see more of her. "

"Don't you even start to turn this thing around on me." BeJo banged her coffee cup down on the table. "I asked you a question."

I grunted out a lie. "I forgot what the damn question even was."

"Are you in love with Rachel?"

The sword dropped. I lowered my head, unable to lie to her face. A noise began to grow in my head. It was becoming a racket, a panic. Say it! I screamed at myself. Just say it. She knows it anyway. I reached out with both hands to hold up the wall.

"Don't bother lying. I can see your answer." Her voice was so low I barely heard her.

The grating noise inside my head disappeared and was replaced by another sound, the final, hollow sound of a rite of passage between BeJo and me.

Chapter 25

The Body Count

[Los Angeles]

August 15, 1975

The phone rang continuously but she never picked up. "Rachel, where are you?" I asked, shaking the receiver in my hand as if I could pry lose an answer from it. My voice was hoarse. I felt strung out. In the gray light of a cloudy morning my *Freep* office with its posters and banners looked out of touch, like yesterday's life.

I hung up and looked through my open doorway at Penny, sitting at her desk across the hall, lost in editing. Her phone rang and she put her papers down to take the call.

Closing my door for privacy, I dialed Rachel's number again. "I've been looking for you since last night," I said to her machine. "I've got great news! I spoke with BeJo….Everything is going to be okay." I paused, hearing my words fall into the silence. "Call me as soon as you get this. I love you."

Where could Rachel be? I'd been calling her for twenty-four hours. If I couldn't reach her by noon, I'd screw my workday and drive to the Saloon to find her. It had been three days since we'd been together. I had to apologize and make things right between us.

"Córdova!" Penny's voice was shrill.

Looking up I saw her sprinting toward my office. Penny never ran. She was the picture of editorial decorum. She swung my door open, her lips stretched tight across her face as she fought for self-control. "Our police mole just called. Joe Tomassi has been shot!"

"Shot?" I stood up, bracing myself against my desk. "Like with a gun?"

"Yes!"

"Where?" I let the shock in. Joe and I had made an appointment for another interview next Monday.

"In front of the Nazi Party Headquarters in El Monte. Quick! Get in your car and go get the story!"

The crowd was thick with Nazis and cops. Tall uniformed shoulders eclipsed my view as I threaded my way toward the front steps of the two-story Nazi headquarters. A rigidly lettered tan sign was planted on the front lawn: American Socialist White People's Party HQ it read in black, no swastikas. The wood-shingled structure was neat, but worn, the peeling white paint the perfect camouflage in this working-class Chicano suburb. The window shades facing the street were drawn, the front grass well kept, weed-less, and otherwise anonymous.

The first part of Joe I saw was his blood. It glistened under the bright sun as it seeped slowly down the sidewalk toward the gutter. Edging closer through the crowd, I knew even before I saw his face that the khaki clad legs lying close to the front steps belonged to Joe.

Medics and police clustered tightly around his chest and face.

"He's been shot in the head," someone close to me gasped. I couldn't see. I didn't want to. My forward push halted, I prayed that the crowd would not part and force me to look at the rest of Joe. The cops hadn't even cordoned off the area yet.

"Is he alive?" I blurted to a creased-faced white man in an LAPD uniform. My voice came out high and thin.

"Don't see how," the cop muttered, glancing at my press badge. "There's his brain all over the sidewalk." The officer pointed ahead of him as he reached out, pushing apart the shoulders of two men standing in front of me. "Look for yourself."

The gray matter wasn't gray at all. The back of Joe's skull, the bone of it, was lying in a pile of mangled, salmon-colored muscle, the texture and color of shelled shrimp. Locks of black curly hair diverted the crimson-colored blood as it ran in rivulets toward the gutter.

I staggered backwards to a patch of grass, and doubled over and vomited. All around me I heard voices hissing: *Tomassi, Tomassi, did you know him?*

Tomassi, Tomassi, yes, I knew him. The boy, the man, the political militant as committed as me, yet on the other side. I knew his passion, his beliefs, and his heated rage. His willingness to die for the world he believed in. Yes, perhaps I knew him too well. Sitting in front of me stabbing chocolate cake, his smile teasing, his shoulders heaving with delight each time he saw that he'd shocked me. The memory of Joe's last words to me rang clearly, so casual yet frighteningly alive: "I don't think I'll live to see my thirtieth birthday."

God damn it. Yes, I knew him.

I picked my clipboard up off the grass and looked back at Joe, squinting so I wouldn't see too much. My Nazi lay on his stomach, his face turned toward me as if to say, "Fuck, I can't make our next interview." I couldn't tell if he was angry or sad. The unforgiving cement was his final resting place.

Averting my eyes, studying his chest, I wondered if he had regrets in the instant he knew death was coming, that he'd put his political life first, ahead of his family, or his girlfriend. I looked around; there were no women here. Did Joe even have a girlfriend?

EXCLUSIVE: LAST INTERVIEW

NAZI LEADER SLAIN

Southern California neo-Nazi leader, Captain Joseph Tomassi. *Los Angeles Free Press, August 1975.*

Did he know how to love? Perspiration poured out of me, I couldn't vomit the acid out of my mouth. My brain stretched for control. You're a reporter, it demanded. Get the story! My emotions taunted, He's dead. There is no story. Just walk away. Leave him in peace.

But Penny had sent me to think and write, not feel. I looked around for someone in charge. Buttoning up my shirt, I approached an officer with stripes on his sleeve.

Clipboard thrust forward, pen in hand, tape recorder switched on, I asked him, "Sergeant, do we know who shot him, or why?"

"Shotgun at close range," the sergeant exhaled, his navy-blue collar beaded with sweat. "They must have wanted him very dead."

"Then you have a suspect?"

"Turned himself in right after he shit in his own pants," the officer snorted. "An eighteen year-old. But we think he was acting on orders from the leader. One of their own. Ain't that always the truth?"

"One of their own?" I prodded further, wondering who inside the Nazi Headquarters would want to take him down.

The sergeant jerked his thumb toward the front porch. "The shooter was standing guard right there, said Tomassi wanted to come back and take back his father's house. Says Tomassi's father left this building to him. But the father signed it over to the Nazis right before he died. But who cares about what these Nazis do. What difference does it make?" The cop dismissed me with annoyance in his gesture.

What difference does it make? The words repeated themselves in my mind as I stared vacantly at the sergeant's chest.

Would it make no difference when it came time for me to die? Would it make no difference when the Feds found and murdered the rest of the SLA and Weather Underground, like they'd done with the Panthers? Would the dead one day include others I'd interviewed, or friends whose secret lives I knew little about? The pigs that represented the law in our so-called democracy had killed student activists at Kent State as easily as the Nazis who had ambushed Joe. Members of the organization he'd built and led had gunned down Tomassi. Maybe if the Feds didn't kill us first, we on the Left would also simply knock each other off, like cannibals eating our own because we were starved for power and freedom. Here we were right now, lesbians pitted against gay men, gay strikers versus a gay Center.

Tears sprang from my eyes as I snapped off my tape recorder, and walked down the sidewalk toward Lionheart. Joe had left me a present. I no longer had to face the FBI's search warrant. As I entered the safety of my cave, bile rose up from my stomach. I fought the urge to vomit again. These months of fighting with Morris, my search to find something enduring with a lover, the endless decade of struggles for gay rights—twenty years from now, would my life have made any difference at all?

Threading the freeways back to L.A., I found myself driving toward the safety of the Women's Saloon. I couldn't shake the image of Joe's almost twitching brain muscle, the sight of his blood. I needed to feel Rachel's arms around me, stroking my face and telling me that somehow in this savage world, everything would be okay because we had each other.

But that could only happen if Rachel forgave me. Replaying the scene of her unclothed body on the front seat of my car, her breasts exposed to the world, I winced with humiliation. I might as well have thrown her a hundred dollar bill.

Reaching the Saloon's parking lot it dawned on me—I was bringing nothing. No flowers. No letter of apology. I dug around in the glove compartment for a shred of paper and leaned over the steering wheel, pen in hand. "Dear Easy," I began, and stopped. Definitely the wrong choice of word. I tore the paper up and reached for another. Tell her you're sorry, I heard Robin's voice. I began again:

My Darling, I came to the Saloon today to find you and to say I'm sorry. About leaving you in the car, about BeJo, about everything else, too. Not being there for you…so many times. I want to make us work. I want to make time for us. I have talked to BeJo. I have good news for us! Please, forgive me.

Reaching back into the glove compartment, I found a roll of scotch tape, sealed the note and entered the Saloon.

It was popping. The strong lights and din of women's voices steadied me. I'd be cool, I decided, and casually talk to others and maybe Rachel would come up to me. I saw the GCSC strikers' table peopled with Pody, June and April, and others. I meandered toward them taking the long way around, moving slowly past the bar and silverware table. No sign of Rachel.

"Hey Córdova, what's happening?" Pody stood up, greeting me with her usual social aplomb.

I smiled, as we hugged. Despite her dating BeJo, there was still warmth between us. After weeks of initial wariness, she and I had resettled into a friendly, though more distant, kind of friendship. After I'd told BeJo that I wanted to spend weekends with Rachel, she'd accepted Pody's invitation to go the San Diego Women's Music Festival this weekend. Now it was me facing a weekend without either BeJo or Rachel.

"Hi dykes!" I called to the strikers, my voice feigning an amiability I didn't feel. Be nice to June, I told myself. I would need her vote, and the votes of her cadre, to get agreement to negotiate with Morris.

Pody glided into another chair, leaving one empty for me. "We just got a letter of support from The Westside Women's Center," said April.

Sitting among them, I marveled at how we'd all come through an ugly summer together and remained, at least politically, cohorts.

"What does the letter say?" June demanded.

April said. "It's addressed to the Gay Community Services Center."

"Do you think they'll ever put the word lesbian in the name of the Center?" Pody taunted.

"In about ten years if we keep pushing them," I joked, sarcastically.

As April read to the group, I craned my neck, looking around. I'd come to find my lover, not get sidetracked by politics. Furtively glancing deep inside the kitchen, I saw her. She sat at a small table next to the silver refrigerators, with Colleen, the owner. *Damn!* Her earth-toned plaid work shirt set off her pale skin. My stomach heaved. I could almost smell her perfume. Watching her twirl a pencil, I was surprised at how calm and concentrated she seemed to be. Was work also Rachel's way of pretending she and I didn't matter?

Suddenly, a dishwasher dropped a large steel pan on the cement floor. The clang made Rachel turn towards the door. Her eyes focused on me. For an instant I saw them come to life. Joy. That's what I saw! But then, before she looked away, I saw grief. Long, deep grief. Quickly, she stood up and dodged behind the refrigerators.

I slumped in my chair, stunned by her avoidance.

April was finishing reading, "...We wish to once again appeal to GCSC to negotiate with the strikers around their demands."

"Cool letter!" Pody said.

"Yeah." I tried to wrench my mind away from Rachel. "I'd like to see Morris Kight have to process like a lesbian feminist. Wouldn't it be right on if The Radical Therapy Collective mediated the negotiation?"

"What negotiation?" June countered. "We haven't voted to sit down with them. We're winning this strike. Now is not the time to negotiate."

I spoke with firmness. "I think maybe it is."

June scowled at April and then at me.

I felt torn between going after Rachel and seizing the moment to convince my comrades. I backed down. "Let's talk about it at the next meeting," Now was not the time to let June distrust me. I'd just seen Rachel's best friend Susan walk into the restaurant. "Excuse me," I said to my gang, standing to leave.

I leaned over to Pody and whispered, "Have a nice weekend with BeJo in San Diego!"

Quickly I strode to the bar and ordered ordered another Coke and a beer. Then I approached Susan's table.

"I was just in the neighborhood," I said lamely, standing in front of her. I held out the beer like a peace offering.

Sitting alone, Susan raised her eyes, tossing her lustrous head of chocolate brown hair with that flick of the neck femmes do to send their locks into a fan of motion.

She pulled out the chair next to her. "That's the nice thing about this place. It's just on the way to everywhere," she replied with an arching of her brows, letting me know she knew the sad state of affairs between Rachel and me.

I sat; grateful I wasn't going to have to climb a jungle gym to get to my topic. "Your best friend is very upset with me," I ventured, my apology note burning in my pocket. "So," I inhaled. "Do you think she still loves me?"

Susan smiled wanly and shook her head. "Maybe you butches change your feelings every two weeks, but we femmes don't."

We sat in silence.

"Did Rachel tell you about the...the thing...in the car?"

"Whatever the thing was, she's quite brokenhearted. I've never seen her so devastated."

Devastated was a strong word. I blinked to cover my emotions. "What can I do to make that go away, Susan?"

"You can't make it go away, Jeanne. Whatever happened seems to have been the last straw to make her evaluate all the other problems you two have."

I had no words. Only shock.

"What if you and Rachel took some distance from each other?" Susan continued. "She got into this relationship with you pretty deeply, pretty quickly. Maybe you two should see others, put some perspective between you."

"Rachel wants to see other people!" My voice rose.

"Just until things cool down between you two."

I leaned forward angrily. "Rachel wants me to see more of her, not less, Susan. She asked me to break things off with BeJo and now I've done that."

Susan's eyes grew large. "Does Rachel know this? Have you told her?"

"I was going to tonight. But she's in the kitchen avoiding me. I want to be with her. I mean capital 'W' with, like monogamously. I'd even cut back on some of my organizing if she wanted more time."

I stopped abruptly. Were these words coming from my subconscious? I hadn't meant to say them.

"Whoa!" Susan seemed shocked too.

I took out my apology note and presented it to Susan. "Maybe you could go and give this to her for me."

Susan smiled gently but she took my note, stood up, and walked determinedly through the kitchen's half-door.

Relief spread through my clenched thigh muscles as I went to the bar counter and a beer for myself. My hand shook with anxiety. Turning around to face the kitchen, I was shocked to see Susan coming toward me. Bad sign. That was too fast.

I swallowed hard. "What did she say?"

"Nothing," said Susan. "I caught her getting into a car out back. I gave her your note. She gave it back to me and drove off."

"Where is she going?" I demanded.

Susan looked down at the floor, as though she were afraid to reply. "She was with…a friend. They're driving down to the music festival in San Diego."

I was out the front door before Susan finished her sentence. I knew exactly what I had to do to show Rachel how much I cared. An hour later, I'd packed a small duffel bag and was swinging onto the San Diego Freeway heading south.

Chapter 26

A Lavender Woodstock

[San Diego]

August 15, 1975

I merged into the fast lane, nearly side-swiping a car. With that scare, I realized I'd never had the chance to ask my dead Nazi the main question for our next interview. What had made him decide to go to war against the world? Very likely, he had no idea, just as I had no idea why I felt so compelled to be at war, with a different enemy, but perhaps with a similar rage. Were we both born to war? My father's violence had taught me war as a survival style. His battery of me as a child taught me that discrimination is inculcated in the abused as a rape of one's self-identity. The rape instills anger or shame and the victim then comes to understand survival as war against the world.

Learning this, I'd also had to embrace the concept of paradox, the ability to hate and love the same person, as well as one's self. I came to understand, as I wondered if Joe did, that these instilled primal fault lines either define or destroy the abused. All wars are paradox, but by now I was comfortable with war as a lifestyle. Sure it was exhausting and dangerous, but also godlike in its creative destruction. To me, war wasn't necessarily a negative state of affairs. It was also a creative chance and ability to redefine Self, myself.

Yet being at constant war left little time for sorting out the rage and the longing, the hate and the love that were tied up in knots inside me. I wished I could understand the war within in my personal life—the war between Rachel and me that prevented us from being there for each other. All I knew was that I had to keep her. This was a war I *had* to win.

I parked Lionheart under a clump of palm trees in a low, dry, mountain meadow surrounded by lemon green hills and forests, part of a dusty horse ranch donated for the weekend festival by a wealthy lesbian. The African sounds of Ajita, Bebe K Roche's master drummer, drifted over on the balmy breeze, welcoming me to the San Diego Women's Music Festival. {1}

The tension of L.A.'s chaos and Joe's death were still in my body muscles as I tried to shift into the mellow tones, and make my way toward the dance of the drums where I'd find the main stage area. Women on the shaven meadow were strolling half-naked, arm in arm, lolling on their sleeping bags reading or kissing, cooking over their campfires, tapping melodies out on pots and fallen logs. It was the heyday of lesbian separatism and I knew I'd see no men this weekend. The publicity had been strident, saying it was verboten to bring testosterone onto the land. Lesbians with boy children past puberty were asked to leave them at home. No amplifiers or speakers allowed. Anything electric was considered male. The organizers had declared this festival would be made in the image and likeness of an all-female world. Women would do everything from nailing the stage together to installing the porta-Johns (called porta-Janes.) Radical stuff, I thought. I was more of a coalition-builder than a separatist. Yet I noticed and enjoyed the deeper essence of a women-only gathering. There was no subcutaneous edge of fear that was always present when men and women were forced together.

Inhaling this life, I followed the trail of bare-breasted dykes, zigzagging from circle to circle searching for Rachel. My organizer's eye counted as many as a thousand lesbians! I slowed down to watch a ten-woman jam session of guitars, kazoos, and a washboard encircled by an audience cathartically singing, "I'm Tired of Fuckers Fuckin' Over Me," a movement favorite. Dozens of semi-clothed dykes wore colorful ethnic beads that contrasted with their tanned skin. This half-naked Lesbian Body was vibrating like a jungle tribe! My beleaguered spirit began to unwind. The sweet odor of cut hay and women's sweat was soothing. I breathed in our lavender Woodstock. To feel complete, I just needed to find Rachel.

Arriving at the crest of a small bluff, I looked down on the stage surrounded by long flying hair, bronzed nipples, swinging breasts, twirling tie-dyed skirts, and girl children dancing in circles. A young mother, bare-breasted and suckling her infant,

Lesbian drummers lead the conga beat at San Diego Women's Music Festival, September 1975. *Photo by EK Waller, Lesbian Tide.*

sat in the dust, cross-legged. The baby wore a white kerchief tied hippie style in a knot at the back of the head, as did her mother. The baby's scarf bore the word *anarchist* lettered in red, and her mother's hands were busy tending her so a woman next to Mom pressed a joint to her lips. Studying the red-faced infant I wondered if Rachel and I could ever have a child together. Maybe someday in such a daughter's lifetime, gays would be allowed to marry. Then our daughter's daughter, a grandchild of dyke militants, would grow up and attend her own lesbian festival in the 21st century!

At this thought I wiped tears of joy out of my eyes as I made my way down to the stage. Lots of L.A. dykes had come, as well as women from as far away as Wyoming and Colorado. Friends and colleagues called out my name every few minutes. Suddenly, a naked body appeared in front of me. I jumped back, startled. There stood *The Tide's* ace music reporter, Rogi Rubyfruit.

"Have you seen Rachel?" I asked, fixing my gaze on Rogi's toes, embarrassed to see someone I knew well, yet not in the Biblical sense, parading nudely before me. I might take off my shirt this weekend on the last day, but I was still Catholic by culture, so that would be my limit.

"No, no have seen," Rogi quipped in her quick, high tones. "But then I haven't been merely socializing. I'm covering this story! What angle are we looking for, chief?"

I squirmed, hoping no one had heard the elitist, distinctly not feminist "chief." "Write about how the music lives inside the Lesbian Body," I instructed Rogi's toes. "Do the metaphor."

"Wheeee! That's great!" She scampered off.

As an organizer, I'd realized two years ago that the new sound of women making music together was shaping a formidable cultural dimension of Lesbian Nation. Women couldn't live on theory alone it seemed—we had to have voice and song. And this woman-sung music was building political cohesion in our community. I was born in a *Sound of Music* family of twelve—minus the music. But I got the political importance of it and was making sure *The Tide* was documenting and interpreting this cultural wave. We were printing interviews with the singers, like Meg Christian and Cris Williamson, and lengthy reviews of concert dynamics in every issue.

Visually, I combed the crowd: no sign of Rachel. The dinner hour was approaching; she could be at a campsite where she and her friends had nested. Or, she could be at any one of the performances, workshops, or dancing areas that were popping up impromptu everywhere. Assuring myself that Rachel wasn't in the sprawled crowd around me, I decided to seek out some friends and beg dinner. In my haste, I hadn't brought any food. But I knew I would find my performer friends, like Robin or Margie Adam, hanging around the food table that a passer-by told me was behind the stage.

I followed the curve of the crest and descended toward the stage, a roughly engineered affair: a twenty by fifteen foot raised platform of nailed-together plywood supported by cubed pilings of cement. I shook my head. For all our protestations, a male-owned forklift company had to have dropped the pilings into place. Rounding the stage, I saw the sun falling into a low sky of red and purple. Finding Rachel after dark would be difficult. I hated the thought of waiting until morning.

"Hello Jai! What's happening?" Margie Adam called to me by her nickname for me. Predisposed as she was to wearing natty blazers, Margie's body language was decidedly foppish. Tall and lean of frame, neither butch nor femme, she called herself androgynous, "a perfect 5" on the butch-femme role-differentiation scale. She threw her arms around my shoulders, hugging me tightly. Her kinky blonde Afro formed a halo around her vibrant smile, accentuating her charismatic warmth. Releasing me, she studied me at arm's length. "What's wrong, Jai? I can hardly feel your energy."

Margie always spoke in that amorphous, touchy feely talk. Half the time I didn't understand what she was saying, but she'd taken her aura-energy lingo onstage. Her intra-song audience raps were littered with odes to all the human forms on the planet and magical animals, so I assumed the rank and file of Lesbian

Singer/songwriter Margie Adam appeared with Holly Near and Cris Williamson topping the charts at women's music festivals and concerts around America, circa 1973 to 1990. *Photo by PGar (Pat Gargaetas).*

Nation derived meaning from her words.

I kissed her cheek and tried to muster better energy. "It's good to see you, Marg."

"Come and have a Tofu burger." Margie led me under a backstage tent to a card table that afforded some privacy. "Spill it to me, Jai, what's depressing your vibe? Are you in love?"

Few people would have dared to ask me such a personal

question, but Margie and I had forged a concrete intimacy since we'd met at the first California women's music conference at a college in Sacramento, in May of '73. I had been aimlessly walking the campus grounds, engulfed by the consuming emotional dysfunction that had gripped me since my troubled National Lesbian Conference the month before. I'd crept purposefully away from the outdoor pack of gyrating Sacramento lesbians and had made my way into one of the empty buildings to be alone. Crouched in a hallway against a classroom wall, my knees drawn to my chest, my head in my hands, I was trying to understand why I felt so exposed and vulnerable simply by being out in public.

That's when I heard a voice calling out to me from an adjoining classroom. The piano-accompanied voice was questioning and wistful, and I was captured by lyrics that seemed to put words to my internal anguish.

"Do you hate yourself, lovable lady?
Can I be of help, beautiful woman?
Your silence is a wall between the two of us,
And your beautiful heart is breaking."

Listening, I dissolved into a small heap on the linoleum floor and started sobbing loudly. The piano went silent. The stranger who was playing came out. Without a word, she sank down on the floor next to me and took me in her arms. I cried myself into an exhausted peace. My new friend's name was Margie Adam.

A week later I moved into her house in Lompoc and Marg and I began a love affair of the pen, the piano, and the soul. A brief stab at being sexual passed as a stumbling moment between two women who were fascinated by the creative core in one another. Marg taught me how writing deeper than a news story could bring about healing. "Look inside, Jai," she told me over and over. "That's where you'll find your poetry." Under her care I'd begun scribbling feverishly. I wrote about how the Pacific beach sand breathed, about the narcissistic nuances of emotional collapse, and about the birth of an emotional child called Lesbian Nation. Marg had been at the UCLA Conference too. She championed my feeble hope that the way out of my feelings of primal personal betrayal and political primal dissonance lay in my writing. In turn, I contributed a line about donuts to a new song she was writing about a magical unicorn.

Six months later, healed and back at *The Tide* in Los Angeles, I produced Margie Adam's first solo concert. I had her double-billed with the *Village Voice's* columnist Jill Johnston, author of a blistering new tome called *Lesbian Nation*. But Johnston had come on stage with an almost empty pint of Southern Comfort and told the audience, "I don't believe in lesbian nation anymore." After that bombshell, Margie stole the show that night, and had gone on to become a national women's music superstar.

Now, down and heartbroken again two years later I told Marg about the state of my love affair with Rachel. My long ago caretaker took my hand. "You're so devoted to politics, Jai. It sounds like your lover's main complaint is that you don't take the time to make her feel special."

I leaned forward over the card table, gripping Margie's hand. "How do you manage to make time for your political singing work and a lover?"

Margie threw back her head, her Afro bobbing. "I don't! My personal life is like a revolving supermarket door. I'm on the road so much, the only time I have to meet someone is on my way up to the stage or down from it. That's why a lot of us are lovers with each other," she finished, referring to the tendency lesbian singers had of sleeping with one another.

"There is no personal peace in revolutionary times, Jai," she said. "I decided I can't give up writing and singing to our lesbian tribe in order to settle down with any one woman."

"I can't give up my political work either, Marg."

"Nor should you!" Margie seemed surprised. "What you do for our movement is too critical, Jai. *The Tide* is our voice!"

I leaned forward and whispered, "You seem to be saying that we activists can't have both. That in fact, you and I have already chosen the political rather than the personal."

"Did I say that?" Margie swallowed hard. "Oh, what a dismal thought!"

I ran my fingers through my dusty windblown hair, and looked around, checking that no one was sitting too close. "I'm coming to the conclusion that this non-monogamy really doesn't work, Marg."

"Oh, Jai, you *are* in love!" Margie laughed. "Come on, let's go outside and listen to the music. The woman who is coming on now is Clytia. She's climactic!"

I threw back my head and laughed too. Lesbian feminists were forever changing their names to suit their inner muse.

As Marg and I squatted on the grass together, Climactic Woman seemed to be singing a song about my new reality, "I'm Feeling Kind of Monogamous over You."

As she finished, a panicked woman ran up to Margie and fell to her knees. "Margie, Holly's piano player has got the runs. Ya gotta play backup for her!"

"I'd be happy to," Margie replied. "Tell her I'm coming." She turned to me with a grin splashed across her freckled face. She placed a mimeographed sheet of paper in my hands. "Take a look at these workshops, Jai. If I don't see you later tonight, I'll meet you at the Role Playing session tomorrow!"

Again she made me laugh. Margie would meet me at the Role Playing gathering only to give me a hard time because I championed the delightful choreography of roles and difference and she did not. The workshop would not talk about butch-femme in any direct or real way. Lesbian feminists felt that the whole subject amounted to nothing more than a heterosexist leftover that should be altogether abolished.

I studied the weekend's roster. There were sessions on Raising Male Children, definitely one I could skip; Anarchy, not in my lifetime; and Racism, Looksism, Ageism, and Fat Oppression. No workshops on how to do relationships successfully, nothing on Romantic Obsession. I tucked the list in my pocket and tried to enjoy the performances.

Holly Near was about to sing. To command a better view, I walked away from the stage and wound my way up through the crowd gathered on the hillside. Holly's vibrant *a capella* and counterculture politics were as pure as the Left ever got. When she broke into the song, "Sister-Woman-Sister," the hillside chorused back to her. Her voice echoed off the hills and the crowd seemed to multiply and push forward. Awed by the landscape of sound, I turned to drink in the faces of the vocal hundreds behind me.

That's when I saw Rachel.

The blonde-gold in her hair, silhouetted against a dark granite boulder on the hill, jumped into my line of vision. Without thinking I called out her name, but the music was too loud. She kept singing with Holly.

I waited and watched. She seemed lighthearted and happy. But something was wrong with this picture. A storm of interference, white noise shooting through adrenaline, was gathering in my head. Her lips and eyes were the same, pale peach underneath the robin-egg blue, but wait—another woman's arm was wrapped around her! The stranger's hand rested on Rachel's neck. Foreign fingers toyed with my lover's curls! I gasped. The alien arm belonged to a butch standing beside her. The dyke had a white Irish-looking face with a mop of dark hair that rested on lumberjack shoulders. She towered over Rachel's small frame. The butch woman's energy seemed to want to wrap Rachel into her bulky body. Now she was leaning down. She kissed my woman on the temple! Rachel didn't seem to notice the kiss. But now she lifted an arm to wave to someone, the very arm that had clung to my neck as we made love in the car less than a week ago!

The pain began in my groin and hammered past my vocal chords. My mouth opened. I couldn't stop my shout, "Raaachel!"

People turned to look at me. So did Rachel. Her eyes found mine, As I came into focus her face turned the color of acid-washed stone. The robin's eggs filled with tears.

I wanted to run to her, but my feet were paralyzed. There

was no more festival and no more song. There was only Rachel and I, a past and a future that yet to shape.

I blinked. And she was gone.

And then I was on top of the hill, leaning against the granite boulder, gasping for air. My eyes were wide and glassy; my fists rose to find the sky. But Rachel and her butch were nowhere. Instead, Susan stood in front of me.

"Where did she go?" I demanded.

She seemed as shocked to see me as I was to see her. "Rachel said you had to work this weekend."

"I didn't have to work!" I screamed. "I saw Rachel standing right here a few seconds ago, Susan!" My voice was dark. "I saw her standing here with another butch!" I slammed my fist into the boulder, and barked at Susan, "Who was she with?"

"With?" Susan stammered, her eyes trying to avoid mine.

"I saw that butch kiss her for fuck's sake, Susan! Who is she seeing?"

"I'm sorry, Córdova!" Susan's gasped. "I thought she'd told you."

As I sped home, northbound on the San Diego Freeway, the thought of Rachel being touched by someone else made me want to smash everything around me, throw glass cups at the metal garage door at Effie Street, crack heads of unknown passers-by with multiple large black typewriters thrown from a freeway overpass.

It occurred to me that I knew Rachel's other lover. That is, if she *was* her lover. Her name was Jacki and she was the lover of my flirting-buddy, Gahan Kelly, co-founder of L.A.'s famous Sisterhood Bookstore. At the Westside Women's Center meeting, I'd bumped into Gahan, who I remembered, had told me that she'd just broken off her long-term relationship with Jacki. Despite having the same taste in women, or maybe because of it, Jacki and I had a competitive acquaintanceship. Now Jacki had what was mine and I wanted it back!

Home in L.A., I left raging messages on Rachel's answering machine. "Is being with another woman what you meant by spending more time together?" I screamed. "God damn it, Rachel, pick up the damn phone. I can't believe you lied to me!"

At midnight on Sunday I drove to her Effie Street house, deciding to confront her in person and make her tell me what the hell was going on. She had to be home from the festival by now. I parked on the downward slope, watching the front door of her bungalow as I waited alone in Lionheart. Had she in fact broken up with me and simply slipped out the back door without telling me? Or was this some kind of non-monogamous trick, a passive-aggressive payback? Her apartment remained dark and shrouded; not a light burned. It was as though she didn't live there anymore.

I dozed and drifted, searching for answers. Did this other woman mean anything to her? As the hours fell away I decided that Jacki was just a revenge date that Rachel had made out of anger after I'd left her in the parking lot on BeJo's birthday. She'd send Jacki packing after this weekend. There was too much passion between us. She loved me too much.

Dawn assaulted Rachel's front porch before I admitted she wasn't coming home. I drove away alternating between rage and bewilderment. Monday I began calling the Saloon, and by Tuesday her boss, Colleen, admitted that Rachel had called in over the weekend saying she'd had a family emergency and had to go out of town for a week. She wasn't scheduled for another shift until the following Sunday. My heart sank. Where and when would I find Rachel?

Chapter 27

By Any Means Necessary

[Los Angeles]

September 3, 1975

The alarm broke through my sleep and I vaulted out of bed—the big day was here. This morning the strikers were scheduled to meet with GCSC for official negotiations.

Standing in front of the bathroom mirror, I looked at myself and managed a proud smile. I had accomplished the almost impossible. Last week, at my insistence, the Strike Steering Committee had met and agreed to go to the table! Still, the universe was continuing to punish me. The meeting had taken place at Rachel's house—even though she wasn't there—due to a scheduling conflict at our lawyer's office. I'd flinched walking in, but at least Joan Baez wasn't playing on the damn stereo.

Pody whispered to me, "Rachel gave me the key to let everyone in. What's more, she gave me her written proxy to vote!"

"Which way?" I asked.

"Whichever way you vote." Pody's eyes twinkled.

I was momentarily disarmed by Rachel's display of political trust. Looking over Pody's shoulder, I found myself facing my lover's bedroom. The door was open. I couldn't staunch the memories, the private nights lying on the queen-sized futon under her multi-colored Nepalese bedspread. I turned away. This had been our world. It seemed only moments ago.

"That's great," I said to Pody, as a mixture of relief and anxiety passed through me. It would be so much easier to concentrate on politics without Rachel's presence. And yet…I hadn't seen her since the festival and longed to be with her.

"Who do you want me to talk to?" Pody asked, her voice low and referring to the lobbying effort I'd started to make sure our faction had enough votes. We'd been talking all week on the phone.

"Talk to Colin," I ordered. "See if we can pin down how that waffle is going to vote."

"Got it!" Pody made a teasing salute as she headed toward Colin.

A half-hour of heated lobbying proceeded until Patton waved for quiet.

"We might as well get right to the main agenda item," she said with authority. "I have reason to believe that the Center wants to sit down and talk settlement."

"No way!" June heckled.

Patton continued, "The president of the Center, Ben Teller, has called us. There is pressure from the community to try and find a settlement."

"Why do you think they want to negotiate now?" asked Enric.

I sighed with relief at how Patton had skirted the question of exactly who had contacted whom first. If it had come up, I was ready to lie outright and say Kight had approached me at another political meeting. But Morris had fulfilled his promise and gotten the president of the Board to call the strikers. This way both sides felt like they'd been first approached by the other. My crossing the line maneuver to make a deal with

Morris would remain a secret. Forever, I hoped.

"I have a hunch," said Patton. "GCSC sees that the September 16 hearing at the Unemployment Benefit Department is coming up. My guess is that the Center thinks they will lose at that hearing, so they want to make an effort to settle before that."

I jumped on her reasoning. "I'll bet they want to use granting us unemployment benefits as a bargaining chip. They'll offer to withdraw their contesting our benefits, in return for us giving them something." Silence fell as everyone focused anxiously on the possibility of finally getting some money. There was desperation in the room. Half the strikers hadn't worked for the last four months.

"They hate the picket line and are desperate to get rid of it," June protested. "That means we're winning. Now is not the time to negotiate!"

Shouting began. The horses were out of the gate! Taunts were thrown between groups. Questions were thrown at Patton: If we settle will we have to give up our lawsuit? Yes. Will we have to give up the picket line? Of course. Will we get our jobs back? No way to know.

An hour later, the room had congealed into the three groups that clearly delineated the political factions within the Gay/Feminist 16. These were now friendship groups, as well as political affinity cadres. June's cadre of Communist Party and Maoist allies, who plain out wanted to force the closure of the Center, were firmly rooted near Rachel's bookcase. These included Dixie Youts, Colin McQueen, Enric Morello, Eddie Culp, and a few others.

Gathered in the middle of the room, against the kitchen's doorjamb was April's group, who had also adopted a labor vs. management interpretation of the strike. They simply wanted their jobs or back pay. April, I hoped, knew as well as I did that the Center wouldn't offer everyone his or her job back. I thought she and her people, Elizabeth "Lizard" Elder, Jesse Crawford, and Terry Pearsy, would settle for receiving weekly unemployment benefits immediately, in lieu of getting their jobs back.

I'd taken my place in the feminist-identified faction, the group that saw GCSC as an important institution that had broken the law and done its employees wrong, but we had never adopted the goal of wanting to close the Center. Gratefully, no one in our all-female group wanted her job back. We no longer wanted to work with men. But there were only five of us: me, Pody, Charlie Jones, Alicia Maddox, and Rachel's sure vote. To carry the day, my group had to win over most of the middling group. But I felt hopeful. Unlike June's group, April and company had nothing to win by letting the strike drag on.

By now, it was eleven at night. Empty bottles and cans crowded each other on Rachel's kitchen table. The haggling had quieted to whispers. I watched Patton place her chair in the middle of the middling group and cross her arms. It occurred to me that she was purposely not running a very shipshape meeting. I wondered if she secretly wanted to let the meeting drag on interminably, hoping that in some exhausted moment before dawn, most of us would leave. Then she could announce that we no longer had a quorum, so no vote could be taken.

I could see the weariness on the faces of my comrades. There was an uncommon sense of deadness in the room as if we were all standing on a ledge, too inert to either fall backwards or forward. Most of us had seen every shirt in each other's closets. In fact, we'd seen way too much of each other. And like all political battles in their end stages, it had been weeks since new people had come to join our ranks. I knew the time was now or never.

I took a deep breath, walked to the center of the room and held up my arms for attention. "The object of a strike is to win something," I said, appealing to the several men in June's group who seemed less shrill. "We can't win anything if we never talk to the other side."

I turned to face the women in April's group. "Doesn't it bother you to see lesbian strikers and lesbian scabs pushing and shoving each other on the picket line? This sistercide is tearing the lesbian community apart. No changes are being made inside GCSC. Let's stop this division and go to the table."

Lastly, I turned to Patton, not about to let her outmaneuver me again. "We're all exhausted and talked out. I demand that we take a democratic vote, by secret, written ballot. Let everyone vote their conscience."

No one said anything. Even June was too embarrassed, or too surprised, to countermand my demand for a secret vote. Up to now, her group had been the loudest and had intimidated others. Now, I put my hopes into a written ballot in which no one would know how their friend, or enemy, voted.

Patton looked around the room, but heard no counter.

"Pody," I called out, "Can you tear up little pieces of paper? Everyone, grab a pen."

Quickly Pody's scraps made their way around the room.

"What's the goddamn question?" June whined.

Patton's voice cut the silence, "A yes vote means we sit down to negotiate. A no vote means no negotiations."

A few conferred with others. Most said nothing. We wrote, folded our paper, and gave it to Patton.

I'd retired to Rachel's back porch to wait for the vote counting. A buoyant moon rose over Rachel's roofline. Numbly, I stared out into the night, wondering which constellation my lover slept under. A large cloud beamed back a silver lining.

"And the ayes have it," I heard Patton scream out. "The vote is ten to six!"

"Blessed be!" Pody yelled.

I rejoined my group in a much-relieved group hug. A smile broke out over Alicia's usually poker face. She grabbed Enric and Eddie and the three of them began jitterbugging in the middle of the room. Someone turned on the radio and blared disco. A male voice started shouting, "Yes! Yes!" to the beat of the music, and for one long beautiful moment we were all just a bunch of dykes and fags, gay-ly happy, all on the same side.

"Everyone! Calm down!" Patton shouted, "We need to pick a negotiating team. Come back to order!"

June yelled out quickly, "Don't nominate me," she said. "I'm too angry and I won't sit at that table. I nominate Enric and Eddie in my place."

The two boys were quickly elected. Next, I was picked to represent my faction. April, ever the diplomat, was chosen as the fourth member of our team.

Now, two days later, I stood in front of the bathroom mirror. Oddly, I had a fleeting impulse to jump back into bed and pull the blankets up over my head. A lump formed in my throat.

Why the sudden cold feet, I wondered, trying to find the part in my hair. I'd been desperate for months to find a politically viable way to resolve the controversial mess I'd helped create. Yet part of me didn't want to go to the negotiation. I'd lived with the reality of the strike primary in my thoughts every waking hour. In a way, I didn't want there to be an end. I'd seen this kind of resistance in others in previous campaigns. A long and deep fight would become so enshrined in an activist's psyche that, at some critical point, the struggle itself became deified instead of the goal. The strike had become a sacred cow in my life, a consuming organism that wanted to live.

"Just put one foot in front of the other," I ordered, as I finished putting my shoes on and stood up to go. "Just find the faith and do the deed."

Forcing myself to walk to the garage, I slipped into Lionheart. Maybe, by this time tomorrow, I could be free of the strike. If the negotiation went well, maybe Rachel would come back and we could reclaim our magic. Maybe when she felt that she wasn't being forced into a political life and the hate and anger this one involved, she'd recover that playful wholeness her personality had when we'd first met. We could then have some peace together. The thought spurred me forward. Today was the beginning of the end of the Great Strike!

The dingy, brown-walled conference room threw off an aura of radical, and therefore noble, impoverished life. Wrangling about where to negotiate—none of us would cross the picket line to meet within the Center—had landed us at the Echo Park People's Law Collective, Patton's office. Other than the cigarette-stained wooden table and eight wobbly chairs, the room was as simple as the issues were complex. Not even a pitcher of drinking water graced the table that separated the two teams.

I strode into the negotiation room projecting cool and confidence, wearing black wraparound sunglasses and a black leather wristband with metal buckles. I was not here for warm and fuzzy. I sat across from Morris and drew a deep breath.

My godfather's negotiating team brought some surprises. Quickly he introduced GCSC's lawyer, Allan Gross, and two strangers. Street rumor had circled back to us that Gross had said that the picket line looked like "a Bolshevik goon squad out of *Doctor Zhivago*." A pleasant-looking young man, with the pale complexion of those recently living on the East Coast, was introduced by Morris as Bob Sirica, the Center's new Executive Director. Morris's fourth team member was a woman named Sharon Corneilson. A new Board member, he said. What the hell is this, I wanted to shout at him. Morris had brought in a brand new Director recently airlifted from another city, and a new activist who I knew still publicly called herself "homosexual"— summer replacements with no background. Why not Dr. Teller or Betty Berzon? Something seemed off.

Patton wore a freshly pressed blouse, but underneath the table her bare feet were encased in leather sandals. Calmly, she introduced our troops. The two teams locked eyes, but nodded politely. I sent Morris a small, knowing smile. He signaled me back. A silence fell. Even Morris seemed afraid to test the atmosphere. It was clear there was to be no small talk. It felt like one wrong move, before the dove of peace had a chance to perch, would send both sides to the door.

Gross, the strong-faced attorney for the Center spoke first. "Let me take a few moments to frame the issues and to say that GCSC is here to propose an out of court settlement to the dissidents," he said.

My team bristled at the center's refusal to call us "the strikers." I faded out on Gross's hundred dollar silk tie and all-American crew cut, not a laminated hair out of place, and turned my attention to Morris. Once again I saw my father's face in him. His blotchy pink and white skin was nothing like my father's olive complexion, but I knew the mind behind the face fed on power. It moved Morris to win by any means necessary. Just like Dad. Morris at least respected my political work. Before the strike, I'd even let myself believe that Morris loved me like a daughter. My father, on the other hand, thought that being a gay activist was tantamount to championing Lucifer's right of return to heaven.

"What we have in front of us is a lawsuit," Patton interrupted Gross.

"Two lawsuits," Gross countered his silk tie bobbing as he spoke. "The Center is countersuing the strikers seeking twenty five thousand dollars in damages that the picket line has cost us in donations."

"Toward the resolution of their lawsuit," Patton cut him off. "My clients wish me to present demands to you for them to be granted unemployment benefits, to be re-instated with back pay, to approve a reinstatement or revision of the Center's Personnel Policies and Procedures that comply with California labor law, and...lastly..." Patton paused, and laid down her paperwork. "A public acknowledgement that their terminations were wrongful. And they want to work with you to restructure management and the Board to reflect feminist representation therein."

Morris spoke. "The Center is proud of its organizational structure. There is no need or desire to change it. What we came to discuss is the abusive and violent picket line and the unsavory boycott of our establishment."

My teeth sank into the pencil between my lips. To calm myself, I drew a lopsided tiara on the edge of my tablet. Kight had brought his venomous queen side. Forgiveness was not in the air.

Modulating my voice, I spoke to Morris warmly. "It would be a definite sign of good faith in these negotiations if the Center would allow us to claim our unemployment benefits."

"That is a most reasonable request!" Morris's tone changed and he waved his arm broadly as though he were granting the benefits on the spot. "If…in a reciprocal sign of good faith, the dissidents would kindly dispense with the picket line."

"The picket line stays until we get our jobs back!" Enric spoke in a flat, hard voice. He leaned forward combatively, a cheetah ready to launch.

"Let's talk about the Center's voided Personnel Policies and Procedures," I interrupted calmly, steering us back onto a workable issue. "We would like them upgraded and reinstated. GCSC cannot continue to operate outside the law."

Morris huffed. "We are a gay institution and the first to offer gay jobs. The Center has achieved national significance by showing the straight world we can shepherd our own!"

"Well, then, some of your lambs have certainly been sacrificed," I retorted.

April ignored me and said with a firm and even tone, "All the more reason to set a nationally significant example."

Sirica popped in, "I'm happy to report —the Personnel Policies have been reinstated."

"How convenient," Enric hissed. "It's comforting to know that you only void them when you need to fire people."

Even I was taken aback by Enric's venom. He hadn't been able to find work all summer. To eat and live, he'd moved in with a friend.

Unruffled, Patton asked, "Are the Personnel Policies & Procedures now in accordance with California labor law?"

"I believe so," Gross replied.

"Are you open to us reviewing them to ensure that they are?" Patton persisted.

"I don't think that's proper!" the new Executive Director interrupted. "For a non-profit organization to allow a group of…of…outside agitators to approve their employee relations guidelines?"

My team glared at him as if he had missed the last two cycles of the moon.

"There's very little that has been proper," I said. "If your Board has indeed rewritten the PP&P's and brought them up to standard, and then we just happened to see them lying around somewhere, we wouldn't be 'approving' them. We would just know that GCSC is now in compliance with labor law."

Morris grunted. Gross looked at him and raised his right eyebrow. Morris nodded back.

"That could be arranged," Gross affirmed.

I gave Patton a quick, small smile. Chalk up one for our side! My brain searched for the next least threatening issue.

Gross offered, "We are willing to drop our lawsuit if you will drop yours."

In the silence I wondered about making the same deal with Rachel. I'll drop my other lovers, if you do the same. If only love were more like politics, predictable and sequential. I sighed.

Patton rejoined, "Your lawsuit is predicated on ours. It's frivolous."

Gross folded his pinstriped arms across his chest.

"What about the unemployment benefits?" I blurted to Morris. "Now that is something you can give easily. Just don't show up at the Department's hearing."

"Paying employment benefits to fifteen people will substantially raise our unemployment tax for a long time to come," Morris refuted.

Eddie shot out of his chair. "You should've thought of that before you fired us!" he yelled.

April grabbed his arm. "The guys and I are going to get some bottles of water," she declared. "It's too hot in here to think. You all go on."

Everyone kicked back for a break. I hadn't expected shouting so early. I watched Morris huddle with his lawyer.

Turning to Patton, I whispered, "How about we offer

to suspend the picket line for one week while we review the Personnel Policies?"

Patton shook her head. "That's not enough. Throw in the unemployment appeal too."

April and the boys returned, passing out Coca-Cola cans to both sides.

Before Morris could open his mouth, I spoke. "We might be willing to call off the picket line for ten days," I said slowly, emphasizing *might* and looking around to gauge the reaction of my own team. April and the boys came to attention. "If..." I dragged the word out, "if the Center drops contesting our benefits, gives us that time to review the PP&P's and talks proceed the following week."

Gross looked at Morris and Morris shrugged. "We can agree to these things," Gross replied.

I knew my eyes danced with delight, so I lowered them quickly. My hope now was that we might be able to solve the thornier issues of jobs and back pay in accordance with my arrangement with Morris.

I was hoping that most of the strikers didn't care about back pay. They had to know, the whole community knew, the Center didn't have any money. Besides, the strike was about issues, not money. But I knew June's faction, represented by Enric and Eddie today, had no interest in the Center's financial health or future. I only hoped that Morris would play his pro forma part and put the job offers on the table. Then I could massage the money issue out of existence. This could be a win-win.

"But..." Morris's drawl hung loudly, puncturing my wishful thinking. "We must ask for more than ten days. That picket line is disrupting our services!"

"And my clients must have their jobs back with financial restitution," Patton cut in.

"The Center has no money," Gross declared.

"You have an annual budget of three hundred and fifty thousand a year," Patton pressed, pointing to the spreadsheet in front of her. I'd never seen the documents she was holding.

Morris spread both his arms at chest height. I saw his otherwise pale neck begin to color. "That *was* our annual budget!" he railed at Patton. "That was the money from the federal grant given to us to run the women's alcohol prevention program. Lillene and I spent months writing that grant. That program and its money have been stolen by you people!" Morris's neck was picking up purple. The veins in his forehead began to show. "We no longer have that money or those projected estimates you have in your hands."

I was speechless, shocked by Patton's use of projection sheets I'd never seen. She and I should have talked. I was sure she was aware that the Center was running on fumes and that its financial situation had been made worse by a bold gamble that Kight and Kilhefner had made two weeks before firing us. They'd taken out a mortgage on GCSC's new Highland property to the tune of two hundred and thirty-five thousand dollars {1}. Now, in addition to that, by my calculations, the Center owed the fired employees some sixty-six thousand dollars in back pay.

"The fate of the alcoholism grant was never part of the strikers' issues," I protested, remembering how the staff of the ACW had piggybacked their mutiny on top of our fight for feminist representation. I'd supported the notion that only women should direct a women's program, but in retrospect, I'd seen that the way the separation was engineered had all but torn the financial guts out of the Center. But none of that was the business of this negotiation.

"ACW was the beginning of all this!" Morris screamed. "Weathers and her gang are the thieves among you. That was the Center's first grant. There is no money!" he finished with an arc of his chin.

I sat back, silenced. While Brenda and her staff were active strike participants, it shocked me to hear that Morris blamed the strikers for ACW's independence revolution. This raw rage was about to derail the negotiations. Had Morris forgotten our private deal? He was acting like the lord of a fiefdom of unruly serfs. It was now or never. I had to put it in his face.

My tone dropped to charming but determined. "What if you just *offered* to give our jobs back?" I said deliberately, using the language of our prior understanding. "And then we strikers were willing to sign an agreement saying that you could pay us our back pay over a long period of time...say three years? That kind of monthly payment wouldn't break you."

I held my breath waiting for Morris to reply.

"That is acceptable..." Morris winked at me.

I sat back, gratified. A smile came to my lips.

"With some reservations," Morris finished.

"What reservations?" Enric growled.

Gross took a single sheet of paper out of his briefcase, and slid it face down over to Patton. She turned it over, read it, and drew in a breath. Her spine stiffened. "These are the reservations?" she asked.

"That is our list of dissidents, the exceptions," Morris began.

"We're strikers! Say strikers!" Enric was on his feet again. He pivoted toward Patton and pounded a clenched fist on the table, "We will make no exceptions!"

"Those names on the page are the ringleaders," Morris continued, his tone dark and flat. "Those are the people we know are out to destroy the Center and overthrow its Board of Directors. We cannot offer their jobs back."

"Read the names, Sylvia," April demanded.

Patton read aloud. "Those dissidents who cannot be rehired are: Jeanne Córdova, June Suwara, Enric Morello, Colin McQueen, Edward Culp, Dick Nash, April Allison, and Alicia Maddox."

With each name my eyebrows reached further into my forehead. I'd warned Morris against singling out any individual names. Now he'd gone and listed every leader. He stared at me without flinching. Then, he turned to Gross and nodded. The lawyer took another single sheet out of his briefcase.

"We agreed to meet with you because we have a formal offer." The attorney mouthed each word slowly. "I have been empowered by the Board of Directors of the Gay Community

Services Center to offer to drop our lawsuit against you and withdraw our appeal against unemployment benefits, in exchange for the dissidents dropping the picket line, the boycott and your lawsuit."

"That's bullshit," Enric screamed, jumping to his feet. This time I joined him, my face red with rage.

My godfather stared at me as if he'd forgotten who I was.

"That's not your only offer, I hope?" I demanded, still incredulous.

Morris cleared his throat. "GCSC is about gay liberation. I can see in retrospect that we shouldn't have hired you feminists in the first place. That was my mistake."

April gasped. I could hardly believe what I'd just heard. Morris had finally been honest. He was saying said GCSC was a *gay* institution and would go feminist over his dead bodyI gripped the metal edge of the table with both hands. Finally, Morris lifted his eyes to mine. A small smile twisted his lips. His normally perceptive blue eyes were the color of slate rock.

Mine were filled with rage. Morris had played me! I'd failed to realize how exclusively Morris loved the body politic of gay maledom and power. Between these two loves of his life, dykes were but a necessary show of political correctness. We were expendable. Feminism would never be part of what motivated Morris Kight.

Patton looked toward Sirica and Corneilson for some glimmer of compromise. "I don't suppose there is a second paragraph to your offer?" she asked. They said nothing. They were window dressing.

"There is nothing further," Gross replied. "This is what I have been empowered to present to you." He closed the manila folder in front of him.

I was still shaking with anger. My thoughts tumbled quickly—my mentor had betrayed me! He'd never intended to offer our jobs back. I saw myself leaning across the table and punching Morris to wipe the near-grin off his placid face. April reached over and put a restraining hand on my forearm.

Gross looked at me nervously. He opened his mouth, speaking haltingly to Patton, "Will we see you at the next scheduled session on September nineteenth?"

Patton replied, "I will take your everything-for-nothing offer to my clients' meeting of the whole. I'm sure you realize it will not be acceptable. I'll call you about the September nineteenth session."

April was the first of our team to stand and walk out. Morris rose up and bowed, like a Japanese emperor giving his subjects permission to self-immolate. He turned and left the room, his retinue scurrying behind him.

My fury dissipated into a deep quiet. I sat glumly, stunned beyond words. Why had the Center agreed to meet with us when it had no intention of offering real compromise? Why this elaborate charade?

The pattern to Morris's plot points piled up in my brain. It was suddenly all too clear. The Center's first hope, to deny our unemployment benefits so we'd eventually quit the picket line to find new jobs, hadn't worked. Now, with the EDD hearing a few days away, they'd come to the negotiating table hoping to mitigate this monetary defeat. They hoped to sucker us, to use this as a bargaining chip, something they would "give" us so the Center could appear magnanimous in the gay press saying they'd "granted" us unemployment benefits. They'd also strategically agreed to talk to us and grant a second token concession to withdrawal of their own frivolous countersuit. If we'd postpone the picket line.

This was vintage Morris, a brilliant subterfuge. I put my elbows on the table and covered my face. I could read the headlines in the next issues of *The Advocate:* "GCSC Grants Benefits; Strikers Reject Offer to Settle!"

Chapter 28

Straws and Absolution

[Los Angeles]

September 3, 1975

I walked out of the negotiation building and onto the beaten-down end of Sunset Boulevard. With the September glare hitting me, my shirt was soon drenched and clinging to my back. Cars flew past me, and I stood on the sidewalk not sure which way to turn.

Rubbing my eyes, I noticed I was on the verge of tears. The Great Strike had lost its greatness. Negotiations were over. There was no more joy, or even righteousness, on the picket line. The strikers would say no to Morris's list. The lawsuit, when it finally had its day in court, would award compensatory damages that would be more than the gay Center could pay. By that time we'd be a pack of wolves circling a crippled prey. Even if GCSC did settle and survive, it would take a decade to heal the antipathy that lesbian feminists felt toward the institution that represented no liberation for women. So much effort—and now defeat.

Looking down at the cactus rock garden next to the sidewalk, I bent over and grasped two white, sun-broiled rocks, one in each fist. The pain stung. I saw myself running madly down the tattered street, hurling the rocks, shattering delicate store windows, laughing crazily at the tinkling sounds of destruction. I felt my inner Great Wall, the heavily fortified mental barrier erected between my politics and my emotions, cracking from fatigue and contradiction. The strike had sapped me. As had Rachel. I was dangerously close to empty. Why had I spent so much time fighting on male turf trying to make the Center co-gender, I wondered bitterly, pacing as I clutched my rocks.

Staring angrily across the street, I realized I was looking at the steeple of a church tucked on a side street. Aha, a church, a place apart, just like the convent. Approaching the front door I read the sign, St. Sebastian's Catholic Church. Sebastian—I remembered my holy card of him. A martyr tied to a post with arrows sticking out of his chest. How appropriate. I entered, genuflected, and made my way to a pew. Placing the rocks on the wooden seat beside me, I knelt in the pew, breathing slowly and consciously, allowing the energy of my defeat to dissipate.

I closed my eyes and Morris's face appeared. He sat on the couch at McCadden Place where I'd crossed the line and met him last month. It was the moment just before we'd shaken hands in agreement—yes, I could see his eyes now, the same cold, emotionless glass they'd been today. The sly smile behind his words had said to me, "This is the house that I built, and it will always be mine!" I should have known then that his Center would never, at least not in this decade, elect avowed feminists to its Board, put the word "lesbian" in its name, or foster a collective management structure.

Grasping for straws and absolution, I considered that perhaps the strike foretold a separation that was destined to happen. At a primal level, feminism and gay liberation were contradictory for many of us. I'd cringed years ago when I'd heard Morris and his Center co-founder, Don Kilhefner, first define gay liberation as "a movement for sexual freedom." To women that sounded like gay men only wanted the freedom to fuck whenever, and whomever, and as much as possible. Permission to fuck was not the movement or the goal to which I'd pledged my life. Radical feminism was about replacing the male order of hierarchical relationships and creating egalitarian structures of shared power. Why couldn't gay male leaders of my generation realize that sexism and misogyny were the basis of their oppression too? That the straight world feared gay men because they'd crossed the line between male power and female submission and they were discriminated against because they "acted like women." Would we women have to wait for a whole new generation of men to realize women's liberation was their liberation too? Today, the uneasy coalition of gay men and lesbians was a double-load freight train waiting to derail.

Even now the memory of Morris's rage during the negotiations took me aback. I hadn't seen rage like that since my father threw Judy and me out of his house, hating me for being different and for daring to bring that difference into his house and trying to change his values so that I could live under his roof with the rest of my family. That attempt had failed, just like this one. But never in the last six years had I regretted leaving my father's domain. Fighting against his constant railing and belittlement of my being gay, I'd found pride in who I was, and I was doing my part to change straight society and show him he was wrong.

Suddenly my mouth fell open. Like Lazarus, a scale fell from my eyes and in this moment the issue was clear! My father *was* wrong, and so was Morris. I'd been trying to get back into my political godfather's house and take it over, or at least make him change his rules for living there. Not leaving with Judy the day Dad threw her out would have meant dying. I didn't choose death then, and I wasn't going to choose it now.

I got up off my knees and picked up my rocks. My tribe of women didn't need to beg entrance to the supposed Holy of Holy place. In order to survive, maybe all of lesbian-kind had to leave the house of the father, the house of men. Maybe we were at a turning point in history when men and women could do more good by working separately. Perhaps the ideology of dyke separatism—the idea that lesbians could only achieve equality by not working with men, gay or straight—was correct, at least for this point in history!

I turned away from the altar, ran down the aisle and out the front door. I had to let go of the GCSC before its contradictions snuffed me out as a lesbian activist. Many of my lesbian activist friends had already given up the movement, left L.A. to live on the land in Santa Cruz and grow carrots for the revolution. I didn't want this burn out to happen to me. I'd be damned if I would spend the rest of my life fighting Morris Kight, or my father. Someday, forces more compelling than the values of lesbian feminism would force Morris to concede, but until that day, the Gay Community Services Center was no longer my problem.

Spying a phone booth, I sprinted toward it, rocks still in hand. I needed to talk out a solution with someone. I wanted to call Rachel. I wanted her to be that someone. I picked up the receiver and dialed her phone number, but something kept me from leaving a message when the answering machine picked up. It was wishful thinking, believing that Rachel would be there for me now when she hadn't returned my phone calls in weeks. Our relationship had been born into a political setting, but Rachel and I didn't have a political relationship.

I dropped in another dime and dialed Robin's number.

The Crest Coffee Shop was a fifties-style joint with fake wood paneling, corners filled with ferns and macramé hangers, and vinyl booths. It was the preferred hangout for Silverlake's non-moneyed activists and intellectuals because the booths offered conversational privacy and the broad bank of windows facing Sunset afforded enough light for writers to read their manuscripts to one another. Also, the price of a full breakfast was two bucks.

"You look bummed out," Robin said, sliding into my booth. She watched me sipping my coffee through a straw I'd twisted into a stick person. Since leaving St. Sebastian's I'd lost some of my revelatory steam.

I smiled. "Glad you came,"

"Why you so convinced the negotiations are over?" she asked, as she pointed to my coffee and nodded to a waitress. "Why can't the strikers compromise more?"

"We can't compromise on an offer of everyone-gets-their-jobs-back-except-the-leadership. That's unprincipled."

"What about continuing the picket line and building pressure to make them come up with a second offer?"

"Short of breaking windows and allowing more violence, I can't see us mounting any more leverage on the line. How many more months can we ask picketers to walk around in a circle without seeing any results? Fewer and fewer are showing up each week. Morris is banking on this attrition and that men's money and donations will win the day in the long run."

Robin mused, "Do you ever think maybe dykes and gay men need to be separate and do their own thing for a while?"

"That's the conclusion I've come to," I said, relieved that Robin was already on the same page. I leaned forward. "And I've also thought about the strike from a dialectic perspective. Gay men versus lesbians are certainly the struggle of opposites. Right now this generation of gay men, having grown up with society's ingrained sexism, constitutes the upper class. As men, they have both the money and the power. But that might not always be so. If men control the means to production, women control the means to reproduction—that means power, too. Someday, women will come into their power. Then today's gender power imbalance will start to level out."

Robin reached across the table and gently pried the stick person out of my hand. "So when are you going to leave the boys to the boys?"

I looked at her soberly and then smiled. "Today?" My eyes danced with excitement, and fear.

Robin studied me. "So, what's stopping you?" She leaned forward and tapped my head. "Get out of your head and into your gut! Your instincts have carried you this far. Look at your track record—*The Tide*, two national conferences, *The Freep*. You've made the right calls for five years. Trust yourself!"

"If I go public with quitting and put it in *The Tide*, and say negotiations are over, it will signal an end to a working relationship between lesbians and gay men in L.A. And if lesbians don't go back to GCSC, we won't get government money for our priorities. Who inside GCSC will agitate for a program to support lesbian mothers' court battles for custody?"

"Government money never made anyone strong." Robin tossed my stick person back to me.

"Christ, Robin, you're such a Libertarian!" I laughed.

"At least I've got you smiling."

"And no closer to doing what needs to be done," I retorted, as the waitress returned with coffee for Robin. She ordered me a Coke float with two scoops.

I began to unravel my stick lady.

Robin nudged, "Are you afraid there'd be a hole in your life if you just quit, or not enough other projects to keep you busy?"

"No, that's not it," I retorted. "The pigs have almost caught Patty Hearst twice in the last few months. Penny is prepping me for an interview with one of the SLA members when the Feds capture them. And I've been talking with Judy Freespirit and Ivy Bottini, you know, the new dyke from New York, about my dream of starting a national lesbian feminist organization…like the Women's Movement has done with N.O.W. I don't have enough time…"

"Then why are you still hesitating?" Robin prodded. "Are you worried about how Rachel will feel if you quit the strike?"

"I don't think so," I hedged. Rachel might well be upset and confused if I dropped out of the lawsuit. She might think I was deserting her. "Hell Robin, I can't let her feelings make this huge political decision for me."

"What about the rest of our community?"

"I'll have some explaining to do to the Westside Women's Center and other lesbian groups. That won't be easy. But it might bring relief too. Lots of dykes are worn out with this."

"*The Tide* and *The Freep* staff will be happy to have your focus come back to them."

I smiled at Robin, feeling blessed that she was trying to frame my angst with a silver lining. A silence fell between us. Joking and making straw stick people were not changing reality.

"So, one more time…" Robin dealt an uppercut. "Why are you afraid to walk away?"

My lips tightened. I looked at Robin, afraid to give words to my thoughts. My shoulders slumped and I laid my stick lady to rest on a napkin coffin. My words came haltingly. "I don't want to have to choose between the woman side of me and the homosexual side of me," I whispered. "I just want to feel whole."

My hands reached up to cover my eyes as I sank into tears. I was so exhausted.

Robin got up and came over to my side of the booth. Instinctively, she shielded me from others in the restaurant by putting her arms around my shoulders and hiding my head on her chest. She knew I didn't want other activists to see me falling apart. But she didn't pull me close or try to shut down my sobbing. My best butch pal handed me some rough paper towels and whispered, "This is good. This needs to be over."

Half an hour later, I stood in front of Patton's building again. My waves of conflict and grief had subsided; I felt lighter and calm. I knelt down on the sidewalk and gave my stones back to the garden. I would throw no rocks today, but I would drop a figurative boulder on my lawyer's desk.

Striding down the corridor to her private office unannounced, I found her door open. "Sylvia," I called out, as I walked up to her desk.

Patton looked up and cocked her chin. Her brow furrowed. "What brings you here, Córdova?"

"I need to let you know. I'm out of here," I said quietly. "The negotiation breaking down this morning was it for me."

"What does that mean?"

"It means I want you to take my name off the lawsuit," I replied, trying to breathe confidence into the tremble in my voice. "It means I won't be on the picket line. It means I'm moving on with my life and I don't want to be part of the strike anymore. It means I quit."

"You're not coming to the next strikers' meeting when I present the Center's offer?"

I shook my head. "We both know there's no point to that. Many of the strikers will vow to keep going. GCSC will continue their stalling and pretending they're the good guys. Right before the lawsuit goes to court in a couple of years, Morris will offer realistic terms. By then GCSC will have solidified their old boys club. It will be too late to make the Center co-gender in its leadership."

Patton objected, "We can't know that will happen."

"It's your job to say that, Sylvia. But it's my job as an organizer to know what's gonna happen and what that means for the future." I stuffed my hands into my pockets, closed my eyes, and took a deep breath. "Dykes and feminists have no more leverage with that institution. The herstory of the Gay Community Services Center has been the history of lesbians leaving it. It will take a cataclysmic event for gay men to accept working equally with women."

She took off her glasses, staring intently at me. "That's what I thought this was."

"Me, too," I said. "We were both wrong."

Patton stood up from behind her desk and took off her glasses. "I wish you wouldn't do this, Córdova," she pleaded.

"There's no future here," I said as I turned and walked out of her office.

Chapter 29

A Fall From Grace

[Los Angeles]

Late September, 1975

After more than a year and a half as fugitives on the run, Patty Hearst and Bill and Emily Harris had finally been captured by the FBI. It was late at night at *The Freep* as I clicked off the Selectric; I'd finally finished my letter of appeal to Emily Harris asking the just-captured revolutionary for her first interview.

Dropping it on Penny's desk I wondered how and when my editor would get my request to Harris's attorney, Leonard Weinglass. That would be Penny's problem, I muttered to myself. It now seemed clear that the well-heeled Hearst family—owner of the *San Francisco Examiner*, the *Seattle Post-Intelligencer*, and the all-American standard, *Good Housekeeping* magazine—wanted their brainwashed daughter to go on trial separately from her SLA mates. It was almost certain that Emily Harris would be tried here in Los Angeles for the robbery of a Melrose convenience store she'd pulled off with Patty and husband Bill. Therefore she'd be held at L.A.'s Sybil Brand

Institute for Women, a short drive from *The Freep*. Emily had
since reiterated her request for a feminist female reporter. For
a host of personal and political reasons, I wanted her to choose
me.

I'd also written yet another letter to Rachel pleading with
her to come back to me emotionally, to choose me again—
rather than the square-jawed butch I'd seen her with at the San
Diego festival. This was my third such epistle.

BeJo had an evening shift tonight so I drove home to Culver
City to lick my wounds in private. Joe's haunting death, Morris's
ultimate betrayal, my decision to quit the strike, and most of all,
Rachel's unexplained abandonment had left crushing voids in
both my political and personal life.

The phone rang, but I ignored it. Only last week BeJo had
bought us a new invention, a small box that recorded incoming
messages if one did not pick up the receiver. A fabulous activist
tool, I grunted as I poured myself another ounce of Jim Beam
and watered it down with Coke. Lying on the sofa, watching
Johnny Carson, I was too bummed to talk to anyone.

"Jeanne," a hushed voice came out of the small box. "It's
Rachel. I don't want to speak into this machine…"

Stunned by the familiar treble, I leapt to pick up the phone.

"I'm here, Rachel!" I said trying to normalize my voice.

"Oh, thank God. I saw on the news a few days ago that
they've captured Patricia Hearst and the other SLA woman. I
thought you must be upset."

"Yes, very," I said, wondering if Rachel's seclusion included
not watching TV for several days. "I'm bummed about that…
and other things."

"I just heard that you quit the strike. I was shocked. Everyone
is mad at you. How are you feeling?"

"Numb, but resolved," I answered, the wound still raw. "I've
made some follow up calls, talked to Pody and others. June and
her crew hate me anyway. I've had some explaining to do to The

Tide Collective and wider community. But I feel free and ready to move on."

I sat down, breathing shallowly. "I'm hoping you didn't call me for the first time in weeks to talk politics?" Deeply wounded, I could barely control my voice. "No. Yes, I mean, no." I heard Rachel's voice break, as though she too was trying to hold on. "Is BeJo there? Can we talk?"

"BeJo won't be home for hours." I paused, not knowing what else to say, afraid to pry into anything that would make her hang up, too angry to deny that the name Jacki was screaming in my head.

"So, how are you and I? Or should I say you and Jacki?" The words blew out despite me.

"There is no me and Jacki," Rachel shot back.

"Is there a you and me?"

"I wish giving up on each other were an option."

"Then, we should see each other."

"Yes," she whispered. "Can you come to me now?"

Walking up Effie Street, I felt once more the giddy high that proximity to Rachel always aroused. Her front door was ajar. Baez's *Diamonds and Rust* jacket lay on the living room floor. The door to the bedroom stood half open.

"You're here!" Her voice called out timidly from the back porch staircase. Rachel came in out of the night.

She wore a low cut olive-colored blouse and my jade heart at the base of her throat. On one of my late night trips looking for her, I'd left the heart on her doorstep hoping she'd take it back. Tonight she looked as lovely as the first time she'd greeted me at Effie.

We stared at one another across the living room's hardwood floor. The distance between us felt like a hardened prairie spent by drought and longing. I rubbed my eyes telling myself that my tension was the product of a rough work week.

Rachel studied the ground between us, and I looked past her

to the landing that crowned the stairwell on which we'd so often made love. Anger, desire and panic swept through me. Should I turn and walk away, I wondered, dump my still unannounced commitment of monogamy, and let the scab that had begun to grow in her absence begin its healing work?

She came toward me with a wide radiant smile. "Would you like me to make you something to eat?" she asked. As she walked past me into the kitchen I heard her chuckle under her breath, "Pretty butch."

I followed her into the kitchen. "I hate when you call me that," I repeated my usual refrain.

"Calm down," she laughed, "I never say it in public. I'll make some eggs. A little protein will help."

Help what? I wondered, as I took my usual seat at her kitchen's yellow Formica table.

I felt strangely ill at ease. My lover shows up with another butch at a public festival, avoids me for a month, then calls out of the blue and shows me an open door. Her behavior felt irrational. So why was I the one who felt like a nutcase? I sat and stared at her Hansel and Gretel porcelain salt shakers, wondering if I should blurt out now that I'd ended my arrangement with BeJo. Or should I wait, get us to make love first, and then talk—when intimate words would come more easily to me?

Rachel cracked eggs against a skillet. "I was shocked to hear that GCSC released our unemployment benefits . They never even went to the hearing." She handed me some plates for our meal as she reported, "June went ballistic when Patton presented Morris's offer. She and Dixie vowed to keep picketing through the winter. April and her followers were sad to hear you'd resigned."

My lover sat down across from me, her lips turned downward. "I had such faith, Jeanne. Both in the Center and then the day you and I went to negotiate with Morris. I cried when Pody told us what Morris did, and how he'd gone back on his promise to you and me."

I studied her face and watched her eyes moisten. "Last fall, when I left my husband and come out and found my job at the Center I thought I'd found a loving family that would help me begin my new gay life. I thought GCSC stood for family. But this battle has felt like a reincarnation of all that was bad in my childhood. My father fighting with my sister and mother, and me trying to come in between and calm everyone down. I don't know if I have the strength to continue." Her voice broke as her tears took control.

The sad catch in her voice melted my resolve to stay removed. I reached and took her hand. "I'm sorry your first movement struggle had to end this way."

Rachel dried her eyes, stood up, and returned to the stove.

I sat back in my chair, afraid to go to her and wrap my arms around her shoulders. "I suppose…" I began but then drifted, distracted by Rachel's lean forearms moving rapidly, one hand scrambling, the other shaking the skillet. The last time I'd studied her body was in Lionheart's front seat at *The Freep*.

"You suppose what?" Rachel repeated, her back toward me.

"Oh?" I came to. "I suppose you'll be happy to get those unemployment checks?"

"You bet!" she laughed. "The Saloon isn't doing so well. Colleen's cut back my hours."

I'd been surprised to receive my unemployment check in the mail since I was getting payment, though irregular, from *The Freep*. Guess the porn boy owners weren't declaring me as salary. I was also getting food stamps from time to time, believing, as all us radicals did, that any accidental funds from the government were small recompense for gays being a disenfranchised class of people with no rights.

"I'm going to stick mine in a piggy bank," I said. "Save to buy a house someday."

She turned from the stove and faced me. "A house for you and BeJo?"

"Of course not. How many times do I need to tell you? BeJo and I are *not* lovers anymore."

Rachel's face clouded over. "So what do you call it when you just live with her and sleep in the same bed?"

I banged a knife on the Formica, my eyes flashing, "I call it not being with the woman I want to make love to!"

She began to laugh. Hearing my own words, I began to laugh too. Rachel and I were together now and that's all that mattered.

Scooping the eggs onto our plates, Rachel said. "Well, for that remark, I should have made us bacon too!"

She sat down across from me. The simple peace of eating together seemed to calm us.

Time passed, but watching her face, the mouth I loved, I couldn't keep my hurt suppressed. I finished the eggs and laid down my fork. "I saw you that weekend at the music festival with her."

Rachel stared at me in silence as though I hadn't said a thing. She titled her head, resting it on her palm, her blue eyes staring into mine. "I adore you," she whispered, "I've never said that to another human being, but just sitting across the table like this and looking at you, I adore you."

My gaze settled on the curve of her upper lip. It had always beckoned. "And her? Tell me—is she your lover?"

"Jacki?" Rachel seemed surprised. "She means little to me, a safe harbor."

The sound of another woman's name on her lips, the lips that had taken my heart before I gave it away, enraged me. "Is that why you're sleeping with her? She's your emotional sugar momma?" I demanded, my fist hitting the table.

Rachel jumped to her feet. "God, you can be so cruel." And she walked away.

I followed her into the big room, grabbing her by the shoulders. "Look at me, Rachel! The cruelty is mutual. How could you leave me for weeks on end? Don't you know how that feels?"

"Yes, I know how that feels, Jeanne!" She shook my hands off her shoulders, "It feels like the sun doesn't come up in the morning."

"Then why?" I screamed, fighting back tears.

She stationed herself in the shadow of the back porch door, placing the room between us once more. "Jacki had been calling me for weeks—to go to the movies and on hikes, to garden in her backyard. She seemed to want my company, unlike some people I know," she added sarcastically.

"I thought you were in love with me?" My voice came out low and dead. "You could have waited for me for a few more months, some people wait years for the one they love."

Rachel slid to the floor, covering my jade heart and her face with her hands. "Oh babe, I didn't know what else to do. The day you left me in the car, you broke my heart. Right after I'd given myself to you in a parking lot! I couldn't face myself after that!"

I rushed to her, going down on my knees. "I'm so fucking sorry, sweetheart. I didn't think about the implications of leaving until afterwards. I don't know what I was thinking. I promise that will never happen again."

"I had to go away." Rachel kept sobbing. "Inside myself, or over to Jacki's house in Venice. Some place where I could think. I need stability in my life. This room, these chairs and pillows," she cried waving her arm around the room, "my house is filled with you and the strike and…too much strife. I told the strikers they can't meet here anymore. I need to calm my life down. I realized that BeJo is not the one keeping Jeanne from me, Jeanne is keeping herself from me! You're married all right, but not to BeJo. You're married to the movement, to politics. You don't want a domestic relationship. That's why I stay at Jacki's sometimes—to get away from all this."

Rachel's reasoning confused me. "So what do you want from me?" I asked, still kneeling beside her crumpled form. "Is tonight about breaking up or coming back together?"

"I thought about breaking it off. But I love you too much. I can't imagine not having you in my life. I can't help but hope, maybe someday your life will settle down and you'll want a fuller relationship. Maybe we just need to give each other time.

In the meantime, maybe if I spend time with others and get some of my needs met, it won't hurt so much that you're so seldom around when I need you. So, I think I should be non-monogamous too."

Her words cut through me like a knife in the ribs. The front of my skull filled with rage, the back with grief. "Are you telling me you want to be non-monogamous, to see other women… like Jacki? Have you fucked her yet?" I asked, cringing at my lack of grace, yet praying I'd hear her denial.

"Don't ask me!" she screamed. "For God's sake, Jeanne, I never asked you."

We sat huddled on the floor inches and miles apart.

Finally, Rachel took a deep breath. "I want to go out with Jacki or whoever makes me feel more centered." Her tone sounded vacant and rehearsed. "Seeing other people will take the pressure off me wanting everything from you. I'll need less from you. Then I can get on with the changes I need to make in my life."

"Changes? What kind of changes?"

Rachel stood up and began to pace. "I don't know what kind of changes! I can't think when my life is screaming all the time. I need a sense of calm."

I looked up at her. "Why didn't you tell me about wanting changes, Rachel, before you went away with another woman?"

"Because I thought you would leave me. If I told you I needed to be non-monogamous, I thought you'd walk out of my life."

Jumping to my feet, I walked to the bookcase, rested my elbows on the top shelf and cradled my head in my hands. It felt like I was drowning, something was compressing the life out of my lungs. Negotiating weekends from BeJo didn't matter to Rachel anymore. Lifting my head, I turned toward Rachel's front door. *Walk through it*, an inner voice told me. *Free yourself*.

But my feet wouldn't move.

Maybe none of these words mattered. Rachel adored me. I was crazy about her. Other people couldn't change that.

I turned back to face her. "So, it's non-monogamy you want?" my hollow voice asked.

"It will make things easier between us, Jeanne." She said, pulling my name out long like she was saying good-bye.

"Easier!" The anger flashed again as I shouted. I grabbed a book out of the bookcase and slammed it against the wall. "It breaks my heart to hear you say these words! Am I supposed to sit around waiting while you screw other women, seeing you every Monday and Friday—make love—and pretend it doesn't tear me up inside?" I looked down to see Andrea Dworkin's hardcover, *Violence Against Women*, hit the floor in front of her. The sharp smack was satisfying. "What kind of easier is that?"

Rachel sobbed louder and ran into the bedroom, screaming, "I can't handle your rage. You're always angry with me."

Running after her, I stood in the bedroom doorway. "I have a right to be angry. You lied to me. You start dating another woman without telling me and now you tell me you want to demote our relationship."

Rachel stood on the other side of the mattress, her face swollen to a dark pink. "Why is non-monogamy a demotion when I do it? You did it for months."

"I didn't use it to distance myself from you!"

"What a goddamn lie, Jeanne! Can you hear yourself?" she yelled.

"BeJo was here before I met you."

"You told me non-monogamy was your preferred lifestyle."

"Not when I'm in love with you!" I pounded my fist against the doorjamb. "Where am I supposed to call you, at Jacki's house?"

"Call me at my house."

"Just drop in like I used to?"

"Don't come here if you don't want to see what you don't want to see."

Suddenly I heard us from afar, as if I were the Goddess listening in, a detached self gazing out the bedroom window.

Córdova didn't want to be alive and hearing these words from the woman she loved. The tiny bedroom wasn't big enough to hold the hurt.

I dropped to my knees, sitting on the edge of the mattress. "What are we doing to each other?" I mumbled through tears.

Rachel came from behind me on the bed and circled her arms around my neck. The sweet pressure of her breasts against my back calmed me.

"I've missed you so much," she whispered, kissing the back of my neck. "I hate it when we fight."

I drank in her patchouli. "When will we see each other?"

"As often as you want to," she promised.

"As often as *I* want?" I retorted, incredulous. "Rachel, why I've been trying to find you these weeks is that I want to spend *every* weekend together. I talked to BeJo. I've broken off our arrangement. I'm free to be with you."

For a long moment Rachel said nothing. She continued to finger-stroke my hair, combing it back over my ears like she liked it.

"I waited months to hear these words from you, Jeanne. I can't keep changing my life again to accommodate yours. Besides, you have so many meetings on Saturdays, you couldn't possibly spend a whole weekend with anyone."

I sighed; Rachel was right about weekend meetings.

"Well then, how about every Saturday night through Monday mornings then?" I reached up, cupping her head. "And at least once during the week. Wednesdays. Every Wednesday night?"

"Whatever night you want." Rachel pulled me backward, down to the mattress, struggling to take off my vest and work her fingers over my shirt buttons. "It's been so long," she breathed into my ear, sending a ripple down my thighs. "Make love to me, babe," she murmured.

Somehow, I wasn't relieved. Something felt wrong… missing…broken. I got up, leaving her alone on the mattress, and went to the fridge to get us some beers. Alcohol never gave me the sweet oblivion it gave Rachel, so I reached into my pocket, grabbed and swallowed another Darvon. The night was young but already I knew I wanted to forget it. No, tonight I couldn't make love to Rachel, but I could certainly fuck.

"I've got some sad news," Penny said, as I stood in her office doorway weeks later. It was November 3rd and I knew by the low pitch in her voice she had another rough assignment for me. I had a much thicker skin than Rachel, but being Human Rights Editor was eroding my human stamina.

Looking down at her desk, she said softly, "Lenny Somberg, the Director of the Free Clinic, was murdered today. At his office. He was just sitting at his desk. Apparently someone broke in maybe looking for cash. When he wouldn't hand it over they shot him. He died before the ambulance got there."

My mind began spinning—more death and loss. Was this an occupational hazard of journalists? My mind flew to Rachel. With life so easily cut short, why were the love of my life and I wasting so much time apart? For six weeks I'd tried to swallow Rachel's non-monogamous announcement like a good feminist, valiantly putting the excruciating images of her in bed with other women out of my mind. I'd run every kind of feminist rationalization through my head—after all, I myself had been non-monogamous, now it was her turn. Jealousy was heterosexual thinking; Rachel didn't belong to me. But our new arrangement, her declaration, had sent my emotional life into a bleak spiral. Being apart from her felt like falling from grace.

As Penny talked on about my covering Somberg's creation of the amazing L.A. Free Clinic and his life and death, all I could think about was writing Rachel a final letter. Returning to my office, I closed and locked the door and pulled the blinds shut. I wanted no interruptions.

My Darling, I typed, *what's happened to our weekends and Wednesday nights? It's November now and I've grown to hate this non-monogamous plan of yours. I can never find you on the phone or even at the Saloon. You don't even seem to be living at your house anymore. It's as though you've disappeared. I've memorized every syllable on your answering machine. Each inflection of your voice feels like a knife paring a hole closer to my heart. Our rare Saturday nights stretch across my life like oases that are too far apart to sustain life. Sometimes you leave me curt phone messages giving me feeble excuses about plans Jacki has made for you two so you can't see me on weekends. And yet, you call me, sometimes from her house, crying, saying how desperately you miss me. Please darling, come back to me so we can share our joy again.*

My private phone line rang off the hook. But I was too absorbed. All I could do was write.

I see you sometimes at demonstrations and you're with her. You look at me with pain and longing. And still, you do nothing. Your actions don't match your words. I don't know which are true anymore. I fear I am beginning to hate you as much as love you. Is this what you call our new relationship?

"Córdova?" Bryan called timidly through my door. "Your friend Rachel has been calling all afternoon."

I stopped banging the Selectric and ran to my door, unlocking it. "Goddamn it, Bryan. Why didn't you interrupt me?"

"I told her you were in a meeting with Penny," he whimpered. "She said to tell you she wants you to come over to her house as soon as you can."

"You should have told me sooner," I barked, as I tore the letter out of my typewriter and jammed it into my back pocket. A minute later I was speeding to her in Lionheart.

The sky was mottled in smog and sunset red. Once more I found the front door to Effie Street left ajar. I found Rachel sitting on the back porch staring across the tiled rooftops and palm forest below. She held a joint pressed between her lips and was dressed in my pale blue button-down shirt, the one I'd left in her closet for overnights.

Wordlessly, I sat down on the step behind her, my legs encircling her small frame, my chest pressed against her back. It was her favorite position. Her delicately pinched fingers held the joint over her shoulder offering it to me as she mouthed a line from Baez about passionate strangers who rescue each other from a lifetime of care.

"No thanks," I murmured, waving the pot away. "I popped a Darvon before I came."

"Of course you did," she retorted, and I reeled from the bitterness in her tone. So it was going to be that kind of night.

"It's nice to see you, Jeanne." Her tone switched to tender as she drew my name out long as if she'd waited all fall to say it.

The heat of her back pressed against my chest, and I stifled an impulse to rip her blouse off and fuck her there on the stairwell. Memories of past times flooded through me. "You could say my name more often, if you'd answer the damn phone when I call."

Rachel picked up a cloth and started dusting the pile of album covers at her feet.

We'd hit a wall. I stood and walked back into the living room to the stereo. Some lighter music might change the mood. She came up behind me.

I turned to face her.

"God, you make me so furious!" she screamed at the top of her lungs, her pent up rage blowing me a step backward. I wondered how much she'd had to drink. Her hands balled into fists as she pounded my chest. "Why did you say we can spend weekends together now, Jeanne? Why *now*? Don't you know how many months I longed for you to admit you wanted to be with me?"

My emotional thermostat was overheating, but I let her hit me until her rage collapsed into bedrock of tears. Then I pulled her close and wrapped my arms around her. "It's going to be all right," I soothed. "Are you saying you used to love me but you don't anymore?"

She pulled away from me, looking as small as a stunned bird. "I love you like I love the mountains, Jeanne. There is no past or present to that."

Her words made me lightheaded and I shook her by the shoulders. "Then leave that woman. Stop seeing her, Rachel!" Roughly, I pressed my mouth against hers.

Her lips slackened and she went limp in my arms. Her forehead rested on my chest as she said dully, "I can't. I can't go forward or backward anymore. I have no more power, Jeanne. The Center won. The Saloon closed. You left me. I'm jobless and can't afford my rent. I can't change anything. All I want to do is run away from my life."

I lifted her head so that our eyes met. "I won't accept your running away, Rachel. Don't cop out on me. You have the power to make us right again. You stood up for lesbian rights at the Center, you came and found me and made me fall in love with you. You *can* change this!"

Rachel sank to the floor, sitting cross-legged.

I squatted beside her, taking her chin gently and studying her eyes. They looked dull and listless. How many bottles or joints had she consumed before I'd arrived? I had to find a way to get through to her. "I am here for you. I want to be monogamous with you. I can do the work for both of us. I'll find us an apartment. We'll live together. I'll be with you all the time."

Rachel slapped me across the cheek. "How dare you say that to me!" Her voice came out cold and strong. "Where were you all summer when I sat here waiting like your goddamn mistress? Knowing you were with BeJo, or at some meeting. Everything was more important to you then. Don't you dare come back to me now and offer me everything I once wanted!" She stood up, using my shoulders to balance her weight as she shrank toward the bedroom.

The sting on my cheek ignited my adrenaline. I bolted to my feet, grabbing Rachel's shirt sleeve. "Don't you dare walk out on me now," I screamed.

"Then fuck me or leave me!" she yelled in my face. "I'm tired of this talk."

"You're drunk!" I yelled back. "I fucked you last time when I was angry and it only made me hate you more when you disappeared again."

She came toward me, defiantly wrapping her arms around my neck; pulling my hair until it hurt, she brought my lips to hers. My body agreed: enough talk. She was right. Only sex was strong enough to break through her self-imposed wall of paralysis. My lips parted and her weight fell against me. I finished ripping off her shirt, my own, and I lifted her off her feet, bringing us both down hard on the bare polished floor.

Being inside her mouth felt bottomless, as always, but this time both of us needed much more. I wanted her to remember my hands when she was with Jacki. And what, I wanted to ask, did she need? But talk was over. My nails raked the ridges of her nipples and her stomach muscles tightened in pain. I turned her over on her stomach and began to caress her back and buttocks, marveling at their whiteness, the color of bone, as I climbed on top of her.

Her body quivered and froze. I could feel her fright. We'd never made love this way before.

"It's me, I'm here," I whispered in her ear, blowing my voice deep into her ear. She lay beneath me her body steeled with trepidation. "I want your mouth," she beckoned and I came to her buffering her face with my hand between her head and the floor, as I waited for her permission or denial.

As her tongue yielded to mine, her spine relaxed against my weight, and she whispered, "Make love to me, darling, like tonight is our forever."

Her words shocked, then drove new rage into my knees as they bruised against the hardwood. When she moaned I knew she was ready. My hands returned to the naked cheeks of her ass, and my fingers probed the recess between her buttocks.

"Hold me!" she called out urgently, but this time I didn't stop.

"Talk to me, baby," she urged.

"Easy," I demanded, using her old nickname as I pushed deeper. "I've got you. Let me in."

"Jeanne," she gasped. She grabbed my other wrist, as I my fingers slid inside her all the way to my palm. Her muscles squeezed my fingers as I began to pump.

"Promise me you won't ever leave me," I demanded in rhythm with my hand, "Promise me."

Her body tightened once more and I saw the shock on her face as pain and pleasure fought one another. I had to knock down her wall and bring her home. I slid past her resistance and felt it yield as abruptly as it had come. Muscles relaxed around my fingers and our bodies went limp. Only then did my left hand go beneath her and find her clit. Slowly, she came back to life. I lifted her hips off the hardwood and stroked her thigh. Her jaw unclenched. Now there was only hunger in her face. Finally, we belonged to each other. Would it be for tonight or as she said, our forever?

"Promise me, Rachel," I repeated as I brought my naked groin hard against her.

Joy swallowed us as we moved together.

"I promise, babe, I'll never leave you."

Her breathing grew rapid and my body climbed quickly to her speed.

"...Jeanne!" she called out, coming with the last syllable of my name.

Later in the night, her mouth on my nipples quelled what was left of my pain.

A noise in the back of my mind roused me slowly. Rachel's telephone was ringing. My eyes flew open. A small shaft of sunlight was peeking in through the window. Somewhere in the night we'd made our way from the hardwood to her bedroom's futon. We lay on her multi-colored bedspread, clutching each other as tightly as two banks hug a river.

I looked at my Timex. It was just past six a.m.

Rachel was asleep, her face luminous, its lines relaxed with joy. Hating to wake her, I mumbled groggily in her ear, "Darling, your phone is ringing. Christ, who would call at this hour?"

She half-opened her eyes and looked at me dreamily and smiled. "You're still here. It can't be important," she cooed, pulling my lips to hers.

Kissing her deeply, a voice broke into our world. "Hi honey, I was calling to wake you up for a kiss and to confirm our picnic today…"

Rachel shot out of bed like an earthquake had catapulted her from it, but not in time to prevent my hearing the woman's voice end with, "Call me back honey."

I heard the click as Rachel snapped off the answering machine. But it was too late. The intimacy in Jacki's voice chilled my heart, made it stop beating long enough for me to fall from grace into despair. I turned over on my stomach and used the pillow to smother my tears. Last night I'd been inside her as no one else had ever been. Last night we were as intimate as two human beings could ever hope to be. Last night we'd promised forever.

Rachel was back in bed, stroking the back of my neck. "Talk to me, babe," she pleaded. "I'm sorry you had to hear that."

The pillow remained between us as my only defense. This was the butt end of non-monogamy, the "slippage" I was never supposed to hear.

"You lied to me." I spoke through the pillow.

"She means nothing to me. We're friends." Rachel tried to pull the pillow away, but I held on tightly. I wanted no living soul to see my hurt. In the blackness I thought about BeJo over the last two years. Had she ever had a moment like this? And Rachel over the summer, surely I hadn't done this to her? Men must have invented non-monogamy. It was a paradigm meant for sex, not love. I wanted to disappear.

"Talk to me, darling," Rachel pleaded.

A stern voice came out of me. "Would you go and make some coffee?"

"What?"

"Make some coffee and toast. Let's have breakfast," the voice instructed.

Rachel got out of our bed. I heard noises in the kitchen. My tears were dry now. Swiftly, I pulled on my jeans and boots, threw the car keys into my pocket.

I paused in the chilled living room, naked from the waist as I looked outdoors through her window trying to find the horizon. This morning's marine layer had vaporized even the palm trees, but not the wall separating Rachel's heart from mine. Last night was over. I couldn't bear to let her see my pain.

My jade shirt was splayed over the avocado beanbag. I put it on, taking time to neatly tuck it under my belt. Then I walked through the kitchen, past Rachel and out the front door.

Chapter 30

The Rage of All Butches

[Los Angeles]

"A lesbian is the rage of all women condensed to the point of explosion." —Radicalesbians NYC, 1970

December 31st, 1975

And yet, I couldn't leave Rachel.

As fall became winter, her words and actions increased in contradiction. She and I saw less and less of each other, but she insisted that her feelings for me remained the same, that she loved me "more than the storybooks speak of love." And it was her words I listened to, returning each time to Effie Street where we sat on the back porch, held each other for hours and stared into the palm-cordoned horizon trying to find our way back to each other.

As her inconsistencies grew, so did my brooding and desperation. A part of me was dying, although the living part found me parked at Effie Street writing her poems and prayers. As Thanksgiving came and went I began to accept that being non-monogamous was not Rachel's way of stabilizing our relationship, it was her way of leaving me. No matter how tender my lovemaking, how desperate my words, nothing reopened her heart. Mine grew more bitter. And I began to hate her as fully as I loved her.

It was finally New Year's Eve, and I was seeing 1975 out as I had lived it, working for the movement. Our annual fundraising dance tonight at the Woman's Building was critical to the financial survival of *The Lesbian Tide*. L.A.'s feminist art institute, the building itself, was the marvel of the night. It had recently moved from the downtown ghetto on South Grandview to the uptown ghetto area of North Spring Street and a former three-story

Lesbian Tide's leaflet advertising annual dance at Woman's Building. 1974

warehouse built in the 1920's by the Standard Oil Company. The night that Angela Davis had spoken had been one of many nights that the old building had been too small and too crowded to house the rapidly growing feminist movement. They'd needed more space.

The new Woman's Building was run by the Feminist Studio Workshop, an art school founded by artist Judy Chicago, art historian Arlene Raven and graphic designer Sheila de Bretteville. Once more the FSW hoped the building would continue to be the center of women's culture in Los Angeles. They didn't have the money to pay carpenters and painters to gut the massive structure and turn it into necessary offices, art galleries, and theater rooms, so the school told their students that the renovation was part of their education. Each pounded nail, all of the newly plastered walls, and every arc and design were the result of women's ingenuity and sweat. Just as our personal lives were the raw materials of our politics, the process of reclamation was as important as the product. This was the feminist way. Over the summer, hundreds of feminists and dykes had knocked down walls, nailed sheet rock, and laid new floors into the former warehouse.

By Christmas the new building was a happening hub. The third floor had been completely denuded of interior walls to make a space for large gatherings and dances. Tonight I was ecstatic to see it densely crowded with upwards of five hundred women. *The Tide* was dependent on the proceeds from this benefit to pay the printer during months when our meager advertising and subscription money ran short. We had no money for a band, so we relied on disco tapes for non-stop dance music throughout the night. Despite the high cover charge of three dollars per dyke, and fifty cents per beer or soda, no one was complaining. They were all *Tide* readers. They all wanted their paper.

Leaning against one of the dozen cement pillars which held up the ceiling, I wondered if I'd ever get to go to a lesbian event and not be responsible for something, or everything, about it. Tonight I'd assigned myself to stay close to the bar, and quarterback the shift changes and restock the fast dwindling supplies of soda and beer. It was 11:45 and the crowd of about four hundred was playfully tipsy.

"Did you wear that hat for me?" The voice was slurred and provocative as Rachel appeared before me.

Instinctively, I reached to my head, unsure what Rachel was talking about. Then I realized I'd worn the flat brimmed, Australian leather hat that I'd had on the day we'd met. "No, I didn't wear it for you," I retorted, my tone surly. What right did she have to approach me so intimately? It had been weeks since we'd been together. "I wear it every winter."

Rachel swirled and twirled around me, dancing playfully, and I could tell she was too lit to hear a word I'd said. "I've always loved that hat on you," she drawled.

I'd spent the last hour wretchedly watching Rachel arrive and dance with Jacki. Rachel's flat-faced carpenter wasn't even butch enough to cut off her hippie pigtail, I noted, heartbroken that Rachel and I were not welcoming in the New Year together. I'd tried to look away and treat the two of them as strangers. But now Rachel had left Jacki and was preening in front of me.

"Since it's only my hat you love," I said, "here, take it." I lowered my head and Rachel snatched the hat and placed it on her own head. The brown leather capped her translucent white face, and I looked down to see a form-fitting black V-neck sweater frame her low neckline. She was giving me that bewitching, come hither smile I knew so well.

"Dance with me," she said, and took my hand, pulling me onto the floor.

"Stop torturing me, leave me alone," I countered, but allowed her to drag me with her.

She brought her body next to mine and wrapped both arms around my neck. Her hair brushed against my cheek as my body responded automatically, losing its center of gravity as it poured into hers. As we moved around the room time and space became other people's reality, as it always did with Rachel.

"Perfect fit," she murmured, tucking her head into my

shoulder. "And you know damn well that I love every part of you, not just your hat!" She played with my fingers, kneading each tip like the edges of raw piecrust. The roughness of her chef-worn calloused palms made my belly tighten.

"Why does our chemistry never die?" I asked.

"I don't know, babe," she sighed. "You're the only one I've ever felt this with." She reached up and began to track my lips with her forefinger. "Whenever I see your face I want to hold it and have you hold me. It doesn't make sense to me how there can be so much love and yet we are not together."

I brushed her fingers off my mouth. "What are you doing, Rachel?"

"I know I shouldn't be here."

"Then why are you?"

The glittering strobe ball lit our faces as if only for each other.

"It's midnight," Rachel replied. "I had to be with you. Jacki is walking her ex-lover out to her car."

"Just a quickie then?" I said, acidly. In the distance I heard someone begin the New Year's countdown.

"I came so you could kiss me," Rachel confessed.

Hoping desperately for some kind of new beginning, I leaned down and kissed her long and hard, my mind going back to the GCSC parking lot, back where we'd begun. My hand fought with her curls as I pressed her lips harder against my own. I felt the familiar shift of weight as her knees buckled. Rocking in each other's arms, we rested with each other, washing away the hurtful months of distance and dissonance. Gradually, I began to feel whole again, resurrected and restored. She burrowed deeper between my shoulders. Sensing something odd, I looked up and saw other couples staring. Like the first time, only rougher, we'd kissed in front of the entire L.A. lesbian community. Everyone knew that Córdova and Rachel were coming back together, and that Rachel belonged to me.

A jostle behind me made my backbone stiffen. "Jacki is coming back," I spoke urgently, clasping Rachel's waist. "Stay with me!"

Her eyes widened as she stood on tiptoe looking over my shoulder. Terror filled them. A hand roughly grasped my shoulder and I knew it wasn't kind. It pulled me backwards away from Rachel. I heard her gasp, "I can't," as she tore herself out of my arms.

My body twisted free from the foreign arm, and I went into a crouch and spun around to face the threat. Dad was coming toward me with his belt. But it was Jacki who stood there, momentarily shocked by my spring into animal defense mode.

I snarled at her, "You gotta stop pushing me around, Jacki. Just because you're bigger than most women, you can't push me around—not with your truck or your body!"

Two weeks ago, Jacki and I had accidentally met at the mouth to the Westside Women's Center's driveway. In her truck, she'd butted me aside, demanding right of way. I'd felt humiliated.

Now she crouched too, and her stance widened. "I didn't push you off the road," Jacki shot back, her black eyes narrowed. "You got in my way!" She stepped toward me, both fists clenched.

"And now you're in my way," I growled, filled with fury.

Jacki crowded closer. Suddenly, my body passed into another state. I was back in my West Covina bedroom, cornered by my father waving his belt. And just as suddenly, I felt my mind alter. I felt no fear. My body was impregnable, my mind sharp and clear.

I lunged forward, a fraction before she did.

Out of nowhere, Robin jumped into the crevice of space between us, her voice shrill, "No fighting! You can't hit me!"

The sight of Robin, the world's most faggy excuse for a butch, standing there, hands above her head, fingers wiggling madly as though she were going to be shot at the OK Corral, brought me up short. How could I slug Jacki with my best friend clowning between us?

The group of women, who'd formed a ragged ring around us, began laughing. Robin was laying on the slapstick heavily. She tiptoed around Jacki and then me as though we were her props in a piece of performance art. Rachel's other butch and I gaped at each other, two gladiators too adrenalin-hyped to know that they'd been saved.

And now, BeJo appeared, her firm arms taking hold of my shoulders and leading me toward the bar. "We're out of sodas and beer, honey," she commanded. "You have to make a run for more. Now!"

Drowning myself, and the whole lesbian community, with a new load of cold beer, I lost the last hour of the dance, and I lost Rachel. It was time to pack up. BeJo and I were in back of the bar, sorting the empty beer cans from the full ones that we'd take back for a refund. BeJo passed me with a trolley of cases heading for the stairs, and she called back, "Don't forget your hat!"

I reached to my head. My hat! Rachel had taken it. It was probably at Jacki's house right now. Jacki's face, a blackness surrounding it, resurfaced in my mind. That numb-nut knew it was mine, that it was my signature Córdova hat. What had she said when she saw Rachel with it? In my mind's eye, I saw Jacki fling my hat into a trashcan in her house when Rachel wasn't looking. Or she was secretly planning to wake up in the middle of the night, throw it into the fireplace and burn it? Wobbling with rage, I reached out to steady myself against the bar counter. Rachel's resurfacing had led me to drink far more than my usual two beers. I was so drunk I could see my hat curling in flames, the once proud crown caving in upon a melting brim. I couldn't let her destroy the only thing that Rachel and I still shared.

A point of light gleamed from the shadowed shelves beneath the bar counter, catching my eye. I stepped forward and bent over. It was a steak knife from BeJo's kitchen. She must have brought it to open the cases of Coke and beer. I held it up. The weapon glinted powerfully in the dimmed third floor loft, its worn wood handle a "perfect fit," as Rachel would say, in my palm.

I thought of Rachel preening in my hat, but she was in Jacki's arms—in Jacki's bed. Rachel, who loved to fuck when she was drunk, just like tonight. Only tonight, she'd fuck Jacki. The thought filled me with a rage I'd never felt before.

I darted past BeJo on the stairs, tore out of the Woman's Building, yelling to her, "I gotta find my hat!"

And I knew exactly where to go to get Córdova's hat. I knew where Jacki lived. Driving west on the 10 Freeway, I got off at the last exit before the ocean, took a sharp right on Olympic, and drove into the residential darkness. There it was. A soggy melon-colored house with a basketball hoop on the garage. Turning into the driveway, I cut my lights and parked in back of Jacki's sorry green-chipped pickup. I should just ram it, I thought. That'd tell her I was here. But it wouldn't get my hat back. Wouldn't get Rachel back. I was determined to get both.

The moon was full and strong, the marine layer was not going to come in tonight to shroud my access. Softly, I closed Lionheart's driver's door and strode quickly toward the front porch, my chest heaving, and my arms swinging loosely. Jacki was bigger and outweighed me by twenty pounds, but I was faster and lighter on my feet. I'd just knock on the front door and tell her to get out of my way.

I paused, wondering, should I knock? What if no one heard me? What if they were both sleeping? The bedroom had to be at the back of the house away from the street. I should try to see if Rachel was in there with Jacki. Maybe Jacki had dropped her off at Effie. I snuck around the front bushes, down the side of the house, opened the gate to the back yard. Crouched down, I made my way to the back door.

Peeking through its screened window, I saw a long hallway that ran from the front of the house to the back. The bedroom had to be to the right. But a tall, thick hedge rose in front of me, blocking access to the bedroom window. No problem, I'd climb right through it. Thorns wouldn't stop me tonight. My senses were acute. I was invulnerable, coarsely alive.

An almost full moon edged over the crown of the house. A sliver of light fell on my hand. Good, I still had the knife. I didn't remember driving with it. Studying it now, I realized it wasn't a steak knife. It was slightly longer, with a serrated edge that had wide scallops. The blade looked firm and cold, devoid of feeling. I breathed heavily, wishing that I could feel as dead as the knife.

Suddenly, the thought of plunging a knife into a body composed of real flesh felt nauseatingly abhorrent. I couldn't even handle the sight of Joe Tomassi's blood. Bile poured into my windpipe and I gripped my stomach and doubled over. Gratefully, my retch was silent. Nothing came out.

Still, the knife looked ferocious enough to plant the fear of God in Jacki—make her give me my hat back. My courage returned. I wasn't afraid of her—or anyone. She had pushed me around for the last time. When I'd left my father's house, I vowed that I'd never let anyone else back me into a corner for the rest of my life. No one would ever humiliate me like that.

The knife glimmered as I held it upwards in my fist, poised to cut the bedroom window screen. Still low to the ground, I listened intently for any sound coming from the supposed bedroom. Nothing. Did I really want to crawl through the window, into the bedroom and see Rachel being held by someone else? No way. And somehow breaking in felt...too low-life and cheap; I might as well just knock.

I retraced my steps to the back door. It was old, its dark blue paint peeling off. A rusted screen protected a window set into it at chest height. The whole structure was frayed and warped by the battering ocean mist. It would break easily against my shoulder.

I kicked the door hard with the toe of my boot.

"Rachel!" I cupped my mouth and shouted through the screened window. "Rachel, it's me. Come out and talk!"

The house was silent. What if Jacki and my lover were out at an all-night restaurant? What if Rachel wasn't here at all? I pressed my face against the window screen trying to peer in. My breath released a hot cloud. "Rachel! Are you in there?"

Overhead, a naked porch light bulb snapped on. I snapped to attention, sucking in my gut and jutting out my chin, like Dad had drilled into us. My backbone went rigid; I was centered and primed, ready for Jacki. This time she wouldn't push me aside.

Through the rust pocked window screen I saw Jacki's face. And she saw mine.

"If you come out here I'll take you apart," I shouted in a cold quiet tone. I brought my fist up to where she could see the knife in my hand. "Go get Rachel!" I commanded.

Jacki's flat face appeared to spasm. Her dark brows rose halfway up her forehead. Her eyeballs fixated on the knife and she whitened with fear. A hoarse scream began in her throat but ended with a whimpering, "Córdova!"

In the dull yellow light, she jumped backwards, mumbling, "Oh my God!"

Then, she disappeared.

Once more, I pressed my face against the screen. Should I cut a hole in it? Wasn't that damaging personal property? Maybe Rachel hadn't heard me. Perhaps she too had been unnerved by our New Year's kiss and had gone to Effie or was sleeping somewhere else in the house like a sofa in the living room. How could she get into someone else's bed after that kiss?

"Rachel?" I shouted again, ensuring I could be heard throughout the house. "Talk to me! Sweetheart, can you hear me?"

Deep in the hallway, at the front end of the house, another light went on. I waited.

A shape in a blur of pink was coming down the hall. Rachel's face appeared through the screen. She saw me and opened the slider window. Her eyes were small and red. She'd been crying. Seeing her, my heart melted and I reached out to touch her cheek. The screen blocked my fingers. "Why are you crying?" I asked.

"Jacki and I had a big fight." She paused, her forehead pressed against the filthy screen, as she whispered, "I miss you, my love." Her voice was sad and broken. "But what are you doing here?" she added.

I brought both hands to the screen forming a private circle

to comfort her.

"Good Lord! Is that a knife?" Rachel asked, horrified.

I looked. The knife was clutched in my fist. I felt foolish and embarrassed. "Don't know why I brought it," I mumbled. "Guess I wanted to scare Jacki into letting me talk to you."

"That was really stupid, darling," Rachel shook her head in wonder.

My insides relaxed. Rachel was with me now. My eyes fell to the small cleft in her chin and down further to the hollow in her neck. She was wearing my jade heart. Her pink nightgown that I knew so well soothed me to be close to it once more.

She opened the door a crack, saying, "Here, give me that thing."

I slipped the knife into the opening between us, wanting to pull her through it too.

"I can't believe you drove out here with a weapon!" Rachel's voice filled my senses. "What were you thinking?"

I grinned for no particular reason. I didn't mind Rachel scolding me. "I came from the dance to get my hat; you forgot to give it back to me."

"You came for your hat?" Her blue eyes widened.

"Yes, and to collect you too," I explained. "I had to go and get supplies, and when I came back you were gone. I know you want to be with me tonight. You said so. It's New Year's Eve."

"Do you know what time it is, babe?"

I sighed and leaned against the rickety door. Talking to each other in the dark felt like old times. "I know it's late, so just go pack your things and come with me. We can go out to breakfast and then home to Effie."

Rachel looked over her shoulder toward the bedroom door into which Jacki had darted. She seemed afraid.

"Open the door, sweetheart," I coaxed, "I need to hold you. Why did you leave me like that at the dance?"

"You've been drinking, Jeanne." Rachel's voice broke and she reached through to take my hand. "I'm so sorry. I didn't mean to do that. God, I didn't mean to do that." She kissed my hand and pushed it back out toward me. "You've got to get out of here."

The dim porch light bathed my lover's face in a stunning yellow hue. I'd never seen her look so beautiful, so hauntingly open. The door between us was only a membrane to be pushed aside.

Jacki's large frame emerged from the bedroom and began coming toward us. "Get away from that door, Rachel!" she roared. "I called the police. They're on their way."

Jacki was going to take Rachel from me once more. I heaved my shoulder against the door. It flew open. And I stepped in to face her.

Rachel stood in between us, frantically looking back and forth.

"Go get my hat and come with me now," I ordered her calmly.

Jacki stepped closer. Rachel balked, paralyzed with fear. She whispered to me, "Your hat isn't here. I stopped and left it at my house. It's safe. I promise. But it's not safe for you here…or for me," she sobbed.

I couldn't fathom her inaction. Why wasn't she coming with me? That's it! Jacki stood between her and her things. "Never mind packing," I pleaded and reached to grab her. "Just come home with me."

Rachel stepped away from my grasp. "I can't!" she screamed, looking wildly at me in front of her and Jacki behind her.

I yelled at Jacki over Rachel's head, "Back off! You're scaring her."

Jacki stood still, watching Rachel's small frame shake.

"Back off," I screamed again, "or I'll come in after you!"

Jacki's large body retreated. She backed away, to the bedroom.

I stepped forward and took Rachel in my arms. "You told me if I waited long enough, we'd get back together. You said we just needed time." My voice tightened. "You said every Wednesday and every weekend. But I think you…you must have lied to me.

Why won't you be with me?"

Rachel looked at me like a small whipped animal. "I'm afraid of the power between us. I can't trust my feelings around you. I can't trust where they will take me."

"What does that mean?" My voice came out hoarse and perplexed. "I can be brave enough for both of us. I can knock Jacki down and go get your things."

"Oh, please don't do that, Jeanne," Rachel whimpered. "You're frightening me!"

The moon's light had darkened behind a growing cloud cover. I heard sirens, piercing background music to the dance of losing Rachel.

"If you love me....don't understand."

Rachel had wrapped her arms around her shoulders and was rocking herself. She took a step backward, sobbing, "I can't handle opening my heart again."

"The cops are coming!" Jacki's soprano trilled from the bowels of the house.

Rachel's face turned gray. "Please go, Jeanne. I'll call you tomorrow from Effie. You can come get your hat. We'll have breakfast; I'll make you scrambled eggs, just the two of us. I'll call you, I promise, at first light."

The sirens were louder now, but the tension in my jaw relaxed into a silly grin. Rachel and I would be together for breakfast. She'd promised. I held my watch up to the porch light. "First light is seven o'clock, that's only a few hours from now, right?"

Rachel nodded. "I promise," she said, pushing me back out into the night, closing the door between us.

I watched her disappear into the blackness.

Her words echoed in my head. I'd gotten what I came for: a promise to return my hat and be together. I tore back through Jacki's side gate and jumped into Lionheart. Driven by hope, I sped away from Venice. The dawn would bring Rachel and me together once more.

Chapter 31

Return of the Hat

[Los Angeles]

January, 1976

New Year's morning dawned clear and sharp, but I was too ashamed to open my eyes. Thankfully, BeJo was pulling a holiday shift, so I heard the front door close behind her. The silk sheets were a comfort for once, and I pulled them up over my head. Today they hid me, and a raging hangover headache, from a world I couldn't face. Was that really me in my memory of last night? How could I have done such a thing? I, who had never felt violence toward a woman before, had gone to another dyke's house, acting like violence was exactly what I intended. Yes, I'd had fantasies about removing my father from the planet, and I had explored my capacity for political violence, but violence out of jealousy? I must have looked like a crazed nutcase. In one blindingly drunk night, I'd lost all control and damaged my sense of self as a woman. And if Jacki told the whole lesbian community, as she had a right to do, my rep as a responsible leader would also be in the toilet.

I threw off the sheets and sat up. Rachel! She'd promised to call at first light. My watch read seven a.m.

In the kitchen, BeJo had left the pot brewing and next to it, a note. *Honey*, it read, *Forget about your hat. It will show up. Try to have yourself a quiet day!*

So BeJo sensed that something extraordinary had happened last night, something she knew better than to ask me about, something I knew I would never tell her.

I reread her note: *Forget about your hat. It will show up.*

Yes, but would Rachel, I wondered, taking a cup of coffee and walking into *The Tide's* office in the second bedroom. Sitting at my desk in my pajamas, my hair standing up like a hedgehog, I lit my first cigarette. Smoking calmed my nerves, gave me the illusion of control. My eyes rifled through the neat stacks piled on the desk. I had to find something compelling to take my mind off the loud quiet of the phone not ringing.

Surveying my well-organized command central, each item from stapler to standing files arranged for maximum efficiency, I spied the red file marked, "National Lesbian Feminist Organization." Aha! Here was a promising distraction.

During the long summer months of the strike, I'd felt repeatedly that lesbians weren't organized enough to command a strong voice. Dykes stood on thin ice, in both the gay men's and women's movement, trying to negotiate power with no leverage. The Women's Movement thought Lesbian Nation was part of the gay movement. Gay male leaders sought to palm dykes off onto the Women's Movement. During the frustrating negotiations with Morris, it had dawned on me that we lesbians needed to harness our power by creating a national political identity rather than just build a separate Amazon culture. Politically, we needed to identify the whereabouts, cohesion, and agenda of Lesbian Nation. {1}

The week after I'd resigned from the Great Strike, I'd gone to work on my new idea. I'd called lesbian leaders on the east coast, in the Midwest and northern Pacific states and detailed my thinking to them: we needed to organize on a national level and create a political power base. The National Lesbian Feminist Organization would be patterned after the nine year old, but already wildly successful, National Organization for Women (NOW). And this time there'd be no huge arguments like at the '73 Conference because this time we'd only invite lesbians who agreed with a simple and defined agenda—creating a national political organization. {2}

The small silver clock on my desk struck eight. I stared at it. Rachel had probably just left Jacki's to return home, intending to call me from Effie Street. Wise of her.

I took out sheets of bond and carbon paper and rolled them into my typewriter. A pressure began to assert itself at my temples, threatening to scatter my thoughts. Too many cheap beers last night. I rarely drank. I stood up and opened a window. Watching the traffic below, I tried to re-read a letter Kate McQueen had sent from Maine. That state's leading lesbian organizer said it would be impossible to find enough minority lesbians to racially balance Maine's delegation to the national convention we were planning. {3} This was in response to an issue from a few big city coastal organizers who felt any national dyke organization would have to seat fifty percent minority women on its governing board. I thought fifty percent was too high. Not only were some places like Maine predominantly white, even where there were a number of third world lesbians, most of them were active in the Black Power and La Raza movements. There weren't enough out-of-the-closet organizers from those communities active in the gay or feminist movements to make a fifty percent goal attainable. Seating one-third, or even twenty-five percent of third world women on the NLFO Board seemed, to me, more realistic. But "realistic" was not a strong suit among lesbian feminists. {4} I sat back down and began a reply to Kate. Leadership was a delicate balance between advising people what to do, and listening to what they wanted to do.

A knock at the door! The clock read nine as I jumped out of the chair. Rachel had never been bold enough to come to the apartment I shared with BeJo. Peeking through the living room window curtains, I saw two neatly dressed men with Bibles in their hands. I reached for and placed BeJo's and my handmade slogan card in the window. "I AM A PAGAN. LEAVE ME ALONE!"

Returning to the *Tide* office, I picked up the phone. The dial tone rang loud and clear. Surely a promise meant something to Rachel? Had she just been trying to placate me and get me away from Jacki's house? Again, I sat down. Of course she'd call. And when she did I'd apologize profusely for last night. I'd tell her I hadn't meant to scare her, or even Jacki, that I'd been drunk and had felt like she played me when she came and kissed me at midnight and then ran away. And then, she'd say she was sorry too and that she realized she couldn't be with anyone else, that she missed me too much. Everything would be like it was last summer.

Smiling to myself, I began replying to another letter to an anarchist leader in Minnesota, this one saying that dykes should not get structured into a hierarchy, even to compete politically in a male world. I was always happy waxing political. Strategy felt solid, grounded in real time and space, and so much more stable than things personal.

Happily I finished and sealed both envelopes. Suddenly, I realized it was almost eleven o'clock. My fingers froze as I licked stamps and stuck them to the envelopes. A thought occurred to me: why would Rachel meet me for breakfast if she wouldn't come with me last night? The two realities were separated only by a few hours. I turned off the typewriter. The silence rang permanent. Rachel wasn't going to call anymore than my desktop was going to magically unbend and straighten itself from the weight of my typewriter. It was permanently deformed, just like my relationship with Rachel. Who was I kidding? There would be no phone call from her this morning.

I banged my fists on the desktop. The rattle shook my framed degrees above it.

Again and again, I pummeled it, wanting to pulverize Jacki… Rachel…anyone.

The pain in my knuckles fed my powerlessness. The desktop swayed on its sawhorses. I stood and screamed aloud. Bitterness felt metallic on my tongue. No! I am not gonna let her leave me. I'd throw on a jacket, go look for her at Effie.

I sped to the closet, never mind my pajamas. But wait. What if she wasn't at Effie, then what? She was probably still at Jacki's. And if she was and I showed up again, what new humiliation would await me this time?

I threw my jacket on the floor and kicked it back into the closet.

It took a few minutes to realize the ringing was not the reverb of my anger. I picked up the receiver.

"Córdova?" the voice demanded.

I was too sad to answer. It was Robin.

"I know it's you," she continued. "I can hear your smoke-filled lungs."

"What do you want, Robin?"

"My, aren't we pissy."

"I'm in a black mood. Go away."

"I know why you're down," my buddy whispered gently. "Listen to me. I want you to put down the phone, get dressed, and come up here immediately. I have something for you."

"I'm not interested," I began to hang up.

"It's from Rachel," Robin added.

"What are you talking about? Have you seen her?"

"I did. This morning. Now get up here." Robin clicked off.

"You look like shit," Robin said when she opened the door. I stumbled into her condo. "I should make you wash and comb your hair before I talk to you."

"Don't push me," I muttered. "Where's the letter from Rachel? And some aspirin. Please, get me some aspirin." I flung myself into the black and silver striped couch of the Chrome Palace.

Robin stared at me, a hand over her mouth. "I've never

seen you drunk. You're such a lightweight on two beers. What's happened?"

"Quit being such a maternal fag," I retorted. "I'm not drunk. I have a headache from not sleeping all night."

Robin sat beside me putting her hand on my thigh. "Rachel told me what you did last night."

"I don't want to talk about it."

"We don't have to. It speaks for itself."

"Just get me her letter and get off my case. I feel bad enough about it."

Robin got up and leaned over to find something behind the couch. She sat back down again with an ungainly plastic bag in her grip. "I never said it was a letter," she said. "Rachel gave me this." She opened the bag and lifted out my hat.

My eyes closed. I couldn't bear to look at it. A tightness began to assault my brain even before Robin crowned me with the leather flat-brim.

"And that's where it belongs," she grunted.

I opened my eyes. "Where did you see Rachel?"

Robin stood up, backing away from me and shifting from foot to foot. "She called me this morning. Asked me to meet her. She said she was in a hurry."

"A hurry?"

"She looked like you, like she'd been to hell and back. We only talked for a minute. She asked me to return your hat."

"She had no message? She said nothing else?" My pitch rose.

"All right." Robin's eyes grew sad. "You won't like this. She said to tell you…by the time you get your hat back…she'd be gone."

"Gone?" I stared up at Robin, my voice a plaintive whisper. "What does that mean?"

"That she had packed all morning and now she was saying good-bye. She's gone."

"Gone where?" I jumped to my feet and shook Robin by her shoulders.

Robin dropped her head, looking down at our feet. "She

said Idaho. Or was it Iowa. Or, maybe—"

"Why the fuck would Rachel go to Idaho?"

"She said her mother lives there."

"What kind of a reason is that to leave her life?"

Robin shrugged. "Maybe she needs her mother."

"Is she going with Jacki?" I lunged to shake Robin by her shoulders.

"No! She's broken inside over you, and the strike. Political life I think. She's running home to mother in a panic."

My heart winced for Rachel in her grief. Then, I leapt toward the front door.

Anticipating my exit, Robin jumped in front of me, knocking us both to the floor. Quickly she disentangled from me and scrambled to her feet and then to the front door, where she threw her back against it, blocking me. We stared at one another.

"Get out of my way or I'm gonna push you out of my way," I warned, glaring.

Robin folded her arms across her chest, but didn't budge, her feet firmly planted. "Rachel's gone," she said. "Córdova, you have to let her go."

"She's still at Effie," I begged. "I can stop her!" I prepared to shove my buddy aside.

"You couldn't stop her last night," Robin said without wavering. "No one can stop someone if they don't want to stay!"

For a fraction of a second my mind climbed out of my body. This was the second time in twenty-four hours that my dearest pal was standing in front of me, trying to stop me. Something was terribly wrong with this picture! Clearly, I was obsessed. I'd never seen Robin so butched out. *She was afraid—not of me, but for me!*

Her words repeated themselves in my brain, *No one can stop someone if they don't want to stay.* A line from a book continued in my head—something about slings and arrows and letting birds go if you really loved them.

Rachel didn't want to stay. I had to let her go.

I crumpled to the floor. Robin slid down next to me.

Together we held the front door closed. Covering my face with my hands, I broke down crying. "Nothing makes sense any more," I whispered, my tears flowing freely onto Robin's lap.

"I know, I know." She took me in her arms. "You'll stay here at my house for a little while. We'll talk till you're out of words. You'll get better."

The room was damp with mid-January's cold. The marine layer, with its shroud of depressing fog, had followed me from Culver City to Robin's condo in the Hollywood Hills. Robin had parked me in her guest bedroom. A black and grey comforter lay over me. Memories tortured me, a catalogue of loss—Morris my mentor and father, the strike battle, Rachel my lover. I was alone in a hole that had taken over my psyche. Where was Idaho anyway? I'd find it. There couldn't be that many states with yellow stones. I could still get on a plane if I could get past Robin. Escape. Find clothes. Pack a suitcase.

Too much effort. Hopelessness begged me to return to sleep. First, rest up for the plane journey. Ah…here it came… sweet darkness.

Rachel would come to me if I just waited long enough. She'd appear in the doorway, come to my bedside, and kiss me good night. As long as I never woke up, Rachel would stay with me forever.

The next time I woke, it was dark. I was still underneath the Chrome Palace quilt. Must not have boarded a plane. Movement caught my eye. Robin must have opened the blinds. Two figures were embracing and kissing on the balcony across from Robin's building. Did one of them have a lover, a husband or wife, somewhere else? Feminism was right, the personal was certainly political. But making the personal fit one's politics, trying to change the nature of jealousy in human beings, would never work. The thought of Rachel with another woman still made me need to vomit. I could never accept that. Yet Rachel had. Or had she? Maybe that's why she left. If I ever felt this way again about someone else, I promised myself, I wouldn't fuck around with non-monogamy. Had I given up BeJo sooner Rachel would be with me today. Now I knew that free love was free only if you weren't *in* love.

Weeks passed, and I had no desire to leave my prison bedroom. Robin came and went, offering solace and trinkets of distraction. BeJo called, Robin said it seemed like daily, but I couldn't go to the phone for anyone. Whenever I was alone I'd find myself reduced to tears. I cried when I woke and I cried in my sleep. I found no reason to leave this haven. Loving Rachel had been a little bit of heaven and a great deal of hell. Mind, body, and soul, I'd finally been in complete harmony when I made love with her. The double bed on the ocean was the most sublime happiness I'd ever know. Less was not worth living for. My grief felt endless, as though it could replenish a long dried-out well. It was better when Robin came in because I couldn't cry in front of her again. Real butches didn't show this kind of grief, even if they were feminists. And the façade of my butchness was all I had left.

I rolled onto my stomach, drew up the quilt and buried myself. Maybe it was time to end my life as I knew it. Move to another city. I'd used up Los Angeles and all the women in it. I could be happy in a tiny village, somewhere in a mountain cave where I would wake up in a year and not remember Rachel. Could I have been so wrong about who I thought I was? Was the mania of political life only my brake pedal against intimacy?

I thought of my .38 caliber that lay in the closet at BeJo's wrapped in the soft rag of an old flannel shirt. Maybe moving was not the solution. Maybe I should just end my fucked up life.

Only BeJo knew I owned a gun, which I'd bought on a whim when I lived in the ghetto with robberies going down weekly on my street.

"Where'd you get this?" she'd screamed the day she'd accidentally found it.

"At a pawn shop," I explained nonchalantly. "They're easy to buy! Everyone's doing it. I didn't even need to show my driver's license."

Knowing how well BeJo knew me, I was sure she'd hidden it by now, just in case I'd come home looking for it.

I awoke in the middle of the night soaked in a cold sweat. No! I couldn't kill myself! How would that look in the headlines of the gay press? "Lesbian Leader Shoots Self Over Ex-Lover." The gay movement couldn't afford a high-profile activist's suicide. We'd seen too many soppy, stereotypical gay movies like the recent *The Killing of Sister George* where the gays died at the end. No, we couldn't handle any more dead dykes.

Killing myself would make a travesty of everything I'd worked for. The movement was more important than my sorry-assed struggles. I would not betray it.

I'd made it through tough times before; feminism had taught me that breakdowns were opportunities for breakthroughs. So, what in my life needed basic change? Somehow I had to find closure with Rachel on my own since she obviously was not going to be around to help. And if I was honest with myself, I'd see what Rachel saw—a life more committed to social change than it could ever be to a single human being. Maybe I needed to learn to love that part of me and stop denying that was who I was. Maybe being a political lifer was positive and great and too valuable to throw away. Something positive *had* to come from quitting the strike and losing Rachel. I'd find a way to break through to the other side of nowhere.

My only job tonight and tomorrow was to live through the seeming emptiness, dump this self-pity, and be on the look out for a crack in a new door that would open someday soon. {5}

Chapter 32

The End of the War

[Los Angeles]

"I want to send my special love and rage to all of my sisters." —Emily Harris, SLA

February, 1976

"Penny's on the phone, Córdova, wake up!" Robin's voice seemed to come from far away, but my bed was rocking. Robin's voice was closer now. "Penny got fired."

"Penny? Fired?" My eyes flew open. Just as suddenly I lost the train of thought and rolled over to go back to sleep. "Tell her I'm on sabbatical."

"I told her that the last three times. And I'm tired of saying the same thing to BeJo and Penny, *Tide* people, and everyone. You've got to talk to your editor this time. You've been lying here for weeks. You're wearing out my linens. Your stay at the Robin Tyler Rest Home for Divorced Butches is over. You're either graduated or flunked. Now get up and go do your own life!" Robin held her cordless phone in front of my face.

I took the phone. "Penny?" I managed weakly, "Did they really give you the ax?"

I heard her suck in her breath and fight for control. "Don and Troy brought me in this morning. They said I was correct in my judgment that either the sexist ads had to go, or I had to. They chose the ads." She offered a small laugh. I could hear the shock in her voice. "I made the sexist pigs gave me one last issue."

Another end of an era, I reflected. Was radicalism dying? "Then it will be my last issue too, Pen."

"You'd better think about that when your head is clear, my friend. But I appreciate the support." Her voice cracked. She paused. I was afraid she was going to cry.

"What can I do to make it better for you?"

"My final issue," she said. "I want this last cover story to be our best."

"What cover story?"

"The prison, SBI called this morning. Emily Harris has chosen *The Freep* and Ms. Magazine to do her only two interviews."

I gulped. So the imprisoned woman-soldier of the SLA had responded to my letter and chosen me! Despite the disintegration of my relationship with Rachel, I'd poured my heart into my appeal to her, sharing my belief in the need for radical systemic change and had included several feminist columns and articles I'd written on Joan Little and Susan Saxe so that she could see the breadth of my political commitment and knowledge. I'd sought to woo Harris with my words, my most powerful weapon according to Rachel, so that Harris would feel safe and confident enough to entrust me with her story. The letter had worked! A wave of hope swept through me.

Sitting up in bed, cradling the phone, I caught my reflection in the mirror. I hadn't combed my hair or bathed in days. I dropped my gaze. "I'm in no kind of mental shape to do such a big interview, Penny. Maybe Tom should step in?"

"Harris said yes to your query letter, not his." Her tone was sharp.

I groaned, falling backwards onto the pillows, picturing

myself trying to pump up my former nothing-scares-Córdova energy. It felt like I'd left my butch arrogance at Jacki's house on that night I was still trying to forget. Could I show up to listen to Emily in a way that I hadn't been able to listen to Rachel?

"We've worked so hard to get this interview, Jeanne."

I sat up. Penny had worked her connections hard for this interview, and picked up my slack at *The Freep* this last month when I'd let it all go to hell. I owed Penny, and I owed Emily Harris, a fellow feminist who had much bigger problems than I did. Besides, a prison seemed like the only place I could go where I wouldn't be the most fucked up human being on the planet. It would be healthy for me to get out of my self-indulgent head and into someone else's. I wanted to interview Emily Harris because she had no voice. Since Rachel's disappearance, I too had lost my voice. And I knew Emily's enforced silence would last a good deal longer than my own. She was just twenty-five, a year younger than I. The capture of the last two members of the SLA had stunned and muted the underground Left.

"Will you help me find my notes?" I asked Penny. "I can't remember where I left them."

"I'll start looking. The interview is the day after tomorrow."

"I'll be ready," I said.

Stumbling into the bathroom, I knew I had to wash off yesterday's dead skin, call BeJo to help me pack and come home to our apartment, and do whatever it took to walk out of Robin's condo and step forward—into the rest of my life.

Sybil Brand Institute for women was a lowdown jail with an uptown name. As I drove up its bluff, the prison began to emerge from the mist like a doctored photo of a boarding school that jailers might send out to comfort parents. It sat on a hill called City Terrace, between the downtown business district and the Latino barrio of East L.A., a fortress separating wealth from the peasantry. From inside, inmates heard the rush of traffic on the San Bernardino Freeway below as the hum of a humanity to which they no longer belonged.

As I reached the blacktop driveway, the marine layer lifted enough to see the fortress's solid walls girdled with steel. The smell of punishment tasted like newly minted lead coin.

I pressed a brass button at the first gate and looked through the chain link at inmates wandering aimlessly in a yard. Black and silver barbed wire straddled the twelve-foot fence.

I wasn't afraid. My bravado had returned. In grad school I'd spent a year interning at Ventura School for Girls, a youth jail, and another year at Terminal Island, California's federal penitentiary for women. I knew the rules. Inmates were instructed to walk, but don't run; speak but never yell; sleep, but don't dream. Repression breeds discontent, I'd tried to tell my superiors. "You are over-identifying with the prisoners," they replied. I'd turned down a career in criminology when I realized that "social work" meant keeping a lid on the garbage can of capitalism's collateral damage. No, I wasn't going to aid and abet the Establishment.

The uniformed female guard greeted me with her eyes on the ground, as if I didn't have a face. I took this as a blessing since I'd forgotten to dress "straight" and had on a boy's shirt and jeans. Although I wouldn't have minded being somehow thrown into SBI's notorious Daddy Tank, a private wing where butch-looking inmates were kept. Think of the stories I'd get, I thought, and the hardcore working class "daddies" I'd meet. Like other jails in America, SBI openly discriminated against masculine women.

The female guard led me, stomping down an antiseptic corridor. She belonged in the Daddy Tank too, I chuckled to myself, wondering if she recognized herself when she locked up butch prisoners. "Wait here," she said, her keys clanging against metal studs on her uniform belt.

I sat on a cement bench in what appeared to be a small, private visiting room. It was really no more than an alcove at the end of a corridor, certainly not the main visiting room. I suspected that they kept political prisoners like Harris separated from the main

Lesbians protest at L.A. County Jail against infamous Daddy Tank—a segregated wing for butch lesbian prisoners. July 1972. *Photo by Bee Ottinger, Lesbian Tide.*

population. They couldn't risk these revolutionaries instigating an inmate civil rights riot. And goddess knows they had no civil rights, as Angela Davis and others had published in stories about the private beatings that went on daily. A vending machine stood in the corner. I noticed it served coffee and soda only in paper cups, no metal cans. No decoration adorned the walls. Floor to ceiling, it was all asylum white, like the white noise inside my mind the last month at Robin's.

Damn. There it was again. A flash from New Year's Eve:

me in a lunge stance outside Jacki's back door. Knife in hand, my violence two parts self-disgust and three parts despair. My stomach torqued with shame. I looked under the bench for a trashcan. Vomit threatened my larynx. I should just let the bile out, I thought, and add throwing up in prison to my repertoire of sad behavior.

A loud bolt slid in its shaft. At the far end of the corridor an iron gate opened and Emily Harris stepped into view clad in prison orange. A short, small-framed white woman with mousy brown curls, she couldn't have weighed more than a hundred pounds. This self-avowed political outlaw had robbed a bank with a shotgun? The petite woman strode the tunnel toward me, her shoulders held high as though she was proud of her self-inflicted outrage. Proud but caged, I thought, wondering once more why I'd chosen to expose capitalism's hypocrisy with the pen while she'd chosen to cripple it with gunpowder.

As Emily came closer, I saw that her eyes were clear, her affect resolute. Her pale face revealed no anger. I reached to take the pencil from behind my ear so she would see me as a sister instead of a journalist.

She offered me her hand. "I'm Emily Harris," she said politely.

For a moment I saw Rachel's face in hers. She had the same girl-next-door innocence.

"Jeanne Córdova. Thank you for choosing me." I smiled broadly, wanting to ask immediately why she had. But that was too personal, too early. Motioning to the cement bench, I said wryly, "Looks like this is all we get."

We sat. I folded my leg across my knee and leaned toward her. "Is Emily Harris your real name?"

She laughed with surprise. It was a soft, normal young woman's laugh, not unlike Rachel's. "No it's not!" she exclaimed. "I was born Emily Montague Schwartz, straight A student from Indiana U. I even pledged Chi Omega sorority."

"Then you didn't go to Wellesley?" I joked.

Our pleasantries continued and Emily relaxed. She had

Volume 12, Number 46 (591), November 14-20, 1975

Free Clinic Director Slain Under Suspicious Circumstances

LOS ANGELES

FREE PRESS

Published Every Friday. An Adjudicated Newspaper

25¢   35¢   50¢
METRO L.A.   ELSEWHERE IN CALIFORNIA   OUTSIDE CALIFORNIA

THE
OUTLAWS
Break ⊔ Loose

Behind The Scenes at Shelter Records

Passionate Scottish Soul: The Average White Band

Emily Harris

Talks About Feminism and the Guerrilla Front

Emily Harris, captured soldier of the Symbionese Liberation Army, issues letter to "my feminist sisters" from her jail cell. *LA Free Press, November 1975*

moved to Berkeley halfway through college and there met fellow student Bill Harris who was an ex-Marine just returned from Vietnam. In northern California, at the politically inflamed UC Berkeley campus, she and Bill had become involved with the radical activist group Venceremos, which visited political prisoners and agitated for prison reform. {1}

"That's where I met Donald," she concluded, referring to

black activist and SLA Field Marshall, Donald DeFreeze, their leader.

"Cinque must have been very charismatic to have pulled together your cadre, a group willing to die for their beliefs?" I probed.

When I used his SLA name, Harris visibly stiffened. Cinque had put a bullet through his own head as two hundred cops surrounded a small house in Watts and in a hail of bullets and tear gas burned alive five of his and Emily's comrades.

"Yes," she replied, her voice numb.

Anguish, I thought, not hostility.

"He was the most committed revolutionary I have ever met. He was also my lover."

I caught my clipboard on its way to the floor, fumbling from the bombshell she just dropped. Newspapers had speculated about personal relationships among the SLA. The lesbian underground knew that Mizmoon and Camilla Hall were lesbian lovers, but little was known about the love life of Cinque. My query letter to Emily had promised that I would not pry into her personal life; yet, I wanted badly to ask more about Cinque and her marriage to Bill, whether the rumored non-monogamy amongst the SLA in general was true. {2}And if it was, did non-monogamy work better for revolutionaries? Had sexual intimacy among them strengthened their willingness to die for their cause, or just added chaos, as it had in mine?

"And your marriage to Bill?" I ventured, holding my breath.

"The three of us were together," Harris confirmed, tight-lipped. "Monogamy is a capitalist tool to keep women as chattel."

I bit my tongue and waited for more.

"And yes," Harris added, as though reading my mind, "we did spend a lot of time and energy dealing with non-monogamy as a radical political stance." She paused, a slight growl in her tone. "I assumed you were a feminist."

"Is that why you chose me?" I countered.

"As a feminist, a Chicana and a lesbian, I thought you would understand me."

For a second I was thrown by her adding "lesbian." The New Left underground was just beginning to see radical gays and lesbians as comrades. I recovered and said, "Yes, I am all those things. And I think I do understand you. I want to."

"Then please don't ask me anymore petit bourgeois psychoanalytic questions."

Clearly I'd been chastened. I flipped a page in my notebook and began again.

"After you were arrested in September, both you and Patty began to refer to yourselves as revolutionary feminists. Was this a new politic that the SLA was coming to, or does it signal your personal evolution?" Shit, was that too personal?

"The liberation of women and the overthrow of capitalism are inextricably entwined," Harris replied. "As soldiers we recognize fighting for the revolution with a gun in hand is not just a man's right." She was now sitting stiffly, her backbone straight, drawing strength from territory she knew well. "Sexism is rooted in the very foundation of U.S. imperialism."

As my tape recorder rolled, it struck me that Harris had gone into another persona. Perhaps the person talking was Yolanda, Emily's chosen political name. Members of the SLA had offed their birth names in favor of more politically meaningful names. I laid down my tablet and offered whoever was speaking to me a cigarette. "This is where I disagree with you socialists," I injected. "You've got the horse before the cart. I believe capitalism is rooted in sexism." I loved being an advocacy journalist for moments like this—I had permission to dissect and challenge my subject's beliefs.

"As a Marxist, I don't think so," Harris shot back. "Let me explain..." She was animated and I could tell that this was nightly dinner table debate within the SLA—that is, if they had a dinner table to sit at while they were on the run.

As we shared coffee and worldviews, there were many places Emily and I held similar opinions, but one on which we did not: murder. Ready to tackle it, I leaned down to flip over my cassette and reset record before turning back toward Emily. "A year and a half ago the SLA issued a communiqué in which the words kill, hate, fascist, insect, pig, dog, and monster appeared twenty-eight times. And your SLA motto says, 'Death to the fascist insect that preys upon the people.' Why so much rage?"

"The military-industrial-complex is guilty of murder, but they call it war," Harris replied angrily. "They rape, and they call it economic development. They are cultural cannibals..."

As Harris ranted it became clear to me that the urban guerilla no longer even thought in personal terms. Name, rank and serial politics, nothing more. She was a walking, talking propagandist. Yet, I began to see a parallel between us. She believed that the capitalist state destroyed civilized society and kept people in bondage as alienated labor. I believed the bigotry of the heterosexual world crippled gays legally and psychologically.

"But why did you pick up a gun?" I finally put it on the table. "Did the situation look that extreme to you?"

"It *is* extreme!" Harris' voice climbed to a higher pitch. "This armed propaganda is an essential complement to mass organizing. The guerilla front is the vanguard. The goal of armed struggle is to form the nucleus of the people's army."

"But why did you pick up a gun?" I repeated.

"Why haven't *you*?" she shot back.

"Fair enough." I spoke slowly, giving myself time to wrestle down my shock. "I'm not a pacifist," I said thoughtfully. "I know people have to die in revolutions. The reason I haven't picked up a gun is because I don't think the revolution is at hand."

"The working class is ready to take to the street," Emily retorted.

"Middle America isn't anywhere near demanding a socialist revolution."

"The middle class is in a perpetual sellout!"

"Even Cesar Chavez is organizing California's Mexicans in the fields for better pay, not the ownership of production."

"Chavez is a liberal and a collaborator!"

Tell that to the growers, I thought, wondering how Harris

would play in Salinas Valley where a finely split hair was used for a child's mattress, not political fodder.

"The working class is desperate enough to hate," Harris continued. "They will lead the middle class when the time comes."

As the sentence left her mouth it frightened me. *Desperate enough to hate.* I'd been *desperate* to end the strike against GCSC, yet never tempted to end it by violence. I felt instinctively that violence would lead only deeper into hatred. My politics were usually governed by rationality: Would this strategy work? What were the likely outcomes? *Desperate* and *hate* were beyond control, the flip side of rational. But ah, my emotional life! It seemed to be governed, if it claimed any governance at all, by feelings of need and rage. What had made me desperate enough to almost assault my lover's other lover?

"The middle class has been blinded into docility by capitalism," Harris continued.

I listened with my journalist's ear but inside I was listening to my childhood's desperation—my father's autocracy, my rage to defend who I was against his constant humiliation. The every day psychological torture of being different, being gay and butch, could have crippled me for life. But somehow, I decided early on that it was society and not me who was wrong. Clutching this faith, I'd channeled my hardened humiliation, made it transform me into being a judicious combatant, fighting the straight world for my people's freedom. Now, Emily Harris was in jail and I was not.

My recorder clicked, signifying the end of my last tape, but I still had one final question. I asked, "Che Guevara said, 'The true revolutionary is guided by feelings of great love.' In your last communiqué, you ended with the salutation, 'I want to send my special love and rage to all sisters.' That's an unusual way to end a political message. What did you mean by that message?"

A deep horn vibrated down the corridor and through the empty alcove. We both shivered. A bolt clanged and the ferric bars slid open at the far end. A voice barked, "Time!"

Harris stood up. "That's dinner bell." She smiled faintly. "Amazingly, it sounds good after a few weeks." But her bottom lip trembled, contradicting her words.

"Is there anything I can do?" I said, standing beside her. I wanted to lift Emily Harris, my sister, bodily out of the clutches of aberrant justice and take her home to a hot bath and BeJo's chocolate chip cookies.

She reached out to hug me. As I felt her in my arms, I almost cried from a sense of helplessness.

"This has been valuable, Jeanne. Just write it all down...and tell my sisters...tell our sisters...it's about rage and it's about love."

A ray from the outside sun fell through a barred window, casting a shadow over her unguarded face. For a few seconds I saw her future in her saddened eyes. Perchance we were both wondering how long it would be before she felt again the freedom to go on with a chosen life.

The last steel door clicked twice behind me as I walked out of Sybil Brand. For her crimes of political passion, Emily Harris would have to trade the remaining years of her youth. My sentence was lighter but perhaps as long. I might never find a mate with whom to share my life, yet, walking toward my car I felt a weight begin to lift. My stride lengthened as I approached Lionheart. As long as I was free to make a political difference in the lives of my people, it was important to go on living.

Under the afternoon sun, I unlocked the driver's door and stretched to take off my denim war jacket. One of the multiple political buttons caught in the door handle. Bending to loosen it, I saw the crisp black and white image of Angela Davis' face. Underneath it read, Free All Political Prisoners. Emily Harris had not come in from the cold soon enough. But I would. {3}

Clearly, radicalism was over, I decided, sitting once more in the driver's seat. So too was Viet Nam, President Nixon, the guerilla front, armed struggle, and the SLA. The new frontrunner for President of the United States, a humble Democrat named Jimmy Carter, had just publicly said that he opposed discrimination on the basis of sexual orientation. This was big! Perhaps it signaled a pivotal change. Maybe our gay and lesbian movement was entering a reformist swing into mainstream politics. I needed to move forward with the National Lesbian Feminist Organization and harness dyke power to work inside the system. Maybe I'd even register as a Democrat and help infiltrate the Democratic Party with hundreds of queers. The 'sixties, with all our half-cocked, messy revolutionary fervor about rights for minorities and women's equality would someday be implemented. The 'seventies would be crowded with battles over restructuring American society. Yes! I felt ready to make the shift and continue the fight, even if it took a lifetime.

Rejoining humanity, westbound on the freeway back to Hollywood, I thought about my mistakes of the last year, both the political and the personal ones. I should have seen the core contradictions in my relationship with Rachel. When we began dating I'd asked her to join *The Tide*, my baby—my first and greatest love—yet she had said no to co-parenting. She didn't understand, or accept, that the movement would always come first in my life. No, passion was not enough to sustain a relationship. Another bitter, but inevitable reality. It was best that she'd left. I could never have chosen between the two.

And I should have seen the same primal contradictions in the battle with the gay Center. I should have walked out of that war the moment my comrades voted to strike. Waging a labor battle, inside a gender war, surrounded by a movement for civil rights, portended an untenable conflict with no exit strategy tied to anything I could have called victory. I would absorb this lesson as a lesbian separatist battle that had to take place somewhere, somehow in Los Angeles—just as it had in multiple cities throughout the gay and lesbian national movement.

I was now old enough to accept that sometimes in the losing is the winning; and in the struggle, is the living.

Epilogue

Dateline: Los Angeles, May 2011

The end of the epic strike against L.A.'s first nationally significant gay center took place in 1978 as lesbians edged closer to achieving equal status in the national lesbian and gay movement. Lesbians began as underdogs in our own liberation struggle and battled more than a decade to convince boomer gay men that women made quality lawyers, activists, journalists, and legislators. Many would argue that gay men still don't recognize women as equals, but having lived alongside a generation of guys raised in the sexist and racist American culture of the '50s and '60s, I know for fact that succeeding generations of men have "come a long way, baby." Today I am amazed by and admiring of the young generation of men, both gay and straight, who walk arm-in—arm in friendship and activism with their lesbian sisters.

It wasn't always so.

Two cataclysmic events had to occur in order for early lesbians to come back to working with gay men. The first originated in Dade County, Florida in 1977 when a newly burgeoning American religious right movement put country and western singer Anita Bryant on its national stage as its anti-gay spokesperson. The conservative backlash grew quickly into a national movement in reaction to the so-called moral decline generated by '60s liberal activists. Bryant sparked America's first anti-gay crusade by convincing Dade County to rescind its recently enacted civil rights laws protecting gays against employment and housing discrimination. As News Editor of

Lesbian Tide, I watched with horror as press releases arrived almost monthly from activists in Dade, St. Paul, Minnesota, Eugene, Oregon, and Wichita, Kansas. Bryant was winning. Gay rights were going down everywhere!

By '78, the queen of Florida's orange juice industry had moved west to California, prompting Orange County senator, John Briggs, to put an initiative on the state ballot which called for the firing from the California public school system of any teacher believed to be homosexual. From Sacramento to San Diego, gay and lesbian leaders panicked. We realized we'd have to raise millions to fight a statewide ballot. Television ads were the only way to reach the heterosexual middle class who would vote for or against us.

But since the strike of '75 lesbians in Southern California were boycotting the gay male Center. What to do? Quickly we realized that to stand a chance of defeating the Briggs Initiative women would have to return to working with the men in order to unite the movement. I called Bob Sirica, the little newbie from '75 who was now Executive Director of GCSC. Bob jumped at the overture saying, "Yes of course. We must meet and bury this strike division." Hastily, Patton and the strikers met with GCSC's Board. Within a week, both sides had settled. The dykes agreed to end the boycott and stop all negative media. The Center agreed to issue a public apology admitting illegally firing the workers, and to pay everyone for back wages and compensation. Each striker was given a $90 token check. The strikers no longer cared about the amount. We were facing a multi-million dollar battle. We had no time to quibble. Ah, timing—the linchpin of politics!

The second historic event which brought gay men and women back into realignment came more horrifically than anyone could have imagined. The catastrophe was the AIDS-HIV epidemic, which arrived, cloaked in mystery, in Los Angeles in 1983. Thousands of lesbians rushed into the streets, and to the bedsides of our gay brothers. Women, both gay and straight, became significant partners in creating ACT UP and dozens of other AIDS organizations.

By 1988 the leadership ranks of gay male activists were decimated by "the gay plague." GCSC couldn't find enough gay men alive from the boomer generation to fill its higher staff positions. But sexist attitudes among gay men had changed, had become more open, and grateful, towards women. Finally, this culminated in 1988 when the Board of Directors of GCSC named lesbian feminist activist Torie Osborn to their top spot, Executive Director.

The "L" Word

After Briggs was defeated, dozens of women continued to lay a more polite siege to the Gay Community Services Center— lobbying from within, petitioning from without, begging, and demonstrating—to add the word Lesbian to its name. By the mid 1980s progressive gay organizations, such as the National Gay Task Force, incorporated the word Lesbian in their titles.

The newly renamed NGLTF decision "marked both the specificity of lesbian life and politics and the coalition between lesbians and gay men," according to NGLTF's archival records. But L.A. could never lay claim to early self-imposed political correctness.

On a hot and humid summer midnight in 1982, three Los Angeles dykes, led by Christi Kissell—a remarkable nineteen year old then on-staff as GCSC's Director of Women's Programming—realized the time had come to take matters into their own hands.

Kissell, who had also been my lover the summer before her heroic reclamation, told me:

"By 1980, the LA Gay Community Services Center was run on a social services model by muscular mustached men with MBAs. This was before the AIDS movement proper. Although each month, the lines at the Health Clinic grew noticeably longer. The Center was swimming with guppies (gay urban professionals) and formerly radical dykes were selling ads in yellow pages. Signs of the times. The gay community and the lesbian community shared the Center's space and occasionally overlapped. There were women's programs and men's programs and a well-maintained room reservation schedule that assured peaceful coexistence. The Center had long added to the illustrious board of directors Lesbian psychotherapists and Lesbian lawyers and Lesbian assistant producers.

"I wasn't alone the night we scrawled '& Lesbian' in pink and purple paint with a caret (^) underneath to signify the squeezing in between 'Gay' and 'Community.' We painted it on a piece of scrap wood and affixed a flat piece, like from a picket fence, with the notion that we would climb to the roof of the building and wedge the sign with professional block letters above the main sign outside the two story building at 1213 North Highland Avenue in Hollywood. I liked the wedge-it-in idea because: (1) no one had to spray paint upside down, (2) once we got up there it would be fast to install and was a good get away plan, and (3) that's what Lesbians were at the center 'wedged in,' awkwardly and late."

To this day no one else knows who drove the dyke getaway car. When the greater L.A. gay community woke up the next morning and saw "& Lesbian" added to the GCSC sign, the news spread a California wildfire through the L.A. basin. By the time the Board of Directors saw the new sign on their building they knew they had a tough choice: publicly erase "Lesbian," or change the name of the place to the Gay & Lesbian Community Services Center. They chose the latter.

After a four decade career in activism, I've learned that identity is a prickly and ever-evolving matter. In 2011, having long ago moved from quaint Highland Avenue into a four-story glass and brick structure the Feds built in the 60s to house the IRS—GCSC is now called the L.A. Gay & Lesbian Center. In this age of irony, some now call the movement itself, Gay Inc.

Before her death in 2006, former Board member Betty Berzon had emerged as an award-winning author of several best-selling therapy books about gays and lesbians in long term relationships. Twenty years after the Great Strike, she parted from Morris as her political mentor, and came to the conclusion that during the strike, "Morris was using me for his own agenda." Berzon then publicly repudiated her role, saying that the mass termination of the Gay/Feminist 16 was "an overreaction and morally wrong." Her apology is a testament to a good activist's valor. We should all admit our mistakes as publicly as we claim our achievements.

My Political Godfather

Morris Kight died peacefully in his sleep in 2003 at the satisfactory age of eighty four. This was the only accomplishment Morris ever managed to pull off peacefully. In the ancient days of the Roman Republic the citizenry occasionally bestowed the title "a great man" upon an individual, usually a conquering political figure, who wrought fundamental change within the Empire. Morris Kight, still credited as one of the pioneer founders of the LBGT movement, was such a great man. He founded, or caused to be built, most of the major gay organizations in Southern California. His strategic concepts and ideas dominated the formation of the radical gay liberation movement. He was a grassroots organizer who was left behind in the early 1990s when the power center of the gay movement went establishment and moved from its city-state structure to Washington D.C.

Morris and I were forced to reconcile, at least politically, to face the Briggs Initiative in '78. We continued working together for another two decades, ending in 1996 when Kight retired and I, as President of the ONE Archive, urged him to give his mammoth collection of papers to a gay archive rather than a University. He managed to thwart me once more, splitting his papers between ONE and UCLA. Although we frequented each other's kitchen table for advice throughout our remaining campaigns, we never spoke about the only battle in which we were on opposite sides.

Our last conversation took place on Christmas Day of 2002 when I woke up that morning realizing that my godfather was old and sick and eighty-two. And we had never said good-bye. Haunted by our lack of personal reconciliation, I dropped in on him unannounced at his Beachwood Canyon apartment.

Morris smiled as he opened his door. "Ah, it's Córdoba!" he bowed and waved me in with a now limp flourish.

I followed him, shocked as he led me through a tiny living room and kitchen crammed with what seemed like one or two million pieces of paper, books and documents. The place was unkempt and sad. It horrified me to see our once great leader living in such disregard. Among the questions I had for him that morning was—how did he feel watching fashionable gay fundraiser attire change from khaki to Prada? But sitting on his tie-dyed sofa, I dropped this idea.

I'd brought him a peace offering, hoping it would ease the way toward my need to talk to him about what stood between us. I presented the package, disguised in seasonally appropriate green and silver wrapping, and he rose immediately out of his tattered armchair. "My, what have we here?" He used the royal plural as always.

Out of the Neiman Marcus box fell a luxurious black and red Bill Blass bathrobe. "Thank you, thank you Jeanne Córdoba!" His blue eyes twinkled as he donned the robe over a ragged white tunic that looked like it was purchased before the Punic Wars.

Fittingly royal, I thought as I leaned back on his dingy sofa, and flung my stinger question at him, "So Morris. I need to know how you feel in retrospect about the Great Strike? Did you ever come to an understanding of why it happened? Do you have any regrets?"

"Oh that." Morris's brows rose and he smiled at me archly, as he twirled and preened in his robe.

My zinger hadn't even made him sit down.

He looked down at me, laughed, and said almost blithely, "If I had understood at the time the essential contradictions between feminism and gay liberation, I would never have hired you people in the first place."

"You old dog!" The disrespectful words fell out of my mouth. After all these years, Morris and I had come to the same conclusion. Thirty years ago, my definition of feminism and his definition of gay liberation were indeed contradictory.

Morris sat beside me, reached out and slapped my knee. As he rocked back and forth amid his hippie furniture, I caught a grin at the corner of his mouth as he said, "My, oh my, we didn't have as much in common as we thought we did. But dear child, didn't we have a wonderful time!"

The Lesbian Tide

As to BeJo, we appear to be ending life as we began it, as ex-lovers and close family, in the lesbian tradition, now thirty-six years later. BeJo left waitressing when *The Tide* folded in 1980 and had a long successful career in print production with FOX. "FOX Movies," she points out, "*not* FOX news." We began as radical activists, but my boomer comrades and lesbian feminists largely went on to become the first generation of women professionals in fields as diverse as astrophysics and college professors of women's and gender studies.

Rachel had a daughter in Idaho, professionalized her commitment to feed the poor by joining the new age grocery industry, and returned to Los Angeles. She entered an alcohol rehabilitation clinic in 2005 and remains sober today. We continue a lifelong intimate friendship.

The best-butch pal of my youth, Robin Tyler, went on to create the famous West Coast Women's Music and Comedy Festivals (see endnote), and became a leading activist in the fight for marriage equality. 1976 was also the dawn of a life-long friendship and decades of political camaraderie with Ivy Bottini who co-founded AIDS Network LA, the first AIDS organization in L.A., became Deputy Director of Southern California's campaign to defeat the Briggs Initiative, and is now known as the lesbian godmother of the City of West Hollywood.

As to my first-born, *The Lesbian Tide* {1}, forty years after her birth she is enjoying a renaissance of popularity in women's and gender studies college courses and among young activists creating historical exhibitions, books, and events. In the *Encyclopedia of LGBT History in America* lesbian archivist Dr. Yolanda Retter Vargas called *The Tide* "arguably the newspaper of record for the lesbian feminist decade, 1970 to 1980."

It was excruciating for me at thirty-two years old to accept the death in 1980 of my first-born as a result of the "times they were a-changing." The lesbian feminist decade was closing down in L.A. Lipstick lesbians were coming into ascendancy and I had no interest in this apolitical phenomenon. In the decades to follow I went on to create several more publications, among them, the first LBGT telephone book in America—*Community Yellow Pages*, and LA's first queer magazine, *Square Peg*—as well as many more campaigns on behalf of lesbian rights and issues. As a mature adult I have come to understand that social revolution is the mother of both birth and death. Even "Córdova" had to grow out of her lame sexist training—by her Latin father and her times—in order to meet and marry her spouse twenty-one years ago. In such peace, I wrote this book and plan to write many more about lesbian history. I remain in service to my people.

Endnotes

Chapter 1: Last Guerilla
{1} National Lesbian Conference
April 13-15, 1973 on campus of UCLA (also known as West Coast Lesbian Conference.) This conference began as a west coast event but in planning stages evolved to include thousands of lesbians from Maine to Seattle, and remains today the largest political gathering of lesbians in history. One of the first major gay events held on a state university campus thanks to the Southwest Regional Lesbian Working Committee, and the behind the scenes approval of the paperwork by UCLA's Associate Dean of Students, Sheila Kuehl. The charismatic Kuehl, child star as "Zelda" on the popular 1960s TV show *The Many Loves of Dobie Gillis*, later became California's first open LGBT State legislator and authored the Dignity for Students Act, which protects students against discrimination based on sexual orientation or gender identity, as well as other crucial LBGT legislation.

Chapter 2: The Hat
{1} Angela Davis
The message of sisterhood and personal politics came late to this superstar of the Left. Davis finally came out as a lesbian in the 1990s. The National Black Gay and Lesbian Leadership Forum invited her to speak at their convention in 1993. In her speech Davis used the phrase "my community" several times when speaking about gays and lesbians. In the winter of 1998, in New York's gay magazine *OUT*, Davis finally answered long-standing rumors about her lesbianism, saying, "It is something I'm fine with as a political statement. But I still want a private

space for carrying out my relationships." Davis said that when she began researching for her book about African-American women who sang the blues, *Blues Legacies & Black Feminism* (1999), she came to understand the role sexual desire played in women's liberation.

Chapter 4: The Tide Rolls Out
{1} Daughters of Bilitis

The Daughters, named after Bilitis, a lover of the legendary Greek poet Sappho of Lesbos, was founded in San Francisco in 1955 by Del Martin and Phyllis Lyon. It was the first organized group of gay women in America. I'd heard its whispered name from dykes on my bar-league softball team, but it took me three years after coming out in 1967 to stumble upon its unpublicized L.A. meeting place. When I joined D.O.B. in 1970 it was a thriving national lesbian non-profit with thirteen chapters spreading from San Francisco to Boston, and a national Board of Directors. For more than two decades, it had been home to five to seven hundred gay women who were committed to one day living openly in a society that recognized homosexuals as positive, productive, and free. For a detailed history of D.O.B. see Marci Gallo's award-winning book, *Different Daughters* (Seal Press: 2007). The demise of The Daughters came about in the early seventies as feminism and its own daughter—lesbian feminism—supplanted D.O.B.'s ideological and organizational centrality.

{2} "A lesbian is the rage of all women condensed to the point of explosion" was the definition of a lesbian offered by the birthmother cell of Lesbian Feminism in 1970. The group—which included later famous activist authors Rita Mae Brown, Charlotte Bunch, Karla Jay and Barbara Love—was based in New York City and called Radicalesbians. This profound, yet singularly politicized, definition of lesbians ignited the Lesbian Feminist Movement.

{3} *Lesbian Tide's* Kissing Cover

The issue with Gudrun Fonfa and Jan Aura kissing was the

August 1974 cover of *The Lesbian Tide*. *The Tide* editors created this cover shot to protest a *Ms. Magazine* cover photo showing a heterosexual couple kissing. I moved the *Tide's* cover fight with it's printer into the 1975 timeframe of my memoir in order to illustrate the hardships *The Tide* went through with printers. During our nine year history (1971-1980) many issues of *The Tide* were contested by sexist printers over "pornography."

Chapter 6: Petition at Midnight
{1} In early 1971 GCSC's co-founders, Kight and Kilhefner, borrowed heavily from the incorporation papers of Del Whan's Gay Women's Community Service Center. Unfortunately that lesbian center would fold in 1973 due to lack of funds.

Chapter 7: The Vote
{1} **Sheldon Andelson**, recruited by Kight as new member of the Board of Directors in 1975, became the first multi-millionaire major donor in Los Angeles to gay causes, bringing others like him into the mainstream of national gay politics. My old pal, Shelly, was named in 1980 by then, and current, California Governor Jerry Brown, to be the first openly gay person to serve as a University of California Regent.

Chapter 9: Cordova's Nazi
{1} Captain Joe Tomassi
Joe Tomassi was admired by Thomas Metzger, the founder of the White Aryan Resistance (WAR), who wrote the following in Tomassi's eulogy:

"Captain Joe was a natural leader of men who did not believe in going completely by the book. Joe recruited a lot of people in the L.A. area and performed many marches. An ordered style loose cell type, his group wore street clothes and surplus military jackets much like the left wing. They grew long hair and many had beards. They could move through the streets of L.A. without notice. No armbands, badges or any other identifying trinkets. They trained in the mountains and the deserts...It is my opinion that if the ideas of organization of Joe's National Socialist Liberation Front would have spread across the nation we would be in a much better situation than we are now in."

{2} LAPD Spy Networks

Since the union building 1920s, and again throughout the black and brown liberation movements of the 1960s and 1970s, the Los Angeles Police Department sought to undermine civil rights activism through its branch called the Red Squad.

There was no outside oversight of any intelligence gathering, since LAPD Chief William H. Parker had declared in 1950 that all intelligence files were "the property of the chief of police," and therefore shielded from subpoena and outside perusal.

In 1965, Los Angeles Police Chief Edward M. Davis formed the Criminal Conspiracy Section (CCS) which became California's secretive political intelligence-gathering operation. In 1970 the CCS evolved into the Public Disorder Intelligence Division (PDID), which was later found to have put together a scandalous record of illegal spying on targeted politicians and political activists. CCS shared information with right-wing extremist groups. By 1975, the PDID was the custodian of almost 2 million dossiers on 55,000 individuals and organizations.

In the course of an ACLU lawsuit filed in 1983, it was discovered that the PDID had *illegally* spied on both individuals and organizations, including myself. Then District Attorney Ira Reiner called these renegade police units "a band of zealot officers (who) believe it is completely appropriate...to abuse every single moral or ethical precept that is involved in society."

Among those targeted by the PDID were two California governors, a state attorney general, a mayor of Los Angeles, a future LAPD chief, City Council members, the National Organization for Women, the PTA and the World Council of Churches. Others discovered to have been spied upon, included: Coalition Against Police Abuse; Alliance for Survival; U.S. Communist Party; Black Panther Party; Teamsters for Democratic Union; Peace and Freedom Party; Progressive Labor Party; Greater Watts Justice Center; Church of

Scientology (L. Ron Hubbard); La Raza Unida; People's College of Law; Democratic Socialists Organizing Committee; Venceremos Brigade; anti-nuclear groups (all of them); American Friends Service Committee; Southern Christian Leadership Conference; United Farm Workers Local 80; American Civil Liberties Union; Community Relations Conference; Juvenile Justice Center; Socialist Workers Party; New Mount Pleasant Baptist Church; and Women For.

Chapter 13: The Women's Saloon
{1} Lexington Six & FBI

The intrusion of the FBI in Lexington, Kentucky took place between January and May of 1975, a few months earlier than this memoir implies. In pursuit of leftist radicals Susan Saxe and Kathy Power, the FBI harassed lesbian compounds in San Francisco, Connecticut and Colorado. Some of the Lexington Six women were convicted of "obstruction of justice" on March 8, 1975. The names of these brave women are: Gail Cohee, Debbie Hands, Carey Junkin, Linda Link, Jill Raymond and Maria Seymour. Some were jailed for 18 months. The May/ June 1975 issue of *The Lesbian Tide* printed "Power or Paralysis" which detailed the harassment of these lesbians. According to an essay in the anthology, *No Middle Ground: Women & Radical Protest*, NYU Press (1997), "Many of the Lexington Six and their supporters defined their radicalism in terms of their homosexuality, co-mingling personal, political, and sexual politics." Susan Saxe was captured shortly after the Lexington women were imprisoned. Katherine Ann Power eluded the FBI for twenty-three years, but suffered a lifelong depression that finally made her turn herself into authorities in 1993.

{2} Camilla Hall

SLA member Camilla Hall's poems were printed in the June 1974 issue of *The Lesbian Tide*. Between the winter of 1974 and the end of 1975, debate over whether to interpret fugitive feminists and lesbians as political sisters, or as common criminals, raged throughout the national lesbian feminist press.

{3} Judy Grahn
"The Common Woman Poems," published by Grahn's Woman's Press Collective in 1973, were popularly quoted and printed on walls in lesbian and feminist spaces. The Saloon quote was from the closing lines of the final poem in the series, "Vera from My Childhood."

Chapter 14: A Somewhat Larger War
{1} Weather Underground Organization
Only one member of the WUO, David Gilbert, remains in jail as of March 2011. Most, like leaders, Bill Ayers and Bernadine Dohrn, had charges against them dropped or received probation and minor jail time. Much of the FBI's evidence against them was thrown out of court because the Feds broke so many laws in collecting this evidence. The Weather Underground was back in the news during the 2008 presidential campaign when Republicans tried to smear Barack Obama or his ties to Bill Ayers via their mutual interest in a Chicago educational foundation. Republican VP candidate Sarah Palin was referring to Ayers when she said Obama was 'palling around with terrorists.'

Coincidently, it was the FBI who palled around with terrorists in the 'sixties and 'seventies. In 1978 two covert FBI agent provocateurs were forced to surface. Agent Richard (Ralph) J. Gianotti and Agent William (Dick) Reagan were outed when they were subpoenaed to testify for the government's case against an L.A. split-off faction of the WUO, The Revolutionary Committee. The agents had infiltrated the RC for six years! The RC was a feminist faction led by Judith "Josie" Bissell and Leslie "Ester" Mullin. The women, based in the Silverlake/Echo Park area, had left the WUO because of its male supremacist behavior toward its women comrades. In 1977 the RC planned to bomb the offices of Orange County California Senator John Briggs, the radically conservative Senator who sponsored the drive to expel gay teachers from California schools. The bombing never came off. Bissell and Mullin were convicted and did time in Federal prison.

{2} My FBI Jacket

My paranoia back in those days turned out to be justified. In 1985 the ACLU gave me a court-discovered document from their 1983 lawsuit, a four-page except from my own FBI file (known as a 'jacket'), which detailed the evening I spent with "John" from the WUO and others. The document confirmed that there was an FBI informant in the room with us that night. All the names in the document, except my own, were blacked out, but in the pages I recognized the location and the Hollywood building I was in that evening.

FBI documents (housed at ONE International Gay & Lesbian Archives in Los Angeles) also reveal that the FEDS had sent undercover informants to both my 1971 Gay Women's West Coast Conference and the 1973 National Lesbian Conference at UCLA. They also attended a number of DOB gay women's meetings in the 1960s thru 1972, including my opening of the first lesbian center at 1910 S. Vermont in 1971. Hoover's FBI believed that radical lesbians were part of a national Leftist conspiracy to overthrow the Establishment. I hope to obtain more details for my next book on lesbian feminist history.

Chapter 15: The Strike

{1} Joan Little (pronounced Jo Ann)

I first wrote about Little —the twenty-year old black woman who had been charged with murder for stabbing her jailer when he tried to rape her a second time—in the *Free Press* in mid April, and in *The Lesbian Tide's* May/June 1975 issue.

Chapter 16: Double Bed on the Ocean

{1} Janis Ian's "Jesse" appears on her 1974 album *Stars*. Jesse was also sung in 1973 by Roberta Flack on her *Killing Me Softly* album, and then in '75 by Joan Baez on *Diamonds & Rust*. Ian came out as a lesbian in 1993 to much rejoicing by the LGBT movement.

Chapter 17: The Gospel According to Joe
{1} Armed Struggle
In his memoir, *Underground: My Life with SDS and the Weathermen* (William Morrow: 2009), WUO co-founder and one time fugitive Mark Rudd said, "I would not trumpet the disastrous strategy of armed revolutionary struggle, which had led me to founding the Weather Underground. How could I? By 1977 I saw the underground as a total failure as well as a tragic mistake...Nor did I still believe in an imminent socialist revolution in the United States, as I once had."

Chapter 18: The Picket Line
{1} McCadden Place Garden
In later decades, Morris Kight would plant dozens of new trees in his historic garden, labeled with names like Schrader, for California State Judge Rand Schrader, and other gay men who died from AIDS. Morris planted a flowering eucalyptus in memory of Truman Capote. A magnolia marked the passing of Tennessee Williams. Years later, a flowering Chinese Magnolia tree was planted in West Hollywood's Triangle Square to honor Morris himself, who died just weeks after his tree's planting in 2002.

Chapter 20: The Plaintiff
{1} The Tide Collective
A "collective" was a feminist group of women who made all decisions by consensus—which meant nothing passed without agreement by all. Small radical feminist groups ran as collective cells, but broader based large organizations, like the National Organization for Women, were organized hierarchically with officers, a president, and majority rule. Consensus was a laborious and time-intensive way to run a newspaper with sharp deadlines. During its long history, the *Lesbian Tide* was run by an Editorial Collective, who at various times included core women like Barbara "BeJo" Gehrke, Sharon MacDonald, Shirl Buss, Barbara McLean, Ann Doczi, Nancy Toder and

others. We determined the paper's voice and content. Scores of other skilled volunteer writers, paste-up artists, and distribution women were also valuable members of the staff.

Chapter 24: The Cuckoo's Nest
{1} The Snuff Movies
These were violent misogynistic films that came to Los Angeles and other American cities from South America, that depicted the death and dismemberment of women rumored to be alive at the time. A guerilla crew I put together in 1975 drove around Hollywood in a car in the early morning dark throwing bricks through the plate glass windows of L.A. theaters showing the snuff movies. It worked. We shut them down.

{2} Socialist Workers Party (SWP)
My experience with Trotskyite ideology dates back to 1972 when I'd begun an affair with Sally Frumpkin-Anderson, who I later learned was the daughter of the Chairman of L.A.'s Socialist Worker's Party. Trying to please her and understand her politics, I took classes with her in Marxist Leninism at the SWP headquarters in Hollywood. The novelty and brilliance of Karl Marx's mind expanded my intellect. Yes, I was a feminist, but my twenty-three year old mind was always searching for more political knowledge.

From my studies I learned that the SWP, the American Communist Party, and most other Marxist Leninist splinter groups of the 1960s-'70s New Left, believed that the path to revolution had to be led by "the workers," who, they said, would at some point take to the streets in mass numbers and topple the American capitalist government. Even back then I personally doubted that American workers, from what I knew of us, were going to revolt in my lifetime. But I drank in world politics. During that summer of '72 Sally also joined the Steering Committee of the National Lesbian Conference which we were planning for April, 1973, on UCLA's campus.

By the winter of '73 my love affair was on the rocks, but the SWP dealt me a surprising card. They sent their top ranking woman, Linda Jenness, to fly out from New York to meet me. Jenness had run for U.S. President in 1972 on the SWP's national ticket. Wondering why the SWP was placing such high value on recruiting me, it dawned on me that Jenness' outreach was because I was the publisher of *The Lesbian Tide*, by then growing into the most influential lesbian paper on the West Coast. By the time I met Jenness however, I'd come to my own studied conclusion that my lover's ideology really despised homosexuality. I was ready to quit. Jenness's attempted coup backfired. Two months before the Conference I quit my associations with the SWP and Anderson. But Anderson, and one other socialist organizer, remained on the Steering Committee.

At the April Conference, a large group of attendees alleged that there were Trotskyite goals implied in the Registration materials, and therefore the organizers were the much hated "Trots." Anderson betrayed me and the other organizers when she and her squad of four SWP lesbians refused to identify themselves as the Trotskyites, and instead allowed us organizers to be publicly attacked as Trots. I have no knowledge as to whether any of the other 2,000 lesbians at the conference were members of the SWP, but the public political betrayal of my recent ex-lover was baffling and extremely painful at the time.

Soon after the Conference, I began to read in lesbian publications out of Boston that the SWP, and groups like it, were seeking to infiltrate the women's and gay liberation movements in order to get feminists and gay and lesbian workers fired up and out on the streets. These "Trots", as the feminist movement called them, didn't really care about the rights of Lesbian mothers, the Equal Rights Amendment, or the struggle for women's reproductive rights. They'd joined our ranks to use our huge numbers and our popular relevance to galvanize their workers' revolution. By this time I agreed with the national mood—the opportunistic Trots were not welcomed in my movements. But, personally and politically I paid a heavy price for too-little-too-late comprehension of wider politics and my inadvertently gullible role in them. As an older activist, I try to teach young queers in the LGBTQ movement to learn more about the politics of friends or lovers before joining them on the streets or under the sheets. Politics can be deceptive.

Chapter 26: A Lavender Woodstock
{1} Women's Music Festivals
This festival took place over the weekend of September 25–27, 1975 and not in mid-August as my narrative implies. I moved the date earlier due to the plotting needs of my story. This San Diego festival was perhaps the earliest precursor of the large national lesbian music festivals, such as the Michigan Womyn's Music Festival, which became the cultural showrooms of our movement over the next two decades. Founded by Lisa Vogel and Barbara Price and their "We Want the Music Collective" in 1976, "Michigan" went on to become the mother of all women's music festivals. Robin Tyler's West Coast Women's Music & Comedy Festival, the second largest festival, ran between 1981 and 1995 in Yosemite National Park. Tyler's Southern Women's Music & Comedy Festival (1986-1993) was the third largest of these lesbian gatherings. Along with smaller regional festivals in the South, New England, and Connecticut, they all eventually circled up and came be known as the women's music festival circuit. A few of them, such as Michigan–despite recent political battles over trans inclusion—still sound the annual call for lesbians and feminists to come and live one week of the year in a world made by women.

Chapter 31: Return of the Hat
{1} Lesbian Nation
A popularly used metaphoric reference to a utopian world peopled only by lesbians and governed by radical feminist principles. Appearing in several books and essays, the term was mainstreamed by Jill Johnston, a columnist at New York's *Village Voice*, when it was used as the title of her 1973 classic lesbian feminist treatise, *Lesbian Nation: The Feminist Solution*. The term

continues through present day as a symbol of political solidarity among lesbians, especially lesbian separatists.

{2} The National Lesbian Feminist Organization
The founding convention of the NLFO took place in 1978. I and others began planning the NLFO in 1976. I've brought the future forward in this memoir in order to show where my future thoughts lay.

{3} "Minority" Lesbians
In the 1970s, people of color were referred to as "minorities." Later, the term "third world" people came into fashion. These earlier terms hint at the extent of systemic racism present in America in those decades, even among liberals. Loretta Ross, *SisterSong* cofounder, recounts how at the National Women's Conference in Houston in 1977 a group of black women activists brought a Black Women's Agenda to substitute for the minority plank in the main agenda. When other minority women, including Latinas, sought to join them, the phrase "Women Of Color" was created in those negotiations to find a new name for the agenda, with a commitment to work in coalition with each other on shared issues.

{4} *La Raza*
This Spanish phrase means "the race," "the cause," or "our people." It was used in the 1960's and '70s by political Latinos/as to refer generically to the goals behind our liberation movement, including the Brown Berets and Cesar Chavez's organization of the farm workers. Today *La Raza* is sometimes politically interpreted by conservatives as a Chicano supremacist slogan, but most Chicanos/Latinos use it to refer to our cause –any cause that helps the progress of Hispanos or Latinos in the United States.

{5} Rachel
I've used a pseudonym for this courageous woman who allowed me to tell our story in great detail.

Chapter 32: The End of the War

{1} *Venceremos*

Venceremos is Spanish for "We shall overcome." The Venceremos Brigade was a New Left activist group well known in the Bay Area during Emily Harris's college days when she became a member. The Brigade, along with other groups that included Angela Davis and many Black and Latino activists, championed the human rights of prison inmates jailed for politically motivated crimes, or under racially discriminatory circumstances.

{2} The SLA, Monogamy & Lesbianism

Shortly after their September 1975 capture with Patty Hearst, press stories began to emerge saying that—in alignment with the non-monogamous politics of the day—most SLA members had slept together. A number of SLA women had intimate relationships with each other and were then, or have since become, lesbians.

{3} Emily Harris

Emily Harris was released from prison in 2008 for the second time, after serving a sentence for a new 2002 conviction for her role in the 1975 death of a woman during the SLA's Crocker National Bank robbery. Harris said the shotgun she held had a hair-trigger and she hadn't meant to pull it. In 2008, I was shocked to hear that Emily and I had been living virtually next door to one another in Altadena, California, a lesbian-friendly hamlet northeast of L.A. I was less shocked to hear that she had divorced husband Bill, is now a lesbian and had been living with her woman lover for the nineteen years between her two terms in prison.

Epilogue

{1} Lesbian Tide

Historically, *The Lesbian Tide* was the successor of *The Ladder*, and a sister in time to the famously doctrinaire *Furies* and the radical feminist D.C. newspaper, *Off Our Backs*. Thousands of lesbians read all three religiously every Sunday morning like people read *The New York Times* today.

Unlike most of the early lesbian feminist publications which carried either politics or poetry, *The Tide* was built on the model of a mainstream weekly newsmagazine, including its 8 ½ x 11 traditional size, and three column format. Each issue carried a broad range of national news stories, investigative reporting, interviews with iconic lesbian musicians and songwriters, concert reviews, short news clips from around the world, photos of the famous and the ordinary, book reviews, one or two poems, and local lists of lesbian bars, restaurants, and shops. At its height *The Tide* printed only 3,000 issues monthly but its "pass along rate" was clocked at 9 per issue. With its strong radical voice and coverage of the primary and most controversial issues, people, and events of its era, the paper played an impactful role in knitting together a sense of national identity among lesbians. Its popular writers included Barbara Love, Karla Jay, Achy Obejas, Jeanne Córdova, Charlotte Bunch, Margie Adam, Sharon MacDonald, Right on Rita Goldberger, Nancy Toder, Shirl Buss, Rogi Rubyfruit, and Ann Doczi—many of whom went on to become successful authors of gay and lesbian books.

In 2004, *The Tide's* rights to digital reproduction were bought by the national college and library service EBSCO which has scanned and makes available all but the first few issues. Sets of *The Tide's* nine year run (1971-1980) are carried at most gay or lesbian archives, among them New York City's Lesbian Herstory Archive, San Francisco's GLBT Historical Society, and L.A.'s ONE International Gay & Lesbian Archive and June L. Mazer Lesbian Archives. Many original internal documents and photos can also be accessed online via the Jeanne Córdova Collection posted on the Online Archive of California site. *Lesbian Tide's* papers, and Córdova's are housed at the ONE Archive in Los Angeles.

Photo by Yvonne Moore

Jeanne Córdova

Jeanne Córdova is a pioneer of the modern American Gay & Lesbian Civil Rights Movement. Born in Germany to Irish and Mexican parents, she is one of twelve siblings and has always enjoyed a large crowd.

Her activism began as L.A. chapter president of the Daughters of Bilitis in 1970, and she went on to found and publish *The Lesbian Tide*, the largest national newsmagazine of the lesbian feminist decade.

After taking her masters degree in Social Work at UCLA, she returned to her alma mater as a key organizer of the National Lesbian Conference (UCLA, 1973). Córdova worked on the campaign to defeat the anti-gay Briggs initiative, (Prop. 6, in 1978), which would have purged LGBT teachers from California schools. One of the first openly gay delegates to the National Democratic Convention, she served as president of the Stonewall Democratic Club in the early 1980s.

In 1986 she became Media Director for STOP 64, the campaign that defeated the California AIDS quarantine ballot measure. Between 1980 and 1999, Córdova continued publishing by founding the Community Yellow Pages, which became the nation's first and largest LGBT telephone directory. During an eight year adventure living in Mexico, Córdova and her partner created a non-profit organization for economic justice, La Palapa Society of Todos Santos, AC. Returning from Mexico living in 2007, Córdova co-founded LEX—The Lesbian Exploratorium, a cultural guerilla group—which created the now famous "GenderPlay in Lesbian Culture" trilogy. She recently organized and chaired the 2010 Butch Voices Regional conference in Los Angeles.

Previous books include a memoir, *Kicking the Habit: A Lesbian Nun Story* (Multiple Dimensions, 1990), and a collection of her *L.A. Free Press* columns, *Sexism: It's a Nasty Affair* (New Way Books, 1974). Her essays appear in numerous award winning anthologies, among them, *Persistent Desire; A Femme Butch Reader* (Alyson Publications, 1992) *Love, West Hollywood* (Alyson Books, 2008) and *Persistence: All Ways Butch & Femme (Arsenal Pulp Press, 2011).*

She lives in the Hollywood Hills among other outlaws, artists, and authors. And invites you to drop in at: jeannecordova.com!